T0233707

Pro Java™ 6 3D Game Development

Java 3D™, JOGL, JInput, and JOAL APIs

Andrew Davison

Apress®

Pro Java™ 6 3D Game Development: Java 3D™, JOGL, JInput, and JOAL APIs

Copyright © 2007 by Andrew Davison

Softcover re-print of the Hardcover 1st edition 2007

All rights reserved. No part of this work may be reproduced or transmitted in any form or by any means, electronic or mechanical, including photocopying, recording, or by any information storage or retrieval system, without the prior written permission of the copyright owner and the publisher.

ISBN-13: 978-1-4302-1186-0

ISBN-10: 1-4302-1186-5

Trademarked names may appear in this book. Rather than use a trademark symbol with every occurrence of a trademarked name, we use the names only in an editorial fashion and to the benefit of the trademark owner, with no intention of infringement of the trademark.

Java and all Java-based marks are trademarks or registered trademarks of Sun Microsystems, Inc. in the United States and other countries. Apress Inc. is not affiliated with Sun Microsystems, Inc. and this book was written without endorsement from Sun Microsystems, Inc.

Lead Editor: Steve Anglin
Technical Reviewers: Chien Yang and Shawn Kendall
Editorial Board: Steve Anglin, Ewan Buckingham, Gary Cornell, Jason Gilmore, Jonathan Gennick, Jonathan Hassell, Chris Mills, Matthew Moodie, Jeffrey Pepper, Paul Sarknas, Dominic Shakeshaft, Jim Sumser, Matt Wade
Project Manager: Denise Santoro Lincoln
Copy Edit Manager: Nicole Flores
Copy Editor: Jennifer Whipple
Assistant Production Director: Kari Brooks-Copony
Senior Production Editor: Laura Cheu
Compositor: Gina Rexrode
Proofreader: Elizabeth Berry
Indexer: Becky Hornyak
Artist: Andrew Davison, April Milne
Cover Designer: Kurt Krames
Manufacturing Director: Tom Debolski

For information on translations, please contact Apress directly at 2560 Ninth Street, Suite 219, Berkeley, CA 94710. Phone 510-549-5930, fax 510-549-5939, e-mail info@apress.com, or visit http://www.apress.com.

The source code for this book is available to readers at http://www.apress.com in the Source Code/ Download section.

It is also available at the author's web site at http://fivedots.coe.psu.ac.th/~ad/jg2/.

To Supatra and John

Contents at a Glance

Contents

PART 1 ▪▪▪ Java 3D

PART 2 ▪▪▪ Nonstandard Input Devices

CHAPTER 10   Navigating a 3D Scene by Waving Your Arm 251

CHAPTER 11   Building a Gamepad Controller with JInput 273

PART 3 ▦▦▦ JOGL

About the Author

 **ANDREW DAVISON** received his PhD from Imperial College in London in 1989. He was a lecturer at the University of Melbourne for six years before moving to Prince of Songkla University in Thailand in 1996. He has also taught in Bangkok, Khon Kaen, and Hanoi.

His research interests include scripting languages, logic programming, visualization, and teaching methodologies. This latter topic led to an interest in teaching games programming in 1999.

His O'Reilly book, *Killer Game Programming in Java*, was published in 2005 and is accompanied by a web site at http://fivedots.coe.psu.ac.th/~ad/jg/.

One of Andrew's favorite hobbies is reading to his son, John, (currently they're on *The Iron Man* by Ted Hughes). He has also been known to play PC and mobile phone games, but purely for research purposes.

About the Technical Reviewers

 **CHIEN YANG** is a software engineer at Sun Microsystems, Inc., where he has worked since 1996. He works on graphics technologies for the Java Client Group. He has worked on the design and implementation of Java 3D API since its inception. He has also done work on graphics features simulation and graphics pipeline software. He holds a BS degree in computer science from the University of Iowa and an MS in computer science from the University of California at Berkeley.

 **SHAWN KENDALL** has developed cutting-edge Java and Java 3D–based game technology demos for Full Sail Real World Education and Sun Microsystems, displayed at various conferences such as GDC and SIG-GRAPH since 1999. In 2002, Shawn founded Immediate Mode Interactive (http://www.imilabs.com), a game technology company dedicated to the use of Java in games. Shawn has been developing in Java since 1995, starting with JDK 1.0 on SGI machines and Java 3D since 1998. Shawn graduated from the University of Central Florida with a BS degree in liberal science in 1995 and a computer science BS in 2002. Shawn maintains several Java 3D content loaders, as well as a host of Java 3D game demo projects.

Acknowledgments

My best regards to the many people at Apress who helped me get this book finished. They include Steve Anglin (Java editor), Denise Santoro Lincoln (project manager), Jennifer Whipple (copy editor), and Laura Cheu (production editor). Thanks also to the astute technical reviewers, Chien Yang and Shawn Kendall. I should also express my gratitude to the numerous people who sent me comments about the early drafts of this book, which are online at http://fivedots.coe.psu.ac.th/~ad/jg2/. Any remaining technical errors or poorly explained gobbledygook are my fault.

I must acknowledge my department (Computer Engineering), faculty (Engineering), and university (Prince of Songkla University) for being so supportive. They've always been understanding and have offered every encouragement. I recommend Thailand as a great place to live and work.

None of this would have been possible, or even worth attempting, without my family, Supatra and John, who I love very dearly.

Introduction

I'll start by answering some questions that might occur to you while you're checking this book out.

Is This Book for Me?

Of course it is! Buy it straightaway, and purchase several copies for your friends. They'll thank you profusely.

If you're not persuaded yet, how about a managerial-style, one-sentence summary of the book: My aim is to describe the key building blocks needed to create fun, exciting 3D games in Java on a PC, with an emphasis on the construction of 3D landscapes that a player can explore.

If that's not enough (gosh, you're a tough customer), cast your eyes over the next section (but really, there's no need; this book was meant for you).

What's This Book About?

This book is divided into three main sections: Java 3D, nonstandard input devices for game playing, and JOGL.

Java 3D is a high-level 3D graphics API based around the construction of a scene graph data structure that contains the objects that appear in the 3D scene. Java 3D topics covered here include how to build your own 3D models, load existing models, create detailed landscapes, display beautiful skies and backgrounds, and have users navigate through the scene, bumping into things as they go.

I examine three nonstandard input devices: the webcam, the gamepad, and the P5 data glove—all fun alternatives to the rather boring PC keyboard and mouse.

JOGL is a Java wrapper around the popular OpenGL 3D graphics API, which offers a less high-level programming abstraction than Java 3D (in particular, there's no scene graph to build). JOGL's closeness to OpenGL means there's a wealth of existing OpenGL examples, tutorials, and programming tips and techniques that can be reused without much recoding. I look at topics similar to those for Java 3D: landscapes, skyboxes, billboards, picking, fog, overlays, and building and loading models.

Another theme of this book is the examination of games-related Java APIs that aren't part of the standard Java distribution (i.e., they're not in the software you get when you download Java SE). I've already mentioned Java 3D and JOGL. Other APIs include JInput (for interfacing Java to nonstandard input devices), JOAL (a Java wrapper around the 3D sound API, OpenAL), JMF (for managing time-based multimedia, which I employ for rapidly taking webcam snaps), and Odejava (a Java layer over the physics API, ODE).

This book examines the latest Java SE 6 features relevant to gaming, including splash screens, JavaScript scripting, and the desktop and system tray interfaces.

What's This Book Not About?

I don't bother introducing Java; there are many books that already do that. Two worth checking out are *Head First Java* by Bert Bates and Kathy Sierra (O'Reilly, 2005) and *Thinking in Java* by Bruce Eckel (Prentice Hall, 2006). An older version of Eckel's book is available free at `http://www.mindview.net/Books/TIJ/`. The sort of background you need for my book is what you'd learn in an introductory course on Java.

This isn't a book about developing a single massive application, such as an FPS (first-person shooter). Instead I describe game elements, building blocks that can be used in a lot of different 3D games.

This book isn't about building a 3D rendering engine; I'm using Java 3D and JOGL for that. If you're interested in creating an engine from the ground up, I recommend *Developing Games in Java* by David Brackeen, Bret Barker, and Laurence Vanhelswue (New Riders Games, 2003).

As I explain JOGL, I also explain the basic features of OpenGL. Unfortunately, I don't have the space to discuss all of OpenGL's wonderful capabilities or the numerous extensions provided by different graphic card vendors. I supply you with pointers to more information when I start on JOGL in Chapter 15.

This isn't a games design book; two great resources are *Game Architecture and Design: A New Edition* by Andrew Rollings and Dave Morris (New Riders Games, 2003) and *Chris Crawford on Game Design* by Chris Crawford (New Riders Games, 2003).

I won't be talking about J2ME games programming on mobile devices. There are some interesting 3D APIs for J2ME (the mobile 3D API and Java bindings for OpenGL ES), but the emphasis of this book is on desktop applications.

Where's the CD/Code?

All the source code can be found at `http://fivedots.coe.psu.ac.th/~ad/jg2/`. I've also uploaded early drafts of the chapters there, including a few that didn't make it into the book.

How Is This Book Different from KGPJ?

KGPJ is the abbreviation for my earlier book, *Killer Game Programming in Java*.

KGPJ is about 2D, 3D, and network games programming, but this book concentrates solely on 3D programming.

KGPJ has sixteen chapters on Java 3D, while this book has eight (roughly half the book), *and* also covers nonstandard input devices and JOGL. Of those eight chapters, four are on topics not covered in *KGPJ*, namely Java SE 6 integration, physics modeling, multitexturing, and mixed-mode rendering. The other four chapters overlap with *KGPJ* to some degree, but it means that this book is completely self-contained; there's no need for you to have to read *KGPJ* before starting here. Also, all the example programs are entirely new.

KGPJ doesn't discuss the range of APIs covered here, such as JOGL, JInput, JOAL, Odejava, and JMF.

KGPJ was published in May 2005, so focuses on J2SE 1.4 and Java 3D 1.3.1, while this book utilizes Java SE 6 and Java 3D 1.5.

If you're still not sure, the best solution, at least the one most pleasing to me, is to *buy both books*. Thank you.

Java for Games Programming: Are You Joking?

Java is a great games programming language. When you learned Java, I'm sure its many advantages were mentioned: an elegant object-oriented paradigm, cross-platform support, code reuse, ease of development, tool availability, reliability and stability, good documentation, support from Sun Microsystems, low development costs, the ability to use legacy code (e.g., C, C++), and increased programmer productivity. That list adds up to my personal reason for programming in Java—*it's fun*, especially when you're programming something inherently good for you, such as games.

Most Java bashers, skipping over the advantages, have the following criticisms:

- Java is too slow for games programming.

- Java has memory leaks.

- Java is too high-level.

- Java application installation is a nightmare.

- Java isn't supported on games consoles.

- No one uses Java to write real games.

- Sun Microsystems isn't interested in supporting Java gaming.

Almost all of these objections are substantially wrong.

Java is roughly the same speed as C++ and has been since version 1.4. Many benchmarks indicate that Java SE 6 is 20% to 25% faster than J2SE 5.

Memory leaks can be avoided with good programming and techniques such as profiling.

Java is high-level but also offers access to the graphics hardware and external devices. Many of the behind-the-scenes speed improvements in Java SE 6 are related to graphics rendering using OpenGL and DirectX.

A variant of the moaning about "high-level" is that Java can't be connected to gaming peripherals such as gamepads. This is nonsense, as shown in Chapters 9–14.

Installation isn't a nightmare. Java applets can be delivered via the Web or downloaded using Java Web Start. There are numerous third-party installers, such as install4j (http://www.ej-technologies.com/products/install4j/overview.html).

There's a growing number of excellent commercial Java games, including *Tribal Trouble, Puzzle Pirates, Call of Juarez, Chrome, Titan Attacks, Star Wars Galaxies, Runescape, Alien Flux, Kingdom of Wars, Law and Order II, Ultratron, Roboforge, IL-2 Sturmovik, Galactic Village, Tiltilation*, and *Wurm Online*. Many are written entirely in Java, others employ Java in subcomponents such as game logic.

Java is used widely in the casual gaming market, where gameplay is generally less complex and time-consuming. Implementation timelines are shorter, budgets are smaller, and the required man power is within the reach of small teams. By 2008, industry analysts predict the casual games market will surpass US$2 billion in the United States alone.

There are numerous Java gaming sites, including a showcase at Sun Microsystems at http://www.java.com/en/games/, community pages at http://community.java.net/games/, a collection of open source gaming tools at https://games.dev.java.net/, the Java Games Factory at http://javagamesfactory.org/, and many very helpful forums at http://www.javagaming.org/.

What About Java on Games Consoles?

If you were paying attention in the last section, you'd have noticed that I didn't disagree with the lack of a games console version of Java. That's a bit embarrassing for a "write once, run anywhere" language.

The Sony PlayStation 2 (PS2) was the dominant games console at the end of 2006, with more than 100 million units sold, dwarfing its competitors such as the Xbox 360, Xbox, Wii, and Game-Cube. Unsurprisingly, there have been many rumors over the years about a Java port for the PS2. In fact, it *is* possible to run Java on Sony's version of Linux, but the OS requires the PS2 to have a hard disk and only offers limited access to the PS2's other hardware.

The good news is that the prospects for Java support on the PlayStation 3 (PS3) are much brighter. Both the basic and premium PS3 versions have 512MB of RAM, a large hard drive, and Linux support, and use an extended version of OpenGL. The PS3's Cell Broadband Engine essentially consists of a central 64-bit PowerPC-based processor (the PPE) and nine data-crunching support chips called SPEs.

Sony's software development chief, Izumi Kawanishi, has spoken of making it easier for individuals to create games on the PS3. One aspect of this is allowing third-party OSes to be installed, with the major restriction that they can't directly access the graphics hardware, which means that only 256MB of RAM is available.

There are currently (March 2007) three versions of Linux known to run on the PS3: Yellow Dog Linux (YDL) 5, Fedora Core 5, and Gentoo, with YDL officially supported by Sony. Installation details for YDL can be found at http://www-128.ibm.com/developerworks/power/library/pa-linuxps3-1/, and information on Fedora and Gentoo is at http://ps3.qj.net/PS3-Linux-The-void-has-been-filled-Full-install-instructions-for-Fedora-Core-5-/pg/49/aid/73144/ and http://ps3.qj.net/Gentoo-Linux-on-your-PS3-With-full-install-instructions-/pg/49/aid/78739/.

Since the PS3 uses a PowerPC chip (the PPE), it should be possible to install the 32-bit or 64-bit PowerPC version of Java for Linux offered by IBM (at http://www-128.ibm.com/developerworks/java/jdk/linux/download.html; select J2SE5.0 for the 32-bit or 64-bit pSeries). As of March 2007, I've heard from one person who has done this (with YDL and the 32-bit J2SE 5.0) and got JBoss running as a test Java application.

A good ongoing thread about Java and the PS3 can be found at javagaming.org (http://www.javagaming.org/forums/index.php?topic=15122.0). It's also worth checking the PS3Forums and Qj.net sites (http://www.ps3forums.com/ and http://ps3.qj.net/).

Java already has a presence on the PS3 as the software for its Blu-ray Disc for high-definition video and data. All Blu-ray drives support a version of Java called BD-J for implementing interactive menus and other GUIs. Also, Blu-ray's network connectivity means that BD-J can be utilized for networking applications such as downloading subtitles, short movies, and adverts.

The present lack of Java on consoles is a serious issue, but the remaining PC market is far from miniscule. The Gartner Group says there were 661 million PC users in 2006 and that the number will hit 953 million at the end of 2008 and cross over the billion mark in 2009.

Games on PCs benefit from superior hardware—such as video cards, RAM, and Internet connections—so can offer more exciting gameplay. There are many more PC games, particularly in the area of multiplayer online games.

PART 1

■■■

Java 3D

CHAPTER 1

Introducing Java 3D

The Java 3D API, a scene graph API developed by Sun Microsystems, provides a collection of high-level constructs for creating, rendering, and manipulating a 3D scene graph. A scene graph makes 3D programming much easier for novices (and even for experienced programmers) because it emphasizes scene design, rather than rendering, by hiding the graphics pipeline. The scene graph supports complex graphical elements such as 3D geometries, lighting modes, picking, and collision detection.

This chapter gives an overview of the main features and strengths of Java 3D, leaving program examples aside for the moment, and addresses the common complaints about the API (which are unfounded).

URLs are included that lead to more information, games, model loaders, games-related libraries, and alternative scene graph systems.

Overview of Java 3D

Prior to the most recent release, version 1.5, there were two Java 3D variants: one implemented on top of OpenGL, the other above DirectX Graphics. OpenGL (the Open Graphics Library) is a cross-language, cross-platform API for 3D (and 2D) computer graphics. The DirectX Graphics API supports a rendering pipeline quite similar (in concept) to OpenGL, describing all geometry in terms of vertices and pixels. It's part of DirectX, a collection of related gaming APIs aimed at Microsoft Windows (http://www.microsoft.com/directx). The other APIs support 3D audio, networking, input device integration, multimedia, and installation management.

Java 3D on Windows uses the OpenGL renderer by default and requires OpenGL 1.3 or later. DirectX rendered can be switched on by the user with a -Dj3d.rend=d3d command-line argument, and requires DirectX 9.0 or later.

A JOGL rendering pipeline was added to Java 3D 1.5, making it easier to develop future Mac versions. JOGL is a thin layer of Java over OpenGL, effectively hiding some of the low-level variations in the OpenGL API across different OSes. The JOGL pipeline also offers a lightweight JCanvas3D class as an alternative to the heavyweight Canvas3D class. Canvas3D is utilized as a drawing surface for rendering a 3D scene but can be tricky to combine with lightweight Swing GUI components; I explain how to safely use Canvas3D in Chapter 2.

One of the main aims of Java 3D 1.6 (due out by the summer of 2008) is to use the JOGL binding to combine OpenGL and Java 3D rendering more closely.

The principal Java 3D web site is https://java3d.dev.java.net/, where Java 3D can be downloaded as a binary installation for various platforms; for example, I retrieved the final release version 1.5 for Windows. Java 3D should be installed after Java SE, with Java SE 5 or later the recommended version. The API documentation and examples are separate (but essential) downloads from the same site.

The Java 3D roadmap site (http://wiki.java.net/bin/view/Javadesktop/Java3DRoadmap) details plans for versions 1.5.1, 1.6, and beyond. For instance, 1.5.1 will mainly add support for Microsoft Vista.

Overview of the Scene Graph

Java 3D uses a scene graph to organize and manage a 3D application. The underlying graphics pipeline is hidden, replaced by a treelike structure built from nodes representing 3D models, lights, sounds, the background, the camera, and many other scene elements.

The nodes are typed, the main ones being Group and Leaf nodes. A Group node has child nodes, grouping the children so that operations such as translations, rotations, and scaling can be applied en masse. Leaf nodes are the leaves of the graph (did you guess that?), which often represent the visible things in the scene, such as 3D shapes, but may also be nontangible entities, such as lighting and sounds. Additionally, a Leaf node may have node components, specifying color, reflectivity, and other attributes of the Leaf.

The scene graph can contain behaviors, represented by nodes holding code that affects other nodes in the graph at runtime. Typical behavior nodes move shapes, detect and respond to shape collisions, and cycle lighting from day to night.

The term *scene graph* is used, rather than *scene tree*, because it's possible for nodes to be shared (i.e., have more than one parent).

Before looking at a real Java 3D scene graph, look at Figure 1-1 that shows how the scene graph idea can be applied to defining the contents of a living room.

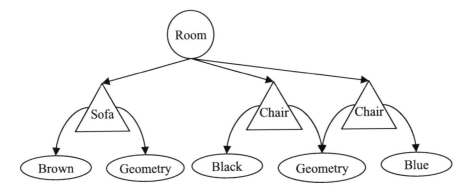

Figure 1-1. *Scene graph for a living room*

The room Group node is the parent of Leaf nodes representing a sofa and two chairs. Each Leaf utilizes geometry (shape) and color node components, and the chair geometry information is *shared*. This sharing means that both chairs will have the same shape but be different colors.

The choice of symbols in Figure 1-1 comes from a standard symbol set (shown in Figure 1-2), used in all of this book's Java 3D scene graph diagrams. I explain the VirtualUniverse and Locale nodes and the Reference relationship in the "HelloUniverse Scene Graph" subsection.

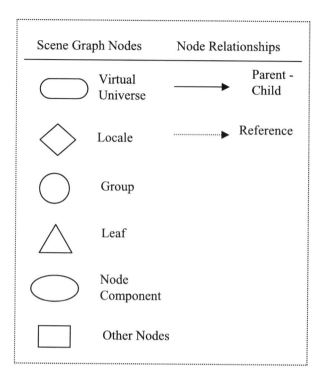

Figure 1-2. *Scene graph symbols*

Some Java 3D Scene Graph Nodes

The Java 3D API can be viewed as a set of classes that subclass the Group and Leaf nodes in various ways. The Leaf class is subclassed to define different kinds of 3D shapes and environmental nodes (i.e., nodes representing lighting, sounds, and behaviors).

The main shape class is called Shape3D, which uses two node components to define its geometry and appearance; these are represented by classes called Geometry and Appearance.

The Group class supports basic node positioning and orientation for its children, and is subclassed to extend those operations. For instance, BranchGroup allows children to be added or removed from the graph at runtime, while TransformGroup permits the position and orientation of its children to be changed.

The HelloUniverse Scene Graph

The standard first code example for a Java 3D programmer is HelloUniverse (it appears in Chapter 1 of Sun's Java 3D tutorial at http://java.sun.com/developer/onlineTraining/java3d and in the Java 3D examples collection at https://java3d.dev.java.net/). The HelloUniverse program displays a rotating colored cube, as shown in Figure 1-3.

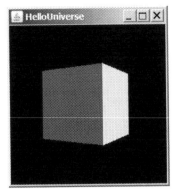

Figure 1-3. *A rotating colored cube*

The scene graph for this application is given in Figure 1-4.

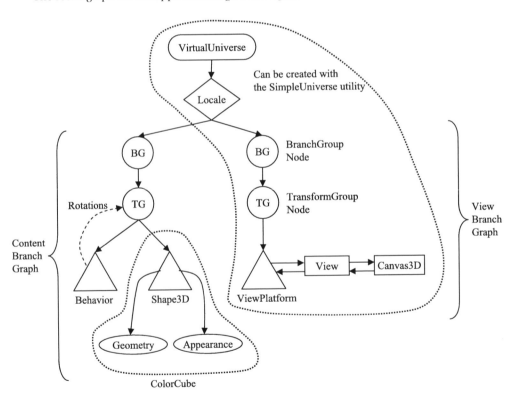

Figure 1-4. *Scene graph for HelloUniverse*

VirtualUniverse is the top node in every scene graph and represents the virtual world space and its coordinate system. Locale acts as the scene graph's location in the virtual world. Below the Locale node there are always two subgraphs.

The left branch is the *content branch graph*, holding program-specific content such as geometry, lighting, textures, and the world's background. The content branch graph differs significantly from one application to another. The ColorCube is composed from a Shape3D node and associated Geometry and Appearance components. Its rotation is carried out by a Behavior node, which affects the TransformGroup parent of the ColorCube's shape.

The right branch below Locale is the *view branch graph*, and specifies the user's position, orientation, and perspective as he looks into the virtual world from the physical world (e.g., from in front of a monitor). The ViewPlatform node stores the viewer's position in the virtual world; the View node states how to turn what the viewer sees into a physical world image (e.g., a 2D picture on the monitor). The Canvas3D node is a Java GUI component that allows the 2D image to be placed inside a Java application or applet.

The VirtualUniverse, Locale, and view branch graph often have the same structure across different applications, since most programs use a single Locale and view the virtual world as a 2D image on a monitor. For these applications, the relevant nodes can be created with Java 3D's SimpleUniverse utility class, relieving the programmer of a lot of graph construction work.

Java 3D Strengths

The core strengths of Java 3D are its scene graph, performance, collection of unique features, Java integration, and extensive documentation and examples.

The Scene Graph

The scene graph has two main advantages: it simplifies 3D programming and speeds up the resulting code. The scene graph hides low-level 3D graphics elements and allows the programmer to manage and organize a 3D scene. The scene graph supports a wide range of complex graphical elements.

At the Java 3D implementation level, the scene graph is used to group shapes with common properties and carry out view culling, occlusion culling, level of detail selection, execution culling, and behavior pruning—all optimizations that must be coded directly by the programmer in lower-level APIs. Java 3D utilizes Java's multithreading to carry out parallel graph traversal and rendering, both very useful optimizations.

Performance

Java 3D is designed with performance in mind, which it achieves at the high level by scene graph optimizations, and at the low level by being built on top of OpenGL or DirectX Graphics.

Some programmer-specified scene graph optimizations are available through capability bits, which state what operations can/cannot be carried out at runtime (e.g., prohibiting a shape from moving). Java 3D also permits the programmer to bypass the scene graph, either totally, by means of the immediate mode, or partially, via the mixed mode. Immediate mode gives the programmer greater control over rendering and scene management, but isn't often required. Mixed mode "mixes" the immediate and retained modes so a program can utilize lower-level rendering and a scene graph together. Retained mode programs (the default Java 3D coding style) only use the scene graph API. Almost all of my Java 3D examples employ retained mode, except in Chapter 9, which looks at mixed mode rendering.

Unique Features

Java 3D's view model separates the virtual and physical worlds (through the ViewPlatform and View nodes). This makes it straightforward to reconfigure an application to utilize a range of output devices, from a monitor to eyeglasses with stereo displays to CAVEs (rooms with projected images covering every wall).

Virtual world behavior is coded with Behavior nodes in the scene graph and triggered by events. Among other things, Behavior nodes offer a different style of animation based on responding to events instead of the usual update-redraw cycle used in most games programs.

The core Java 3D API package, javax.media.j3d, supports basic polygons and triangles within a scene graph, while the com.sun.j3d packages add a range of utility classes, including ColorCube and SimpleUniverse, mouse and keyboard navigation behaviors, audio device handling, and loaders for several 3D file formats.

Geometry compression is possible, often reducing size by an order of magnitude. When this is combined with Java's NIO (new I/O capabilities present since version 1.4) and networking, it facilitates the ready transfer of large quantities of data between applications, such as multiplayer games.

Java 3D supports both of the popular programmable shader languages, OpenGL's GLSL (the default), and NVIDIA's Cg. This allows the programmer to create specialized rendering effects—such as bump mapping and shadows—very easily.

Java 3D offers 2D and 3D audio output, with ambient and spatialized sound. Unfortunately, there are bugs in the sound system, so spatialized sound isn't available by default in Java 3D 1.5. Version 1.6 will probably include a JOALMixer class instead, which will act as a programming interface to a JOAL-based audio device. JOAL is a Java binding for a 3D audio API called OpenAL, which is supported by many sound cards. As of January 2007, there's a partially completed version of JOALMixer at the j3d-incubator site (https://j3d-incubator.dev.java.net/). In Chapter 13, I develop a JOAL sound class that can be used with Java, Java 3D (in Chapter 14), and JOGL (Chapter 17).

Java Integration

Java 3D is Java, so it offers object orientation (classes, inheritance, polymorphism), threads, exception handling, and more. Java 3D can easily make use of other Java APIs, such as Java Media Framework (JMF) and Java Advanced Imaging (JAI). The JMF includes mechanisms for playing audio and video segments and can be extended to support new forms or audio and video (http://java.sun.com/products/java-media/jmf). JMF is utilized alongside Java 3D in Chapters 9 and 10. JAI provides many additional image processing features, including more than 100 imaging operators, tiling of large images, network-based capabilities, and the means to add new forms of image processing (JAI can be found at http://java.sun.com/products/java-media/jai).

Documentation and Examples

The Java 3D distribution doesn't come with any programming examples, which are a separate download at https://java3d.dev.java.net/; the 40-plus small to medium examples are a great help, but somewhat lacking in documentation.

Sun's Java 3D tutorial, available at http://java.sun.com/developer/onlineTraining/java3d, is quite old, dating from 2002 and focusing on version 1.2, but still useful for understanding Java 3D's core features.

Ben Moxon has a very nice introductory Java 3D tutorial based around getting a 3D figure to move over a hilly terrain (http://www.benmoxon.info/Java3d/); it's called "The Little Purple Dude Walks."

I recommend three Java 3D textbooks as supplemental reading:

- *Java 3D API Jump-Start* by Aaron E. Walsh and Doug Gehringer (Prentice Hall, 2001)
- *Java 3D Programming* by Daniel Selman (Manning Publications, 2002)
- *Java Media APIs: Cross-Platform Imaging, Media, and Visualization* by Alejandro Terrazas, John Ostuni, and Michael Barlow (Sams, 2002)

The Walsh and Gehringer text is an excellent overview using code snippets rather than page after page of listings. It complements the Java 3D tutorial.

The Selman book is more advanced. For the games enthusiast, Selman describes a *Doom*-like world, utilizing first-person perspective keyboard navigation and scene creation from a 2D map. The world contains bookcases, pools of water, flaming torches, and animated guards.

Terrazas is involved in virtual reality research and business, so there's a heavy slant in the 3D part of his book toward less common topics such as sensors and head tracking, and a bit on CAVEs. There's an example combining Java 3D and JMF to create a 3D video chat room.

Criticisms of Java 3D for Games Programming

The misconceptions and complaints about Java 3D closely match those used against Java, which I mention in the introduction to this book. I'll focus on three criticisms specific to Java 3D:

- Java 3D is too high-level.
- No one uses Java 3D to write real games.
- There is a lack of support for Java 3D.

Java 3D's Level of Abstraction

Java 3D's scene graph is often considered a source of unreasonable overheads, especially by programmers with experience of OpenGL or DirectX. Although it does introduce some overheads, they should be judged against the optimizations that the scene graph brings. These optimizations can be implemented in a low-level API by an experienced programmer, but at what cost in time and maintainability?

Most large OpenGL and DirectX applications need a data structure like a scene graph in order to manage code complexity, so the scene graph versus no scene graph argument is often invalid.

A powerful, high-level, and flexible 3D graphics API needs both a scene graph and a way to efficiently access the graphics pipeline. These two mechanisms are aimed at different levels in 3D graphics programming, sometimes called the *entity level* and the *rendering level*. An application's entity level requires a data structure for organizing the scene objects, while the rendering level handles light mapping, shadows, radiosity, vertex shading, and so on. Great games are designed at the entity level, in terms of game play, characters, scenarios, and story elements. The look and feel of a great game—the light and dark, the atmosphere—is created at the rendering level.

Although Java 3D is best known for entity-level programming (via the scene graph), it also supports rendering-level coding. For example, Java 3D can perform vertex and pixel shading using either the GLSL or Cg shading languages. It's also possible to achieve some striking effects by employing multitextures, rendering attributes, and blending functions, as I show in Chapter 6.

The high-level nature of the scene graph makes Java 3D code harder to tune for speed, unlike programs using OpenGL or DirectX directly. However, a programmer does have the option of moving to Java 3D's mixed or immediate modes.

The hiding of the low-level graphics API makes it harder for a programmer to code around bugs in the APIs or the drivers.

Java 3D Games

Java 3D has been employed in relatively few games, but they include best sellers and award-winners, including the following:

- *Law and Order II* (http://www.lawandordergame.com). This is a detective game based on the TV show.
- *Pernica* (http://www.starfireresearch.com/pernica/pernica.html). This is a sword-and-sorcery role-playing world.
- *RoboForge* (http://www.roboforge.com/). Build and fight robots.
- *FlyingGuns* (http://www.flyingguns.com/). World War I planes dogfight in the skies.
- *CazaPool3D* (http://cazapool3d.sourceforge.net/cazapooljws/Pool.html). Want to shoot some pool?
- *Cassos* (http://www.la-cfd.com/cassos/english/index.php). Race monkeys with a dragon.
- Games by IMI Labs (http://www.imilabs.com/). Several impressive game demos over the years include *Java 3D Grand Prix* (a racing game), *JAMID* (a first-person shooter in the *Quake* mold), and *Underworld Assault* (a two-person fighting game). The latest is *Cosmic Birdie*, a networked racing game using the Sun Game Server.
- *Out of Space* (http://www.geocities.com/Psionic1981/oos.html). This features jet-packed flying and shooting with explosions.
- *StreamGlider* (http://www.streamglider.net/). Blow up space gliders.
- *The Virtual FishTank* (http://www.virtualfishtank.com/main.html). This is a distributed simulation of a 24,000 gallon aquarium, rendered to 13 large projection screens and running on 15 networked machines.

The "Useful Sites" page at http://www.j3d.org/sites.html is a good source for Java 3D examples and includes a games and demos section. Other good general lists of code examples can be found at http://java3d.virtualworlds.de/projects.php and the Java 3D Users Wiki at http://wiki.java.net/bin/view/Javadesktop/Java3DUsers.

The games listed at the Java Games Factory, http://javagamesfactory.org/, can be viewed by technology categories, which include several 3D-related sections.

The third-year computer graphics course in the Computer Science Department of the University of Applied Sciences in Biel, Switzerland, maintains a site of student projects using Java 3D (https://prof.hti.bfh.ch/swc1/DemoJ3D/). Many of them are games, including *Battleship3D-Net* (a networked version of the *Battleships* game), *Billard-3D* (pool), *Glymp3D* (role-playing action), *JBomba* (based on *Bomberman*), and *TriChess* (3D-networked chess).

A good strategy for finding Java 3D games and source code is to visit SourceForge (http://sourceforge.net/search/) and freshmeat.net (http://freshmeat.net/) and search for keywords such as *Java*, *3D*, and *game*.

Sun's Project Darkstar (http://games-darkstar.dev.java.net/) is aimed at developing tools for supporting massive multiplayer online games. The Sun Game Server is its server-side platform, and there are client APIs for C++, Java SE, and Java ME. The first two demos, *Battle Trolls* and *Cosmic Birdie* (mentioned previously), both use Java 3D.

Two very exciting Java 3D projects that aren't really games are the following:

- Project Looking Glass (https://lg3d.dev.java.net/). This is a prototype 3D desktop offering rotating transparent windows, multiple desktop workspaces, and an API for developing applications.

- The Mars Rover Mission (http://www.sun.com/aboutsun/media/features/mars.html). Java 3D and JAI are being used to render and interpret the real-time images captured by the rover. There's also a rover simulator implemented in Java 3D, which is a sort of game (http://www.distant-galaxy.com/MERalizer/MERalizer.html).

Java 3D Model Loaders for Games

A *loader* is an essential tool for quickly populating a game with people, artifacts, and scenery. A good first stop for loader listings is the j3d.org page at http://java3d.j3d.org/utilities/loaders.html. All the model loaders in the following list are for popular game formats, and they all support animation:

- Quake Loaders (http://www.newdawnsoftware.com/). The loaders support id Software's *Quake II* MD2 and BSP, and *Quake III* MD3 formats. A morphing animation example using the MD3 loader can be found at http://www.la-cfd.com/cassos/test/md3/index.html.

- The Java XTools (http://www.3dchat.org/dev.php). This package offers a range of Java 3D extras, including loaders for Renderware, Caligari TrueSpace, and Wavefront OBJ and MTL files. Other elements include a lens flare mechanism, a text-to-texture converter, and a sky box class.

- NWN Java3d Loader (http://nwn-j3d.sourceforge.net/). It handles *Neverwinter Nights* models, including animation and emitters.

- 3DS Java3D Loader (http://sourceforge.net/projects/java3dsloader/). The loader supports 3D Studio Max models, including cameras, point and directional lights, animation, and hierarchy textures.

- Anim8orLoader (http://anim8orloader.sourceforge.net/). It can load 3D models and scenes saved in the Anim8or file format. Anim8or is a 3D modeling and character animation program (http://www.anim8or.com/main/index.html).

- Xj3D (http://www.xj3d.org/). The loader implements the X3D standard, a successor to VRML 97, and provides for keyframe animation. Xj3D also contains its own OpenGL renderer, which is reportedly much faster than the one inside Java 3D.

Extra Gaming Libraries

Three places to start looking for additional games-related libraries/APIs for Java 3D are the following:

- The j3d-incubator project (https://j3d-incubator.dev.java.net/) is for sharing examples and utility code.

- The j3d.org Code Repository (http://code.j3d.org/) includes code (or partial code) for ROAM terrain rendering, particle systems, and 2D overlays. ROAM (Real-Time Optimally Adapting Meshes) automatically adjusts the amount of terrain detail that's rendered, depending on its distance from the user's viewpoint. This speeds up rendering times considerably for large landscape.

- The Java Games Middleware project (`https://games-middleware.dev.java.net/`) contains game engines and special-purpose libraries.

Specialized add-ons include the following:

- Yaarq (`http://www.sbox.tugraz.at/home/w/wkien/`). Yaarq, by Wolfgang Kienreich, offers APIs for several gaming-related features, including texturing, bump maps, reflection maps, overlays, and particle systems. It also demonstrates how to achieve stable frame rates.

- Various lighting examples (`http://planeta.terra.com.br/educacao/alessandroborges/java3d.html`). Java 3D is often criticized for lacking sophisticated lighting effects. Alessandro Borges has developed several examples showing how to utilize bump maps to generate irregular surface lighting and cube map textures for reflection effects. Mike Jacobs wrote a JDJ article on bump mapping at `http://mnjacobs.javadevelopersjournal.com/bump_mapping_in_java3d.htm`, and Joachim Diepstraten has one at `http://java3d.j3d.org/tutorials/quick_fix/dot3_bumps.html`.

- Comic/cel shaders (`http://www.antiflash.net/java3d/comicshader.html`). This demonstrates how simple cartoon-style shading can be added to shapes.

- A constructive solid geometry (CSG) API (`http://www.geocities.com/danbalby/`). A new shape is created using set operations (e.g., union, intersection, difference) applied to groups of simpler shapes.

- jgeom (`https://jgeom.dev.java.net/`). This is a 3D geometry library including NURBS, subdivision surfaces, and boolean operators. NURBS are used to define smooth curves and surfaces.

- skinandbones (`https://skinandbones.dev.java.net/`). This is a skeletal animation and skinning system.

- Odejava (`https://odejava.dev.java.net/`). This is an ODE binding for Java. ODE (Open Dynamics Engine) is a rigid body physics library suitable for simulating articulated rigid body dynamics, such as ground vehicles and legged creatures. I describe how it can be used with Java 3D in Chapter 5.

- java3dgamessdk (`https://java3dgamesdk.dev.java.net/`). The extra functionality includes a menu to let the user choose between full-screen and window mode. There is support for a game mouse, and a collision box for the precise steering of objects.

- Genesis FX (`http://www.indietechnologies.com/`). This is a commercial particle system for 3D game special effects. There's a full-featured version for personal use, which is free to the community. The techniques are explained in Mike Jacobs' JDJ article at `http://jdj.sys-con.com/read/99792.htm`.

Java 3D Support

If *support* means a pool of knowledgeable people ready to offer advice and large archives of technical information, Java 3D has an abundance of support.

Java 3D is a community project managed by the Java Media, Imaging, and Graphics (JMIG) Group at Sun, with more than 400 registered members. Java 3D's license allows developers to download the source code and to contribute bug fixes and utilities. Modifications are allowed for research purposes, and there is a no-fee commercial license.

An important aspect of a community project is that much of the implementation work comes from the community, a strategy also successfully employed to develop the JOGL, JOAL, and JInput APIs. JOGL is considered in Chapters 15 through 17, JOAL is utilized in Chapters 13, 14, and 17, and JInput, to connect a game pad to Java 3D, is in Chapters 11 and 12.

Popular Java 3D forums include the following:

- The forum in Java.Net's Java Desktop Technologies category: http://forums.java.net/jive/forum.jspa?forumID=70
- The Java Games forum: http://www.javagaming.org/forums/index.php?board=14.0
- The forum at the Sun Developer Network site: http://forum.java.sun.com/forum.jsp?forum=21

Other information sources include the following:

- The Wiki page at http://wiki.java.net/bin/view/Javadesktop/Java3D, which includes installation details, a roadmap for future versions, pointers to good books, and a great list of applications.
- The old Java 3D product page at http://java.sun.com/products/java-media/3D/, with links to demos, a basic FAQ, and several application sites such as the Virtual FishTank.
- The Java 3D Interest Mailing list, which was closed in July 2005 but still contains years of good advice. It can be searched from http://archives.java.sun.com/archives/java3d-interest.html and http://www.mail-archive.com/java3d-interest@java.sun.com/.
- The Java 3D Programming forum hosted at Manning Publications at http://www.manning-sandbox.com/forum.jspa?forumID=31. This is a good place to contact Daniel Selman, the author of *Java 3D Programming* published by Manning.
- The Java 3D section of j3d.org (http://java3d.j3d.org), which has a great FAQ, a large collection of tutorials, utilities, and a code repository. Some of the information is a bit out of date.
- Java 3D at VirtualWorlds (http://java3d.virtualworlds.de/), which is a German/English site with sections on loaders, input devices, add-on libraries, documentation links, and a forum.
- The USENET newsgroup comp.lang.java.3d, which can be searched and mailed to from Google's Groups page, http://groups.google.com/groups?group=comp.lang.java.3d.

Alternatives to Java 3D

There are many ways of programming in 3D with Java without employing Java 3D. One major approach is to use a more direct Java binding to OpenGL, as typified by JOGL, covered in Chapters 15 through 17, or the Lightweight Java Game Library (LWJGL).

The following lists 3D graphics APIs based around the scene graph idea:

- Xith3D (http://xith.org) uses the same basic scene graph structure as Java 3D but can also directly call OpenGL operations. Since the high-level APIs of Xith3D and Java 3D are so similar, porting Java 3D code over to Xith3D is fairly straightforward. There are versions of Xith3D that run on top of JOGL and LWJGL.
- jME (jMonkey Engine) (http://www.mojomonkeycoding.com/) was inspired by the scene graph engine described in *3D Game Engine Design* by David H. Eberly (Morgan Kaufmann, 2000). jME is built on top of LWJGL.
- JAVA is DOOMED (http://javaisdoomed.sourceforge.net) includes loaders for *Quake II* MD2 and 3D Studio Max 3DS files. The implementation uses JOGL, and the distribution includes *Escape*, a *Doom*-like game.

- Aviatrix3D (`http://aviatrix3d.j3d.org/`) is a retained-mode Java scene graph API above JOGL. Its tool set is aimed at data visualization rather than gaming, and supports CAVEs, domes, and head-mounted displays.

- JView (`http://www.rl.af.mil/tech/programs/JVIEW/`) is another visualization API, supporting both 2D and 3D graphics, developed by the U.S. Air Force Research Lab. GL4Java, an older low-level Java API for OpenGL, was used to build it.

- Espresso3D (`http://www.espresso3d.com/`), a games-oriented library, includes OpenAL audio, sprites, collision detection, input, and rendering support. It's built using LWJGL.

- AgentFX (`http://www.agency9.se/products/agentfx/`) includes character animation, shader support using Cg, and texture compression. It's a commercial product, implemented using JOGL.

Summary

This chapter summarized the main features of Java 3D, including its many strengths (the scene graph, performance, its unique features, integration with Java, and an extensive body of documentation and examples). I examined the criticisms of Java 3D (i.e., being too high-level, not being used for "real" games, and having a lack of support), and found them to be groundless. I finished by briefly listing some of the alternatives to Java 3D; the most popular, JOGL, is the subject of Chapters 15 through 17.

This chapter contains many URLs leading to more information on Java 3D, including games, model loaders, and games-related libraries.

■ ■ ■

CHAPTER 2

Get a Life (in 3D)

This chapter introduces a number of programming techniques that you will see again frequently in upcoming chapters. We will integrate Java 3D's Canvas3D class (where a scene is rendered) with a Swing-based GUI and display the scene in a full-screen window. We will build a Java 3D scene graph that is lit with ambient and directional lights, has a blue-sky background, and is filled with multi-colored spheres. The spheres gradually rotate, change color, and fade in and out of view. These dynamic elements are driven by a simple subclass of Java 3D's Behavior acting as a timer, which triggers updates to the scene every 50 milliseconds. The user's viewpoint (the camera) can be zoomed in and out, panned, and rotated with the mouse and control keys (courtesy of Java 3D's OrbitBehavior class). We will then convert the example into a screensaver with the help of JScreenSaver, a Java-based Microsoft Windows screensaver loader.

The Game of Life

The application described in this chapter is a 3D version of British mathematician John Conway's *Game of Life,* a well-known cellular automaton. The game concept is simple to understand, but displaying the game's execution in 3D is more complicated; for this reason it makes a good introductory example.

The original game consists of an infinite 2D grid of cells, each of which is either *alive* or *dead.* At every time "tick," a cell evaluates rules involving the current state of its immediate neighbors to decide whether to continue to live, to die, to stay dead, or be born. The rules in Conway's game are the following:

- Any living cell with fewer than two neighbors, or more than three, dies.

- Any living cell with two or three neighbors continues living.

- Any dead cell with exactly three neighbors comes to life.

All the cells in the grid are updated simultaneously in each time tick, so the entire grid moves to a new state (or *generation*) at once. The infinite grid is usually implemented as a finite 2D array, with cells at an edge using the cells at the opposite edge as neighbors.

An important factor is the initial configuration of the grid (i.e., which cells start as alive). Another variable is the shape of the grid: 1D and 3D (my interest) are possible, as are special shapes.

Although Conway's game is only a game, cellular automata have found application in more serious areas, such as computability theory and theoretical biology. I include links to more information at the end of the chapter.

Running Life3D

My 3D version of the game, called Life3D, is shown in action in Figures 2-1 and 2-2; the screenshots were taken several generations apart.

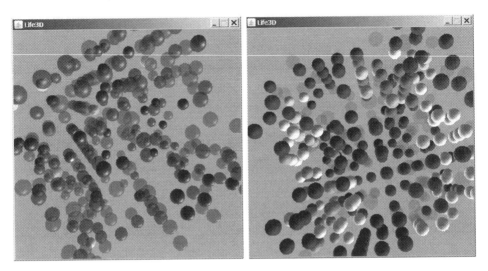

Figure 2-1. *Life3D in action*   **Figure 2-2.** *Life3D still in action*

Each cell is represented by a sphere, and the grid is a 10-by-10-by-10 lattice. When a cell is first born (or reborn) it is painted blue, then gradually changes color as it ages, through green, yellow, orange, and finally to red. When a cell dies, it fades away, and when one is born, it gradually appears.

The grid is rotating by random amounts along the x-, y-, and z- axes during all of this, causing it to change direction at regular intervals.

Configuring Life3D

Life3D is configured using a properties file, life3DProps.txt. A properties file is a series of key=value pairs that can be read and updated easily with Java's Properties class. life3DProps.txt stores information on seven attributes: whether it's full-screen or not; the window's width and height (if it's not full-screen); the rotation speed of the grid; the scene's background color; and the game's birth and die ranges. For example, my current version of life3DProps.txt contains the following attributes:

```
fullscreen=false
width=512
height=512
speed=fast
bgColour=blue
birth=5
die=3 4 5 6
```

I'll explain how the birth and die ranges are used to initialize the game rules when I get to the CellsGrid class in the "Managing the Grid" section later in the chapter. Since the properties file is text, it can be edited directly. However, Life3D includes a configuration screen (see Figure 2-3), which is displayed when the application is started with the -edit option:

```
$ java Life3D -edit
```

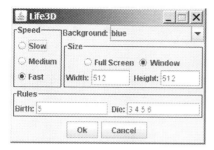

Figure 2-3. *The configuration screen*

The adjusted properties are saved back to life3DProps.txt when the OK button is pressed. Next time Life3D is started, it will use the new settings.

A Life3D Screensaver

It may seem a little strange that Life3D has two modes of operation: to display the 3D life lattice, and to access and change configuration details. Why not utilize two distinct applications instead?

The main reason for integrating the configuration screen into Life3D is to make it fit the requirements of JScreenSaver, a Java-based Windows screensaver loader, which I'm using to execute Life3D as a screensaver.

Figure 2-4 shows Window XP's Display Properties window with the Screensaver tab ready to start Life3D.

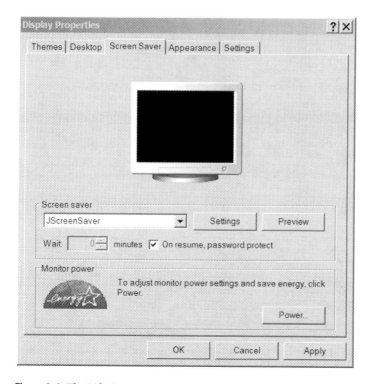

Figure 2-4. *The Life3D screensaver*

To be honest, there's not much to see in Figure 2-4, since JScreenSaver doesn't support drawing to the preview miniscreen in the middle of the tab. However, JScreenSaver is shown as the currently selected saver.

Clicking the Settings button brings up the configuration screen shown in Figure 2-3, while the Preview button starts Life3D proper (e.g., as shown in Figures 2-1 and 2-2).

I talk more about how to convert Life3D into a screensaver module at the end of this chapter in the "Time for Screensavers" section and discuss some other ways of making screensavers.

An Overview of the Life3D Classes

Figure 2-5 shows the class diagrams for the Life3D application. Only the public methods are shown, and I've left out superclasses and listeners.

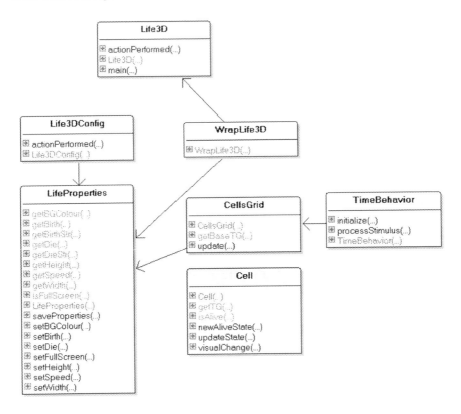

Figure 2-5. *Class diagrams for Life3D*

Life3D is a subclass of JFrame and manages the creation of the configuration screen (handled by Life3DConfig) or the 3D scene (in WrapLife3D) depending on whether the command line includes -edit. Both Life3DConfig and Wrap3DLife are subclasses of JPanel.

Life3DConfig is a conventional mix of Swing controls for building the interface shown in Figure 2-3. It uses LifeProperties as an interface to the properties file, calling various get and set methods for the seven properties. I won't explain the Life3DConfig or LifeProperties classes in this chapter, since they're quite standard examples of using Swing and properties; both classes are fully documented.

WrapLife3D is the home for Java 3D's rendering of the scene, which is displayed in a Canvas3D object surrounded by WrapLife3D's JPanel. WrapLife3D handles many elements of the scene, including the background, lighting, and moving the camera. WrapLife3D delegates the creation of the cells grid to the CellsGrid class, which represents each cell (sphere) with a Cell object.

The TimeBehavior class (a subclass of Java 3D's Behavior) periodically calls the update() method in CellsGrid, triggering generational change in the grid.

In the rest of this chapter, I look at each of these classes in more detail.

Deciding How to Start

Life3D can progress in three ways:

1. If -edit is supplied on the command line, a configuration screen managed by Life3DConfig is slotted into Life3D's JFrame.

2. If the Java 3D API is found on the machine, the 3D application is started.

3. If Java 3D isn't found, Life3D reports the problem and terminates.

The three-way *if* branch corresponding to these choices is located in Life3D's constructor:

```
public Life3D(String[] args)
{
  super("Life3D");

  LifeProperties lifeProps = new LifeProperties();

  Container c = getContentPane();
  c.setLayout( new BorderLayout() );

  if (args.length > 0 && args[0].equals("-edit")) {
    // view/change application properties
    Life3DConfig l3Ctrls = new Life3DConfig(lifeProps);
    c.add(l3Ctrls, BorderLayout.CENTER);
  }
  else if (hasJ3D()) {
    // start the Life3D application
    WrapLife3D w3d = new WrapLife3D(this, lifeProps);
    c.add(w3d, BorderLayout.CENTER);
    if (lifeProps.isFullScreen())
      setUndecorated(true);   // no menubar, borders
  }
  else
    reportProb(c);

  setDefaultCloseOperation( JFrame.EXIT_ON_CLOSE );
  pack();
  setResizable(false);    // fixed size display

  // center this window
  Dimension screenDim = Toolkit.getDefaultToolkit().getScreenSize();
  Dimension winDim = this.getSize();
  this.setLocation( (screenDim.width-winDim.width)/2,
                    (screenDim.height-winDim.height)/2);

  setVisible(true);
} // end of Life3D()
```

> **▓Note** Code shown in bold in a listing (e.g. the call to has J3D()) will be explained in more detail later in the chapter.

The constructor creates a LifeProperties object to act as the interface to the properties file. A reference to this object is passed to both JPanels (Life3DConfig and Wrap3DLife), and is also used inside Life3D.

If the properties specify full-screen rendering, the JFrame decorations (its menu bar and borders) are switched off. The resizing of the window is done indirectly by the resizing of Wrap3DLife's JPanel, as you'll see when I get to that class.

Since the Java 3D API is not part of the standard Java SE 6 distribution, it's a good idea to check for it and try to "die" gracefully when the API isn't found.

hasJ3D() checks for the presence of a key Java 3D class—SimpleUniverse—although any Java 3D class would do:

```
private boolean hasJ3D()
// check if Java 3D is available
{
  try {    // test for a Java 3D class
    Class.forName("com.sun.j3d.utils.universe.SimpleUniverse");
    return true;
  }
  catch(ClassNotFoundException e) {
    System.err.println("Java 3D not installed");
    return false;
  }
} // end of hasJ3D()
```

reportProb() reports on Java 3D using a JPanel filled with a label and a nonfunctioning button showing the Java 3D home URL (see Figure 2-6). I'll make the button start a browser using Java SE 6's new Desktop API in the next chapter.

Figure 2-6. *The error reporting screen*

Displaying the 3D Game

If Java 3D is present, WrapLife3D's constructor is called. Its main tasks are to integrate Java 3D's Canvas3D class into its JPanel and to create the scene graph that's rendered inside the Canvas3D. Two lesser jobs are to fix the size of the JPanel (full-screen or a specific size) and to set up keyboard processing.

Integrating Java 3D and Swing

The Canvas3D view onto the 3D scene is created using the following code:

```
// inside the WrapLife3D constructor
setLayout( new BorderLayout() );

GraphicsConfiguration config =
            SimpleUniverse.getPreferredConfiguration();
Canvas3D canvas3D = new Canvas3D(config);
add("Center", canvas3D);
```

Some care must be taken when using Canvas3D, since it's a heavyweight GUI element (a thin layer over an OS-generated window). Heavyweight components aren't easily combined with Swing controls, which are lightweight (the controls are mostly generated by Java itself). Problems are avoided if the Canvas3D object is embedded in a JPanel (as here); then the panel can be safely integrated with the rest of the Swing-built application.

There's a detailed discussion of the issues related to combining Canvas3D and Swing at j3d.org (http://www.j3d.org/tutorials/quick_fix/swing.html).

Java 3D 1.5 offers an experimental JCanvas3D class, a lightweight version of Canvas3D. The JOGL rendering pipeline (another 1.5 innovation) allows JCanvas3D to be accelerated, but its performance doesn't yet match that of Canvas3D.

The Canvas3D object is initialized with a configuration obtained from getPreferredConfiguration(); this method queries the hardware for rendering information. Some older Java 3D programs don't bother initializing a GraphicsConfiguration object, using null as the argument to the Canvas3D constructor instead; this isn't good programming practice.

Window Sizing

WrapLife3D checks the properties file (via the LifeProperties object) to see whether the application should be full-screen or not, and sets the size of the JPanel accordingly:

```
// global
private LifeProperties lifeProps;

// in the WrapLife3D constructor
if (lifeProps.isFullScreen())
  setPreferredSize( Toolkit.getDefaultToolkit().getScreenSize() );
else {   // not full-screen
  int width = lifeProps.getWidth();
  int height = lifeProps.getHeight();
  setPreferredSize( new Dimension(width, height));
}
```

The window's width and height are obtained from the properties file.

The changes to the JPanel's dimensions will affect the parent JFrame since it is tied to the size of the JPanel by its call to Window.pack().

Processing Key Presses

WrapLife3D gives focus to the Canvas3D object, called *canvas3D*, so that keyboard events will be visible to behaviors in the scene graph. This is a good general strategy since most applications require user input to be directed to the code controlling the scene graph. However, the scene dynamics in Life3D are driven by a time-triggered behavior, so it's not really necessary to set the focus. I've left these lines in since they're needed in almost every other program we'll consider.

Keyboard input is utilized in Life3D, but only as a quick way to terminate the application. This feature becomes essential when Life3D is shown in full-screen mode, since there isn't a menu bar with a close box.

A key listener is attached to the canvas and calls Window.dispose() in the top-level JFrame:

```
// global
private Life3D topLevel;   // the JFrame


// in the WrapLife3D constructor
canvas3D.setFocusable(true);
canvas3D.requestFocus();
   // the canvas now has focus, so receives key events
```

```
canvas3D.addKeyListener( new KeyAdapter() {
// listen for esc, q, end, ctrl-c on the canvas to
// allow a convenient exit from the full-screen configuration
  public void keyPressed(KeyEvent e)
  { int keyCode = e.getKeyCode();
    if ((keyCode == KeyEvent.VK_ESCAPE) ||
        (keyCode == KeyEvent.VK_Q) ||
        (keyCode == KeyEvent.VK_END) ||
        ((keyCode == KeyEvent.VK_C) && e.isControlDown()) ) {
      topLevel.dispose();
      System.exit(0);
      // exit() alone isn't sufficient most of the time
    }
  }
});
```

The call to dispose() ensures that all the screen resources are released, which doesn't seem to be the case when the key listener only calls System.exit().

Scene Graph Creation

The scene graph is created by the WrapLife3D constructor after instantiating the Canvas3D object:

```
// globals
private SimpleUniverse su;
private BranchGroup sceneBG;


// inside the WrapLife3D constructor
su = new SimpleUniverse(canvas3D);

createSceneGraph();
initUserPosition();        // set user's viewpoint
orbitControls(canvas3D);   // controls for moving the viewpoint

su.addBranchGraph( sceneBG );
```

The SimpleUniverse object, called *su*, very kindly generates a standard view branch graph and the VirtualUniverse and Locale nodes of the scene graph for me, but I have to do the rest. createSceneGraph() sets up the lighting, the sky background, the floor, and the cells grid, while initUserPosition() and orbitControls() handle viewer issues. The three method calls in bold are explained in more detail later: createSceneGraph() is described next, initUserPosition() in the "Viewer Positioning" section, and orbitControls() in the "Viewer Movement" section.

createSceneGraph() builds the application scene graph below a sceneBG BranchGroup, which is connected to the graph made by SimpleUniverse by calling addBranchGroup():

```
// globals
private static final int BOUNDSIZE = 100;  // larger than world

private BranchGroup sceneBG;
private BoundingSphere bounds;   // for environment nodes


private void createSceneGraph()
{
```

```
sceneBG = new BranchGroup();
bounds = new BoundingSphere(new Point3d(0,0,0), BOUNDSIZE);

lightScene();        // add the lights
addBackground();     // add the sky
addGrid();           // add cells grid

sceneBG.compile();   // fix the scene
} // end of createSceneGraph()
```

Various methods add subgraphs to sceneBG to build up the content branch graph. sceneBG is compiled once the graph has been finalized to allow Java 3D to optimize it. The optimizations may involve reordering the graph and regrouping and combining nodes. For example, a chain of TransformGroup nodes containing different translations may be combined into a single node.

The *bounds* variable is a global BoundingSphere used to specify the influence of environment nodes for lighting, background, and the OrbitBehavior object. The bounding sphere is placed at the center of the scene and affects everything within a BOUNDSIZE units radius. Bounding boxes and polytopes are also available.

The scene graph created by WrapLife3D is shown in Figure 2-7.

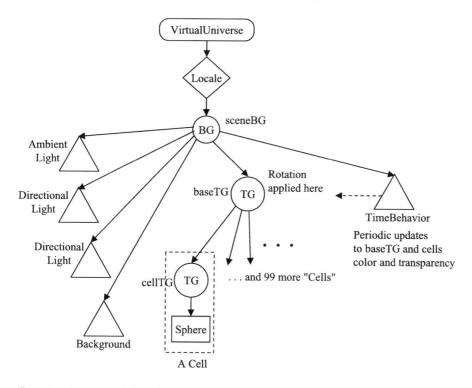

Figure 2-7. *Scene graph for Life3D*

The three lights are created by lightScene(), the Background node by addBackGround(), and the subgraph starting at the baseTG TransformGroup by addGrid(). The TimeBehavior object is also instantiated in addGrid().

The view branch part of the scene graph is missing from Figure 2-7, since it's created by the SimpleUniverse object in WrapLife3D.

Lighting the Scene

One ambient and two directional lights are added to the scene by lightScene(). An ambient light reaches every corner of the world, illuminating everything equally:

```
private void lightScene()
{
  Color3f white = new Color3f(1.0f, 1.0f, 1.0f);

  // Set up the ambient light
  AmbientLight ambientLightNode = new AmbientLight(white);
  ambientLightNode.setInfluencingBounds(bounds);
  sceneBG.addChild(ambientLightNode);

  // Set up the directional lights
  Vector3f light1Direction  = new Vector3f(-1.0f, 1.0f, -1.0f);
        // light coming from left, up, and back quadrant
  Vector3f light2Direction  = new Vector3f(1.0f, 1.0f, 1.0f);
        // light coming from right, up, and front quadrant

  DirectionalLight light1 =
          new DirectionalLight(white, light1Direction);
  light1.setInfluencingBounds(bounds);
  sceneBG.addChild(light1);

  DirectionalLight light2 =
      new DirectionalLight(white, light2Direction);
  light2.setInfluencingBounds(bounds);
  sceneBG.addChild(light2);
}  // end of lightScene()
```

The color of the light is set and the ambient source is created along with bounds and added to the scene. The Color3f() constructor takes red/green/blue (RGB) values between 0.0f and 1.0f (1.0f being "full-on").

A directional light mimics a light from a distant source, hitting the surfaces of objects from a specified direction. The main difference from an ambient light is the requirement for a direction, such as in the following:

```
Vector3f light1Direction  = new Vector3f(-1.0f, 1.0f, -1.0f);
    // light coming from left, up, and back quadrant
```

The direction is the vector starting at the specified coordinate, pointing toward (0, 0, 0); the light can be imagined to be multiple parallel lines with that direction, originating at infinity.

Point lights and spotlights are the other forms of Java 3D lighting. Point lights position the light in space, emitting in all directions. Spotlights are focused point lights aimed in a particular direction.

The Scene's Background

A background for a scene can be specified as a constant color (as in the method given next), a static image, or a texture-mapped shape such as a sphere:

```
private void addBackground()
/* The choice of background color is obtained from the
```

```
    properties file (blue, green, white, or black). */
{
  Background back = new Background();
  back.setApplicationBounds( bounds );

  int bgColour = lifeProps.getBGColour();
  if (bgColour == LifeProperties.BLUE)
    back.setColor(0.17f, 0.65f, 0.92f);     // sky blue color
  else if (bgColour == LifeProperties.GREEN)
    back.setColor(0.5f, 1.0f, 0.5f);        // grass color
  else if (bgColour == LifeProperties.WHITE)
    back.setColor(1.0f, 1.0f, 0.8f);        // off-white
  // else black by default
  sceneBG.addChild( back );
}  // end of addBackground()
```

The code is complicated by the need to check with the LifeProperties object to determine the currently specified color, as represented by the constants LifeProperties.BLUE, LifeProperties.GREEN, LifeProperties.WHITE, and LifeProperties.BLACK. addBackground() maps these to RGB values.

Building the Cells Grid and Making It Behave

The work required to create the scene graph for the grid is left to a CellsGrid object. addGrid() creates the object and a TimeBehavior instance for triggering grid changes:

```
// time delay (in ms) to regulate update speed
private static final int TIME_DELAY = 50;


private void addGrid()
/*  Create the cells grid and a time behavior to update
    it at TIME_DELAY intervals. */
{
  CellsGrid cellsGrid = new CellsGrid(lifeProps);
  sceneBG.addChild( cellsGrid.getBaseTG() );

  TimeBehavior tb = new TimeBehavior(TIME_DELAY, cellsGrid);
  tb.setSchedulingBounds(bounds);
  sceneBG.addChild(tb);
}  // end of addGrid()
```

The LifeProperties object, lifeProps, is passed to the CellsGrid object since the properties include the rotation speed for the grid and the birth and die ranges, which CellsGrid handles.

Viewer Positioning

The scene graph in Figure 2-7 doesn't include the view branch graph; that branch is shown in Figure 2-8.

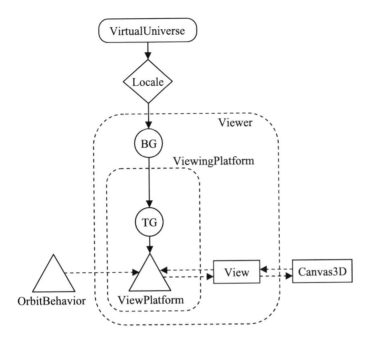

Figure 2-8. *The view branch graph*

Most of the branch is generated by a call to the SimpleUniverse constructor in the WrapLife3D() constructor:

```
su = new SimpleUniverse(canvas3D);
```

SimpleUniverse offers simplified access to the view branch graph via the ViewingPlatform and Viewer classes, which are mapped to the graph (shown as dotted boxes in Figure 2-8).

ViewingPlatform is used in initUserPosition() to access the TransformGroup above the ViewPlatform node:

```
// global
private static final Point3d USERPOSN = new Point3d(-2,5,10);
  // initial user position


private void initUserPosition()
/* Set the user's initial viewpoint using lookAt()   */
{
  ViewingPlatform vp = su.getViewingPlatform();
  TransformGroup steerTG = vp.getViewPlatformTransform();

  Transform3D t3d = new Transform3D( );
  steerTG.getTransform( t3d );

  t3d.lookAt( USERPOSN, new Point3d(0,0,0), new Vector3d(0,1,0));
  // args are: viewer posn, where looking, up direction
  t3d.invert();

  steerTG.setTransform(t3d);
}  // end of initUserPosition()
```

lookAt() is a convenient way to set the viewer's position (i.e., the camera position) in the virtual world. The method requires the viewer's intended position, the point that she is looking at, and a vector specifying the upward direction. In this application, the viewer's position is USERPOSN (the (-2, 5, 10) coordinate); she is looking toward the origin (0, 0, 0), and "up" is along the positive y-axis. This is illustrated by Figure 2-9.

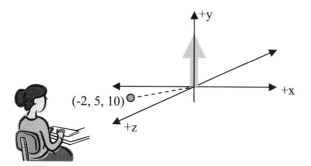

Figure 2-9. *lookAt() depicted graphically*

invert() is required since the position is relative to the viewer rather than an object in the scene.

Viewer Movement

The user is able to move through the scene by connecting a Java 3D OrbitBehavior object to the view graph (the ViewPlatform triangle in Figure 2-8). It offers a combination of control keys and mouse button presses to pan, zoom, and rotate the viewer's position.

The behavior is set up in orbitControls() in WrapCheckers3D:

```
private void orbitControls(Canvas3D c)
{
  OrbitBehavior orbit =
        new OrbitBehavior(c, OrbitBehavior.REVERSE_ALL);
  orbit.setSchedulingBounds(bounds);

  ViewingPlatform vp = su.getViewingPlatform();
  vp.setViewPlatformBehavior(orbit);
}  // end of orbitControls()
```

The REVERSE_ALL flag ensures that the viewpoint moves in the same direction as the mouse.

There are numerous other flags and methods for affecting the rotation, translation, and zooming characteristics, explained in the OrbitBehavior class documentation.

The Java 3D classes, MouseRotate, MouseTranslate, and MouseZoom, are similar behavior classes that appear in many examples; their principal difference from OrbitBehavior is that they affect the objects in the scene rather than the viewer.

Most games, such as first-person shooters, require greater control over the viewer's movements than these utility behaviors can offer, so I'll be implementing my own behaviors in later chapters.

Behaviors in Java 3D

A Behavior object is used to monitor and respond to events occurring in a Java 3D application, such as key presses, the rendering of frames, the passage of time, the movement of the user's viewpoint,

Transform3D changes, and collisions. These events, called *wakeup criteria*, activate the Behavior object so it can carry out specified tasks.

A typical Behavior subclass has the following format:

```
public class FooBehavior extends Behavior
{
  private WakeupCondition wc;    // what will wake the object
  // other global variables

  public FooBehavior(…)
  { // initialise globals
    wc = new ...  //  create the wakeup condition
  }

  public void initialize()
  // register interest in the wakeup condition
  {  wakeupOn(wc);  }


  public void processStimulus(Enumeration criteria)
  {
     WakeupCriterion wakeup;
     while (criteria.hasMoreElements() ) {
       wakeup = (WakeupCriterion) criteria.nextElement();
       // determine the type of criterion assigned to wakeup;
       // carry out the relevant task;
     }
     wakeupOn(wc);  // re-register interest
   } // end of processStimulus()

} // end of FooBehavior class
```

A subclass of Behavior must implement initialize() and processStimulus(). initialize() should register the behavior's wakeup condition, but other initialization code can be placed in the constructor for the class. processStimulus() is called by Java 3D when an event (or events) of interest to the behavior is received. Often, the simple matter of processStimulus() being called is enough to decide what task should be carried out (e.g., as in TimeBehavior in the next section). In more complex classes, the events passed to the object must be analyzed. For example, a key press may be the wakeup criterion, but the code will also need to determine which key was pressed.

A common error when implementing processStimulus() is to forget to reregister the wakeup condition at the end of the method:

```
wakeupOn(wc);  // re-register interest
```

If this is skipped, the behavior won't be triggered again.

A WakeupCondition object can be a combination of one or more WakeupCriterion. There are many subclasses of WakeupCriterion, including the following:

- *WakeupOnAWTEvent*: An AWT event is generated when a key or the mouse is manipulated (e.g., a key is pressed, or the mouse is moved).

- *WakeupOnElapsedFrames*: An event can be generated after a specified number of renderings. This criterion should be used with care since it may result in the object being triggered many times per second.

- *WakeupOnElapsedTime*: An event can be generated after a specified time interval. WakeupOnElapsedTime is used in TimeBehavior in the next section.

Another common mistake when using Behaviors is to forget to specify a scheduling volume (or *region*) with Behavior.setSchedulingBounds(). A Behavior node is only active (and able to receive events) when the user's viewpoint intersects a Behavior object's scheduling volume. If no volume is set, the Behavior will never be triggered.

The volume for TimeBehavior is set in addGrids() when the behavior object is created.

A Time-Based Behavior

The TimeBehavior class is pleasantly short since processStimulus() doesn't need to examine its wakeup criteria:

```
public class TimeBehavior extends Behavior
{
  private WakeupCondition timeOut;
  private int timeDelay;
  private CellsGrid cellsGrid;


  public TimeBehavior(int td, CellsGrid cg)
  { timeDelay = td;
    cellsGrid = cg;
    timeOut = new WakeupOnElapsedTime(timeDelay);
  }

  public void initialize()
  {  wakeupOn(timeOut);  }

  public void processStimulus(Enumeration criteria)
  { cellsGrid.update();   // ignore criteria
    wakeupOn(timeOut);
  }

}  // end of TimeBehavior class
```

The wakeup condition is an instance of WakeupOnElapsedTime, making TimeBehavior the Java 3D equivalent of a timer that fires every timeDelay milliseconds. It calls the update() method in CellsGrid to change the grid.

Managing the Grid

CellsGrid creates and controls a 10-by-10-by-10 grid of Cell objects centered at (0, 0, 0) in the scene.

TimeBehavior periodically calls CellsGrid's update() method to update the grid. Since I'm interested in using Life3D as a screensaver later on, an update can trigger either a state change *or* a visual change. Figure 2-10 shows the general idea: a state change is followed by a series of visual changes, and then the sequence repeats. The number of changes is determined by the MAX_TRANS value plus 1.

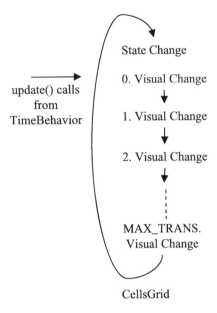

State Change

0. Visual Change

1. Visual Change

2. Visual Change

MAX_TRANS.
Visual Change

update() calls
from
TimeBehavior

CellsGrid

Figure 2-10. *Updates causing state and visual changes*

A state change changes the grid's cells state by applying game rules using birth and die ranges. I describe what these ranges are later in this section.

Most updates trigger visual changes to the cells, which affect their visibility or color. A visual transition is spread out over several updates, so a sphere gradually appears, disappears, or changes color based on its current age. The choice of transition depends on the current visual state of the cell, which I explain when I describe the Cell class in "The Cell" section later in the chapter.

Every update also causes the grid to rotate, and the rotation axis is periodically changed, so the grid moves in a random manner.

Accessing Properties

The birth and die ranges and the grid rotation speed are specified by properties obtained from a LifeProperties object. The code is located in the CellsGrid constructor:

```
// globals
private LifeProperties lifeProps;

// birth and die ranges used in the life rules
boolean[] birthRange, dieRange;

public CellsGrid(LifeProperties lps)
{
  lifeProps = lps;

  // load birth and die ranges
  birthRange = lifeProps.getBirth();
  dieRange = lifeProps.getDie();

  setTurnAngle();
```

```
      // scene graph creation code
}  // end of CellsGrid() constructor
```

setTurnAngle() reads a speed constant from the properties file (it may be SLOW, MEDIUM, or FAST), and converts it into a rotation angle:

```
// globals
// grid rotation amount
private static final double ROTATE_AMT = Math.toRadians(4);
                                         // 4 degrees
private double turnAngle;

private void setTurnAngle()
{
  int speed = lifeProps.getSpeed();

  if (speed == LifeProperties.SLOW)
    turnAngle = ROTATE_AMT/4;
  else if (speed == LifeProperties.MEDIUM)
    turnAngle = ROTATE_AMT/2;
  else  // fast --> large rotation
    turnAngle = ROTATE_AMT;
}  // end of setTurnAngle()
```

The grid's turning angle is larger for faster speeds.

Creating the Grid Scene Graph

The CellsGrid constructor is also responsible for building the scene graph branch for the cells. This corresponds to the branch below the baseTG TransformGroup node in Figure 2-7, which is repeated here again as Figure 2-11 for convenience.

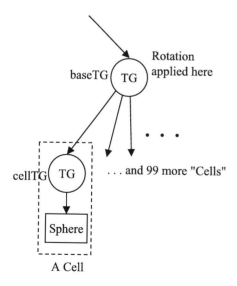

Figure 2-11. *The cells grid part of the scene graph*

The code for creating the cells is the following:

```
// globals
// number of cells along the x-, y-, and z- axes
private final static int GRID_LEN = 10;

private Cell[][][] cells;         // cells storage
private TransformGroup baseTG;    // used to rotate the grid


// in the CellsGrid constructor
/* Allow baseTG to be read and changed at runtime (so
   it can be rotated). */
baseTG = new TransformGroup();
baseTG.setCapability(TransformGroup.ALLOW_TRANSFORM_READ);
baseTG.setCapability(TransformGroup.ALLOW_TRANSFORM_WRITE);

// initialize the grid with Cell objects
cells = new Cell[GRID_LEN][GRID_LEN][GRID_LEN];
for (int i=0; i < GRID_LEN; i++)
  for (int j=0; j < GRID_LEN; j++)
    for (int k=0; k < GRID_LEN; k++) {
      cells[i][j][k] =
          new Cell(i-GRID_LEN/2, j-GRID_LEN/2, k-GRID_LEN/2);
          // subtract GRID_LEN/2 so grid is centered
      baseTG.addChild( cells[i][j][k].getTG() );  //connect to baseTG
    }
```

The runtime manipulation of scene graph nodes is only possible if those nodes have the desired capabilities switched on with setCapability() calls. The orientation of the baseTG TransformGroup will be read and changed at runtime, necessitating two setCapability() calls.

Each cell is managed by a Cell object that is passed a coordinate derived from its position in the cells[][][] array. The subtraction of GRID_LEN/2 from i, j, and k means that the 10-by-10-by-10 grid is centered on the origin.

To understand this, it helps to recall how the viewer is orientated with respect to the axes (see Figure 2-12).

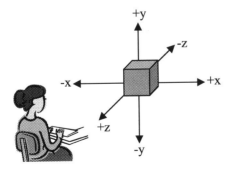

Figure 2-12. *Axes in Java 3D*

If a cell is positioned using only the i, j, and k values, it would be located too close to the viewer, too far to the right, and too far up. The subtraction of GRID_LEN/2 moves the cell back toward a central region around the origin.

Updating the Cells States

As shown in Figure 2-10, an update() call either triggers a state change or a visual change. The cycling through the changes is done using a counter, called transCounter, which is incremented from 0 to MAX_TRANS, then repeats. When transCounter is 0, the state of the grid's cells is updated, and for other values, the cells' visuals are changed. The grid is rotated at every update, irrespective of the transCounter value:

```
// globals
// number of updates used to complete a visual transition
public static final int MAX_TRANS = 8;

// transition (transparency/color change) step counter
private int transCounter = 0;
private Random rand = new Random();


public void update()
{
  if (transCounter == 0) {   // time for grid state change
    stateChange();
    turnAxis = rand.nextInt(3);  // change rotation axis
    transCounter = 1;
  }
  else {   // make a visual change
    for (int i=0; i < GRID_LEN; i++)
      for (int j=0; j < GRID_LEN; j++)
        for (int k=0; k < GRID_LEN; k++)
          cells[i][j][k].visualChange(transCounter);

    transCounter++;
    if (transCounter > MAX_TRANS)
      transCounter = 0;   // reset counter
  }

  doRotate();   // rotate in every update() call
}  // end of update()
```

A visual change is handled by iterating over the cells[][][] array and calling Cell.visualChange() for each cell. The current value of transCounter is supplied, and Cell has access to the MAX_TRANS constant as well, since it's declared public in CellsGrid.

The state change performed by stateChange() is a two-stage affair. First, it determines the state of each cell in the next generation. Only when every cell has been examined is each updated. The state update includes the first visual change to a cell (see Figure 2-10):

```
private void stateChange()
{
  boolean willLive;

  // calculate next state for each cell
  for (int i=0; i < GRID_LEN; i++)
    for (int j=0; j < GRID_LEN; j++)
      for (int k=0; k < GRID_LEN; k++) {
        willLive = aliveNextState(i, j, k);
        cells[i][j][k].newAliveState(willLive);
      }
```

```
   // update each cell
   for (int i=0; i < GRID_LEN; i++)
     for (int j=0; j < GRID_LEN; j++)
       for (int k=0; k < GRID_LEN; k++) {
         cells[i][j][k].updateState();
         cells[i][j][k].visualChange(0);
       }
 }  // end of stateChange()
```

The next state for a cell is determined by calling aliveNextState(), and the value is stored in the cell by calling Cell.newAliveState(). However, the cell doesn't actually use the state until Cell.updateState() is called inside the second for-loop block.

Will the Cell Live or Die?

There are many ways of specifying how a cell's state may change. The state diagram in Figure 2-13 shows the four possible transitions between the alive and dead states.

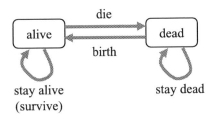

Figure 2-13. *Cell state changes*

CellsGrid utilizes rules that specify reasons to *die* (i.e., move from the alive state to dead), and reasons for *birth* (i.e., from dead to alive). If these rules can't be applied to a particular cell, it stays in its current state.

The coding uses birth and die ranges, which specify the *number* of cell neighbors that can cause a birth or die transition. For example, the birth and die ranges might be the following:

```
birth range = {5, 10}
die range = {3, 4, 5, 6}
```

These ranges state that a dead cell is born if it has five or ten living neighbors, and an alive cell dies if it has three, four, five, or six living neighbors.

On the Life3D configuration screen (see Figure 2-3), these ranges can be changed by typing in new numbers separated by spaces. Figure 2-3 shows that the birth range has been changed to only use five neighbors.

The birth and die ranges are encoded as boolean arrays in the CellsGrid code. For the birthRange[] array, if birthRange[i] is true, then i living neighbors are needed to bring a cell to life. Each array has 27 elements, large enough for the 26 neighbors of a 3D cell, with the 0th entry employed when having *no* living neighbors will trigger the transition.

For the previous example, birthRange[5] and birthRange[10] will be true, and its other elements will be false. The dieRange[] array will contain true at index positions 3, 4, 5, and 6.

aliveNextState() uses the birth and die ranges by first collecting two pieces of information for the cell at coordinate position (i, j, k) in the cells[][][] array: the number of its living neighbors, and its current state (i.e., alive or dead):

```
private boolean aliveNextState(int i, int j, int k)
{
  // count all the living neighbors, but not the cell itself
  int numberLiving = 0;
  for(int r=i-1; r <= i+1; r++)  // range i-1 to i+1
    for(int s=j-1; s <= j+1; s++)  // range j-1 to j+1
      for(int t=k-1; t <= k+1; t++) {  // range k-1 to k+1
        if ((r==i) && (s==j) && (t==k))
          continue;   // skip self
        else if (isAlive(r,s,t))
          numberLiving++;
      }

  // get the cell's current life state
  boolean currAliveState = isAlive(i,j,k);

  // ** Life Rules **: calculate the cell's next life state

  if (birthRange[numberLiving] && !currAliveState)
    return true;    // to be born && dead now --> make alive
  else if (dieRange[numberLiving]  && currAliveState)
    return false;  // to die && alive now --> kill off
  else
    return currAliveState;  // no change
}  // end of aliveNextState()
```

aliveNextState() returns true or false, representing alive or dead, and this value becomes the cell's new state when it is updated.

isAlive() gets the cell's current state by calling Cell.isAlive(), and also deals with grid edge cases, when the neighbor is on the opposite side of the grid:

```
private boolean isAlive(int i, int j, int k)
{
  // deal with edge cases for cells array
  i = rangeCorrect(i);
  j = rangeCorrect(j);
  k = rangeCorrect(k);
  return  cells[i][j][k].isAlive();
}  // end of isAlive()


private int rangeCorrect(int index)
/* if the cell index is out of range then use the index of
   the opposite edge */
{
  if (index < 0)
    return (GRID_LEN + index);
  else if (index > GRID_LEN-1)
    return (index - GRID_LEN);
  else // make no change
    return index;
}  // end of rangeCorrect()
```

Rotating the Grid

The baseTG TransformGroup stores its position, rotation, and scaling information in a 4-by-4 matrix. Thankfully, we can manipulate it using Java 3D's Transform3D class, which offers numerous methods for translating, rotating, and scaling.

The programming strategy is to copy the matrix from a TransformGroup node as a Transform3D object, apply an operation to it (e.g., a rotation), then write the changed Transform3D back in to the TransformGroup. When the scene is next rendered, the node will be changed accordingly.

baseTG highlights an important advantage of the scene graph hierarchy. Since all the cells are children nodes of baseTG (see Figure 2-11), they'll be affected by the transformation applied to baseTG. This means that only baseTG needs to be rotated in order to turn the entire grid.

doRotate() is called at the end of the update() method:

```
// globals
// reusable Transform3D object
private Transform3D t3d = new Transform3D();
private Transform3D rotT3d = new Transform3D();

private int turnAxis = 0;

private void doRotate()
// rotate the object turnAngle radians around an axis
{
  baseTG.getTransform(t3d);  // get current rotation
  rotT3d.setIdentity();       // reset the rotation transform object

  switch (turnAxis) {    // set rotation based on the current axis
    case 0: rotT3d.rotX(turnAngle); break;
    case 1: rotT3d.rotY(turnAngle); break;
    case 2: rotT3d.rotZ(turnAngle); break;
    default: System.out.println("Unknown axis of rotation"); break;
  }

  t3d.mul(rotT3d);            // 'add' new rotation to current one
  baseTG.setTransform(t3d);   // update the TG
}  // end of doRotate()
```

The transformation matrix is copied into t3d using TransformGroup.getTransform(), and written back with TransformGroup.setTransform() at the end of the method. t3d is utilized each time that doRotate() is called, rather than repeatedly creating a temporary object, to reduce garbage collection and so improve the application's efficiency.

doRotate() applies a rotation around either the x-, y-, or z- axis using the turnAngle value (which was set in getTurnAngle()). The rotation direction can be determined using *the right-hand rule*: point the thumb of your right hand along the positive axis being used for the rotation, and the turning direction will be the direction of your closed fingers (as shown in Figure 2-14).

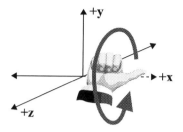

Figure 2-14. *The right-hand rule for rotation*

Figure 2-14 illustrates the direction of a positive rotation around the x-axis.

The choice of axis depends on the turnAxis value, which is randomly changed whenever there's a state change (the code is in update()). The rotation is stored in rotT3d, another reusable Transform3D object, using Transform3D.rotX(), rotY(), or rotZ() to store an x-, y-, or z- axis rotation.

If you run Life3D, it seems that the rotations are much more varied than just turns around the three axes. The apparent variety is because a rotation around one axis affects the position of the other axes. This makes subsequent rotations using those axes appear different.

For instance, when the rotation in Figure 2-14 is carried out on baseTG, it turns its y- and z- axes as well: the +y-axis rotates forward, and the +z-axis downward. If a subsequent rotation is applied around those axes, it will be relative to their new orientations.

The rotT3d rotation is applied to the existing transformation in t3d by multiplying the objects together:

```
t3d.mul(rotT3d);
```

This is t3d = t3d * rotT3d, which multiplies the object's matrices together. This has the effect of *adding* the rotT3d rotation to the rotation in t3d.

baseTG's initial orientation is specified when it's created in the CellsGrid constructor:

```
baseTG = new TransformGroup();
```

The Transform3D component is set to be the identity matrix, which means that the node is positioned at the origin and is unrotated and unscaled.

The Cell

A good way to understand how a cell works is to consider its possible states. In terms of the *Life* game, a cell can be either alive or dead, as shown in Figure 2-13. However, the picture becomes more complex when I add the possible visual changes:

- Gradually fading out when the cell dies
- Gradually fading in as the cell is born
- Changing color as the cell gets older

The state chart in Figure 2-15 represents these visual states as the internal structure for the alive and dead states.

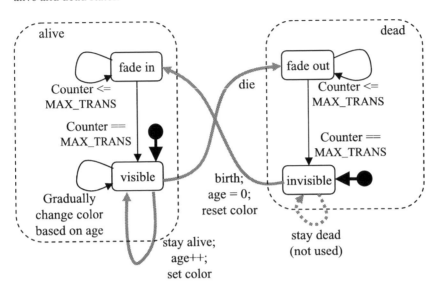

Figure 2-15. *Life and visual states for a cell*

The transitions between the life states are drawn as the thicker arrows in Figure 2-15, while the visual state transitions are normal thickness. The stay dead transition is dotted to indicate that it's not used in my code.

When a cell is created it will be alive or dead. If alive, it will start in the visible visual state, if dead it will start in the invisible state. These two start states are indicated by the solid circles with thick arrows in Figure 2-15.

When the cell's life state changes from alive to dead, the cell's visual state switches from visible to fade out. Subsequent visual change requests by CellsGrid trigger a fading away of the cell over CellsGrid.MAX_TRANS updates followed by a transition from fade out to invisible.

When the cell's state changes from dead to alive, it switches its visual state from invisible to fade in, and its age is reset to 0. Subsequent visual change requests by CellsGrid trigger a gradual fade in of the cell over CellsGrid.MAX_TRANS updates until it switches from fade in to visible.

If a state change keeps the cell alive (i.e., it survives), its age is incremented and it is assigned a new color at certain ages. This will trigger a series of visual transitions that gradually change the cell's color from its old value to the new one, spread over CellsGrid.MAX_TRANS updates.

Another aspect of the cell is its scene graph branch; the "cell" box in Figure 2-11 can be expanded to become Figure 2-16.

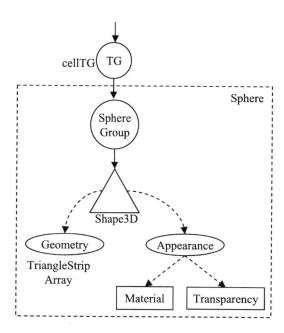

Figure 2-16. *The scene graph for a cell*

Much of the sphere's scene graph is created automatically by Java 3D's Sphere class, but the Material and Transparency node components need to be added by me.

Building the Cell's Scene Graph

The primary job of the following Cell constructor is to build the scene graph shown in Figure 2-16:

```
// globals
// length of cell side (== diameter when the cell is a ball)
private final static float CELL_LEN = 0.5f;

// space between cells : a factor multiplied to CELL_LEN
private final static float SPACING = 1.5f;


private boolean isAlive;      // cell state information
private Appearance cellApp;
private TransformGroup cellTG;


public Cell(int x, int y, int z)
{
  isAlive = (Math.random() < 0.1) ? true : false;
    // it's more likely that a cell is initially dead (invisible)
```

```
      // create appearance
      cellApp = new Appearance();
      makeMaterial();
      setVisibility();

      // the cell shape as a sphere
      Sphere cellShape = new Sphere(CELL_LEN/2,
                              Sphere.GENERATE_NORMALS, cellApp);

      // fix cell's position
      Transform3D t3d = new Transform3D();
      double xPosn = x * CELL_LEN * SPACING;
      double yPosn = y * CELL_LEN * SPACING;
      double zPosn = z * CELL_LEN * SPACING;
      t3d.setTranslation( new Vector3d(xPosn, yPosn, zPosn) );

      // build scene branch
      cellTG = new TransformGroup();
      cellTG.setTransform(t3d);
      cellTG.addChild(cellShape);
  }  // end of Cell()
```

The arguments of the Sphere constructor are the sphere's radius, the GENERATE_NORMALS flag to have Sphere add normals to the shape, and its appearance. Normals are needed so the sphere can reflect light. The other requirements for light to affect the shape's color are a Material component in the Appearance object, and that light is enabled in the Material object. Both of these are handled by makeMaterial() described in the next section.

The Sphere's geometry is stored in a Java 3D TriangleStripArray, which specifies the sphere as an array of connected triangles. Fortunately, the intricacies of building this mesh are dealt with by Sphere.

The Appearance node is a container for a variety of information, including geometry coloring, line, point, polygon, rendering, transparency, and texture attributes. The attributes needed here are added in setMaterial() and setVisibility().

The positioning of the sphere is done with the cellTG TransformGroup, using a Transform3D object containing a position. The position is based on the (x, y, z) coordinate passed in to the constructor, but scaled up to take account of the sphere's diameter (CELL_LEN) and the space between the cells (SPACING).

It's quite easy to change the cell shape by employing one of the other shape utility classes in Java 3D's com.sun.j3d.utils.geometry package (it contains Sphere, Box, Cone, and Cylinder). For example, cellShape can be defined as a cube with the following:

```
Box cellShape = new Box( CELL_LEN/2, CELL_LEN/2, CELL_LEN/2,
                         Box.GENERATE_NORMALS, cellApp);
```

Each box will have CELL_LEN long sides, include normals for lighting, and have the same appearance characteristics as the spherical cell. Figure 2-17 shows Life3D with boxes instead of spheres.

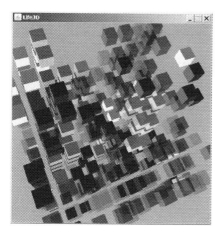

Figure 2-17. *Life3D with boxes*

Coloring the Cells

The coloring of a cell is complicated by the need to change it as the cell ages and to reset it to blue when the cell is reborn. makeMaterial() creates the Color3f objects needed during these changes and calls resetColours() to initialize them to blue:

```
// globals
private final static Color3f BLACK = new Color3f(0.0f, 0.0f, 0.0f);
private final static Color3f WHITE = new Color3f(0.9f, 0.9f, 0.9f);

// appearance elements
private Material material;
private Color3f cellCol, oldCol, newCol;


private void makeMaterial()
{
  cellCol = new Color3f();
  oldCol = new Color3f();
  newCol = new Color3f();

  // set material
  material = new Material(WHITE, BLACK, WHITE, WHITE, 100.f);
            // sets ambient, emissive, diffuse, specular, shininess

  material.setCapability(Material.ALLOW_COMPONENT_WRITE);
  material.setLightingEnable(true);
  resetColours();
  cellApp.setMaterial(material);
}  // end of makeMaterial()
```

The three Color3f objects are required for the color changes that gradually modify the cell's color (stored in cellCol) from the old color (stored in oldCol) to a new color (stored in newCol).

The Java 3D Material constructor controls what color a shape exhibits when lit by different kinds of lights:

```
Material mat = new Material(ambientColour, emissiveColour,
                           diffuseColour, specularColour, shininess);
```

The ambient color argument specifies the shape's color when lit by ambient light; this gives the object a uniform color. The emissive color contributes the color that the shape produces itself (akin to the light emitted by a lightbulb); frequently, this argument is set to black (equivalent to off). The diffuse color is the color of the object when lit, with its intensity depending on the angle the light beams make with the shape's surface.

The intensity of the specular color parameter is related to how much the shape reflects from its "shiny" areas. This is combined with the shininess argument, which controls the size of the reflective highlights.

The specular color is often set to white, matching the specular color produced by most objects in the real world.

In Life3D there are two directional lights, which create two shiny patches on each sphere.

The ambient and diffuse values in makeMaterial() are "dummies"; their real values are set in resetColours() and setMatColours():

```
// globals
private final static Color3f BLUE = new Color3f(0.0f, 0.0f, 1.0f);


private void resetColours()
// intialization of the material's color to blue
{
  cellCol.set(BLUE);
  oldCol.set(cellCol);    // old and new cols are blue as well
  newCol.set(cellCol);

  setMatColours(cellCol);
}  // end of resetColours()


private void setMatColours(Color3f col)
// the ambient color is a darker shade of the diffuse color
{
  material.setAmbientColor(col.x/3.0f, col.y/3.0f, col.z/3.0f);
  material.setDiffuseColor(col);
}  // end of setMatColours()
```

This unusual separation of tasks is due to the need to call resetColours() whenever the cell is reborn, to make it blue again. setMatColours() is called whenever the cell changes color. The darker ambient color helps to highlight the curvature of the spheres.

Setting the Cell's Visibility

A cell's visibility is controlled by a TransparencyAttributes instance. If the cell starts in the alive state, that means it will be in the visible visual state; while if it starts as dead, it must be invisible. The capabilities of the TransparencyAttributes object must also be set to allow its value to change at runtime. setVisibility() handles these tasks:

```
// globals
// possible visual states for a cell
private final static int INVISIBLE = 0;
private final static int FADE_IN = 1;
private final static int FADE_OUT = 2;
private final static int VISIBLE = 3;

private int visualState;
```

```
private void setVisibility()
{
  // let transparency value change at runtime
  transAtt = new TransparencyAttributes();
  transAtt.setTransparencyMode(TransparencyAttributes.BLENDED);
  transAtt.setCapability(TransparencyAttributes.ALLOW_VALUE_WRITE);

  if (isAlive) {
    visualState = VISIBLE;
    transAtt.setTransparency(0.0f);      // opaque
  }
  else  { // dead so invisible
    visualState = INVISIBLE;
    transAtt.setTransparency(1.0f);    // totally transparent
  }

  cellApp.setTransparencyAttributes(transAtt);
}  // end of setVisibility()
```

The visual states of Figure 2-15 are encoded as values for the visualState integer.

Changing a Cell's Life State

CellsGrid updates the grid in two stages. First it evaluates the rules for all its cells and stores a new state in each one. When all the cells have been examined, the grid is updated in a second pass.

The Cell class helps with the initial evaluation stage by offering methods to get and set the cell's state:

```
// globals
private boolean isAlive, newAliveState;

public boolean isAlive()
{  return isAlive;  }

public void newAliveState(boolean b)
{  newAliveState = b;  }
```

The "trick" is that the cell's isAlive boolean is *not* updated by a newAliveState() call; instead the value is stored in a second boolean, newAliveState. The updating of isAlive occurs during CellsGrid's second pass when it calls Cell.updateState().

Figure 2-15 shows the three transitions that change the cell's life state: die, birth, and stay alive (they're the thicker arrows). The code representing these transitions is located in updateState():

```
// globals
private int age = 0;

public void updateState()
{
  if (isAlive != newAliveState) {  // there's a state change
    if (isAlive && !newAliveState)  // alive --> dead (die)
      visualState = FADE_OUT;   // from VISIBLE
    else {  // dead --> alive (birth)
      visualState = FADE_IN;    // from INVISIBLE
      age = 0;    // reset age since born again
      resetColours();
    }
```

```
    }
  else { // current and new states are the same
    if (isAlive) {    // cell stays alive (survives)
      age++;    // get older
      ageSetColour();
    }
  }
}  // end of updateState()
```

The current cell state (in isAlive) and the new state (in newAliveState) are examined to determine which transition to apply.

ageSetColour() changes the newCol object if the age has reached certain hardwired values:

```
// global material colors
private final static Color3f RED = new Color3f(1.0f, 0.0f, 0.0f);
private final static Color3f ORANGE = new Color3f(1.0f, 0.5f, 0.0f);
private final static Color3f YELLOW = new Color3f(1.0f, 1.0f, 0.0f);
private final static Color3f GREEN = new Color3f(0.0f, 1.0f, 0.0f);
private final static Color3f BLUE = new Color3f(0.0f, 0.0f, 1.0f);


private void ageSetColour()
{
  if (age > 16)
    newCol.set(RED);
  else if (age > 8)
    newCol.set(ORANGE);
  else if (age > 4)
    newCol.set(YELLOW);
  else if (age > 2)
    newCol.set(GREEN);
  else
    newCol.set(BLUE);
} // end of ageSetColour()
```

Visual Changes to a Cell

Figure 2-10 shows that a state change by CellsGrid is followed by MAX_TRANS+1 visual changes; these are carried out by CellsGrid repeatedly calling Cell.visualChange(). There are five possible visual changes represented by five thinner arrows in Figure 2-15, which correspond to the possible transitions between the visual states, fade in, visible, fade out, and invisible.

The three looping transitions, which return to the same state they leave, are handled by an if-test inside visualChange():

```
public void visualChange(int transCounter)
{
  float transFrac = ((float)transCounter)/CellsGrid.MAX_TRANS;

  if(visualState == FADE_OUT)
    transAtt.setTransparency(transFrac);  // 1.0f is transparent
  else if (visualState == FADE_IN)
    transAtt.setTransparency(1.0f-transFrac);
  else if (visualState == VISIBLE)
    changeColour(transFrac);
  else if (visualState == INVISIBLE) {}
    // do nothing
  else
```

```
        System.out.println("Error in visualState");

    if (transCounter == CellsGrid.MAX_TRANS)
      endVisualTransition();
}  // end of visualChange()
```

transFrac is assigned a number between 0 and 1 based on the current transCounter value, which increases from 0 to CellsGrid.MAX_TRANS.

changeColour() sets the current cell's color to be a mix of its old and new colors (if the two are different):

```
private void changeColour(float transFrac)
{
  if (!oldCol.equals(newCol)) {  // if colors are different
    float redFrac = oldCol.x*(1.0f-transFrac) + newCol.x*transFrac;
    float greenFrac = oldCol.y*(1.0f-transFrac) + newCol.y*transFrac;
    float blueFrac = oldCol.z*(1.0f-transFrac) + newCol.z*transFrac;

    cellCol.set(redFrac, greenFrac, blueFrac);
    setMatColours(cellCol);
  }
}  // end of changeColour()
```

The mix uses the transFrac value so that as transCounter increases, the current color migrates toward the new color.

visualChange() ends with a test:

```
if (transCounter == CellsGrid.MAX_TRANS)
  endVisualTransition();
```

endVisualTransition() handles the two visual transitions not dealt with by the if-test in visualChange():

```
private void endVisualTransition()
{
  // store current color as both the old and new colors;
  // used when fading in and when visible
  oldCol.set(cellCol);
  newCol.set(cellCol);

  isAlive = newAliveState;    // update alive state

  if (visualState == FADE_IN)
    visualState = VISIBLE;
  else if (visualState == FADE_OUT)
    visualState = INVISIBLE;
}  // end of endVisualTransition()
```

The visual states are changed and the new life state is finally stored as the cell's current life state in isAlive. The old and new colors are also updated to be the current color.

Time for Screensavers

JScreenSaver is a Windows screensaver loader that can execute Java programs. It was written by Yoshinori Watanabe, and is available at http://homepage2.nifty.com/igat/igapyon/soft/jssaver.html and http://sourceforge.net/projects/jssaver/.

JScreenSaver has three components:

- jssaver.scr, an SCR executable that Windows calls when it wants the JScreenSaver screen-saver to start

- jssaver.cfg, a text-based configuration file that specifies the JAR file that jssaver.scr will invoke

- jssaver.jar, an example JAR file

Windows XP looks for SCR executables in c:\windows\system32, so the three files should be moved there (XP also looks in c:\windows, so you actually have a choice).

The configuration file is very simple; it must include the name of the JAR and the class where main() is found, as in this example:

```
-classpath
jssaver.jar
SimpleRssSaver
```

The -classpath argument, the JAR name, and the class name must be on separate lines.
The configuration can be understood by considering its command-line equivalent:

```
java -classpath jssaver.jar SimpleRssSaver
```

This command is executed when the screensaver starts or if the Preview button is pressed in Windows' screensaver tab (see Figure 2-4). If the Settings button is pressed, jssaver.scr calls the equivalent of the command line:

```
java -classpath jssaver.jar SimpleRssSaver -edit
```

The simplicity of Watanabe's interface means that jssaver.scr can invoke any JAR file, including ones using nonstandard APIs such as Java 3D. The only requirement is that the application under-stands the -edit command-line argument. Life3D illustrates one approach to this: the -edit option causes a configuration screen to be displayed, which edits properties in the life3DProps.txt file; this file is also utilized by the main application.

Changing Life3D into a Screensaver

JScreenSaver requires its screensaver application (Life3D in my case) to be packaged as a JAR:

```
javac *.java
jar cvfm Life3D.jar mainClass.txt *.class
```

mainClass.txt contains the name of the class containing main(), information that's added to the JAR's manifest:

```
Main-Class: Life3D
```

A nice feature of Watanabe's approach is that the JAR, the configuration screen, and main application can be tested separately from the SCR application by executing their equivalent java command lines directly. So I tested the Life3D configuration screen with the following:

```
java -classpath Life3D.jar Life3D -edit
```

and the main application with this:

```
java -classpath Life3D.jar Life3D
```

The jssaver.cfg file must be modified to refer to Life3D:

```
-classpath
```

```
Life3D.jar
Life3D
```

Also, Life3D.jar *and* life3DProps.txt must be copied to the same system directory as jssaver.scr and jssaver.cfg.

Problems with Screensavers

Many people have reported problems with screensavers in Windows XP; a good (but somewhat poorly organized) list of tips for getting things to work can be found at `http://www.softwaretipsandtricks.com/windowsxp/articles/573/1/Windows-XP-FAQ-S`, starting under the heading "Screen Savers."

The SaverBeans SDK

One drawback of JScreenSaver is that it only works with Windows. Another is that it doesn't support all of the Windows SCR functionality; most notable is that a preview of the screensaver isn't shown in the little computer screen at the top of the Screensaver tab (see Figure 2-3).

A possible solution is the excellent SaverBeans Screensaver SDK (`https://jdic.dev.java.net/documentation/incubator/screensaver/`), a Java screensaver development kit for creating cross-platform screensavers. Currently Windows, Linux, and Solaris are supported, but not the Mac.

The programmer writes Java classes and an XML description of the screensaver settings and uses the SDK tools to produce a screensaver.

The main reason I didn't choose SaverBeans is that it doesn't currently support Java 3D. However, it's an excellent choice if you're writing 2D screensavers or ones using JOGL.

Joshua Marinacci wrote an informative introduction to SaverBeans at the end of 2004 that you can read at `http://today.java.net/pub/a/today/2004/11/01/jdic2.html`. There's also a SaverBeans forum at `https://screensavers.dev.java.net/servlets/ForumMessageList?forumID=698`. A collection of SaverBeans screensavers is available at `http://screensavers.dev.java.net/`.

SaverBeans is a part of the larger JDesktop Integration Components (JDIC) project (`https://jdic.dev.java.net/`), which aims to integrate native OS applications with Java. JDIC components include access to the OS's web browser, system tray, file and system utilities, and floating dock. Some elements of JDIC functionality have been added to Java SE 6, which I discuss in the next chapter.

More Life Required?

Conway's *Game of Life* is deceptively simple *and* addictive. Paul Callahan has written a nontechnical introduction to the 2D game at Math.com (`http://www.math.com/students/wonders/life/life.html`) with pointers to information on the game's creator, and some great math books.

The Wikipedia entry (`http://en.wikipedia.org/wiki/Conway's_Game_of_Life`) has a good explanation, fun animations, and a lot of links (as you might expect). It employs a birth/survive ranges notation for the rules, which is a fine alternative to my birth and die ranges. One link worth following is to more information on cellular automata, `http://en.wikipedia.org/wiki/Cellular_automata`.

The Conway's *Game of Life* FAQ site (`http://cafaq.com/lifefaq/index.php`) explains matters well and has a link to Martin Gardner's *Scientific American* article, which started the *Life* craze.

There's a lot of free software available for running Conway's game, such as *Life32* by Johan Bontes (http://psoup.math.wisc.edu/Life32.html), and *MCell* by Mirek Wojtowicz (http://www.mirwoj.opus.chelm.pl/ca/index.html), a general-purpose 1D and 2D cellular automata package.

The 3D aspects of *Life* have been explored in several papers by Carter Bays (see his list at http://www.cse.sc.edu/~bays/articles.html). His team developed a 3D *Life* applet with many controls at http://www.cse.sc.edu/~bays/d4d4d4/guide.html.

Robert Trujillo has a comprehensive list of 3D cellular automata links at http://www.geocities.com/robisais/3dca.html. Two 3D versions of *Life* that I've tried are *Life3D* by Michael Shelley (http://wwwcsif.cs.ucdavis.edu/~shelley/projects/), which is fun to play with, and the *Kaleidoscope of 3D Life* applet at http://www.people.nnov.ru/fractal/Life/Game.htm, which has very nice controls and includes examples. I got the idea of using birth and die ranges for my game rules from this site.

Summary

I introduced Java 3D programming in this chapter. I showed how to integrate the Java 3D Canvas3D class (where the 3D scene is drawn) with Swing components. I built a Java 3D scene graph, which includes ambient and directional lights, a colored background, and camera movement. I filled the scene with a grid of spheres by reusing Java 3D's Sphere class. The spheres change color, adjust their transparency, and rotate. These changing elements are governed by a Java 3D behavior subclass, which is the standard way of adding dynamic behavior to a scene.

I converted Life3D into a screensaver with the help of JScreenSaver, a Java-based windows screensaver loader written by Yoshinori Watanabe.

I haven't finished with Life3D just yet. In Chapter 3, I employ Java SE 6 features to add a splash screen, access the system tray and desktop, and integrate JavaScript.

CHAPTER 3

■■■

Get a Life (the Java 6 Way)

The Life3D example from Chapter 2 is utilized again in this chapter. Just to remind you, Life3D is a 3D version of Conway's *Game of Life,* a simple cellular automaton game whose visualization demonstrates many of Java 3D's basic capabilities. This time around I'll change the application a little to discuss four new Java SE 6 features that are useful for gaming: splash screens; the system tray API; the desktop API; and scripting integration.

This chapter's version of the Life3D example still displays a rotating 3D grid of cells that obey the game's rules. Indeed, the graphics code is mostly unchanged, so I won't explain it again.

Life3D Basics

The two most significant things that I've removed from Life3D (shown in Figure 3-1) are the configuration window (and its properties configuration file) and full-screen rendering. The application starts with hardwired values for its window size, background color, grid rotation speed, and birth and die ranges.

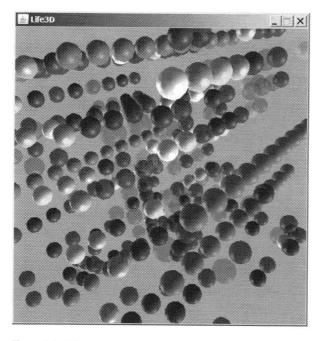

Figure 3-1. *Life3D once again*

The most visible new elements in the new version of Life3D are a splash screen, which includes an animated clock picture (see Figure 3-2) and a popup menu accessible from a system tray icon (Figure 3-3).

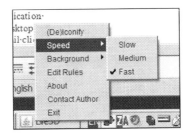

Figure 3-2. *Life3D splash screen*   **Figure 3-3.** *Life3D popup menu*

The popup menu allows the user to modify Life3D in various ways at runtime. This includes the grid's rotation speed and the scene's background color. The application can also be iconified/deiconified and closed. The menu utilizes Java's new desktop API to let the user access the system's default web browser, a text editor, and an e-mail client.

One of the exciting elements of Java SE 6 is its ability to communicate with scripting languages. In Life3D, JavaScript if-then rules are employed to control how cells change over time. Also, the user can edit those rules at runtime to dynamically change the grid's behavior.

An Overview of the Life3D Classes

Figure 3-4 shows the class diagrams for this version of Life3D. Only the public methods are shown, and I've left out the listeners used by the Life3D and Life3DPopup classes.

A quick comparison with the class diagrams for Life3D in Chapter 2 reveals most of the high-level changes: the configuration classes are gone (Life3DConfig and LifeProperties), and Life3DPopup and ClockAnimator are new. Many classes appear in both versions; Cell and TimeBehavior are unchanged, but Life3D, WrapLife3D, and CellsGrid are modified.

Life3D starts by creating an instance of ClockAnimator, which displays the animated clock in the bottom right of the splash screen (see Figure 3-2). It then creates the popup menu in the system tray using Life3DPopup (Figure 3-3), and renders the 3D scene with WrapLife3D.

The state and visual updates to the grid are controlled by periodic calls to CellsGrid.update() by TimeBehavior, and each cell in the grid is managed by a Cell object.

The user can modify Life3D's execution in various ways by selecting items from the popup menu in the system tray. Life3DPopup responds by calling methods in Life3D (changeIconify()) and WrapLife3D (adjustColour() and adjustSpeed()).

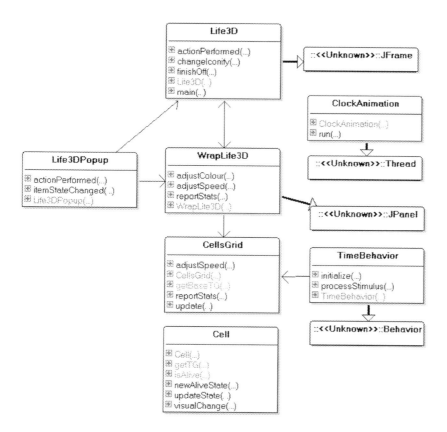

Figure 3-4. *Class diagrams for Life3D*

The user can edit a rules script file (rules.js), which is automatically reloaded by CellsGrid when it's been changed. rules.js contains JavaScript if-then rules, such as the following:

```
// rules.js
var beBorn = false;
var toDie = false;

if (states[4])
  beBorn = true;

if (states[5] && states[6] && states[17] && states[14])
  toDie = true;

if (numberLiving > 5)
  toDie = true;
```

I'll explain the meaning of these rules later when I consider CellsGrid in the "Scripting in Life3D" section.

Making a Splash

Adding a splash screen to an application is very easy: just add **-splash <image filename>** to the command line, as in this example:

```
java -splash:lifeSplash.jpg LifeSplashTest
```

You can use GIF, JPEG, and PNG files for the splash image. Animated GIFs and transparency (in GIF or PNG files) are supported. The splash is positioned at the center of the screen and displayed until the application's JFrame is made visible.

The splash effect can be made a little fancier by using the new Java SE 6 SplashScreen class to treat the splash as a drawing surface. The class also has methods to close the splash screen, change the image, and get the image's position and size.

The LifeSplashTest class listed here is a test rig for the SplashScreen functionality in my ClockAnimation class, which is utilized by Life3D:

```java
public class LifeSplashTest
{
  public static void main(String args[])
  {
    // add a ticking clock to the splash screen
    ClockAnimation ca = new ClockAnimation(7,7);
    ca.start();

    try {
      Thread.sleep(5000);    // 5 secs asleep
    }
    catch (InterruptedException ignored) {}

    // make a window
    JFrame frame = new JFrame("Life3D");
    frame.setDefaultCloseOperation(JFrame.EXIT_ON_CLOSE);
    JLabel label = new JLabel("Life3D has started", JLabel.CENTER);

    frame.add(label, BorderLayout.CENTER);
    frame.setSize(300, 95);

    // center the window
    Dimension screenDim =
            Toolkit.getDefaultToolkit().getScreenSize();
    Dimension winDim = frame.getSize();
    frame.setLocation( (screenDim.width-winDim.width)/2,
                    (screenDim.height-winDim.height)/2);

    frame.setVisible(true);  // splash screen will close now
  } // end of main()

} // end of LifeSplashTest class
```

LifeSplashTest calls ClockAnimation to draw a ticking clock at the bottom right of the splash screen. The clock's offset from the bottom right is determined by the x- and y- values passed to the ClockAnimation constructor (two 7s).

LifeSplashTest sleeps for 5 seconds before creating a JFrame holding a label. The call to Window.setVisible() at the end of main() causes the splash screen to become invisible.

Animating a Clock

The animated clock effect is created using a series of eight GIFs with transparent backgrounds, stored in clock0.gif to clock7.gif; they're shown in Figure 3-5.

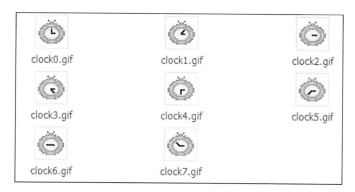

Figure 3-5. *The clock images*

The main task of the ClockAnimation constructor is to load these images from the clocks/ subdirectory:

```
// globals
private static final int NUM_CLOCKS = 8;

private ImageIcon clockImages[];  // stores the clock images
private int currClock = 0;
private int clockWidth, clockHeight;
private int offsetX, offsetY;
                // offset of images from bottom right corner


public ClockAnimation(int oX, int oY)
{
  offsetX = oX; offsetY = oY;

  // load the clock images
  clockImages = new ImageIcon[NUM_CLOCKS];
  for (int i = 0; i < NUM_CLOCKS; i++)
    clockImages[i] = new ImageIcon(
        getClass().getResource("clocks/clock" + i + ".gif"));

  // get clock dimensions; assume all images are same size
  clockWidth = clockImages[0].getIconWidth();
  clockHeight = clockImages[0].getIconHeight();
} // end of ClockAnimation()
```

The images are stored in an ImageIcon array. The call to the ImageIcon constructor uses getClass().getResource() to identify the full path to the images. This is only required if the class and images are going to be packaged up inside a JAR.

Drawing onto a Splash

It's possible to draw on top of the splash screen image. First a reference is obtained to the splash screen using the SplashScreen.getSplashScreen() static method:

```
SplashScreen splash = SplashScreen.getSplashScreen();
```

Then a graphics context is obtained, which refers to the splash screen's drawing surface:

```
Graphics2D g = splash.createGraphics();
```

Drawing can now commence.

It's also useful to know the size of the splash, so the drawing area can be constrained:

```
Dimension splashDim = splash.getSize();
```

Animation effects are coded using a loop, which should terminate when the splash disappears from the screen, after the JFrame is made visible. This change can be detected by calling SplashScreen.isVisible().

Drawing the Clocks

The ClockAnimation run() method gets the splash's graphic context then loops through the clock images, drawing each one in turn. When the end of the images array is reached, the drawing starts back at the beginning. There's a short pause between each drawing while run() sleeps:

```
// globals
private static final int MAX_REPEATS = 100;
private static final int TIME_DELAY = 250;    // ms


public void run()
{
  // get a reference to the splash
  SplashScreen splash = SplashScreen.getSplashScreen();
  if (splash == null) {
    System.out.println("No splash screen found");
    return;
  }

  // get a reference to the splash's drawing surface
  Graphics2D g = splash.createGraphics();
  if (g == null) {
    System.out.println("No graphics context for splash");
    return;
  }

  /* calculate a (x,y) position for the clock images near the
     the bottom right of the splash image. */
  Dimension splashDim = splash.getSize();
  int xPosn = splashDim.width - clockWidth - offsetX;
  int yPosn = splashDim.height - clockHeight - offsetY;

  // start cycling through the images
  boolean splashVisible = true;
  for (int i = 0; ((i < MAX_REPEATS) && splashVisible); i++) {
    clockImages[currClock].paintIcon(null, g, xPosn, yPosn);
    currClock = (currClock + 1) % NUM_CLOCKS;
```

```
    // only update the splash if it's visible
    if (splash.isVisible())   // turns invisible when appl. starts
      splash.update();
    else
      splashVisible = false;

    try {
      Thread.sleep(TIME_DELAY);
    }
    catch (InterruptedException e) {}
  }
}  // end of run()
```

The two-step access to the graphic context at the start of run() detects problems, such as there not being a splash image.

The drawing loop can terminate in two ways: either when the splash becomes invisible (splashVisible is set to false) or after the loop has repeated MAX_REPEATS times. The second test ensures that the ClockAnimation thread will definitely stop after a certain period. Relying only on the application's visibility is a bit dangerous since the JFrame might never be made visible if there are initialization problems.

JAR Packaging

The command-line specification of the splash image isn't possible if the application is wrapped up inside a JAR. Instead, the image's filename is added to the JAR's manifest.

The JAR is created in the standard way:

```
jar -cvfm LifeSplashTest.jar mainClass.txt *.class clocks lifeSplash.jpg
```

Note that the list of files includes the clocks/ subdirectory and the splash image file, lifeSplash.jpg. mainClass.txt contains the extra manifest information:

```
Main-Class: LifeSplashTest
SplashScreen-Image: lifeSplash.jpg
```

The resulting JAR file, LifeSplashTest.jar, can be executed by double-clicking its icon or by typing this:

```
java -jar LifeSplashTest.jar
```

Adding ClockAnimation to Life3D

Life3D is called with the -splash command-line argument:

```
java -splash:lifeSplash.jpg Life3D
```

The ClockAnimation thread is created at the beginning of the Life3D constructor:

```
public Life3D()
{
  super("Life3D");

  // start the clock animation that appears with the splash screen
  ClockAnimation ca = new ClockAnimation(7,7);
  ca.start();

  // rest of the Life3D initialization
}
```

The Desktop API

The new java.awt.Desktop class allows a Java application to do the following:

- Launch the host system's default browser with a specific Uniform Resource Identifier (URI)
- Launch the host system's default e-mail client
- Launch applications to open, edit, or print files associated with those applications

The Desktop API relies on the operating system's file-type associations for your machine to decide which applications are employed. On Windows, these associations map file extensions (e.g., .doc) to programs (e.g., Microsoft Word).

Unfortunately, the Desktop API doesn't support a mechanism for viewing or changing these associations, so the actual application started when a web page is loaded, or e-mail created, or file opened, is outside of the programmer's control.

Life3D uses the Desktop API in two places: the Life3D class starts a browser to display the Java 3D home page if Java 3D isn't installed on the machine, and the popup menu lets the user open and edit text files and send e-mail. I discuss the popup menu when I get to the Life3DPopup class in the "Building the Popup Menu" section.

Using the Desktop Browser

The Life3D constructor creates a Desktop instance, but only after checking whether the functionality is supported:

```
// global
private Desktop desktop = null;

// in the Life3D constructor, get a desktop ref
if (Desktop.isDesktopSupported())
  desktop = Desktop.getDesktop();
```

This desktop reference is used to start a browser when the user clicks the URL in the "Java 3D not installed" window (shown in Figure 3-6).

Figure 3-6. *The "Java 3D not installed" window*

The reportProb() method creates the window's label and button, just as in Chapter 2. The difference is that an action listener is attached to the button if the desktop reference is capable of starting a browser:

```
// global
private JButton visitButton;


// inside reportProb()
String visitText = "<html><font size=+2>" +
                   "Visit https://java3d.dev.java.net/" +
                   "</font></html>";
```

```
visitButton = new JButton(visitText);
visitButton.setBorderPainted(false);

if ((desktop != null) &&
    (desktop.isSupported(Desktop.Action.BROWSE)) )
  visitButton.addActionListener(this);

reportPanel.add(visitButton);
```

The Desktop.isSupported() method tests whether a particular OS action is available. The *actions* are defined as constants in the Desktop.Action class.

The action listener starts the system's browser with Desktop.browse():

```
// global
private static final String J3D_URL = "https://java3d.dev.java.net/";


public void actionPerformed(ActionEvent e)
{
  if (e.getSource() == visitButton) {
    try {   // launch browser
      URI uri = new URI(J3D_URL);
      desktop.browse(uri);
    }
    catch (Exception ex)
    { System.out.println(ex); }
  }
} // end of actionPerformed
```

What Other Browser Capabilities Are There?

Desktop.browse()is the only browser-related method in the Desktop class, which is somewhat disappointing when compared to the features in the JDesktop Integration Components (JDIC) project (http://jdic.dev.java.net/); JDIC was the inspiration for the Desktop class.

JDIC includes a browser listener class, which permits a page download to be monitored. The browser's navigation controls can be accessed to move backward and forward through the history, and for a page to be reloaded, or a download to be aborted. It's possible to access and change the HTML text of a page and execute JavaScript against it. There's a WebBrowser class, which lets the rendering part of the native browser be embedded in the Java application as a Canvas; WebBrowser is intended to be a replacement for Java's aging JEditorPane.

JDIC can also manipulate OS file-type associations, which means, for example, that it's possible to specify which browser is used to download a page.

A good JDIC overview by Michael Abernethy can be found at http://www-128.ibm.com/developerworks/java/library/j-jdic/index.html?ca=drs, or you can browse information at the JDIC site (https://jdic.dev.java.net/documentation/).

An informative article on JDIC's file-type associations by Jack Conradson is at http://java.sun.com/developer/technicalArticles/J2SE/Desktop/jdic_assoc/.

The System Tray

The system tray is the strip of icons on the right of the Windows taskbar and is sometimes called the Notification Area . The tray is in a similar place in Linux (at least in KDE) and is up on the menu bar in Mac OS X.

The new java.awt.SystemTray class represents the desktop's system tray. If tray functionality is offered by your OS (checkable with SystemTray.isSupported()), it can be accessed with SystemTray.getSystemTray().

SystemTray holds one or more TrayIcon objects, which are added to the tray using the add() method and removed with remove(). A TrayIcon object is represented by an icon in the tray and may also have a text tooltip, an AWT popup menu, and assorted listeners.

When the tray icon is right-clicked it displays the popup menu. When the mouse hovers over the icon, the tooltip appears.

Creating Life3D's Popup Menu

Life3D delegates the hard work of managing the tray icon and popup menu to the Life3DPopup class, which is instantiated in Life3D's constructor:

```
// globals
private WrapLife3D w3d = null;
private Desktop desktop = null;


// in the Life3D constructor
Life3DPopup lpop = new Life3DPopup(this, w3d, desktop);
```

The constructor's references to Life3D (this) and the WrapLife3D object (w3d) are needed for method calls from the popup menu. It can call the Life3D method changeIconify() to iconify or deiconify the application, and finishOff() to terminate the application. It can call the WrapLife3D method adjustSpeed() to adjust the rotation speed of the grid and adjustColour() to change the scene's background color.

The Desktop reference is required so the menu can start the OS's default text editor and e-mail client.

The Menu Contents

Figure 3-3 shows the Speed submenu, while Figure 3-7 was snapped when the Background submenu was open.

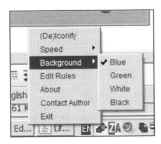

Figure 3-7. *The popup menu with Background selected*

The menu items are the following:

- (De)Iconify iconifies or deiconifies the application. The user can also double-click the tray icon to do the same thing.

- Speed changes the grid's rotation speed. There are three choices in the submenu: Slow, Medium, and Fast (see Figure 3-3).

- Background changes the scene's background color. Figure 3-7 shows the possible colors: Blue, Green, White, and Black.

- Edit Rules opens a text editor using the Desktop API so the user can modify rules.js. The rules are reloaded after the file has been saved.

- About starts a text editor to display the contents of the about.txt file.

- Contact Author opens an e-mail client with the Desktop API. The message will be sent to the address adNOT@fivedots.coe.psu.ac.th.

- Exit causes the Life3D application to exit.

Creating the TrayIcon

The Life3D constructor calls makeTray() to create a TrayIcon object:

```
// globals
private Life3D applWindow;
private WrapLife3D w3d;
private Desktop desktop;      // for accessing desktop applications
private TrayIcon trayIcon;


public Life3DPopup(Life3D top, WrapLife3D w3d, Desktop d)
{
  applWindow = top;      // used to (de-)iconify, and closing the appl.
  this.w3d = w3d;        // used to change speed and background
  desktop = d;           // used for text editing & opening, and e-mail

  if (SystemTray.isSupported())
    makeTrayIcon();
  else
    System.err.println("System tray is currently not supported.");
}  // end of buildTray()


private void makeTrayIcon()
// the tray icon has an image, tooltip, and a popup menu
{
  SystemTray tray = SystemTray.getSystemTray();

  Image trayImage =
      Toolkit.getDefaultToolkit().getImage("balls.gif");
  PopupMenu trayPopup = makePopup();

  trayIcon = new TrayIcon(trayImage, "Life3D", trayPopup);
  trayIcon.setImageAutoSize(true);

  // double left clicking on the tray icon causes (de-)iconification
  ActionListener actionListener = new ActionListener() {
    public void actionPerformed(ActionEvent e)
    { applWindow.changeIconify(); }
  };
  trayIcon.addActionListener(actionListener);

  try {
    tray.add(trayIcon);
```

```
  }
  catch (AWTException e)
  { System.err.println("TrayIcon could not be added.");  }
}  // end of makeTrayIcon()
```

The TrayIcon object is initialized with an image (which appears in the system tray), a "Life3D" string as the text for the tray icon's tooltip, and a popup menu created with makePopup(). The balls.gif image is shown in Figure 3-8; it can be seen in the system tray in Figures 3-3 and 3-7.

Figure 3-8. *The TrayIcon image*

The TrayIcon action listener is triggered by a double-click of the left mouse button. In response, the changeIconify() method is called over in Life3D:

```
// in the Life3D class
public void changeIconify()
// iconify or deiconify the application
{
  if ((getState() & JFrame.ICONIFIED) == JFrame.ICONIFIED)
    setState(Frame.NORMAL);    // deiconify
  else
    setState(Frame.ICONIFIED);  // iconify
} // end of changeIconify()
```

changeIconify() toggles the window between iconified and normal size.

Building the Popup Menu

A disappointing aspect of the TrayIcon class is that its popup menu must be built with the old AWT components: PopupMenu, MenuItem, and CheckboxMenuItem, rather than the modern Swing versions, JPopupMenu, JMenuItem, and JCheckBoxMenuItem. There's also no equivalent of JRadioButtonMenuItem, which means that I had to code up radio button group behavior in Life3DPopup.

By comparison, JDIC's system tray API does use Swing components (JDIC can be found at http://jdic.dev.java.net/).

The PopupMenu object consists of a series of MenuItems except for the Speed and Background submenus, which are represented by Menu objects containing CheckboxMenuItems. makePopup() creates the MenuItems and uses them to build the PopupMenu object:

```
// globals
private static final int DEFAULT_SPEED = 2;    // fast
private static final int DEFAULT_COLOUR = 0;   // blue

private static final String[] speedLabels =
                        {"Slow", "Medium", "Fast"};
private static final String[] colourLabels =
                        {"Blue", "Green", "White", "Black"};

private MenuItem iconifyItem, rulesItem, aboutItem,
                 authorItem, exitItem;
private CheckboxMenuItem[] speedItems;    // for speed values
private CheckboxMenuItem[] colourItems;   // for background colors
```

```
private PopupMenu makePopup()
{
  PopupMenu trayPopup = new PopupMenu();

  iconifyItem = new MenuItem("(De)Iconify");
  iconifyItem.addActionListener(this);
  trayPopup.add(iconifyItem);

  // -------------- speed items -----------------------

  Menu speedMenu = new Menu("Speed");
  trayPopup.add(speedMenu);

  speedItems = new CheckboxMenuItem[speedLabels.length];
  for(int i=0; i < speedLabels.length; i++) {
    speedItems[i] = new CheckboxMenuItem( speedLabels[i] );
    speedItems[i].addItemListener(this);
    speedMenu.add( speedItems[i] );
    if (w3d == null)   // if no 3D scene, then cannot change speed
      speedItems[i].setEnabled(false);
  }
  speedItems[DEFAULT_SPEED].setState(true);    // default is 'fast'


  // ------------ background color items ---------------

  Menu bgMenu = new Menu("Background");
  trayPopup.add(bgMenu);

  colourItems = new CheckboxMenuItem[colourLabels.length];
  for(int i=0; i < colourLabels.length; i++) {
    colourItems[i] = new CheckboxMenuItem( colourLabels[i] );
    colourItems[i].addItemListener(this);
    bgMenu.add( colourItems[i] );
    if (w3d == null)   // if no 3D, then cannot change background
      colourItems[i].setEnabled(false);
  }
  colourItems[DEFAULT_COLOUR].setState(true);    // default is 'blue'


  // -----------------------------

  rulesItem = new MenuItem("Edit Rules");
  if ((desktop != null)&&(desktop.isSupported(Desktop.Action.EDIT)) )
    rulesItem.addActionListener(this);  // if text editing possible
  else
    rulesItem.setEnabled(false);
  trayPopup.add(rulesItem);

  aboutItem = new MenuItem("About");
  if ((desktop != null)&&(desktop.isSupported(Desktop.Action.OPEN)) )
    aboutItem.addActionListener(this);  // if text opening possible
  else
    aboutItem.setEnabled(false);
  trayPopup.add(aboutItem);
```

```
  authorItem = new MenuItem("Contact Author");
  if ((desktop != null)&&(desktop.isSupported(Desktop.Action.MAIL)) )
    authorItem.addActionListener(this);    // if e-mail possible
  else
    authorItem.setEnabled(false);
  trayPopup.add(authorItem);

  MenuShortcut exitShortcut = new MenuShortcut(KeyEvent.VK_X,true);
    // ctrl-shift-x on windows
  exitItem = new MenuItem("Exit", exitShortcut);
  exitItem.addActionListener(this);
  trayPopup.add(exitItem);

  return trayPopup;
}  // end of makePopup()
```

The CheckboxMenuItems utilized in the Speed and Background submenus are meant to act as radio buttons, so that the selection of one will disable the previous selection. speedItems[] stores all the check boxes for the Speed menu, and colourItems[] all the background color check boxes. These arrays are manipulated by the itemStateChanged() method to simulate the behavior of radio buttons.

The Edit Rules, About, and Contact Author menu items require the Desktop API, so the GUI code checks for its presence before attaching the action listener. It also uses Desktop.isSupported() to determine whether the API supports the action required by the menu item: Edit Rules needs text editing; About utilizes text viewing; and Contact Author requires an e-mail client. If the checking fails, the menu item is disabled.

The Exit menu is assigned a key combination shortcut (Ctrl-Shift-x) as a MenuShortcut object. Unfortunately, it doesn't work in the version of Java SE I'm using, v.1.6.0. (By the way, Ctrl is replaced by the Command key on the Mac.)

The five menu items ((De)Iconify, Edit Rules, About, Contact Author, and Exit use an action listener, while the Speed and Background check boxes use an item listener.

Listening for Actions

The actionPerformed() method in Life3DPopup reacts differently depending on which of the five menu items activated it:

```
// globals
// rules file, author e-mail, and about file
private static final String SCRIPT_FNM = "rules.js";
private static final String AUTHOR_EMAIL =
                            "adNOT@fivedots.coe.psu.ac.th";
private static final String ABOUT_FNM = "about.txt";


public void actionPerformed(ActionEvent e)
{
  MenuItem item = (MenuItem) e.getSource();
            // all the actions come from MenuItems

  if (item == iconifyItem)
    applWindow.changeIconify();
  else if (item == rulesItem)
    launchFile(SCRIPT_FNM, Desktop.Action.EDIT);
  else if (item == aboutItem)
    launchFile(ABOUT_FNM, Desktop.Action.OPEN);
```

```
    else if (item == authorItem)
      launchMail(AUTHOR_EMAIL);
    else if (item == exitItem)
      applWindow.finishOff();
    else
      System.out.println("Unknown Action Event");
  }  // end of actionPerformed()
```

The (De)Iconify menu item is processed by calling changeIconify() in Life3D, duplicating the action of double-left clicking the tray icon.

The Edit Rules and the About menu items are processed by calling launchFile(), which uses the Desktop API to start a text editor, either to edit or view the supplied file.

The Contact Author menu item triggers a call to launchMail(), which starts the e-mail client with the address argument.

When the Exit item is pressed, finishOff() is called in Life3D:

```
// in Life3D
// global
private WrapLife3D w3d = null;

public void finishOff()
{ if (w3d != null)
    w3d.reportStats();
  System.exit(0);
}
```

The application is terminated after printing statistics related to the 3D scene:

```
// in WrapLife3D
// global
private CellsGrid cellsGrid;

public void reportStats()
{  cellsGrid.reportStats(); }
```

The necessary information is located in CellsGrid, so the reportStats() call is passed along to that class:

```
// in CellsGrid
// globals used in the timing code
private long totalTime = 0;
private long numUpdates = 0;


public void reportStats()
{ int avgTime = (int) ((totalTime/numUpdates)/1000000);  // in ms
  System.out.println("Average update time: " + avgTime +
                     "ms;  no. updates: " + numUpdates);
}
```

reportStats() prints the average update time, which measures how long it takes for a new grid generation to be calculated in CellsGrid's update() method. This information is useful for adjusting the time delay used by TimeBehavior. For instance, if an update takes 100 ms, there's no point having TimeBehavior fire off update() calls every 50 ms; its interval should be 100 ms or longer.

The reported average varies quite a lot on my slowish Windows XP test machines, with values ranging between 50 ms and 100 ms. One factor is the complexity of the script being executed.

Using a Text Editor

launchFile() opens up a text file in the OS's default text editor, after checking that the file exists. Errors are reported as popup messages using TrayIcon.displayMessage():

```
private void launchFile(String fnm, Desktop.Action action)
{
  File f = null;
  try {
    f = new File(fnm);
  }
  catch (Exception e)
  { trayIcon.displayMessage("File Error",
      "Could not access " + fnm, TrayIcon.MessageType.ERROR);
    return;
  }

  if (!f.exists()) {
    trayIcon.displayMessage("File Error",
      "File " + fnm + " does not exist", TrayIcon.MessageType.ERROR);
    return;
  }

  if (action == Desktop.Action.OPEN)
    openFile(fnm, f);
  else if (action == Desktop.Action.EDIT)
    editFile(fnm, f);
}  // end of launchFile()
```

Figure 3-9 shows the popup error message when about.txt (displayed by the About menu item) cannot be found.

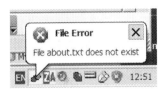

Figure 3-9. *Popup error message*

openFile() and editFile() are quite similar, differing in the File tests they apply before calling the Desktop API. openFile() checks whether the file can be read (with File.canRead()), while editFile() makes sure that the file can be edited (with File.canWrite()). The editFile() method is the following:

```
private void editFile(String fnm, File f)
{
  if (!f.canWrite()) {
    trayIcon.displayMessage("File Error",
        "Cannot write to file " + fnm, TrayIcon.MessageType.ERROR);
    return;
  }
  else {  // can write
    try {
      desktop.edit(f.getAbsoluteFile());
    }
    catch (Exception e)
```

```
      { trayIcon.displayMessage("File Error",
          "Cannot edit file " + fnm, TrayIcon.MessageType.ERROR);
      }
    }
}  // end of editFile()
```

editFile() employs Desktop.edit() and requires an absolute filename. openFile() calls Desktop.open() in a similar manner.

Launching an E-mail Client

launchMail() converts the supplied e-mail address (adNOT@fivedots.coe.psu.ac.th) into a mailto URI, then calls Desktop.mail():

```
private void launchMail(String addr)
{
  try {
    URI uriMail = new URI("mailto", addr +
                          "?SUBJECT=Life 3D Query", null);
    desktop.mail(uriMail);
  }
  catch (Exception e)
  { trayIcon.displayMessage("E-mail Error",
        "Cannot send e-mail to " + addr, TrayIcon.MessageType.ERROR);
  }
}  // end of launchMail()
```

A mailto URI can include header lines after the e-mail address. I added a SUBJECT header, which initializes the subject line in the e-mail client (see Figure 3-10).

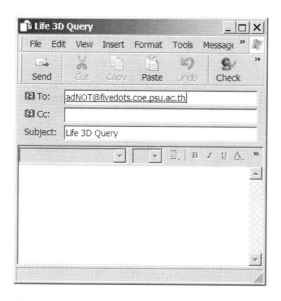

Figure 3-10. *The e-mail client*

Details on the mailto URI can be found in its Internet Society specification at ftp://ftp.isi.edu/in-notes/rfc2368.txt.

Listening for the Check Boxes

The Speed and Background menus are populated with check box menu items, and Life3DPopup implements an itemStateChanged() method to listen to them:

```
// globals
private static final String[] speedLabels =
                          {"Slow", "Medium", "Fast"};
private static final String[] colourLabels =
                          {"Blue", "Green", "White", "Black"};

private CheckboxMenuItem[] speedItems;   // for speed values
private CheckboxMenuItem[] colourItems;  // for background colors

private WrapLife3D w3d;


public void itemStateChanged(ItemEvent e)
{
  CheckboxMenuItem item = (CheckboxMenuItem) e.getSource();
  int posn = -1;

  // speed checkbox items
  if ((posn = findItem(item, speedItems)) != -1) {
    switchOffItems(posn, speedItems);
    if (w3d != null)
      w3d.adjustSpeed( speedLabels[posn] );
  }
  // color checkbox items
  else if ((posn = findItem(item, colourItems)) != -1) {
    switchOffItems(posn, colourItems);
    if (w3d != null)
      w3d.adjustColour( colourLabels[posn] );
  }
  else
    System.out.println("Unknown Item Event");
} // end of itemStateChanged()
```

findItem() searches for the selected CheckboxItem in the supplied array of CheckboxItems, returning its index position, or -1 if the item isn't found.

If the item is found, switchOffItems() iterates through the CheckboxItems array, setting the state of the other items to false (i.e., unchecking them). In this way the selection of an item causes any previously checked items to be unchecked.

If a Speed check box is selected, adjustSpeed() is called in WrapLife3D with a speed string argument (Slow, Medium, or Fast):

```
// in WrapLife3D
public void adjustSpeed(String speedStr)
{ cellsGrid.adjustSpeed(speedStr);  }
```

CellsGrid uses the speed to affect its rotation:

```
// in CellsGrid
// globals
private static final double ROTATE_AMT = Math.toRadians(4);
private double turnAngle = ROTATE_AMT;
```

```
public void adjustSpeed(String speedStr)
{
  if (speedStr.equals("Slow"))
    turnAngle = ROTATE_AMT/4;
  else if (speedStr.equals("Medium"))
    turnAngle = ROTATE_AMT/2;
  else  // fast --> large rotation
    turnAngle = ROTATE_AMT;
} // end of adjustSpeed()
```

A faster speed string is converted into a larger rotation angle, which makes the grid turn faster.

If a Background check box is selected in Life3DPopup, adjustColour() is called in WrapLife3D with a color string argument (Blue, Green, White, or Black):

```
// in WrapLife3D
public void adjustColour(String colourStr)
{
  if (colourStr.equals("Blue"))
    back.setColor(0.17f, 0.65f, 0.92f);   // sky blue color
  else if (colourStr.equals("Green"))
    back.setColor(0.5f, 1.0f, 0.5f);      // grass color
  else if (colourStr.equals("White"))
    back.setColor(1.0f, 1.0f, 0.8f);      // off-white
  else   // black by default
    back.setColor(0.0f, 0.0f, 0.0f);      // black
}  // end of adjustColour()
```

Scripting in Java SE 6

One of the most interesting (and powerful) new features of Java SE 6 is its support for scripting languages such as JavaScript. Java SE 6 includes the Mozilla Rhino engine (http://www.mozilla.org/rhino/), an implementation of JavaScript. Other scripting languages can be easily added to the JRE, so long as they conform to the JSR-233 scripting specification (http://www.jcp.org/en/jsr/detail?id=223). The list of conformant engines at https://scripting.dev.java.net/ includes AWK, Python, Ruby, Scheme, and Tcl, and is growing rapidly.

There are several reasons for employing scripts in a Java application:

- Scripts are more powerful and flexible than having the user interact with the application through configuration screens or property files.

- Scripts can easily interact with the application's Java code, so can add to or extend its functionality.

- Writing application add-ons with scripting languages is generally less complex than using Java, especially if the coder is unfamiliar with Java.

- Many scripting languages have large libraries, which can be useful for the Java application.

Adding scripting capabilities to an application isn't always necessary, but if the application is meant to be extensible, giving the user the ability to add or change substantial features, scripting is an ideal approach.

A downside of using scripts is their speed, a problem that can be partly overcome by compilation.

Life3D utilizes Java SE 6's built-in JavaScript support (i.e., the Rhino engine) to allow the user to modify cell rules. The rules are simple if-then statements, which hide the complexities of the CellsGrid class. As soon as the rules file has been edited and saved (via the Edit Rules popup menu item), the modified rules start to be applied and the behavior of the cells changes. To improve speed, the rules script is compiled.

Before I explain CellsGrid's scripting elements, I'll go through several smaller scripting examples.

Executing a Script

Executing a script is a three-step process:

1. Create a ScriptEngineManager object.

2. Retrieve a scripting engine of your choice as a ScriptEngine object.

3. Evaluate the script using the engine.

The ScriptingEx1 class shows these steps:

```
import java.io.*;
import javax.script.*;

public class ScriptingEx1
{
  public static void main(String[] args)
  {
    // create a script engine manager (step 1)
    ScriptEngineManager factory = new ScriptEngineManager();

    // get the JavaScript engine (step 2)
    ScriptEngine engine = factory.getEngineByName("js");

    try {
      // evaluate a JavaScript string (step 3)
      engine.eval("println('hello world')");
    }
    catch(ScriptException e)
    { System.out.println(e);  }
  } // end of main()

} // end of ScriptingEx1 class
```

There are several ways of obtaining an engine at step 2, via its name, file extension, or even MIME type.

The output from ScriptingEx1 is the following:

```
java ScriptingEx1
hello world
```

It's not much more difficult to evaluate code loaded from a file, as ScriptingEx2 illustrates:

```
public class ScriptingEx2
{
  public static void main(String[] args)
  {
    // create a script engine manager
    ScriptEngineManager factory = new ScriptEngineManager();

    // create JavaScript engine
    ScriptEngine engine = factory.getEngineByName("js");
```

```
    // evaluate JavaScript code from a file
    evalScript(engine, "hello.js");
  } // end of main()


  static private void evalScript(ScriptEngine engine, String fnm)
  {
    try {
      FileReader fr = new FileReader(fnm);
      engine.eval(fr);
      fr.close();
    }
    catch(FileNotFoundException e)
    {  System.out.println(fnm + " not found");  }
    catch(IOException e)
    {  System.out.println("IO problem with " + fnm);  }
    catch(ScriptException e)
    {  System.out.println("Problem evaluating script in " + fnm);  }
    catch(NullPointerException e)
    {  System.out.println("Problem reading script in " + fnm);  }
  }  // end of evalScript()

} // end of ScriptingEx2 class
```

evalScript() uses a variant of the ScriptEngine.eval() method with a FileReader source. It's made longer by having to deal with multiple possible exceptions.

The hello.js script file contains one line:

```
println('hello world');
```

The execution of ScriptingEx2 produces the following output:

```
java ScriptingEx2
hello world
```

Communicating with a Script

Java can pass data into a script, get a result back, and retrieve the changed data. The following example passes an integer and an array of integers into the sums.js script. The communication is achieved by storing variable bindings in the script engine:

```
public static void main(String[] args)
{
  // create a script engine manager
  ScriptEngineManager factory = new ScriptEngineManager();

  // create JavaScript engine
  ScriptEngine engine = factory.getEngineByName("js");

  int age = 40;
  int[] nums = { 1, 2, 3, 4, 5, 6, 7};   // sum is 28

  // pass values to JavaScript
  engine.put("age", age);
```

```
  engine.put("nums", nums);

  // evaluate script from a file
  evalSummer(engine, "sums.js");

  // more code, explained below
} // end of main()
```

The integer and array bindings are stored in the engine through calls to ScriptEngine.put():

```
engine.put("age", age);
engine.put("nums", nums);
```

The age integer is copied into an age variable inside the script, while a *reference* to the nums[] array (an object) is assigned to the nums[] array inside the script.

sums.js compares the input age with the sum of the numbers in nums[], and returns true or false depending on whether the age is bigger than the sum:

```
// sums.js
println("age = " + age);
println("nums[6] = " + nums[6]);

var sum = 0;
for(var i=0; i < nums.length; i++)
  sum += nums[i];

println("sum = " + sum);

age > sum;
```

The boolean result of the final expression (age > sum) becomes the return result for the script.

evalSummer() evaluates the sums.js script:

```
static private void evalSummer(ScriptEngine engine, String fnm)
// evaluate script from a file
{
  boolean isBigger = false;

  try {
    FileReader fr = new FileReader(fnm);
    isBigger = (Boolean) engine.eval(fr);
            // converts returned Object to a boolean
    fr.close();
  }
  catch(FileNotFoundException e)
  {  System.out.println(fnm + " not found");  }
  catch(IOException e)
  {  System.out.println("IO problem with " + fnm);  }
  catch(ScriptException e)
  {  System.out.println("Problem evaluating script in " + fnm);  }
  catch(NullPointerException e)
  {  System.out.println("Problem reading script in " + fnm);  }

  // javascript number mapped to Double
  double sum = (Double) engine.get("sum");
  System.out.println("(java) sum = " + sum);

  System.out.println("age is bigger = " + isBigger);
} // end of evalSummer()
```

This method is quite similar to evalScript() in ScriptingEx2 but shows two ways of getting data out of a script.

ScriptEngine.eval() returns an object of type Object , which stores the value of the last executed expression. The last expression in sums.js is a boolean, so evalSummer() converts the Object to a Boolean, and then to a boolean assigned to isBigger.

The other way of obtaining data is with ScriptEngine.get(), which copies the value of a specified script variable. The call to get() in evalSummer() retrieves the sum variable from sums.js as a Double. It's cast to a double, and assigned to sum.

The call to evalSummer() produces the following output:

```
age = 40
nums[6] = 7
sum = 28
(java) sum = 28.0
age is bigger = true
```

The output shows that the Java age value and the nums[] array are accessible to the script, and that the script's boolean result and its sum value are accessible back in the Java code.

The meaning of ScriptEngine.put() depends on whether the value is a simple type (e.g., int, boolean) or an object (e.g., an array, String). The script gets a *copy* of the value of a simple type, such as age, but a *reference* to an object, such as num[]. This means that subsequent changes to the object will be visible to the Java code and the script without the need for put() or get() calls. This is illustrated by a second call to evalSummer():

```
// change age and nums[] values, and re-evaluate script
age = 50;        // increased by 10
nums[6] = 27;    // increased by 20, so sum should be 48
evalSummer(engine, "sums.js");
```

The resulting output from evalSummer() is this:

```
age = 40
nums[6] = 27
sum = 48
(java) sum = 48.0
age is bigger = false
```

The script "sees" the change to nums[] but not the new age value (which it thinks is still 40).

ScriptEngine.put() must be called again to update the age copy used by the script. This is shown by the third call to evalSummer():

```
// explicitly copy age value into engine
engine.put("age", age);
evalSummer(engine, "sums.js");
```

The output is the following:

```
age = 50
nums[6] = 27
sum = 48
(java) sum = 48.0
age is bigger = true
```

The script uses the new age value (50).

Speeding Things Up

If a script is going to be used repeatedly, its execution speed can be improved by compilation. This capability is an optional part of JSR 223 but is available in Java SE 6's Rhino engine. The next example executes a compiled version of sums.js:

```java
public static void main(String[] args)
{
  // create a script engine manager
  ScriptEngineManager factory = new ScriptEngineManager();

  // create JavaScript engine
  ScriptEngine engine = factory.getEngineByName("js");

  // load and compile the script
  CompiledScript cs = loadCompile(engine, "sums.js");

  int age = 40;
  int[] nums = { 1, 2, 3, 4, 5, 6, 7};   // sum is 28

  // pass values to script
  engine.put("age", age);
  engine.put("nums", nums);

  // evaluate compiled script
  evalCSummer(cs, engine);
} // end of main()
```

Script compilation requires a Compilable version of the engine, and the compiled script is stored as a CompiledScript object. These tasks are done by loadCompile():

```java
static private CompiledScript loadCompile(ScriptEngine engine,
                                            String fnm)
// load the script from a file, and compile it
{
  Compilable compEngine = (Compilable) engine;

  CompiledScript cs = null;
  try {
    FileReader fr = new FileReader(fnm);
    cs = compEngine.compile(fr);
    fr.close();
  }
  catch(FileNotFoundException e)
  {  System.out.println(fnm + " not found");  }
  catch(IOException e)
  {  System.out.println("Could not read " + fnm);  }
  catch(ScriptException e)
  {  System.out.println("Problem compiling script in " + fnm);  }
  catch(NullPointerException e)
  {  System.out.println("Problem reading script in " + fnm);  }

  return cs;
}  // end of loadCompile()
```

A compiled script is executed using CompiledScript.eval(), but data is passed to the script and retrieved from it with the same mechanisms employed in ordinary scripts. evalCSummer() contains the following code:

```
static private void evalCSummer(CompiledScript cs,
                                ScriptEngine engine)
// evaluate compiled script
{
  boolean isBigger = false;
  try {
    isBigger = (Boolean) cs.eval();   // converts Object to boolean
  }
  catch(ScriptException e)
  { System.out.println("Problem evaluating script");  }

  // js number mapped to Double
  double sum = (Double) engine.get("sum");
  System.out.println("(java) sum = " + sum);

  System.out.println("age is bigger = " + isBigger);
  System.out.println();
}  // end of evalCSummer()
```

Calling Script Functions

It's useful to organize longer, more complex scripts into functions and then call specific script functions from the Java side. This is possible with the Invocable interface, another optional part of the JSR 223 specification, which is supported by the Rhino engine.

First, the script is stored in the engine, then its functions can be called after casting the engine to an Invocable object, as shown here:

```
// store the script function
engine.eval("function sayHello(name) {" +
            " println('Hello ' + name);" +
            "}");

// invoke the function
Invocable invocableEngine = (Invocable) engine;
Object[] fnArgs = {"Andrew"};  // function argument
try {
  invocableEngine.invokeFunction("sayHello", fnArgs);
}
catch(NoSuchMethodException e)
{ System.out.println(e);  }
catch(ScriptException e)
{ System.out.println(e);  }
```

If a function requires input arguments, they must be supplied in an Object[] array. In the example, sayHello() takes a single string argument; I supplied **Andrew**, and the function printed "Hello Andrew."

Letting a Script Use Java

I've concentrated on explaining how Java can call scripts, but it's possible for scripts to use Java. The Rhino engine has an importPackage() function, which imports Java packages so that Java objects can be created. The following code snippet shows the use of the Date class from the java.util package:

```
engine.eval("importPackage(java.util); " +
            "today = new Date(); " +
            "println('Today is ' + today);");
```

Also, if an object reference is passed to a script, its class methods can be called. The following script changes a String object to uppercase using String.toUpperCase(), and prints it:

```
String name = "Andrew Davison";
engine.put("name", name);

engine.eval("nm2 = name.toUpperCase();" +
            "println('Uppercase name: ' + nm2)");
```

More Scripting Information

Here are two informative articles on Java SE 6 scripting:

- "Scripting for the Java Platform," by John O'Conner, July 2006, `http://java.sun.com/developer/technicalArticles/J2SE/Desktop/scripting/`

- "The Mustang Meets the Rhino: Scripting in Java 6," by John Ferguson Smart, April 2006, `http://www.onjava.com/pub/a/onjava/2006/04/26/mustang-meets-rhino-java-se-6-scripting.html`

"Scripting for the Java Platform" by Mike Grogan, A. Sundararajan, and Joe Wang at `http://developers.sun.com/learning/javaoneonline/2005/coreplatform/TS-7706.pdf` is an older overview of scripting, presented at JavaOne 2005.

It's possible to create new scripting languages for Java, as long as they follow the JSR 223 specification. The article "Build Your Own Scripting Language for Java" by Chaur Wu at `http://www.javaworld.com/javaworld/jw-04-2006/jw-0424-scripting.html` outlines how to create a boolean expressions language.

A good online introduction to JavaScript by Simon Willison can be found at `http://simon.incutio.com/archive/2006/03/07/etech`. The Wikipedia page on JavaScript has more overview and background with many links (`http://en.wikipedia.org/wiki/JavaScript`).

Scripting in Life3D

All the Life3D scripting code is located in CellsGrid, which performs the same tasks as the version of Life3D in Chapter 2. It manages a grid of Cell objects, and TimeBehavior periodically calls its update() method to update that grid. An update either triggers a state change or a visual change.

The state of the grid's cells can be changed either by applying birth and die ranges (as in Chapter 2) or by employing rules loaded (and compiled) from a script. This version of CellsGrid doesn't use a properties configuration file, so the birth and die ranges are fixed.

As you saw in Life3DPopup, the user can modify the rules at runtime via the system tray popup menu. When the rules file is saved, it's reloaded and recompiled by CellsGrid.

Timings shows that the compiled script rules are about 10 to 16 times slower than using birth and die ranges; an update using rules takes about 60 ms to 100 ms on average, versus around 6 ms for the ranges.

I won't explain all of CellsGrid again, only the parts affected by the addition of the script rules.

Initializing the Grid

The CellsGrid constructor has to decide whether to use birth and die ranges or script rules, and then initialize the required data structures:

```
// globals
private static final String SCRIPT_FNM = "rules.js";
                              // holds the life rules
private boolean usingScript;


public CellsGrid()
{
  // will the rules come from a script or be predefined ranges?
  usingScript = hasScriptFile(SCRIPT_FNM);
  if (usingScript)
    initScripting();
  else
    initRanges();

  // more initailization code
}  // end of CellsGrid
```

hasScriptFile() checks whether the script file is available and assigns a File object to the scriptFile global:

```
// global
private File scriptFile;


private boolean hasScriptFile(String fnm)
{
  scriptFile = null;
  try {
    scriptFile = new File(fnm);
  }
  catch (NullPointerException e) {
    System.out.println("Could not access " + fnm);
    return false;
  }
  if (!scriptFile.exists()) {
    System.out.println("No script file " + fnm);
    return false;
  }
  return true;
}  // end of hasScriptFile()
```

Scripting initialization consists of obtaining a compilable JavaScript engine and adding a states[] array to the engine for later use by the rules:

```
// globals
private static final int NUM_NEIGHBOURS = 26;
```

```
private ScriptEngine engine;
private Compilable compEngine;
private CompiledScript lifeScript = null;

private boolean[] states;


private void initScripting()
{
  // states array used by the scripting rules
  states = new boolean[NUM_NEIGHBOURS+1];    // includes self state
  for (int i=0; i <= NUM_NEIGHBOURS; i++)
    states[i] = false;

  // create a script engine manager
  ScriptEngineManager factory = new ScriptEngineManager();
  if (factory == null) {
    System.out.println("Could not create script engine manager");
    usingScript = false;
    return;
  }

  // create a JavaScript engine
  engine = factory.getEngineByName("js");
  if (engine == null) {
    System.out.println("Could not create javascript engine");
    usingScript = false;
    return;
  }

  // create a compilable engine
  compEngine = (Compilable) engine;
  if (compEngine == null) {
    System.out.println(
            "Could not create a compilable javascript engine");
    usingScript = false;
    return;
  }

  // add states[] array reference to engine
  engine.put("states", states);
} // end of initScripting()
```

The states[] array has 27 elements, one for each cell neighbor and one for the cell itself.

The states[] array is added to the engine at the end of initScripting(). Since it's an object, any future changes to the data in states[] will be seen by the script when it's executed.

Changing the Grid's State

As in the previous version of CellsGrid, state change is a two-stage operation: first the next state is calculated for every cell, and then all the cells are updated. The first stage may use rules or birth and die ranges:

```
// globals
// number of cells along the x-, y-, and z- axes
private final static int GRID_LEN = 10;
```

```
// storage for the cells making up the grid
private Cell[][][] cells;


private void stateChange()
{
  boolean willLive;

  // calculate next state for each cell

  if (!usingScript) {    // no script, so using ranges
    for (int i=0; i < GRID_LEN; i++)
      for (int j=0; j < GRID_LEN; j++)
        for (int k=0; k < GRID_LEN; k++) {
          willLive = aliveNextState(i, j, k);
          cells[i][j][k].newAliveState(willLive);
        }
  }
  else {  // using a script
    if (isScriptModified())
      loadCompileScript(SCRIPT_FNM);    // if it's been modified

    for (int i=0; i < GRID_LEN; i++)
      for (int j=0; j < GRID_LEN; j++)
        for (int k=0; k < GRID_LEN; k++) {
          willLive = aliveScript(i, j, k);
          cells[i][j][k].newAliveState(willLive);
        }
  }

  // update each cell
  for (int i=0; i < GRID_LEN; i++)
    for (int j=0; j < GRID_LEN; j++)
      for (int k=0; k < GRID_LEN; k++) {
        cells[i][j][k].updateState();
        cells[i][j][k].visualChange(0);
      }
}  // end of stateChange()
```

The birth and die ranges use aliveNextState() to calculate each cell's new state, a method unchanged from Chapter 2. Also, the nested for-loops for updating the cells are the same at the end of stateChange().

When rules are available (i.e., when usingScript is true), they're applied to each cell with the aliveScript() method. However, if the rules file has been modified since it was last accessed, it's loaded and recompiled first.

Change is detected by comparing the file's current modification time stamp with the time stored when the file was last loaded:

```
// global
private long lastModified = 0;


private boolean isScriptModified()
{
  long modTime = scriptFile.lastModified();
  if (modTime > lastModified) {
    lastModified = modTime;
```

```
      return true;
  }
  return false;
} // end of isScriptModified()
```

The compilation uses the compilable version of the engine:

```
// globals
private Compilable compEngine;
private CompiledScript lifeScript = null;


private void loadCompileScript(String fnm)
{
  System.out.println("Loading script from " + fnm);
  lifeScript = null;

  try {
    FileReader fr = new FileReader(fnm);
    lifeScript = compEngine.compile(fr);
    fr.close();
  }
  catch(FileNotFoundException e)
  {  System.out.println("Could not find " + fnm);  }
  catch(IOException e)
  {  System.out.println("Could not read " + fnm);  }
  catch(ScriptException e)
  {  System.out.println("Problem compiling script in " + fnm);  }
  catch(NullPointerException e)
  {  System.out.println("Problem reading script in " + fnm);  }
} // end of loadCompileScript()
```

Any compilation problems will leave lifeScript with a null value.

This code has a slight chance of being affected by a threaded execution issue: the Compilable.compile() call may occur at the same time that the user saves the script via Life3D's popup menu. This might cause the compilation to be inconsistent due to changes to the file while FileReader is reading it in. Actually, it's quite unlikely, bearing in mind that the file is read and compiled in a few milliseconds. For that reason, I have not bothered including any file-locking code.

Once the compiled script has been generated the file is only consulted again when state-Change() detects that the file's modification time has changed.

Executing the Script Rules

The rules script is given two inputs:

- The states[] array, which holds the states for all the cell's neighbors and the cell itself.

- A numberLiving variable, which contains the number of alive states in states[]. (A cell can be alive or dead.)

The script calculates values for the beBorn and toDie boolean variables, and their values are copied from the script at the end of its execution. Those booleans and the cell's current state are used to calculate the cell's next state:

```
private boolean aliveScript(int i, int j, int k)
{
```

```
  if (lifeScript == null)    // no script so just return current state
    return isAlive(i,j,k);

  /* collect states and number of living cells for all
     the neighbors, and the cell */
  int w = 0;
  int  numberLiving = 0;
  for(int r=i-1; r <= i+1; r++)  // range i-1 to i+1
    for(int s=j-1; s <= j+1; s++)  // range j-1 to j+1
      for(int t=k-1; t <= k+1; t++) {  // range k-1 to k+1
        states[w] = isAlive(r,s,t);
        if (states[w])
          numberLiving++;
        w++;
      }

  // store input values in the engine
  // engine.put("states", states);     // no need to update object
  engine.put("numberLiving", numberLiving);

  // execute the script and get the beBorn and toDie results
  boolean beBorn = false;   // default values
  boolean toDie = false;
  try {
    lifeScript.eval();
    beBorn = (Boolean) engine.get("beBorn");
    toDie = (Boolean) engine.get("toDie");
  }
  catch(ScriptException e)
  {  System.out.println("Error in script execution of " +
                                              SCRIPT_FNM);
     lifeScript  = null;  //stops this error appearing multiple times
  }


  // get the cell's current state
  boolean currAliveState = isAlive(i,j,k);

  // Life Rules: adjust the cell's state
  if (beBorn && !currAliveState)   // to be born && dead now
    return true;    // make alive
  else if (toDie  && currAliveState)  // to die && alive now
    return false;   // kill off
  else
    return currAliveState;   // no change
} // end of aliveScript()
```

The isAlive() function, which returns a cell's state, is unchanged from Chapter 2. It's used to fill the states[] array and increment numberLiving.

The ordering of the nested for-loops in aliveScript() means that the ordering of the cells in states[] is as shown in Figure 3-11.

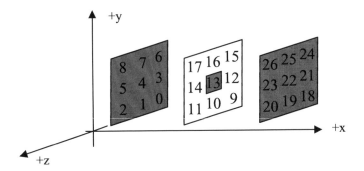

Figure 3-11. *The ordering of the cells in states[]*

For example, states[13] holds the state of the current cell, while states[0] is its left-hand neighbor in the bottom y-axis row at the back.

Only numberLiving needs to be explicitly copied over to the script, since it's a simple int type. The values in the states[] array will be visible without another call to ScriptEngine.put().

beBorn and toDie are copied from the completed script and then applied to the current state to decide the state's next value. If something goes wrong with the copying, both variables have default values of false.

The Rules Script

rules.js can utilize the states[] array and numberLiving integer in any way it chooses. However, the script should assign boolean values to beBorn and toDie.

Following is a typical set of script rules:

```
var beBorn = false;
var toDie = false;

if (states[4])
  beBorn = true;

if (states[5] && states[6] && states[17] && states[14])
  toDie = true;

if (numberLiving > 5)
  toDie = true;
```

This illustrates that scripts offer the user a great deal of flexibility for changing the behavior of the application, without the user needing to know the intricacies of the implementation, or even how to program in Java.

Summary

Life3D from Chapter 2 was given a Java 6 makeover, with the addition of an animated splash screen, the use of the system tray and desktop APIs, and the integration of scripting to enhance the application's configurability.

The desktop API was utilized to start the OS's default browser, open an e-mail client to send a message to the author, and to read text files. These features are accessible through a Life3D system tray icon that leads to nested popup menus for configuring different aspects of the application.

One of the highlights of Java 6 is its scripting capabilities, which were introduced through a series of small, self-contained examples. Life3D uses scripting to let the user change *cell rules* governing when cells are created and terminated. Any changes take effect immediately, and the rules are compiled to increase their speed by a factor of 10 to 15 times.

CHAPTER 4

■■■

The Colliding Grabbers

This chapter looks at how to use Java 3D's built-in Box, Cylinder, and Sphere shapes to create *articulated models*. The shapes are linked together by Java 3D TransformGroups nodes acting as joints, which can be rotated and moved. This functionality is essential if you want to build humanoid figures with operational limbs or machinery with working parts.

Building Articulated Arms

The articulated model built in this chapter consists of two arms (*grabbers*). Each grabber can rotate at its "elbow" around the x-, y-, and z- axes. A grabber's forearm ends with two "fingers" that can open and close. The grabbers can slide in unison over the floor forward, backward, left or right, but the two arms always stay the same distance apart. The application is called Arms3D.

Figures 4-1 and 4-2 show the grabbers in different poses.

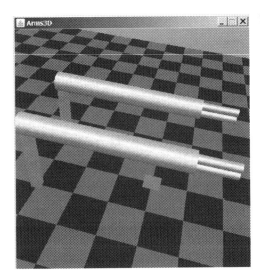
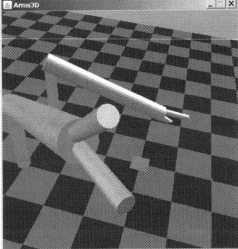

Figure 4-1. *The grabbers' initial pose*   **Figure 4-2.** *After moving the grabbers*

Figure 4-3 highlights a grabber's elbow and finger joints.

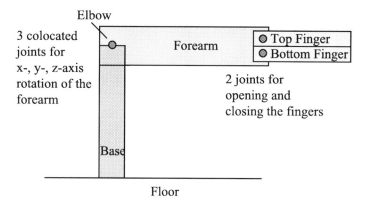

Figure 4-3. *A grabber's joints*

Articulated models also need *collision detection* abilities to prevent them from moving through objects in the scene. Arms3D demonstrates a simple form of collision detection and recovery, which stops the grabbers from rotating through each other. The detection code also reports when a grabber's fingers touch or pass through the floor (but doesn't stop the fingers).

Rotation and translation commands entered at the keyboard are caught by a Java 3D Behavior. Another Behavior subclass is used to monitor the grabbers' joints and trigger collision checking.

The grabbers' appearance is a combination of a shiny metallic Java 3D Material object and a texture (a GIF image) to add extra detail.

The x- and z- axes of the checkerboard floor are labeled with 2D text, which is useful when positioning the grabbers. I'll be reusing the floor code in several later examples.

Arms3D employs the same lighting scheme and background color as in Life3D. Java 3D's OrbitBehavior class is again utilized to move the camera around the scene.

Class Diagrams for Arms3D

Figure 4-4 shows the class diagrams for the Arms3D application. Only the public methods are shown for each class.

Arms3D creates the application's JFrame and calls WrapArms3D to render the 3D scene in a JPanel. The checkerboard floor is built by CheckerFloor, with the help of ColouredTiles to make (and group together) floor tiles of the same color.

The Grabbers class manages the grabbers and carries out tasks common to both, such as moving them about the floor. It creates two Grabber instances to handle grabber-specific work, such as rotating a particular grabber's elbow or fingers. Collision detection is supported by a GrabberBounds object assigned to each grabber.

The KeyBehavior object passes the user's key presses to the Grabbers class for processing, while JointsBehavior monitors the joints of both grabbers and triggers collision detection and recovery code in GrabberBounds.

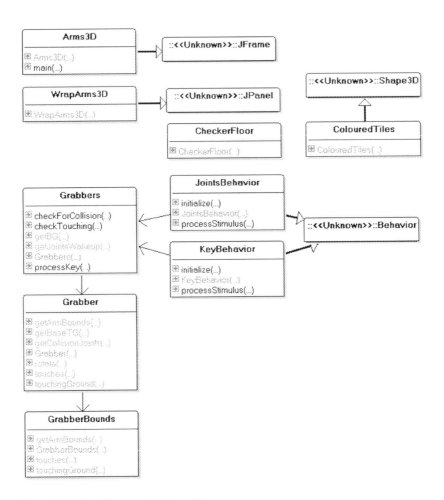

Figure 4-4. *Class diagrams for Arms3D*

Creating the Application Window

Arms3D creates a nonresizable JFrame to hold the JPanel where the 3D scene is rendered:

```
public Arms3D()
{
  super("Arms3D");
  Container c = getContentPane();
  c.setLayout( new BorderLayout() );
  WrapArms3D w3d = new WrapArms3D();   // panel holding 3D canvas
  c.add(w3d, BorderLayout.CENTER);

  setDefaultCloseOperation( JFrame.EXIT_ON_CLOSE );
  pack();
  setResizable(false);    // fixed size display
  setVisible(true);
} // end of Arms3D()
```

If the application needs additional GUI elements, such as buttons or menus, they can be added to Arms3D.

Drawing the 3D Scene

WrapArms3D wraps Java 3D's heavyweight Canvas3D component inside a lightweight Swing JPanel, thereby protecting the rest of the application's GUI:

```
// globals
private static final int PWIDTH = 512;    // size of panel
private static final int PHEIGHT = 512;

private SimpleUniverse su;


public WrapArms3D()
{
  setLayout( new BorderLayout() );
  setOpaque( false );
  setPreferredSize( new Dimension(PWIDTH, PHEIGHT));

  GraphicsConfiguration config =
                  SimpleUniverse.getPreferredConfiguration();
  Canvas3D canvas3D = new Canvas3D(config);
  add("Center", canvas3D);
  canvas3D.setFocusable(true);    // give focus to the canvas
  canvas3D.requestFocus();

  su = new SimpleUniverse(canvas3D);

  createSceneGraph();
  initUserPosition();        // set user's viewpoint
  orbitControls(canvas3D);   // controls for moving the viewpoint

  su.addBranchGraph( sceneBG );
} // end of WrapArms3D()
```

The WrapArms3D constructor sets up the user's viewpoint and the Java 3D OrbitBehavior in a similar way to WrapLife3D. Unlike WrapLife3D, there's no KeyListener for capturing key presses. Keystrokes are still sent to the Canvas3D instance because of the setFocusable() call, but they're dealt with by the KeyBehavior instance.

createSceneGraph() sets up a bounding sphere for the environment nodes, initializes the top-level BranchGroup, called sceneBG, and compiles the scene, all in a similar manner to Life3D. However, the scene graph created below sceneBG is quite different:

```
// globals
private BranchGroup sceneBG;
private BoundingSphere bounds;   // for environment nodes


private void createSceneGraph()
{
  sceneBG = new BranchGroup();
  bounds = new BoundingSphere(new Point3d(0,0,0), BOUNDSIZE);

  lightScene();          // add the lights
```

```
   addBackground();        // add the sky
   sceneBG.addChild( new CheckerFloor().getBG() );  // add the floor
   addGrabbers();          // add grabbers and behaviours

   sceneBG.compile();    // fix the scene
} // end of createSceneGraph()
```

Figure 4-5 shows the scene graph constructed by the calls to lightScene(), addBackground(), the CheckerFloor() instance, and addGrabbers().

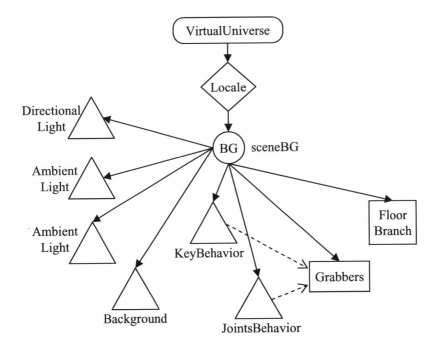

Figure 4-5. *The scene graph for Arms3D*

lightScene() creates an ambient light and two directional sources, and addBackground() adds a light-blue sky.

The "Floor Branch" box hides the details of floor creation, which I'll explain when I get to the CheckerFloor class in "The Floor" section later in this chapter.

The two behaviors and the "Grabbers" box are created in addGrabbers():

```
private void addGrabbers()
{
  Grabbers grabbers = new Grabbers( new Vector3f(0,0,3), 1.0f);
       /* Supply the position of the grabbers center point, and
          each grabber's x-axis offset from that point. */
  sceneBG.addChild( grabbers.getBG() );

  // the keyboard controls
  KeyBehavior kb = new KeyBehavior(grabbers);
```

```
    kb.setSchedulingBounds(bounds);
    sceneBG.addChild(kb);

    // the joints collision detection behavior
    JointsBehavior jb = new JointsBehavior(grabbers);
    jb.setSchedulingBounds(bounds);
    sceneBG.addChild(jb);
}  // end of addGrabbers()
```

The "Grabbers" box in Figure 4-5 hides the complicated scene branch constructed for the two grabbers.

The Vector3f argument of the Grabbers constructor can be any (x, y, z) position, so it's entirely possible to place the grabbers in midair or below the floor's surface. But once they're in place, they can only move parallel to the XZ plane, not up or down. Also, the grabbers always stay facing along the negative z-axis; I explain how to rotate them when I revisit Arms3D in Chapter 12.

The second constructor argument is the x-axis offset of each grabber from the midpoint between them. In this example, the grabbers will be two units apart.

Processing the Keys

KeyBehavior waits for a key to be pressed, then sends its details to Grabbers. The WakeupCondition is an AWT key press, specified in the constructor and registered in initialize():

```
// globals
private WakeupOnAWTEvent keyPress;
private Grabbers grabbers;


public KeyBehavior(Grabbers gs)
{ grabbers = gs;
  keyPress = new WakeupOnAWTEvent( KeyEvent.KEY_PRESSED );
}

public void initialize()
{ wakeupOn( keyPress ); }
```

processStimulus() checks that the waking criteria is an AWT event and responds to a key press:

```
public void processStimulus(Enumeration criteria)
{
  WakeupCriterion wakeup;
  AWTEvent[] event;

  while( criteria.hasMoreElements() ) {
    wakeup = (WakeupCriterion) criteria.nextElement();
    if( wakeup instanceof WakeupOnAWTEvent ) {
      event = ((WakeupOnAWTEvent)wakeup).getAWTEvent();
      for( int i = 0; i < event.length; i++ ) {
        if( event[i].getID() == KeyEvent.KEY_PRESSED )
          processKeyEvent((KeyEvent)event[i]);
      }
    }
  }
  wakeupOn( keyPress );
} // end of processStimulus()
```

All the testing and iteration through the event[] array leads to a call to processKeyEvent():

```
private void processKeyEvent(KeyEvent eventKey)
{
  grabbers.processKey(eventKey.getKeyCode(),
                      eventKey.isShiftDown(),
                      eventKey.isAltDown() );
}
```

The key code, and whether the Alt and Shift keys are pressed, are delivered to processKey() in Grabbers.

Monitoring Grabber Joints

JointsBehavior monitors TransformGroups, which implement grabber joints. Not every joint is watched, only those that may cause collisions when they change.

Grabbers creates the wake-up condition, a Java 3D WakeupOr object, which contains a list of WakeupOnTransformChange criteria. JointsBehavior retrieves the object from Grabbers, then registers it:

```
// globals
private WakeupOr jointsWakeup;
private Grabbers grabbers;


public JointsBehavior(Grabbers gs)
{ grabbers = gs;
  jointsWakeup = grabbers.getJointsWakeup();
}

public void initialize()
{ wakeupOn( jointsWakeup ); }
```

processStimulus() is called when any of the TransformGroups in the wakeup condition change (i.e., a joint is rotated). The rotation *may* cause a collision between the grabbers or between a grabber and the floor. These possibilities are checked by calls to checkForCollision() and checkTouching() in Grabbers:

```
public void processStimulus(Enumeration criteria)
{
  WakeupCriterion wakeup;
  TransformGroup tg;

  while( criteria.hasMoreElements() ) {
    wakeup = (WakeupCriterion) criteria.nextElement();
    if( wakeup instanceof WakeupOnTransformChange ) {
      // reportTG(wakeup);
      grabbers.checkForCollision();
      grabbers.checkTouching();
    }
  }
  wakeupOn( jointsWakeup );
} // end of processStimulus()
```

JointsBehavior doesn't need to know which TransformGroup woke it up, but it isn't hard to find out. reportTG() prints the name of the joint:

```
private void reportTG(WakeupCriterion wakeup)
{
  TransformGroup jointTG =
          ((WakeupOnTransformChange)wakeup).getTransformGroup();
  String name = (String) jointTG.getUserData();
  if (name == null)
    System.out.println("Joint has no name");
  else
    System.out.println(name + " moved");
} // end of reportTG()
```

A reference to the TransformGroup is obtained by calling WakeupOnTransformChange.getTransformGroup(). Only printing the object's reference isn't very informative, so in Grabber, I label each TransformGroup with SceneGraphObject.setUserData(). reportTG() reads a label with getUserData().

There are specialized versions of these set/get methods for Strings only (setName() and getName()), introduced in Java 3D 1.4.

In a more complex application, the TransformGroup labels could be passed to checkForCollision() and checkTouching(), to allow them to focus collision detection upon a particular joint.

Managing the Grabbers

The Grabbers class does four main jobs:

- It creates two Grabber objects and ties their scene branches to the rest of the scene graph.

- It processes keyboard commands. Translation commands are handled by Grabbers itself, while joint rotation requests are passed to the relevant Grabber instance.

- It asks each Grabber instance for a collection of TransformGroup joints, which may potentially cause collisions when they're rotated. It combines the two collections into a single wake-up condition and makes it available to JointsBehavior.

- Grabbers methods are called by JointsBehavior to check whether a collision has occurred and to fix it if it has.

Adding the Grabbers to the Scene Graph

Figure 4-6 supplies the contents of the "Grabbers" box in Figure 4-5.

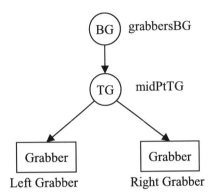

Figure 4-6. *The scene branch for the grabbers*

midPtTG in Figure 4-6 is the position of the midpoint between the grabbers.

I explain the scene graph branches made by each Grabber instance when I consider the Grabber class in "The Grabber" section later in this chapter.

The code that generates Figure 4-6 is located in the Grabbers constructor:

```
// globals
private final static String TEX_FNM = "images/steel.jpg";

// reusable objects for calculations
private Transform3D t3d, toMove;
private Vector3f moveVec;

// scene graph elements
private BranchGroup grabbersBG;
private TransformGroup midPtTG;
private Grabber leftGrabber, rightGrabber;


public Grabbers(Vector3f posnVec, float grabOffset)
{
  t3d = new Transform3D();
  toMove = new Transform3D();
  moveVec = new Vector3f();

  grabbersBG = new BranchGroup();

  // position the grabbers midpoint at posnVec
  t3d.set(posnVec);
  midPtTG = new TransformGroup(t3d);
  midPtTG.setCapability(TransformGroup.ALLOW_TRANSFORM_READ);
  midPtTG.setCapability(TransformGroup.ALLOW_TRANSFORM_WRITE);
    // let midPtTG be read and changed at runtime
  grabbersBG.addChild(midPtTG);
```

```
Texture2D tex = loadTexture(TEX_FNM);  // used by both grabbers

// add the grabber left of the midpoint
leftGrabber = new Grabber("left", tex, -grabOffset);
midPtTG.addChild( leftGrabber.getBaseTG() );

// add the grabber right of the midpoint
rightGrabber = new Grabber("right", tex, grabOffset);
midPtTG.addChild( rightGrabber.getBaseTG() );

buildWakeUps();
}  // end of Grabbers()
```

The t3d, toMove, and moveVec objects are used repeatedly in Grabbers to hold translation information. Reusing objects isn't difficult and avoids the garbage collection overheads associated with creating many short-lived temporary objects.

Grabbers moves the grabbers by applying translations to the midPtTG TransformGroup, which is the midpoint between the grabbers and the parent node for both grabber scene branches. In order for midPtTG to be read and changed at runtime, its ALLOW_TRANSFORM_READ and ALLOW_TRANSFORM_WRITE capability bits must be set.

Since Java 3D 1.4, all the read capability bits for scene graph objects are on (true) by default. Read capability bits have the form ALLOW_*_READ, and also include Geometry.ALLOW_INTERSECT. This means that it's not strictly necessary to set TransformGroup.ALLOW_TRANSFORM_READ in Grabbers(); I've included it for backward-compatibility.

Mapping a texture to a model wraps the model in the texture's image, making the model look more colorful and detailed. I use a "steel" texture to give the grabbers' cylinders and boxes a realistic metallic look.

A texture is made in two stages in Java 3D. First, a TextureLoader object is created for the file holding the texture image, then the texture is extracted from that object:

```
private Texture2D loadTexture(String fn)
{
  TextureLoader texLoader = new TextureLoader(fn, null);
  Texture2D texture = (Texture2D) texLoader.getTexture();
  if (texture == null)
    System.out.println("Cannot load texture from " + fn);
  else {
    System.out.println("Loaded texture from " + fn);
    texture.setEnable(true);
  }
  return texture;
}  // end of loadTexture()
```

TextureLoader can handle JPEGs and GIFs (which are useful if transparency is required), and it can be employed in conjunction with JAI (Java Advanced Imaging) to load other formats, such as BMP, PNG, and TIFF files. The loader can include various flags, such as one for creating textures at various levels of resolution for rendering onto small areas.

The if-test in loadTexture() checks if the texture is successfully created. A common reason for the texture being null is the source image's dimensions being invalid. It's generally safest—if the image is square—when its dimensions are a power of two. Keeping this in mind, I made the size of the steel texture image be 128 by 128 pixels. Figure 4-7 shows the contents of the steel.gif file.

Figure 4-7. *The steel.gif file*

Since version 1.5, Java 3D supports textures whose dimensions are not a power of two, but the feature is only available if the underlying graphics driver offers it.

The call to Texture2D.setEnable() switches on texture mapping, which allows the texture to be wrapped around a shape. The wrapping will be carried out in the Grabber class when *limbs* are created from Java 3D's Box and Cylinder classes.

Processing Keyboard Commands

An unusual aspect of this application is the large number of different input commands. A grabber can rotate its elbow around the x-, y-, and z- axes and open and close its fingers, which requires eight commands, since the joints and fingers can rotate in both the positive and negative directions; this doubles to 16 when both grabbers are considered. With the inclusion of the translations possible for the entire grabbers model (forward, backward, left, and right), the number of commands reaches 20.

I use the letter keys X, Y, and Z, for positive rotations of the x-, y-, and z- axis joints for the left grabber, and F to open its fingers. F is enough for both finger joints, since they open and close together.

If Alt is pressed as well, the meaning switches to a negative rotation. If Shift is included, the commands refer to the right grabber.

The keyboard's arrow keys are utilized for forward, backward, left, and right movements of both grabbers.

Admittedly, all these key combinations are somewhat confusing, and this is one reason why I revisit Arms3D in Chapter 12, to replace the keyboard with a gamepad.

As explained earlier, KeyBehavior obtains the letter (or arrow) key, sets booleans if the Alt and Shift keys are pressed, and calls Grabbers' processKey():

```
// global
private boolean moveNeedsChecking = false;

public void processKey(int keyCode, boolean isShift, boolean isAlt)
{ if (!moveMidPt(keyCode) && !moveNeedsChecking)
    rotateJoint(keyCode, isShift, isAlt);
}
```

moveMidPt() tries to translate the grabbers. If the supplied key code isn't an arrow key, moveMidPt() returns false and rotateJoint() is called. It attempts to rotate a joint and looks at the key code and the Alt and Shift booleans to determine the grabber, joint, and direction.

The moveNeedsChecking boolean is set to true when the previous command rotates a joint, which *may* cause a collision. Until the situation is checked, moveNeedsChecking will be true, thereby preventing any new joint rotations being carried out by rotateJoint().

Translating the Grabbers

moveMidPt() contains a series of if-tests to determine which arrow key was pressed and to respond accordingly:

```
// globals: the translation key codes
private final static int forwardKey = KeyEvent.VK_DOWN;
private final static int backKey = KeyEvent.VK_UP;
private final static int leftKey = KeyEvent.VK_LEFT;
private final static int rightKey = KeyEvent.VK_RIGHT;

// step size for moving the base
private final static float STEP = 0.1f;


private boolean moveMidPt(int keyCode)
// move the grabbers midpoint if the keyCode is the right type
{
  if(keyCode == forwardKey) {
    moveBy(0, STEP);
    return true;
  }
  if(keyCode == backKey) {
    moveBy(0, -STEP);
    return true;
  }
  if(keyCode == leftKey) {
    moveBy(-STEP, 0);
    return true;
  }
  if(keyCode == rightKey) {
    moveBy(STEP, 0);
    return true;
  }
  // not a move keyCode
  return false;
}  // end of moveMidPt()
```

moveBy() moves the grabbers' midpoint position by a step composed of a move in the x- and z- axis directions.

```
// reusable global objects for calculations
private Transform3D t3d, toMove;
private Vector3f moveVec;


private void moveBy(float x, float z)
// add (x,z) to the grabbers midpoint position
{
  moveVec.set(x,0,z);
  midPtTG.getTransform(t3d);
  toMove.setTranslation(moveVec);
  t3d.mul(toMove);   // t3d = t3d * toMove
  midPtTG.setTransform(t3d);
}
```

midPtTG's current transformation (its translation from the origin) is copied into t3d. The x- and z- step values are stored in a vector (with the y- value == 0), and from there are copied into toMove.

The effect of multiplying toMove to t3d is to *add* the (x, z) step to t3d's translation. The changed t3d is put back into midPtTG, making it move by that (x, z) step when the scene is next rendered.

Rotating a Grabber Joint

If the key code isn't an arrow key, moveMidPt() returns false and rotateJoint() is called (if moveNeedsChecking is false). rotateJoint() decides which grabber is to be affected and the direction of the rotation:

```
// globals that store the keyboard info for the last joint command
private int keyCode;
private boolean isShift, isAlt;


private void rotateJoint(int keyCode, boolean isShift, boolean isAlt)
{
  // store keyboard info for the joint command
  this.keyCode = keyCode;
  this.isShift = isShift;
  this.isAlt = isAlt;

  // SHIFT means the right grabber
  Grabber grabber = (isShift) ? rightGrabber : leftGrabber;

  if(isAlt)    // ALT means a negative rotation
    rotJoint(grabber, keyCode, Grabber.NEG);
  else
    rotJoint(grabber, keyCode, Grabber.POS);
} // end of rotateJoint()
```

rotateJoint() also stores the keyboard information for the joint command, which will be useful later if a collision needs to be undone.

rotJoint() decides which of the joints of the selected grabber should be rotated based on the supplied key code:

```
// globals
// keys for rotating a grabber's joints
private final static int rotXKey = KeyEvent.VK_X;
private final static int rotYKey = KeyEvent.VK_Y;
private final static int rotZKey = KeyEvent.VK_Z;

// key for rotating a grabber's fingers
private final static int rotfinKey = KeyEvent.VK_F;


private void rotJoint(Grabber grabber, int keycode, int dir)
{
  boolean done;
  if(keycode == rotXKey) {
    done = grabber.rotate(Grabber.X_JOINT, dir);
    if (done)
      mmoveNeedsChecking = true;  // move needs checking
  }
  else if(keycode == rotYKey) {
    done = grabber.rotate(Grabber.Y_JOINT, dir);
    if (done)
      moveNeedsChecking = true;
```

```
    }
    else if(keycode == rotZKey)  // no checking for z- and finger
      grabber.rotate(Grabber.Z_JOINT, dir);
    else if(keycode == rotfinKey)
      grabber.rotate(Grabber.FING_JOINT, dir);
  } // end of rotJoint()
```

The four joints are referred to using the Grabber constants X_JOINT, Y_JOINT, Z_JOINT, and FING_JOINT. If either X_JOINT or Y_JOINT are rotated, moveNeedsChecking is set to true. This prevents further joint command keys from being processed until the rotation has been checked by JointsBehavior calling checkForCollision().

X_JOINT and Y_JOINT are singled out since X_JOINT swings a grabber's forearm left and right and Y_JOINT moves the forearm up and down. These movements may bring a grabber in contact with the other grabber or the floor.

Z_JOINT and FING_JOINT aren't considered since Z_JOINT rotates the forearm around its major axis and FING_JOINT opens and closes the fingers. It's unlikely that either will cause collisions.

As you'll see later, this same distinction is applied when collecting collision joints for JointsBehavior. The joints for X_JOINT and Y_JOINT are included, but not Z_JOINT and FING_JOINT. This reduces the number of times that JointsBehavior is woken up, reducing the overhead of including collision detection in Arms3D.

Collecting the Collision Joints

The Grabbers constructor finishes with a call to buildWakeUps(). References to the collision-causing TransformGroups are converted into a series of "wake-up" criteria, and packed into a wake-up condition for JointsBehavior:

```
// global
private WakeupOr jointsWakeup;


private void buildWakeUps()
{
  TransformGroup[] leftJoints = leftGrabber.getCollisionJoints();
  TransformGroup[] rightJoints = rightGrabber.getCollisionJoints();

  WakeupOnTransformChange[] jointCriteria =
      new WakeupOnTransformChange[leftJoints.length +
                                 rightJoints.length];

  // fill the criteria array with the TGs from both grabbers
  int i = 0;
  for (int j=0; j < leftJoints.length; j++) {
    jointCriteria[i] = new WakeupOnTransformChange( leftJoints[j]);
    i++;
  }
  for (int j=0; j < rightJoints.length; j++) {
    jointCriteria[i] = new WakeupOnTransformChange( rightJoints[j]);
    i++;
  }

  jointsWakeup = new WakeupOr(jointCriteria);  // make the condition
} // end of buildWakeUps()
```

JointsBehavior should be triggered when any of the TransformGroups is rotated, so the WakeupOnTransformChange objects are wrapped in a WakeupOr instance.

The condition is retrieved by JointsBehavior calling Grabbers' getJointsWakeup() method:

```
public WakeupOr getJointsWakeup()
{ return jointsWakeup; }
```

Collision Detection and Recovery

When JointsBehavior is woken up, it calls checkForCollision() and checkTouching() in Grabbers.

checkForCollision() generates bounds information for the grabbers and checks whether they intersect. If there's a collision, it's undone by "reversing" the joint rotation command that caused it. The keyboard information for that command is utilized to create a new command that reverses the original's rotation direction:

```
// globals: last key command for moving a joint
private int keyCode;
private boolean isShift, isAlt;

private int touchCounter = 1;


public void checkForCollision()
{
  // SHIFT means the right grabber
  Grabber grabber = (isShift) ? rightGrabber : leftGrabber;

  // check if the grabber's bounding spheres intersect
  BoundingSphere[] bs = rightGrabber.getArmBounds();
  if (leftGrabber.touches(bs)) {
    System.out.println((touchCounter++) + ") Arms are touching");

    // reverse the previous joint rotation command
    if(isAlt)
      rotJoint(grabber, keyCode, Grabber.POS);   // was NEG
    else
      rotJoint(grabber, keyCode, Grabber.NEG);   // was POS
  }

  moveNeedsChecking = false;  // since move has been checked
}  // end of checkForCollision()
```

Why Bother with JointsBehavior?

At first glance, JointsBehavior seems like a needless complication. Since Grabbers processes the rotation command in rotateJoint(), why can't it just call checkForCollision() itself at the end of that method?

The reason is *frame delay*; it takes the Java 3D system two scene redraws (two frame renders) to update the application's TransformGroups. The rotation operation called by rotateJoint() doesn't change a joint immediately, and so rotateJoint() cannot immediately call checkForCollision(). The joints must be monitored by separate code, which waits until they are updated, which is the role of JointsBehavior.

Touching the Floor

JointsBehavior also calls checkTouching() in Grabbers. It examines each grabber to see if its fingers are touching the floor:

```
public void checkTouching()
{
  if (leftGrabber.touchingGround())
    System.out.println("Left Grabber's fingers are
                                touching the ground");
  if (rightGrabber.touchingGround())
    System.out.println("Right Grabber's fingers are
                                touching the ground");
}  // end of checkTouching()
```

The Grabber

Figures 4-1 and 4-2 show the grabbers in action, and a grabber's joints are highlighted in Figure 4-3.

A grabber has a vertical base, a forearm, and two fingers. Its forearm points along the negative z-axis and can turn left/right, up/down, and spin around its main axis. Its two fingers are vertically aligned and can open and close. There are three joints at the elbow between the base and the forearm for rotating the forearm around the x-, y-, and z- axes, and one joint for each finger.

The Grabber class performs three tasks:

- It builds the grabber's scene graph, which includes TransformGroups for the joints, Java 3D Cylinders and a Box for its shape, and a shiny metallic material and texture for its appearance.

- It processes rotation commands, moving specified joints, but only within hardwired limits. For example, a finger can only rotate open to a maximum of 20 degrees.

- It supports bounds detection for its forearm and fingers. However, most of the hard work is done by the GrabberBounds object.

Making the Grabber's Appearance

The constructor sets the grabber's appearance first, then builds the scene graph:

```
// global
private Appearance grabberApp;


public Grabber(String name, Texture2D tex, float xPos)
{ makeAppearance(tex);
  makeGrabber(name, xPos);
}


private void makeAppearance(Texture2D tex)
// shiny metallic appearance, combining a material and texture
{
  grabberApp = new Appearance();

  // combine texture with material and lighting of underlying surface
  TextureAttributes ta = new TextureAttributes();
```

```
ta.setTextureMode( TextureAttributes.MODULATE );
grabberApp.setTextureAttributes( ta );

// shiny metal material
Color3f alumDiffuse = new Color3f(0.37f, 0.37f, 0.37f);
Color3f black = new Color3f(0.0f, 0.0f, 0.0f);
Color3f alumSpecular = new Color3f(0.89f, 0.89f, 0.89f);

Material armMat =
    new Material(alumDiffuse, black, alumDiffuse, alumSpecular, 17);
            // sets ambient, emissive, diffuse, specular, shininess
armMat.setLightingEnable(true);
grabberApp.setMaterial(armMat);

// apply texture to the shape
if (tex != null)
  grabberApp.setTexture(tex);
}  // end of makeAppearance();
```

The material and texture are combined with the TextureAttributes.MODULATE mode, which merges the material's lighting effects with the texture's detailing. The best effects are achieved when the material's ambient and diffuse colors are close to the main color of the texture (in this case, gray).

Figure 4-8 shows the grabber's appearance when the texture (shown in Figure 4-7) is applied without a material component.

Figure 4-8. *Textured grabbers without material*

Figure 4-9 shows the grabbers with the metallic material but no texturing.

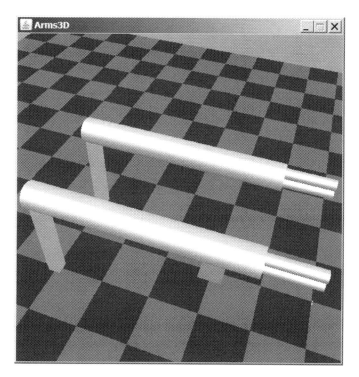

Figure 4-9. *Grabbers with a material but no texture*

Figures 4-1 and 4-2 show the grabbers covered with the material and texture.

The Grabber Shape

The grabber is built from four shapes: a tall, skinny boxlike base; a cylindrical forearm; and two fingers also made from cylinders. They're linked together by several TransformGroups, with the main ones shown in Figure 4-10.

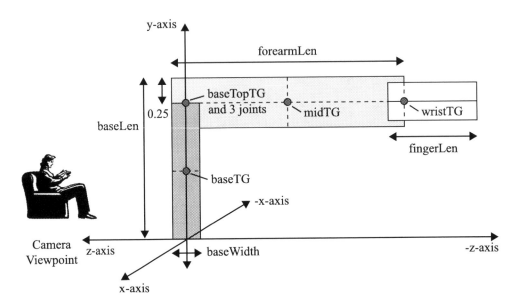

Figure 4-10. *The elements of a grabber*

When Arms3D starts, the camera is facing down the negative z-axis, but Figure 4-10 shows the view from the right, facing along the negative x-axis.

The baseTG TransformGroup positions the base so it's resting on the XZ plane. baseTopTG connects the base and forearm and is the parent of the forearm's three elbow joints (TransformGroups). midTG positions the forearm cylinder so it extends from the left side of the base. wristTG connects the grabber fingers to the forearm, although the fingers use other TransformGroups to rotate (which aren't shown in Figure 4-10).The scene graph corresponding to Figure 4-10 is given in Figure 4-11. Copies of it occupy the "Grabber" boxes in Figure 4-6.

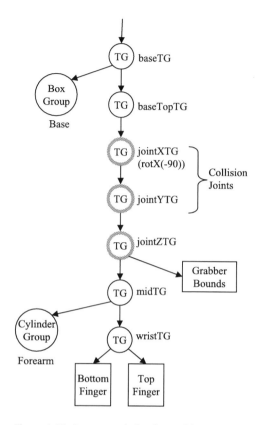

Figure 4-11. *Scene graph for the grabber*

The three TransformGroups for rotating the forearm are jointXTG, jointYTG, and jointZTG, and the first two are monitored by JointsBehavior.

The "Grabber Bounds" box refers to the scene graph branch made by the GrabberBounds object, which handles collision detection. The "Bottom Finger" and "Top Finger" boxes hide the details of how the fingers are represented.

The graph in Figure 4-11 is built by makeGrabber():

```
// globals
private TransformGroup baseTG;  // top-level TG

// for collision detection
private GrabberBounds grabberBounds;
private TransformGroup[] collisionJoints;
      // joint TGs that may cause collisions

// grabber's joints
private TransformGroup jointXTG, jointYTG, jointZTG,
                    topFingTG, botFingTG;


// reusable objects for calculations
private Transform3D t3d = new Transform3D();
private Transform3D toRot = new Transform3D();
```

```java
private void makeGrabber(String name, float xPos)
{
  // limb dimensions
  float baseWidth = 0.24f;
  float baseLen = 2.0f;
  float foreArmLen = 4.0f;

  /* position baseTG at the base limb's midpoint, so the limb
     will rest on the floor */
  t3d.set( new Vector3f(xPos, baseLen/2, 0));
  baseTG = new TransformGroup(t3d);

  // make base limb
  com.sun.j3d.utils.geometry.Box baseLimb =
      new com.sun.j3d.utils.geometry.Box(baseWidth/2,
                   baseLen/2, baseWidth/2,
                   Primitive.GENERATE_NORMALS |
                   Primitive.GENERATE_TEXTURE_COORDS, grabberApp);
  baseTG.addChild(baseLimb);

  // move to top of base limb
  t3d.set( new Vector3f(0, baseLen/2, 0));
  TransformGroup baseTopTG = new TransformGroup(t3d);
  baseTG.addChild(baseTopTG);

  /* add jointXTG for left/right swings, start it rotated
     by 90 degrees so the rest of the grabber points along
     the negative z-axis */
  t3d.rotX(Math.toRadians(-90));
  jointXTG = new TransformGroup(t3d);
  jointXTG.setCapability(TransformGroup.ALLOW_TRANSFORM_READ);
  jointXTG.setCapability(TransformGroup.ALLOW_TRANSFORM_WRITE);
  jointXTG.setUserData(name + "-X");   // identify the joint
  baseTopTG.addChild(jointXTG);

  // add jointYTG for up/down swings
  jointYTG = new TransformGroup();
  jointYTG.setCapability(TransformGroup.ALLOW_TRANSFORM_READ);
  jointYTG.setCapability(TransformGroup.ALLOW_TRANSFORM_WRITE);
  jointYTG.setUserData(name + "-Y");   // identify the joint
  jointXTG.addChild(jointYTG);

  // add jointZTG for spinning the forearm
  jointZTG = new TransformGroup();
  jointZTG.setCapability(TransformGroup.ALLOW_TRANSFORM_READ);
  jointZTG.setCapability(TransformGroup.ALLOW_TRANSFORM_WRITE);
  jointYTG.addChild(jointZTG);

  // set up bounds checking for the grabbers forearm and fingers
  grabberBounds = new GrabberBounds(jointZTG,
                                    (1.0f - baseWidth/2), 0.25, 7);

  /* Move to the middle of forearm limb - half width of baseLimb.
     This ensures that the end of the forearm will coincide with the
     left side of the base limb when drawn. */
  t3d.set( new Vector3f(0, (foreArmLen/2 - baseWidth/2), 0));
```

```
TransformGroup midTG = new TransformGroup(t3d);
jointZTG.addChild(midTG);

// make forearm limb
Cylinder foreArmLimb = new Cylinder(0.25f, foreArmLen,
                Primitive.GENERATE_NORMALS |
                Primitive.GENERATE_TEXTURE_COORDS, grabberApp);
midTG.addChild(foreArmLimb);

// move to end of forearm
t3d.set( new Vector3f(0, foreArmLen/2, 0));
TransformGroup wristTG = new TransformGroup(t3d);
midTG.addChild(wristTG);

float fingerRadius = 0.1f;

// create topFingTG for up/down rotation of the top finger
topFingTG = new TransformGroup();
makeFinger(fingerRadius, wristTG, topFingTG);

// create botFingTG for down/up rotation of the bottom finger
botFingTG = new TransformGroup();
makeFinger(-fingerRadius, wristTG, botFingTG);

// store references to the joints that _may_ cause collisions
collisionJoints = new TransformGroup[2];
collisionJoints[0] = jointXTG;
collisionJoints[1] = jointYTG;
    // don't bother with jointZTG and the finger joints
}  // end of makeGrabber()
```

makeGrabber() makes repeated use of the t3d Transform3D object to hold the translations used in the different TransformGroups. This avoids the creation of many temporary objects, which Java would then have to spend time garbage collecting.

The joint TransformGroups (jointXTG, jointYTG, and jointZTG) have their ALLOW_TRANSFORM_READ and ALLOW_TRANSFORM_WRITE capability bits switched on so their positions can be read and changed at runtime.

jointXTG and jointYTG have strings stored with them as *user data* via calls to setUserData(). This data is read by JointsBehavior to identify the joint that woke it.

The base, the forearm cylinder, and the fingers are initialized with GENERATE_TEXTURE_COORDS. The generated texture coordinates are used to wrap the steel texture over the shapes.

The GrabberBounds object that deals with collision detection is explained later in the "Implementing Collision Detection" section. Another part of collision processing is the storage of references to jointXTG and jointYTG in the collisionJoints[] array. This array is retrieved by the Grabbers object and used to create the WakeupOnTransformChange conditions for JointsBehavior.

Local and Global Coordinate Systems

The positioning of the TransformGroups and shapes relies on the scene graph nodes having both local and world coordinates.

A node's local coordinate system always has the x-axis running left to right, the y-axis straight up, and the z-axis pointing out of the page, as in Figure 4-12. A new node is positioned at (0, 0, 0) by default. Translations, rotations, or scaling affect the node according to this local system.

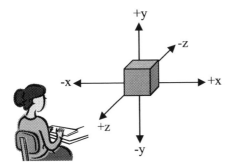

Figure 4-12. *Local coordinate axes for a node*

The world coordinates for a node give its position in the coordinates system for the entire 3D scene and depend not only on the node's own transformations but on those applied to its ancestors in the scene graph. For instance, baseTopTG is moved up the y-axis by half the base's height in its local coordinates system:

```
t3d.set( new Vector3f(0, baseLen/2, 0));
TransformGroup baseTopTG = new TransformGroup(t3d);
baseTG.addChild(baseTopTG);
```

In world coordinates, its position also includes the translation of its parent TransformGroup, midTG (shown in Figure 4-11), which is moved up by half the base height as well. This means that baseTopTG is actually located at (0, baseLen, 0) in the world coordinates system.

The effects of ancestor TransformGroups also include rotations and scaling. For example, jointXTG is initialized with the rotation:

```
t3d.rotX(Math.toRadians(-90));
jointXTG = new TransformGroup(t3d);
```

The right-hand rule can be used to determine the direction of the negative 90-degree rotation: clench your right hand, and point your thumb along the positive x-axis (in Figure 4-10, that's pointing straight out of the page). The direction of your fingers will be the direction of a positive rotation: to the left in Figure 4-10. Therefore a negative rotation is to the right.

This rotation not only affects jointXTG but all the other nodes below it in the Figure 4-11 scene graph. It means that the forearm and fingers shapes, and the child TransformGroups, are rotated to the right in the world coordinates system.

The local x-, y-, and z- axes are rotated so they are orientated as in Figure 4-13.

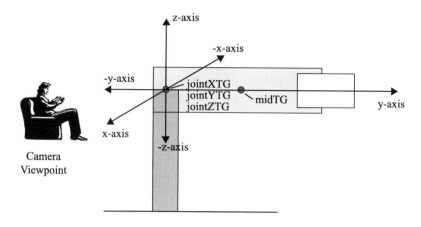

Figure 4-13. *Axes after jointXTG's rotation*

This explains why the translation from jointZTG to midTG is along the y-axis:

```
// y-axis translation from jointZTG to midTG
t3d.set( new Vector3f(0, (foreArmLen/2 - baseWidth/2), 0));
TransformGroup midTG = new TransformGroup(t3d);
jointZTG.addChild(midTG);
```

jointZTG's positive y-axis is pointing to the right because of the rotation of its grandparent, jointXTG.

Making the Fingers

Each finger is created using makeFinger() and connected to the forearm as in Figure 4-14. Figure 4-14 is a close-up of the fingers part of Figure 4-10.

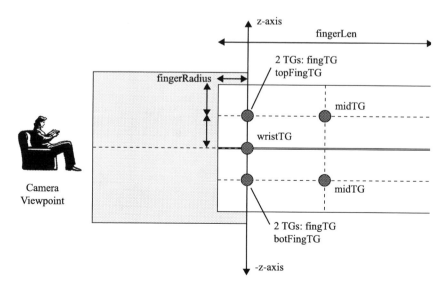

Figure 4-14. *Connecting the fingers to the forearm*

wristTG connects the fingers to the forearm, but each finger uses a separate rotation TransformGroup, topFingTG, and botFingTG.

Each finger is linked to midTG (which is locally declared in makeFinger()). midTG is positioned so that the left end of the finger overlaps the forearm by fingerRadius units. This ensures that when the finger rotates around topFingTG (or botFingTG) that its left edge doesn't come into view.

The z-axis is aligned vertically because of the rotation in jointXTG. The scene graph for both fingers is shown in Figure 4-15; it replaces the "Bottom Finger" and "Top Finger" boxes in Figure 4-11.

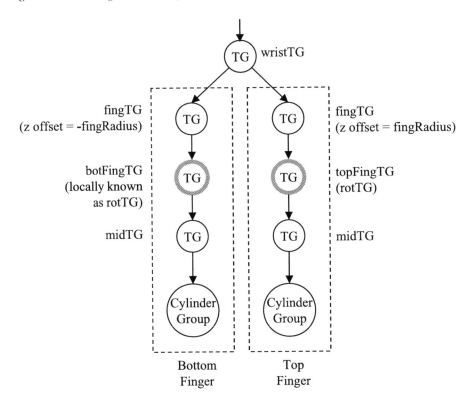

Figure 4-15. *Scene graph for the fingers*

Two calls to makeFinger() in makeGrabber() build the scene graph in Figure 4-15:

```
private void makeFinger(float offset, TransformGroup wristTG,
                                      TransformGroup rotTG)
{
  // finger dimensions
  float fingerRadius = Math.abs(offset);
  float fingerLen = 1.0f;

  // move finger by offset towards the forearm's edge
  t3d.set( new Vector3f(0,0,offset));  // along local z-axis
  TransformGroup fingTG = new TransformGroup(t3d);
  wristTG.addChild(fingTG);

  // add in finger rotation TG
  rotTG.setCapability(TransformGroup.ALLOW_TRANSFORM_READ);
```

```
    rotTG.setCapability(TransformGroup.ALLOW_TRANSFORM_WRITE);
    fingTG.addChild(rotTG);

    /* forward to middle of finger - radius of finger.
       This will mean that the finger will be drawn with one end
       embedded in the forearm. */
    t3d.set( new Vector3f(0, (fingerLen/2 - fingerRadius), 0));
    TransformGroup midTG = new TransformGroup(t3d);
    rotTG.addChild(midTG);

    // make finger limb
    Cylinder finger = new Cylinder(fingerRadius, fingerLen,
                    Primitive.GENERATE_NORMALS |
                    Primitive.GENERATE_TEXTURE_COORDS, grabberApp);
  midTG.addChild(finger);
}  // end of makeFinger()
```

Handling Rotation Commands

The Grabbers object passes rotation commands to the Grabber instances. Each command is sent to
the relevant grabber and includes the joint name (X_JOINT, Y_JOINT, Z_JOINT, or FING_JOINT) and
the rotation direction (POS or NEG). Grabber's rotate() method converts the direction to an angle
(in both degrees and radians), tests if the request is within the rotation limits of the joint, and then
carries it out:

```
// globals
// joint rotation amount
private final static int ROTATE_DEG = 2;   // degrees
private final static double ROTATE_AMT = Math.toRadians(ROTATE_DEG);

// rotation joint names (used by Grabbers)
public static final int X_JOINT = 0;
public static final int Y_JOINT = 1;
public static final int Z_JOINT = 2;
public static final int FING_JOINT = 3;

// rotation directions (used by Grabbers)
public static final int POS = 0;
public static final int NEG = 1;

// rotation joints current angle (in degrees)
int xCurrAngle, yCurrAngle, zCurrAngle, fingCurrAngle;


public boolean rotate(int rotType, int dir)
{
  int degAngle;    // angle in degrees
  double angle;    // angle in radians

  // test if the rotation is possible
  if (dir == POS) {
    degAngle = ROTATE_DEG;
    if (!withinRange(rotType, degAngle))
      return false;  // do nothing
    angle = ROTATE_AMT;
  }
```

```
  else {   // dir == NEG
    degAngle = -ROTATE_DEG;
    if (!withinRange(rotType, degAngle))
      return false;   // do nothing
    angle = -ROTATE_AMT;
  }

  // carry out the rotation; store the new joint angle
  if (rotType == X_JOINT) {        // left/right movement
    doRotate(jointXTG, X_JOINT, angle);
    xCurrAngle += degAngle;
  }
  else if (rotType == Y_JOINT) {   // up/down movement
    doRotate(jointYTG, Y_JOINT, angle);
    yCurrAngle += degAngle;
  }
  else if (rotType == Z_JOINT) {   // spinning around forearm
    doRotate(jointZTG, Z_JOINT, angle);
    zCurrAngle += degAngle;
  }
  else if (rotType == FING_JOINT) {    // up/down of fingers
    doRotate(topFingTG, Y_JOINT, angle); //up (or down) of top finger
    doRotate(botFingTG, Y_JOINT, -angle);//down (up) of bottom finger
    fingCurrAngle += degAngle;
  }
  else {
    System.out.println("Did not recognise rotation type: "+ rotType);
    return false;
  }

  return true;
}  // end of rotate()
```

Representing the angle as an integer degree makes the coding of withinRange() simpler, while the radian value is used by the Java 3D built-in methods.

FING_JOINT is mapped to two rotations, since the fingers use two TransformGroups (topFingTG, botFingTG) as joints.

Checking the Rotation

withinRange() employs hardwired numerical ranges to determine whether a rotation should be carried out. The intended rotation is added to the current joint angle to see whether the range is exceeded:

```
private boolean withinRange(int rotType, int degAngle)
{
  int nextAngle;

  if (rotType == X_JOINT) {
    nextAngle = xCurrAngle + degAngle;
    return ((nextAngle >= -45) && (nextAngle <= 45));
  }
  else if (rotType == Y_JOINT) {
    nextAngle = yCurrAngle + degAngle;
    return ((nextAngle >= -45) && (nextAngle <= 45));
  }
  else if (rotType == Z_JOINT) {
```

```
      nextAngle = zCurrAngle + degAngle;
      return ((nextAngle >= -90) && (nextAngle <= 90));
    }
    else if (rotType == FING_JOINT) {
      nextAngle = fingCurrAngle + degAngle;
      return ((nextAngle >= 0) && (nextAngle <= 20));
    }

    System.out.println("Did not recognise rotation type: " + rotType);
    return false;
  }  // end of withinRange()
```

Doing the Rotation

The joint name is mapped to an axis, and the rotation is applied around that axis:

```
// global reusable objects for calculations
private Transform3D t3d = new Transform3D();
private Transform3D toRot = new Transform3D();

private void doRotate(TransformGroup tg, int rotType, double angle)
// rotate the tg joint by angle radians
{
  tg.getTransform(t3d);

  if (rotType == X_JOINT)
    toRot.rotZ(angle);      // left/right == rotation around z-axis
  else if (rotType == Y_JOINT)
    toRot.rotX(angle);      // up/down == rotation around x-axis
  else    // must be Z_JOINT
    toRot.rotY(angle);      // spin == rotation around y-axis

  t3d.mul(toRot);      // t3d = t3d * toRot, which adds the rotation
  tg.setTransform(t3d);
}
```

X_JOINT is the jointXTG joint, which swings the forearm left and right. A quick look at Figure 4-13 shows that this means a rotation about the z-axis. The right-hand rule means that a positive rotation is a swing to the left (from the camera's viewpoint). The same reasoning can be used to understand the Y_JOINT and Z_JOINT rotation choices in doRotate().

To save on temporary objects, the rotation is stored in an existing toRot Transform3D and then multiplied to the joint's current Transform3D. Once this is stored back in the joint's TransformGroup, the effect is to "add" the rotation to the joint's current orientation.

Collision Detection

Grabber delegates the collision detection processing to its GrabberBounds object, which it created in makeGrabber(). The following methods are called by Grabbers:

```
// global
private GrabberBounds grabberBounds;
```

```
public BoundingSphere[] getArmBounds()
{  return grabberBounds.getArmBounds();  }

public boolean touches(BoundingSphere[] bs)
{  return grabberBounds.touches(bs); }

public boolean touchingGround()
{  return grabberBounds.touchingGround();  }
```

Implementing Collision Detection

GrabberBounds generates an array of TransformGroups that extend from the Grabber's forearm to its fingers. Whenever the grabber moves, the world coordinates for these TransformGroups are recalculated and used to initialize an array of Java 3D bounding spheres. These spheres are employed for collision detection with bounding spheres in the other grabber.

The last TransformGroup in the array is near the tip of the fingers, so is also used to detect if the fingers are touching the ground.

The positioning of the TransformGroups is shown in Figure 4-16.

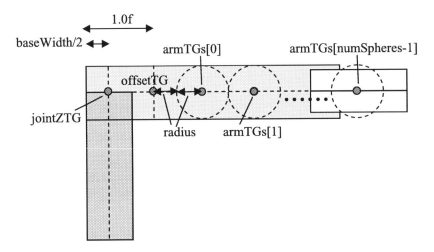

Figure 4-16. *GrabberBounds' TransformGroups*

armTGs[] contains the TransformGroups positioned down the forearm and fingers, starting at offsetTG.

The Java 3D bounding spheres created for each TransformGroup are shown as dotted circles in Figure 4-16. Each circle's radius is stored in the radius variable, and the TransformGroups are spaced radius*2 units apart, so the spheres just touch each other.

The scene graph made by a GrabberBounds instance is shown in Figure 4-17; it occupies the "GrabberBounds" box in Figure 4-11.

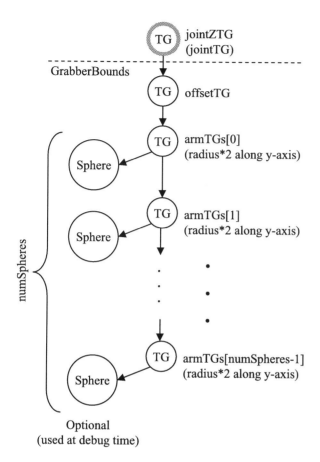

Figure 4-17. *The GrabberBounds scene graph*

The Sphere circles in Figure 4-17 are *not* Java 3D bounding spheres but sphere shapes. I use them as visual representations of their parent TransformGroups when debugging the collision detection code. Sphere creation is commented out in the final version of Arms3D.

Each TransformGroup is moved radius*2 units along the y-axis due to the jointXTG rotation shown in Figure 4-13.

Figure 4-17 is constructed by makeArmTGs():

```
// globals
private double radius;     // of the bounding spheres
private int numSpheres;

// reusable object for calculations
private Transform3D t3d;

// TGs used for generating the bounding spheres
private TransformGroup offsetTG;
private TransformGroup[] armTGs;


private void makeArmTGs(TransformGroup jointTG, float offset)
{
  Appearance blueApp = makeSphereApp();  // sphere's blue appearance
```

```
// move to offset position, along the arm
t3d.set( new Vector3f(0, offset, 0));
offsetTG = new TransformGroup(t3d);
jointTG.addChild(offsetTG)

/* Create TGs chain after offsetTG. Start at the last one
   and move backward toward the offsetTG. This makes it easier
   to attach a child TG to its parent. */
armTGs = new TransformGroup[numSpheres];
for (int i=(numSpheres-1); i >= 0; i--) {
  t3d.set( new Vector3f(0, (float)(radius*2), 0));
  armTGs[i] = new TransformGroup(t3d);
  armTGs[i].setCapability(TransformGroup.ALLOW_TRANSFORM_READ);
  armTGs[i].setCapability(
                  TransformGroup.ALLOW_LOCAL_TO_VWORLD_READ);
  if (i != numSpheres-1)
    armTGs[i].addChild( armTGs[i+1] );
  // armTGs[i].addChild( new Sphere((float)radius, blueApp) );
           // optionally add a sphere for TG visibility
}

offsetTG.addChild(armTGs[0]);
}  // end of makeArmTGs()
```

offsetTG is connected to jointTG (jointZTG in Grabber), the last joint at the start of the forearm. offsetTG is positioned along the forearm after jointTG at a distance determined by the offset variable passed to makeArmTGs().

The commented-out line

```
armTGs[i].addChild( new Sphere((float)radius, blueApp) );
```

adds a blue sphere to each TransformGroup. Figure 4-18 shows the grabbers with these spheres (I've also reduced the radius of the forearm cylinders so the spheres are more visible).

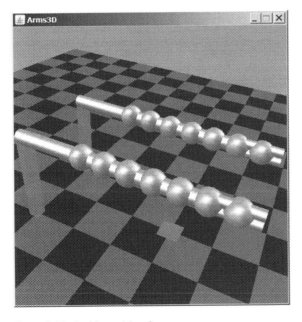

Figure 4-18. *Grabber with spheres*

Initializing the Bounding Spheres

For efficiency reasons, the bounds calculations reuse existing bounding spheres, which are initialized by the GrabberBounds constructor calling initBS():

```
// globals
private BoundingSphere[] armBounds;

private void initBS()
{
  armBounds = new BoundingSphere[numSpheres];
  for (int i=0; i < numSpheres; i++) {
    armBounds[i] = new BoundingSphere();
    armBounds[i].setRadius(radius);
  }
}  // end of initBS()
```

The array of bounding spheres give a specified radius (which will always stay the same) and are positioned at (0, 0, 0) by default. Before collision detection is performed, their positions are updated with the current locations of the armTGs[] TransformGroups.

Positioning the Bounding Spheres

When a joint moves, JointsBehavior calls checkForCollision() in Grabbers. It calls getArmBounds() in the right-hand grabber and tests the returned bounds against those in the left-hand grabber with touches():

```
// in checkForCollisions() in Grabbers
BoundingSphere[] bs = rightGrabber.getArmBounds();
if (leftGrabber.touches(bs)) {
  System.out.println((touchCounter++) + ") Arms are touching");
```

There's no particular reason for calling getArmsBounds() on the right-hand grabber and touches() on the left-hand one. The test result would be the same if the grabbers were reversed.

The getArmBounds() and touches() calls pass through Grabber to be processed by GrabberBounds:

```
// in Grabber
public BoundingSphere[] getArmBounds()
{  return grabberBounds.getArmBounds();  }

public boolean touches(BoundingSphere[] bs)
{  return grabberBounds.touches(bs); }
```

getArmBounds() in GrabberBounds updates the positions of the bounding spheres with the locations of the TransformGroups:

```
// global
private Point3d wCoord;   // world coordinate


public BoundingSphere[] getArmBounds()
{
  for (int i=0; i < numSpheres; i++) {
    setWCoord(armTGs[i]);  // wCoord gets this TG's center point
    armBounds[i].setCenter(wCoord);
  }
  return armBounds;
}
```

setWCoord() calculates the given TransformGroup's position in world coordinates and stores it in wCoord:

```
// globals
// reusable objects for the TG --> world coordinate calculations
private Transform3D t3d, t3d1;
private Vector3f posnVec;
private Point3d wCoord;


private void setWCoord(TransformGroup tg)
{
  tg.getLocalToVworld(t3d);
          // position, not including this node's transform
  tg.getTransform(t3d1);      // get this TG's transform
  t3d.mul(t3d1);              // 'add' it in

  t3d.get(posnVec);     // extract the position
  wCoord.set(posnVec);  // store it in wCoord
}
```

Java 3D's Node.getLocalToVWorld() returns the world coordinates transformation for the specified node. This combines all the transformations (i.e., translations, rotations, scaling) made by the node's ancestors into a single Transform3D object. Rather confusingly, it doesn't include the transformations applied to the node itself. They have to be obtained with TransformGroup.getTransform() and then multiplied to the first Transform3D to get the complete transformation. The position component is extracted with Transform3D.get() and assigned to wCoord.

touches() tests whether one of the spheres in the supplied array intersects with one of the object's own bounding spheres:

```
public boolean touches(BoundingSphere[] bs)
{
  BoundingSphere[] myBS = getArmBounds();

  for (int i=(bs.length-1); i >= 0; i--)
    for (int j=(myBS.length-1); j >=0; j--)
      if (bs[i].intersect(myBS[j]))
        return true;
  return false;
}
```

A minor optimization is that the spheres are checked in reverse order in the arrays, which means the spheres nearer the fingers are checked first. This will often find a collision sooner, since it's more likely that the grabbers will touch lower down their arms.

Touching the Ground

JointsBehavior calls checkTouching() in Grabbers:

```
// in Grabbers
public void checkTouching()
{
  if (leftGrabber.touchingGround())
    System.out.println("Left Grabber's fingers are
                                      touching the ground");
  if (rightGrabber.touchingGround())
    System.out.println("Right Grabber's fingers are
                                      touching the ground");
}
```

Grabber's touchingGround() calls GrabberBounds's touchingGround():

```
// in Grabber
public boolean touchingGround()
{  return grabberBounds.touchingGround();  }
```

The following is GrabberBounds's touchingGround():

```
public boolean touchingGround()
{
  setWCoord(armTGs[numSpheres-1]);  // set wCoord for last TG

  boolean touchingGround = (wCoord.y-radius <= 0);
  if (touchingGround)
    printTuple("last ball touching ground; center: ", wCoord);
  return touchingGround;
}
```

touchingGround() calculates the world coordinates for the last TransformGroup in the armTGs[] array and checks whether its y-value is less than or equal to 0, which means that its center is on or below the floor.

This code is less complex than a calculation involving the floor's geometry. But it's also less accurate, since the center of the last TransformGroup is several units back from the grabber's fingertips, as shown in Figure 4-18.

The Floor

The floor is made up of multiple blue and green tiles and a single red tile created with my ColouredTiles class and axis labels made with the Java 3D Text2D class. A close-up of the floor is shown in Figure 4-19.

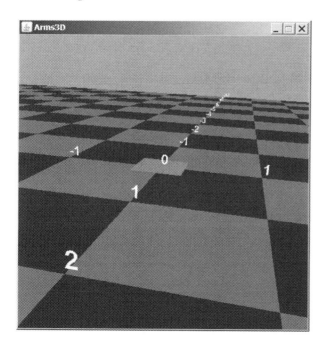

Figure 4-19. *Close-up of the floor*

Figure 4-20 shows the floor branch, previously hidden inside the "Floor Branch" box in Figure 4-5.

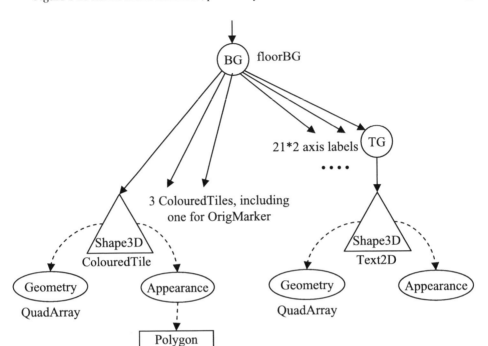

Figure 4-20. *Floor branch of the scene graph*

The floor subgraph is constructed with an instance of my CheckerFloor class and made available via the getBG() method:

```
// in createSceneGraph() in WrapArms3D
sceneBG.addChild( new CheckerFloor().getBG() );  // add the floor
```

The CheckerFloor() constructor uses nested for-loops to initialize two ArrayLists. The blueCoords list contains all the coordinates for the blue tiles, and greenCoords holds the coordinates for the green tiles. Once the ArrayLists are filled, they're passed to ColouredTiles objects, along with the color that should be used to render the tiles. A ColouredTiles object is a subclass of Shape3D, so it can be added directly to the floor's graph:

```
floorBG.addChild( new ColouredTiles(blueCoords, blue) );
floorBG.addChild( new ColouredTiles(greenCoords, green) );
```

The red square at the origin (visible in Figure 4-19) is made in a similar way:

```
Point3f p1 = new Point3f(-0.25f, 0.01f, 0.25f);
Point3f p2 = new Point3f(0.25f, 0.01f, 0.25f);
Point3f p3 = new Point3f(0.25f, 0.01f, -0.25f);
Point3f p4 = new Point3f(-0.25f, 0.01f, -0.25f);

ArrayList<Point3f> oCoords = new ArrayList<Point3f>();
oCoords.add(p1); oCoords.add(p2);
oCoords.add(p3); oCoords.add(p4);

floorBG.addChild( new ColouredTiles(oCoords, medRed) );
```

The square is centered at (0, 0) on the XZ plane and raised a little above the y-axis (0.01 units) so that it's visible above the tiles.

Each side of the square is of length 0.5 units. The four Point3f points in the ArrayList are stored in a counterclockwise order. This is also true for each group of four points in blueCoords and greenCoords. Figure 4-21 shows the ordering of the square's points.

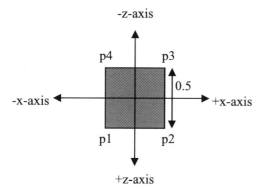

Figure 4-21. *OrigMarker viewed from above*

The Colored Tiles

My ColouredTiles class extends Shape3D and defines the geometry and appearance of tiles with the same color. The geometry uses a Java 3D QuadArray to represent the tiles as a series of quadrilaterals (quads). The following is the constructor:

```
QuadArray(int vertexCount, int vertexFormat);
```

The vertex format is an ORed collection of static integers that specify the different aspects of the quad to be initialized later, such as its coordinates, color, and normals. In ColouredTiles, the QuadArray plane is created using this line of code:

```
plane = new QuadArray(coords.size(),
            GeometryArray.COORDINATES | GeometryArray.COLOR_3 );
```

The size() method returns the number of coordinates in the supplied ArrayList. The coordinate and color data is supplied in createGeometry():

```
int numPoints = coords.size();
Point3f[] points = new Point3f[numPoints];
coords.toArray( points );   // ArrayList-->array
plane.setCoordinates(0, points);

Color3f cols[] = new Color3f[numPoints];
for(int i=0; i < numPoints; i++)
  cols[i] = col;
plane.setColors(0, cols);
```

The order in which a quad's coordinates are specified is significant; the front of a polygon is the face where the vertices form a counterclockwise loop. Knowing front from back is important for lighting and hidden-face culling and, by default, only the front face of a polygon will be visible in a scene. In this application, the tiles are oriented so their fronts are facing upward along the y-axis.

It's also necessary to make sure that the points of each quad form a convex, planar polygon, or rendering may be compromised. However, each quad in the coordinates array doesn't need to be connected or adjacent to the other quads, which is the case for these tiles.

Since a quad's geometry doesn't include normal information, a Material node component can't be used to specify the quad's color when lit. I could use a ColoringAttributes, but a third alternative is to set the color in the geometry, as done in the previous code fragment (with plane.setColors (0, cols);). The geometry color will be constant, unaffected by the scene lighting.

Once finalized, the Shape3D's geometry is set with the following:

```
setGeometry(plane);
```

The shape's appearance is handled by createAppearance(), which uses a Java 3D PolygonAttribute component to switch off the culling of the back face. PolygonAttribute can also be employed to render polygons in point or line form (i.e., as wire frames), and to flip the normals of back-facing shapes:

```
Appearance app = new Appearance();
PolygonAttributes pa = new PolygonAttributes();
pa.setCullFace(PolygonAttributes.CULL_NONE);
app.setPolygonAttributes(pa);
```

Once the appearance has been fully specified, it's fixed in the shape with the following:

```
setAppearance(app);
```

The Floor's Axes Labels

The floor's axes labels are generated with the labelAxes() and makeText() methods in CheckerFloor(). labelAxes() uses two loops to create labels along the x- and z- axes. Each label is constructed by makeText() and then added to the floor's BranchGroup (see Figure 4-20):

```
floorBG.addChild( makeText(pt,""+i) );
```

makeText() uses the Text2D utility class to create a 2D string of a specified color, font, point size, and font style:

```
Text2D message = new Text2D(text, white, "SansSerif", 36, Font.BOLD);
                        // 36 point bold Sans Serif
```

A Text2D object is a Shape3D object with a quad geometry (a rectangle) and appearance given by a texture map (image) of the string, placed on the front face. By default, the back face is culled; if the user moves behind an axis label, the object becomes invisible.

The point size is converted to world units by dividing by 256. Generally, it's a bad idea to use too large a point size in the Text2D() constructor since the text may be rendered incorrectly. Instead, a TransformGroup should be placed above the shape and used to scale it to the necessary size.

The positioning of each label is done by a TransformGroup above the shape:

```
TransformGroup tg = new TransformGroup();
Transform3D t3d = new Transform3D();
t3d.setTranslation(vertex);    // the position for the label
tg.setTransform(t3d);
tg.addChild(message);
```

setTranslation() only affects the position of the shape. The tg TransformGroup is added to the floor scene graph.

Summary

This chapter described an articulated model (two grabber arms), built using Java 3D's shape classes (Box, Cylinder, and Sphere), and linked together with TransformGroups acting as joints. It also explained how to deal with collision detection and recovery by employing Java 3D's BoundingSphere and Behavior classes. Commands to move and rotate the arms are sent from the keyboard and processed using another Behavior subclass. The arms use a mix of Material color and texture to make them look more realistically steellike.

The checkerboard floor includes x- and z- axes, which are useful when positioning things in the scene; the floor will appear several times more in future chapters.

This example is revisited in Chapter 12, when a gamepad is used as the primary input device. It greatly simplifies the user's experience, replacing a bewildering mix of key combinations with a more intuitive set of game controls. Chapter 12 also examines an alternative form of collision detection, a *try-it-and-see* approach, and adds obstacles to the scene.

■■■

CHAPTER 5

When Worlds Collide

An important physics-related gaming problem is how to handle object collisions. It can be difficult to decide how a 3D object should rebound or bounce, especially when mass, linear and angular velocity, gravity, friction, and other forces are taken into account.

In this chapter I show you how to use the physics API ODE to do the heavy lifting; to be more precise, I will employ Odejava, a Java binding for ODE. You will create physics-based models of the objects and let Odejava calculate how they should move. Position and orientation details are read from the models and used to update a game's graphical entities. This is a *dual-model* approach to coding, where the implementation of the physics and graphical elements are largely separate.

I explain this dual-model approach later in the chapter with the help of a simple application called Balls3D, where balls bounce off each other and the walls of a box. This chapter's title refers to the balls that are texture-wrapped with images of the earth, the moon, and Mars.

Before I describe Balls3D, I will go through a simpler Odejava program. It implements the physics for a single ball bouncing on a floor.

Odejava and ODE

I'll be using Odejava, a Java binding for the ODE (Open Dynamics Engine) physics API for my programming. Odejava can be found at `https://odejava.dev.java.net`, and ODE is at `http://www.ode.org`.

ODE's application domain is the physics of articulated rigid bodies, such as a person's skeleton and muscles, or a car's suspension. A rigid body's properties include its position, orientation, mass, and any applied forces, accelerations, and velocities (e.g., gravity and friction). Complex bodies are built by connecting simpler bodies together using different types of *joints*, such as hinges, balls and sockets, and pistons.

ODE bodies don't have a visual appearance; it's best to think of them as sets of equations applied to invisible, connected masses. An ODE system is executed by advancing time in discrete steps; at each time step, the equations are applied to the bodies, changing their position and orientation.

ODE also has a collision detection engine based around *geoms* (geometries), which have shape and size attributes. Basic geoms include spheres, boxes, and meshes, with more complex geoms built by combining simpler ones. An ODE body can be involved in collisions if it's been assigned a geom.

As an ODE simulation progresses, body collisions are detected when their associated geoms intersect. A contact is represented by a temporary *contact joint*, which permits velocities and accelerations to be transferred between the bodies.

Although geoms have shape, size, position, and orientation, they don't have a visual represen-tation. This can make debugging an ODE program somewhat difficult, since there's no built-in view of the bodies and geoms. However, it also means that ODE can be utilized with a variety of visuali-zation APIs. For example, Odejava has been employed with Java 3D, Xith3D, and jME (the jMonkey Engine).

It's possible to create geoms that have no corresponding body, which can't be affected by veloc-ities or accelerations. Bodiless geoms are often used to represent walls and floors, which can be collided with but can't move themselves.

A typical ODE program has two separate models: a graphical (perhaps 3D) scene, and a physics-based representation of all or some of the objects in that scene. This *dual-model* approach is also true for Odejava, which offers much the same programming API as ODE, but in the form of Java methods.

One advantage of this dual-model approach is that the two models can be developed inde-pendently. For example, the visual versions of the container and balls in Balls3D were developed first, without any physics elements. The physics was added after the graphical parts had been com-pleted.

Figure 5-1 shows Balls3D in action.

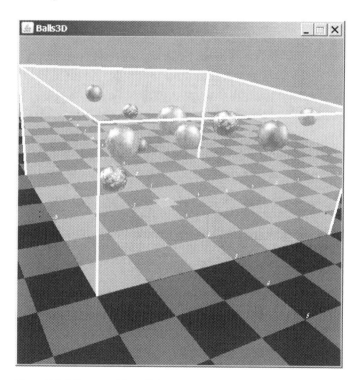

Figure 5-1. *When worlds collide*

There's no requirement that the physics components model everything in the scene. In Balls3D only the container and the balls have Odejava representations, since they're the only things involved in collisions. Odejava isn't needed for the checkerboard floor, the axis labels, or the blue background.

The visual and physics-based components of an object can be quite different from each other. For instance, a game monster may be represented by a large 3D model but have a comparatively simple ODE body made of 10 to 20 hinged parts.

Odejava is a Java wrapper over ODE's C/C++ API. Odejava offers both a low-level interface and a more object-oriented API; I'll be using the latter.

Installing Odejava

The Odejava API can be obtained at `https://odejava.dev.java.net/`. The Odejava snapshot is available in the 2006-01-15_cvs (1) folder, accessed via the web site's Documents & Files menu item. The snapshot is a zipped file containing Odejava's platform-independent JARs (and a lot more stuff as well). Extract odejava.jar from the odejava\odejava subdirectory, and log4j-1.2.9.jar from odejava\odejava\lib. You may also want the vecmath.jar file, but Java 3D already contains that JAR, so I didn't need it.

The platform-dependent elements are a separate download from the same web site. Grab the Windows Binaries ZIP file from the 004-10-30 natives (4) folder and extract the odejava.dll file from its windows\release subdirectory.

At this point, you should have three files: odejava.dll, odejava.jar, and log4j-1.2.9.jar. The two JARs should be copied to <JAVA HOME>\jre\lib\ext, and the DLL to <JAVA HOME>\jre\bin. On my machine, <JAVA HOME> is c:\Program Files\Java\jdk1.6.0.

If you've installed the JRE as well, then also copy the JARs and DLL into the corresponding directories below <JRE HOME>. On my machine, <JRE HOME> is c:\Program Files\Java\jre1.6.0.

One of Odejava's optional extras are classes that can semiautomatically map geoms to displayable entities in a particular graphics API. The main developer of Odejava, William Denniss, is also involved in Xith3D, and so the Odejava snapshot contains a Xith3D subdirectory holding classes for mapping geoms to Xith3D. A similar API for Java 3D, by Paul Byrne, can be found at `https://odejava.dev.java.net/` in the contrib (0)\java3d-binding (1) folder.

These mapping classes are rather difficult to understand and use and are perhaps better suited for complex geometries. I won't be using the Java 3D binding, since Balls3D only utilizes spheres.

Documentation, Examples, and Online Help

The Odejava API documentation can be downloaded as a ZIP file from `http://odejava.org/OdejavaDocs` or can be viewed online at `http://odejava.org/javadoc/`. There's also a version in the Odejava snapshot, but it's combined with Xith3D API information, which I don't need.

It's a good idea to download the ODE user guide, which explores ODE concepts and its API in detail. This is useful since much of the Odejava API is closely related to ODE. The user guide can be found at `http://www.ode.org/ode-docs.html` in HTML or PDF formats.

The Odejava snapshot contains several example folders in the subdirectory odejava\odejava\src\org\odejava\test\. The simple\ folder is the place to start, and my Bouncer.java example (discussed in the next section) is a variant of its HighLevelApiExample.java. The car\ folder contains an example that models how a car moves over a bumpy terrain.

The best source for help on Odejava is the Game Physics forum at `http://www.javagaming.org/forums/index.php?board=11.0`.

For ODE advice, there's a community page at the ODE site (`http://www.ode.org/community.html`), which includes a link to an ODE mailing list archive at `http://ode.org/pipermail/ode/`. Unfortunately, there's no search feature at the ODE.org site, but Google can be employed instead by including **site:ode.org** in search queries (e.g., type **xode site:ode.org** to scan the mailing list for references to *xode*, an XML data format for ODE).

Another ODE forum, this one directly searchable, is at `http://ode.petrucci.ch/`.

The GameDev.net site has an informative physics forum (http://www.gamedev.net/community/forums/forum.asp?forum_id=20) and other general physics resources. Another good forum is at http://www.continuousphysics.com/Bullet/phpBB2/index.php.

Bouncing a Ball

Bouncer.java is a small Odejava example that doesn't use any Java graphics (thereby keeping the code nicely simple). A sphere drops onto a floor, and its position and other information is printed out periodically. Whenever the sphere hits the floor it bounces. The simulation continues until it has been updated 1,000 times and then stops.

The following partial output shows what happens when the ball (which has a radius of 1) drops from a height of 4 meters under a gravity of 0.2 m/s^2.

The *pos* value is the position of the ball's center, and the *angle* is the ball's rotation around the y-axis. Information is printed every ten simulation updates (steps):

```
> java Bouncer
0    [main] INFO  odejava  - Odejava version 0.2.4
Step 10) Pos: (0, 4, 0), angle: 0
Step 20) Pos: (0, 3.9, 0), angle: 0
Step 30) Pos: (0, 3.8, 0), angle: 0
Step 40) Pos: (0, 3.6, 0), angle: 0
Step 50) Pos: (0, 3.4, 0), angle: 0
Step 60) Pos: (0, 3.1, 0), angle: 0
Step 70) Pos: (0, 2.8, 0), angle: 0
Step 80) Pos: (0, 2.4, 0), angle: 0
Step 90) Pos: (0, 2, 0), angle: 0
Step 100) Pos: (0, 1.5, 0), angle: 0
Step 110) Pos: (0, 1, 0), angle: 0
Step 120) Pos: (0, 1.4, 0), angle: 0
Step 130) Pos: (0, 1.8, 0), angle: 0
Step 140) Pos: (0, 2.1, 0), angle: 0
     :
Step 920) Pos: (0, 1, 0), angle: 0
Step 930) Pos: (0, 1, 0), angle: 0
Step 940) Pos: (0, 1, 0), angle: 0
Step 950) Pos: (0, 1, 0), angle: 0
Step 960) Pos: (0, 1, 0), angle: 0
Step 970) Pos: (0, 1, 0), angle: 0
Step 980) Pos: (0, 1, 0), angle: 0
Step 990) Pos: (0, 1, 0), angle: 0
```

The ball drops from (0, 4, 0) until it reaches the floor at step 110 and then bounces up to a reduced height. The bounces continue, but by step 990 the ball is at rest.

The Odejava API is simple enough that it's easy to modify the ball's behavior. In the second run shown next, the sphere has a linear velocity of 2 m/s along the x-axis, and an angular velocity around the y-axis of 1 m/s. Friction is also included to slow the ball down:

```
> java Bouncer
0    [main] INFO  odejava  - Odejava version 0.2.4
Step 10) Pos: (1, 4, 0), angle: 28.6
Step 20) Pos: (2, 3.9, 0), angle: 57.3
Step 30) Pos: (3, 3.8, 0), angle: 85.9
Step 40) Pos: (4, 3.6, 0), angle: 114.6
```

```
Step 50) Pos: (5, 3.4, 0), angle: 143.2
Step 60) Pos: (6, 3.1, 0), angle: 171.9
Step 70) Pos: (7, 2.8, 0), angle: 200.5
Step 80) Pos: (8, 2.4, 0), angle: 229.2
Step 90) Pos: (9, 2, 0), angle: 257.8
Step 100) Pos: (10, 1.5, 0), angle: 286.5
Step 110) Pos: (11, 1, 0), angle: 315.1
Step 120) Pos: (11.7, 1.4, -0), angle: 318
Step 130) Pos: (12.4, 1.8, -0), angle: 281.5
Step 140) Pos: (13.2, 2.1, -0), angle: 236.8
Step 150) Pos: (13.9, 2.4, -0), angle: 190.5
Step 160) Pos: (14.6, 2.6, -0), angle: 143.9
   :
Step 920) Pos: (69.2, 1, -0.7), angle: 36.1
Step 930) Pos: (70, 1, -0.7), angle: 61.5
Step 940) Pos: (70.7, 1, -0.7), angle: 104.8
Step 950) Pos: (71.4, 1, -0.7), angle: 151.1
Step 960) Pos: (72.1, 1, -0.7), angle: 198.1
Step 970) Pos: (72.8, 1, -0.7), angle: 244.8
Step 980) Pos: (73.5, 1, -0.7), angle: 289.2
Step 990) Pos: (74.3, 1, -0.7), angle: 321.8
```

The ball bounces as before and moves at a slowly decreasing speed to the right along the x-axis. The ball also drifts slightly down the negative z-axis (ending at -0.7), due to its spin around the y-axis and the presence of friction.

The rotation angle increases until the ball bounces, then the change in the ball's direction causes the angle to start decreasing. This continues until the ball begins falling again, at which time the angle starts increasing again.

Much more tweaking is possible, such as changing the gravity, the bounce velocity, and the friction applied to the ball.

Three-Stage Simulation

An Odejava simulation passes through three stages: setup, execution, and cleanup, which can be seen in the Bouncer() constructor:

```
// globals
private static final int MAX_STEPS = 1000;  // simulation steps
private DecimalFormat df;      // used for reporting


public Bouncer()
{
  df = new DecimalFormat("0.#");  // 1 dp

  // set-up
  Odejava.getInstance();
  initWorld();
  initStatics();
  initDynamics();

  simulate(MAX_STEPS);  // carry out the simulation

  cleanUp();
} // end of Bouncer()
```

The setup involves the initializations of the rigid body and collision detection engines (in init-World()), and the creation of static and dynamic objects. A *static* object is a geom without a body, so it can't move. A *dynamic* object is a body, so it can be affected by forces, accelerations, and velocities. A body may have an associated geom to let it get involved in collisions.

simulate() steps the simulation forward until MAX_STEPS (1,000) steps have been carried out. The cleanup phase closes down the ODE engines.

Initializing the Engines

The rigid body engine is accessed through the World class, while collision detection utilizes HashSpace, JavaCollision, and Contact:

```
// globals
private World world;

// for collisions
private HashSpace collSpace;       // holds collision info
private JavaCollision collCalcs;   // calculates collisions
private Contact contactInfo;       // for accessing contact details


private void initWorld()
{
  world = new World();
  world.setGravity(0f, -0.2f, 0);  // down y-axis (9.8 is too fast)

  // max interactions per step (bigger is more accurate, but slower)
  world.setStepInteractions(10);

  // set step size (smaller is more accurate, but slower)
  world.setStepSize(0.05f);

  // create a collision space for the world's geoms
  collSpace = new HashSpace();

  collCalcs = new JavaCollision(world);   // collision calculations
  contactInfo = new Contact( collCalcs.getContactIntBuffer(),
                             collCalcs.getContactFloatBuffer());
}  // end of initWorld()
```

The World object acts as an environment for the bodies and joints, and manages gravity and step-related parameters.

The HashSpace object is a collision space for geoms. Collision testing involves examining pairs of geoms in the space to see if they intersect. It's possible to create multiple collision spaces, which improves collision testing performance since testing is only done between geoms within the same space.

JavaCollision performs the collision testing on geoms in a particular space. The tests generate a list of contact points, and the details relating to a particular point can be manipulated with the Contact object, contactInfo.

Initializing Static Objects

As I mentioned earlier, static objects are geoms with no bodies, so the simulation can't change the objects' positions or orientations. Static objects are often employed for modeling boundaries in a scene, such as walls and the floor—objects that can be collided with, but can't move themselves.

The only static entity in Bouncer is the floor, which is represented by a GeomPlane object with its normal facing up the y-axis:

```
private void initStatics()
{
  // the floor, facing upward
  GeomPlane groundGeom = new GeomPlane(0, 1.0f, 0, 0);
  collSpace.add(groundGeom);
}
```

Since the floor plays a part in the collision calculations, it's added to the collision space, collSpace.

Initializing Dynamic Objects

Dynamic objects have bodies, so the simulation can move them. If a body also has a geom, it can collide with other objects. The geom defines the object's shape, while the body specifies the object's mass, position, orientation, and the forces, velocities, and accelerations being applied to it.

initDynamics() creates a body and a geom for the ball. Its body has a mass, position, and linear and angular velocities. Odejava has other methods for specifying force and torque, which I haven't used here:

```
// globals for the sphere's body and geom
private Body sphere;
private GeomSphere sphereGeom;


private void initDynamics()
{
  // a sphere of radius 1, mass 1
  sphereGeom = new GeomSphere(1.0f);
  sphere = new Body("sphere", world, sphereGeom);
  sphere.adjustMass(1.0f);

  sphere.setPosition(0, 4.0f, 0);      // starts 4 unit above the floor
  sphere.setLinearVel(2.0f, 0, 0);     // moving to the right
  sphere.setAngularVel(0, 1.0f, 0);    // velocity around y-axis

  collSpace.addBodyGeoms(sphere);
} // end of initDynamics()
```

The sphere is added to the collision space, since it'll be involved in collisions with the floor.

Executing the Simulation

simulate() repeatedly calls step() to advance the simulation. Information about the sphere is printed every tenth simulation step:

```
// globals for holding sphere info
private Vector3f pos = new Vector3f();
private AxisAngle4f axisAng = new AxisAngle4f();


private void simulate(int maxSteps)
{
  int step = 1;
  while (stepCount < maxSteps) {
```

```
    step();
    // print sphere's details every 10th step
    if ((stepCount % 10) == 0) {
      pos = sphere.getPosition();
      sphere.getAxisAngle(axisAng);
      System.out.println("Step " + stepCount + ") Pos: (" +
              df.format(pos.x) + ", " + df.format(pos.y) + ", " +
              df.format(pos.z) + "), angle: " +
              df.format( Math.toDegrees(axisAng.angle)) );
              // ", quat: " + sphere.getQuaternion() );
    }
    stepCount++;
/*
    // sleep a bit
    try {
      Thread.sleep(50);    // ms
    }
    catch(Exception e) {}
*/
  }
} // end of simulate()
```

The Odejava Body class has numerous get methods, and three are shown in simulate().
Body.getPosition() returns the sphere's current position as a Vector3f object. Body.getAxisAngle()
returns the axis angle (a rotation in radians) around a direction vector. Body.getQuaternion() is
another way of obtaining the body's rotation as a quaternion.

The pos and axisAng objects are global so that new, temporary Vector3f and AxisAngle4f objects
don't need to be created in every iteration of the simulation loop.

The simulation step (0.05 ms) defined in initWorld() is an elapsed time within the simulation
and has no effect on the running time of the Bouncer application. A simple way of slowing down the
simulate() loop is to call Thread.sleep(), as shown in the commented code in the simulate() method
above.

Performing a Simulation Step

step() detects collisions, creates contact joints, and advances the simulation:

```
private void step()
{
  collCalcs.collide(collSpace);    // find collisions
  examineContacts();               // examine contact points
  collCalcs.applyContacts();       // apply contacts joint

  world.stepFast();                // make a step
}
```

JavaCollision.collide() examines the geoms in the collision space to determine which ones are
touching each other, and their contact points are collected.

examineContacts() converts the interesting contact *points* into contact *joints*. These joints act
as temporary links between the bodies attached to the geoms.

JavaCollision.applyContacts() applies the forces, acceleration, and velocity equations of the newly formed contact joints to their associated bodies, and then the joints are deleted.

Finally the simulation is stepped forward, moving the bodies and their geoms.

Examining the Contact Points

In Bouncer, the only contact point is the one made by the sphere when it touches the floor. examineContacts() finds the contact point and converts it into a "bouncy" contact joint:

```
private void examineContacts()
{
  for (int i = 0; i < collCalcs.getContactCount(); i++) {
    contactInfo.setIndex(i);    // look at the ith contact point

    // if the contact involves the sphere, then make it bounce
    if ((contactInfo.getGeom1() == sphereGeom) ||
        (contactInfo.getGeom2() == sphereGeom)) {
      contactInfo.setMode(Ode.dContactBounce);
      contactInfo.setBounce(0.82f);        // 1 is max bounciness
      contactInfo.setBounceVel(0.1f);      // min velocity for a bounce
      contactInfo.setMu(100.0f);           // 0 is friction-less
    }
  }
} // end of examineContacts()
```

The contact point in the list is accessed via the Contact object, contactInfo.

A contact point involves a pair of geoms, referenced via Contact.getGeom1() and Contact.getGeom2(). If either one is the sphere, a bouncing contact joint is created. The joint's mode is set to be Ode.dCountBounce, and the amount of bounciness is specified. If the sphere's velocity is below 0.1 meters/seconds (m/s), no bounce will occur and friction is added in to slow the sphere down.

Cleaning Up

At the end of the simulation (after 1,000 steps have been executed), cleanUp() is called from Bouncer():

```
private void cleanUp()
{
  collSpace.delete();
  collCalcs.delete();
  world.delete();
  Ode.dCloseODE();
}
```

It switches off the rigid body and collection detection engines and terminates ODE.

Visualizing Balls in a Box

Figure 5-2 shows a snapshot of the Balls3D application:

Figure 5-2. *More ball collisions*

Most of the visual elements in Balls3D are taken from the Arms3D example in Chapter 4, including the checkerboard floor, the numbered axes, the blue background, the two directional lights, and the OrbitBehavior for moving the user's viewpoint around the scene. I won't bother explaining them again, so look back at Chapter 4 if that material is unfamiliar to you.

The new elements are the translucent box with yellow edges and the ten textured bouncing spheres. The box and the spheres have Odejava models, as does the floor, so that collision detection can be carried out. The class diagrams for Balls3D are shown in Figure 5-3; only the public methods are listed for each class.

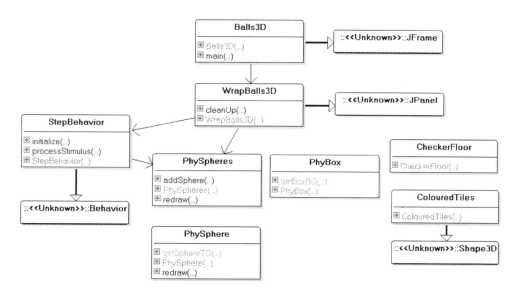

Figure 5-3. *Class diagrams for Balls3D*

Balls3D is the top-level JFrame, while WrapBalls3D does the work of creating the 3D scene. This includes setting up the graphical elements borrowed from Arms3D, such as the floor, the background, and the lighting. The floor is created with the help of the CheckerFloor and ColouredTiles classes taken from Arms3D.

Each sphere has a graphical and physics component, which are wrapped up in the PhySphere class. PhySpheres manages the PhySphere objects.

The Java 3D and Odejava aspects of the translucent box are created by PhyBox.

The simulation is executed by a Behavior subclass, StepBehavior, which is triggered every 30 ms to perform a simulation step.

Creating the Scene

WrapBalls3D initializes the physics system, creates the box and spheres, and starts StepBehavior. These tasks are carried out from createSceneGraph():

```
// globals
private BranchGroup sceneBG;
private BoundingSphere bounds;    // for environment nodes


private void createSceneGraph()
{
  sceneBG = new BranchGroup();
  bounds = new BoundingSphere(new Point3d(0,0,0), BOUNDSIZE);

  lightScene();         // add the lights
  addBackground();        // add the sky
  sceneBG.addChild( new CheckerFloor().getBG() );   // add the floor

  initPhysWorld();     // start the physics engines
  addPhysObjects();    // add the box and spheres
  addStepper();        // step behaviour for simulation

  sceneBG.compile();   // fix the scene
} // end of createSceneGraph()
```

Initializing the Engines

initPhysWorld() starts Odejava's rigid body and collision detection engines:

```
// global physics objects
private World world;
private HashSpace collSpace;       // holds collision info
private JavaCollision collCalcs;  // calculates collisions


private void initPhysWorld()
{
  Odejava.getInstance();

  world = new World();
  // world.setGravity(0f, -0.2f, 0);
  world.setStepInteractions(10);
  world.setStepSize(0.05f);
```

```
  // create a collision space for the world's box and spheres
  collSpace = new HashSpace();

  collCalcs = new JavaCollision(world);  // for collision calcs
}
```

The gravity setting has been commented out so the spheres won't fall to the bottom of the box.

The Physics Objects

The details of the spheres and the box are hidden away inside their own objects, which
addPhysObjects() creates:

```
// globals
private static final int NUM_SPHERES = 10;
private PhySpheres spheres;      // manages the bouncing spheres


private void addPhysObjects()
{
  PhyBox box = new PhyBox(6.0f, 3.0f, 6.0f, collSpace);
  sceneBG.addChild( box.getBoxBG() );    // add the box to the scene

  // create the spheres
  spheres = new PhySpheres(sceneBG, world, collSpace);
  for(int i=0; i < NUM_SPHERES; i++)
    spheres.addSphere();
}
```

The first three arguments of PhyBox() are the box's width, height, and depth. The box's visual
representation (the translucent space with yellow edges) is returned via PhyBox.getBoxBG() and
added to the scene graph.

NUM_SPHERES (10) spheres are created at random places inside the box by repeatedly calling
PhySpheres.addSphere(). The Java 3D spheres are attached to the scene graph inside PhySpheres,
which is passed sceneBG.

Starting the Simulation

The simulation is driven by a StepBehavior object created in addStepper():

```
// global
private StepBehavior stepBeh;


private void addStepper()
{
  stepBeh =
    new StepBehavior(30, spheres, world, collSpace, collCalcs);
      // it will be triggered every 30ms (== about 33 frames/sec)

  stepBeh.setSchedulingBounds( bounds );
  sceneBG.addChild( stepBeh );
}
```

The behavior is triggered every 30 ms, according to the first argument of its constructor.
StepBehavior also takes a reference to the PhySpheres object, called *spheres*, so it can request that
the spheres' visual components be redrawn.

The Box

The PhyBox class manages the graphical and physics elements of a box whose dimensions are specified by width, height, and depth values supplied in the PhyBox() constructor. The box is centered at the origin, with its base resting on the XZ plane.

The graphical box is translucent, and its edges are highlighted with thick yellow lines (apart from those edges resting on the floor.) See Figures 5-1 and 5-2 for screenshots.

The physics box is defined by a geom plane on the XZ plane and five geom boxes for the walls and ceiling.

The dual nature of PhyBox is highlighted in its constructor:

```
public PhyBox(float width, float height, float depth, HashSpace collSpace)
{
  makeBox(width, height, depth);          // makes the graphical parts
  makeBoxGeom(width, height, depth, collSpace);     // physics parts
}
```

makeBox() handles the Java 3D graphics, while makeBoxGeom() generates the Odejava geoms.

The Graphical Box

WrapBalls3D supplies the dimensions (6, 3, 6) for the box's width, height, and depth, and makeBox() creates a Java 3D Box object like the one in Figure 5-4.

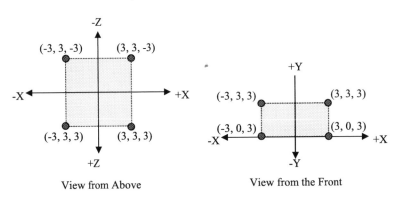

Figure 5-4. *The Box's dimensions*

By default, a Java 3D Box object is centered at the origin. makeBox() must move the box 1.5 units up the y-axis to make its base sit on the XZ plane. The box also needs to be made semitransparent.

The following is the makeBox() method:

```
// global
private BranchGroup boxBG;  // for holding the box's graphical parts


private void makeBox(float width, float height, float depth)
{
  float xDim = width/2.0f;
  float yDim = height/2.0f;
  float zDim = depth/2.0f;

  Appearance app = new Appearance();
```

```
// switch off face culling
PolygonAttributes pa = new PolygonAttributes();
pa.setCullFace(PolygonAttributes.CULL_NONE);
app.setPolygonAttributes(pa);

// semi-transparent appearance
TransparencyAttributes ta = new TransparencyAttributes();
ta.setTransparencyMode( TransparencyAttributes.BLENDED );
ta.setTransparency(0.7f);      // 1.0f is totally transparent
app.setTransparencyAttributes(ta);

// position the box: centered, sitting on the XZ plane
Transform3D t3d = new Transform3D();
t3d.set( new Vector3f(0, yDim+0.01f,0));
  /* the box is a bit above the floor, so it doesn't visual
     interact with the floor. */
TransformGroup boxTG = new TransformGroup(t3d);
boxTG.addChild(
   new com.sun.j3d.utils.geometry.Box(xDim, yDim, zDim, app));
        // set the box's dimensions and appearance

Shape3D edgesShape = makeBoxEdges(xDim, height, zDim); // edges

// collect the box and edges together under a single BranchGroup
boxBG = new BranchGroup();
boxBG.addChild(boxTG);
boxBG.addChild(edgesShape);
}  // end of makeBox()
```

Aside from making the Box's Appearance node use transparency, culling is also switched off. Then if the user moves the camera inside the box, the box's sides will still appear translucent.

The translation upward is by height/2 (yDim), plus a small amount (0.01), so the box's base doesn't overlap with the checkerboard floor.

makeBoxEdges() creates the yellow box edges by utilizing a Shape3D object. The Box, the box's TransformGroup, and the edges (stored in edgesShape) are collected together under a single BranchGroup, resulting in the scene graph branch shown in Figure 5-5.

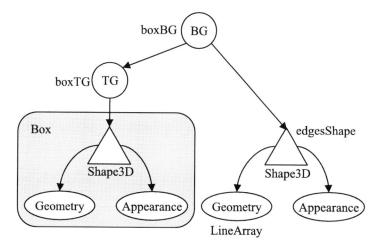

Figure 5-5. *The scene graph branch for the onscreen Box*

A close look at Figures 5-1 and 5-2 shows that the highlighting only appears on the eight box edges above the floor. The simplest way of creating these edges is as lines in a Java 3D LineArray. This data structure can be used to initialize the Shape3D node.

Eight lines requires 16 points in the LineArray:

```
private Shape3D makeBoxEdges(float x, float y, float z)
{
  LineArray edges = new LineArray(16, LineArray.COORDINATES |
                                      LineArray.COLOR_3);

  Point3f pts[] = new Point3f[16];
  // front edges
  pts[0] = new Point3f(-x, 0, z);    // edge 1 (left)
  pts[1] = new Point3f(-x, y, z);

  pts[2] = new Point3f(-x, y, z);    // edge 2 (top)
  pts[3] = new Point3f( x, y, z);

  pts[4] = new Point3f( x, y, z);    // edge 3 (right)
  pts[5] = new Point3f( x, 0, z);

  // back edges
  pts[6] = new Point3f(-x, 0,-z);    // edge 4 (left)
  pts[7] = new Point3f(-x, y,-z);

  pts[8] = new Point3f(-x, y,-z);    // edge 5 (top)
  pts[9] = new Point3f( x, y,-z);

  pts[10] = new Point3f( x, y,-z);   // edge 6 (right)
  pts[11] = new Point3f( x, 0,-z);

  // top edges, running front to back
  pts[12] = new Point3f(-x, y, z);   // edge 7 (left)
  pts[13] = new Point3f(-x, y,-z);

  pts[14] = new Point3f( x, y, z);   // edge 8 (right)
  pts[15] = new Point3f( x, y,-z);

  edges.setCoordinates(0, pts);

  // set the edges colour to yellow
  for(int i = 0; i < 16; i++)
    edges.setColor(i, new Color3f(1, 1, 0));

  Shape3D edgesShape = new Shape3D(edges);

  // make the edges (lines) thicker
  Appearance app = new Appearance();
  LineAttributes la = new LineAttributes();
  la.setLineWidth(4);
  app.setLineAttributes(la);
  edgesShape.setAppearance(app);

  return edgesShape;
} // end of makeBoxEdges()
```

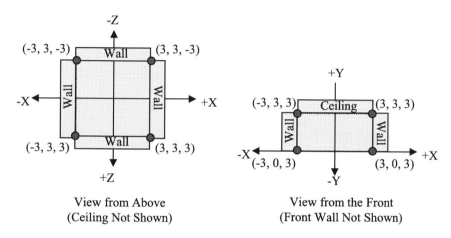

The color of the lines is set as part of the geometry, while their thickness is achieved with a LineAttributes object in the shape's appearance.

The Physics-Based Box

The box geometry manufactured in makeBoxGeom() consists of a geom plane for the floor, four geom boxes for the walls, and a fifth one for the ceiling. The geom plane coincides with the XZ plane, while the boxes surround the space occupied by the translucent Java 3D box. This notion is illustrated in Figure 5-6.

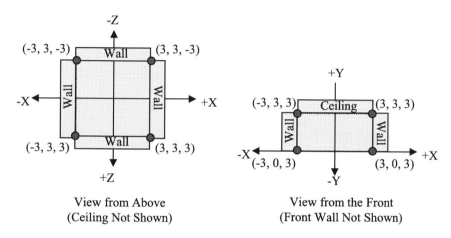

Figure 5-6. *The placing of the geoms around the box*

The trickiest aspect is positioning the geom boxes correctly. By default, each box is centered at the origin so it needs to be repositioned. Each box is THICKNESS (1.0) units thick, an arbitrary value:

```
// global
private static final float THICKNESS = 1.0f;

private void makeBoxGeom(float width, float height, float depth,
                                        HashSpace collSpace)
{
  float xDim = width/2.0f;
  float yDim = height/2.0f;
  float zDim = depth/2.0f;
  float midWall = THICKNESS/2.0f;

  collSpace.add( new GeomPlane(0, 1.0f, 0, 0));    // floor

  // the four walls
  GeomBox rightWall = new GeomBox(THICKNESS, height, depth);
  rightWall.setPosition(xDim+midWall, yDim, 0);
  collSpace.add(rightWall);

  GeomBox leftWall = new GeomBox(THICKNESS, height, depth);
  leftWall.setPosition(-(xDim+midWall), yDim, 0);
  collSpace.add(leftWall);
```

```
    GeomBox frontWall = new GeomBox(width, height, THICKNESS);
    frontWall.setPosition(0, yDim, zDim+midWall);
    collSpace.add(frontWall);

    GeomBox backWall = new GeomBox(width, height, THICKNESS);
    backWall.setPosition(0, yDim, -(zDim+midWall));
    collSpace.add(backWall);

    // the ceiling
    GeomBox ceiling = new GeomBox(width, THICKNESS, depth);
    ceiling.setPosition(0, height+midWall, 0);
    collSpace.add(ceiling);
}  // end of makeBoxGeom()
```

Since the floor, walls, and ceiling will be involved in collision detection, they're added to the collision space, collSpace.

Managing the Spheres

The main task of the PhySpheres object is to create multiple PhySphere spheres using a randomly generated radius, position, and linear velocity. Each sphere is also assigned a texture chosen at random.

The textures are loaded by PhySpheres at initialization time, so each PhySphere object can use one immediately, without the overhead of loading it.

PhySpheres has a redraw() method for all its spheres, which the StepBehavior class calls.

Initializing PhySpheres

The constructor creates an empty array list for holding future PhySphere objects and uses loadTextures() to load the earth, moon, and Mars textures, storing them as Texture2D objects in an array:

```
// globals
private BranchGroup sceneBG; // the scene graph
private World world;         // physics elements
private HashSpace collSpace;

private ArrayList<PhySphere> spheres;
private Random rand;


public PhySpheres(BranchGroup sg, World w, HashSpace cs)
{
  sceneBG = sg;
  world = w;
  collSpace = cs;

  spheres = new ArrayList<PhySphere>();
  rand = new Random();

  loadTextures();
}  // end of PhySpheres()
```

Adding a Sphere

addSphere() (called from WrapBalls3D) utilizes random numbers to set the texture, radius, position, and velocity for a new sphere:

```
// globals
private Texture2D[] textures;    // holds the loaded textures


public void addSphere()
{
  Texture2D planTex = textures[ rand.nextInt(textures.length) ];
  float radius = rand.nextFloat()/4.0f + 0.2f; // between 0.2 & 0.45

  PhySphere s = new PhySphere(world, collSpace, "planet "+counter,
                    planTex, radius, randomPos(), randomVel());

  sceneBG.addChild( s.getSphereTG() );
  spheres.add(s);  // add to ArrayList
  counter++;
}  // end of addSphere()
```

PhySphere creates a Java 3D sphere, which is accessed via PhySphere.getSphereTG() and linked to the scene graph.

randomPos() and randomVel() generate random position and velocity vectors within prescribed ranges:

```
private Vector3f randomPos()
{ Vector3f pos = new Vector3f();
  pos.x = rand.nextFloat()*5.0f - 2.5f;    // -2.5 to 2.5
  pos.y = rand.nextFloat()*2.0f + 0.5f;    // 0.5 to 2.5
  pos.z = rand.nextFloat()*5.0f - 2.5f;    // -2.5 to 2.5
  return pos;
}  // end of randomPos()

private Vector3f randomVel()
{ Vector3f vel = new Vector3f();
  vel.x = rand.nextFloat()*6.0f - 3.0f;    // -3.0 to 3.0
  vel.y = rand.nextFloat()*6.0f - 3.0f;
  vel.z = rand.nextFloat()*6.0f - 3.0f;
  return vel;
}  // end of randomVel()
```

The position values are hardwired to be somewhere within the translucent space, while the velocity numbers produce a reasonable speed in most cases.

Helping StepBehavior

StepBehavior periodically needs to redraw the visual components of the spheres. It does this with PhySpheres' redraw() method:

```
public void redraw()
{ for(PhySphere ps: spheres)
    ps.redraw();
}
```

A Sphere

A PhySphere sphere has two parts: a Java 3D visualization and an Odejava body. This is highlighted by the method calls in the constructor that builds them:

```
// globals
private Transform3D t3d;    // used for accessing a TG's transform
private DecimalFormat df;   // for printing data


public PhySphere(World world, HashSpace collSpace, String name,
                          Texture2D tex, float radius,
                          Vector3f posVec, Vector3f velVec)
{ t3d = new Transform3D();
  df = new DecimalFormat("0.##");  // 2 dp

  makeSphere3D(tex, radius, posVec);     // makes the graphical part
  makeSphereBody(world, collSpace, name, radius, posVec, velVec);
                                    // physics part
}
```

The Graphical Sphere

The graphical sphere is textured and lit and hangs below two TransformGroups (TGs) that control its position and orientation. The configuration is shown in Figure 5-7.

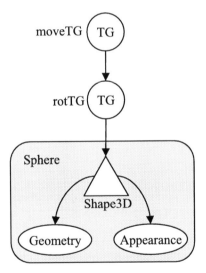

Figure 5-7. *The scene graph branch for an onscreen Sphere*

The moveTG TransformGroup is used to translate the sphere, and rotTG rotates it. I could have used a single TransformGroup instead, but separating the two operations makes them easier to understand.

makeSphere3D() also constructs the Java 3D Sphere and sets its appearance:

```
// globals
// sphere colours
private static final Color3f BLACK = new Color3f(0.0f, 0.0f, 0.0f);
private static final Color3f GRAY = new Color3f(0.6f, 0.6f, 0.6f);
private static final Color3f WHITE = new Color3f(0.9f, 0.9f, 0.9f);

// TGs which the sphere hangs off:
private TransformGroup moveTG, rotTG;


private void makeSphere3D(Texture2D tex, float radius, Vector3f posVec)
{
  Appearance app = new Appearance();

  // combine texture with material and lighting of underlying surface
  TextureAttributes ta = new TextureAttributes();
  ta.setTextureMode( TextureAttributes.MODULATE );
  app.setTextureAttributes( ta );

  // assign gray material with lighting
  Material mat= new Material(GRAY, BLACK, GRAY, WHITE, 25.0f);
     // sets ambient, emissive, diffuse, specular, shininess
  mat.setLightingEnable(true);
  app.setMaterial(mat);

  // apply texture to shape
  if (tex != null)
    app.setTexture(tex);

  // make the sphere with normals for lighting, and texture support
  Sphere sphere = new Sphere(radius,
                       Sphere.GENERATE_NORMALS |
                       Sphere.GENERATE_TEXTURE_COORDS,
                       15, app);    // default divs == 15

  // create a transform group for rotating the sphere
  rotTG = new TransformGroup();
  rotTG.setCapability(TransformGroup.ALLOW_TRANSFORM_READ);
  rotTG.setCapability(TransformGroup.ALLOW_TRANSFORM_WRITE);
  rotTG.addChild(sphere);

  // create a transform group for moving the sphere
  t3d.set(posVec);
  moveTG = new TransformGroup(t3d);
  moveTG.setCapability(TransformGroup.ALLOW_TRANSFORM_READ);
  moveTG.setCapability(TransformGroup.ALLOW_TRANSFORM_WRITE);
  moveTG.addChild(rotTG);
}  // end of makeSphere3D()
```

The Physics-Based Sphere

The Odejava sphere combines GeomSphere and Body objects. The GeomSphere is for detecting collisions with other spheres and the box. The Body object stores the mass, position, and the linear and angular velocities.

The position and linear velocity come from PhySpheres, the mass is derived from the sphere's radius, and the angular velocity is hardwired to produce a clockwise spin around the y-axis:

```
// globals
// radius --> mass conversion
private static final float MASS_FACTOR = 5.0f;

private Body sphereBody;


private void makeSphereBody(World world, HashSpace collSpace,
                           String name, float radius,
                           Vector3f posVec, Vector3f velVec)
{
  sphereBody = new Body(name, world, new GeomSphere(radius));

  sphereBody.adjustMass(MASS_FACTOR*radius);
  sphereBody.setPosition(posVec);  // same as graphical sphere
  sphereBody.setLinearVel(velVec);
  sphereBody.setAngularVel(0, 2.0f, 0);  // clockwise around y-axis

  collSpace.addBodyGeoms( sphereBody );  // add to collision space
} // end of makeSphereBody()
```

Care must be taken that the Odejava and Java 3D spheres start at the same position. Also, the Odejava sphere must be added to the collision space so it can take part in collision detection.

Redrawing the Sphere

redraw() is where changes in the Odejava sphere affect the Java 3D sphere.

StepBehavior calls PhySpheres' redraw() at the end of its simulation step after the physics-based spheres have been moved.

PhySpheres calls redraw() in each PhySphere to update the position and orientation of the Java 3D sphere with the position and orientation of the corresponding Odejava sphere:

```
public void redraw()
{
  // get position and orientation from the physics sphere
  Vector3f posVec = sphereBody.getPosition();
  Quat4f quat = sphereBody.getQuaternion();

  // update the TGs in the graphical sphere
  t3d.set(posVec);
  moveTG.setTransform(t3d);  // translate the sphere

  t3d.set(quat);
  rotTG.setTransform(t3d);  // rotate the sphere
} // end of redraw()
```

The mapping from Odejava to Java 3D is quite straightforward. The position and orientation details of the Odejava sphere are extracted as a Vector3f vector and a Quat4f quaternion and applied to the moveTG and rotTG TransformGroups of the Java 3D sphere.

An important reason for the simplicity is that Odejava and Java 3D use the same vector and matrix classes, so data can be readily shared.

I'm Steppin' Out...

StepBehavior advances the simulation a step at a time, once every timeDelay milliseconds.

The simulation step performs collision detection, creates contact joints, and redraws the Java 3D spheres:

Initializing the Behavior

The StepBehavior constructor stores references to the PhySpheres object, the rigid body and collision engines, and the Java 3D WakeupCondition object, which will periodically trigger the behavior:

```
// globals
private WakeupCondition timeOut;
private PhySpheres spheres;

private World world;
private HashSpace collSpace;      // holds collision info
private JavaCollision collCalcs;  // calculates collisions
private Contact contactInfo;      // for accessing contact details


public StepBehavior(int timeDelay, PhySpheres ps,
                          World w, HashSpace cs, JavaCollision cc)
{
  timeOut = new WakeupOnElapsedTime(timeDelay);
  spheres = ps;
  world = w;
  collSpace = cs;
  collCalcs = cc;
  contactInfo = new Contact( collCalcs.getContactIntBuffer(),
                      collCalcs.getContactFloatBuffer());
}
```

Java 3D calls the behavior's initialize() method to set it waiting until the specified time has elapsed:

```
public void initialize()
{ wakeupOn( timeOut ); }
```

Responding to a Wake-Up Call

The behavior is woken by Java 3D calling its processStimulus() method, where the step execution code is located:

```
public void processStimulus( Enumeration criteria )
{
  // step through the simulation
  collCalcs.collide(collSpace);   // find collisions
  examineContacts();                // examine contact points
  collCalcs.applyContacts();
                  // add contacts to contactInfo jointGroup
  world.stepFast();                    // advance the simulation

  spheres.redraw();   // redraw the graphical spheres

  wakeupOn( timeOut );  // wait for the next wake-up
} // end of processStimulus()
```

The contact points are found and converted to joints, and the physics simulation is advanced, thereby changing the position and orientation of the physics spheres. redraw() is called in PhySpheres to use those changes to modify the graphical sphere's position and orientation.

examineContacts() loops through the contact points and converts those involving spheres into bouncing contact joints:

```
private void examineContacts()
{
  for (int i = 0; i < collCalcs.getContactCount(); i++) {
    contactInfo.setIndex(i);      // look at the ith contact point

    // if contact involves a sphere, then make the contact bounce
      if ((contactInfo.getGeom1() instanceof GeomSphere) ||
          (contactInfo.getGeom2() instanceof GeomSphere)) {
      contactInfo.setMode(Ode.dContactBounce);
      contactInfo.setBounce(1.0f);       // 1 is max bounciness
      contactInfo.setBounceVel(0.1f);  // min velocity for a bounce
      contactInfo.setMu(0);              // 0 is friction-less
    }
  }
} // end of examineContacts()
```

The contact point details in contactInfo include references to the geoms involved in the collision. StepBehavior checks if either of them is a GeomSphere before configuring the joint to be very bouncy and frictionless.

Another slightly more general way of identifying a geom is to examine its name using Geom.getName(). In Balls3D, all the sphere names start with *Planet*, followed by a number, so they are easy to recognize. makeSphereBody() in PhySphere assigns the name to the sphere's Body object, which gets taken up by its associated geom.

A Note of Application Development

A useful way of structuring the development of a Java 3D/Odejava application is to split it into two stages. The first stage involves the creation of the visual elements only—the Java 3D scene *without* the physics.

In the case of Balls3D, I implement the PhyBox and PhySphere classes without their Odejava methods (makeBoxGeom() and makeSphereBody()). I also leave out the StepBehavior and PhySpheres classes.

This approach allows the graphical features of an application to be tested and debugged without the extra complexity of physics simulation.

The second stage adds in the physics elements. Since the Odejava bodies and geoms are closely linked to their Java 3D counterparts, it's quite easy to decide which classes need augmenting.

The basic StepBehavior class is always the same: a behavior using an elapsed time WakeupCondition. The code in processStimulus() is fairly standard, although the details of examineContacts() will vary depending on what geoms are of interest.

Another advantage of developing the graphical side of the application first, is that it can show how things look when various parameters, such as gravity, friction, and the amount of bounce, are tweaked.

Summary

This chapter looked at Odejava, a Java binding for the ODE physics API, and how it can be utilized with Java 3D. Odejava is a collision detection engine based around bodies, geoms, and joints. Bodies and geoms represent shapes but have no visual representation, which leads to a *dual-model* approach in the code, separating the physics and graphical elements.

The Balls3D example models a collection of spheres bouncing around inside a box, and the dual-model technique can be seen at work in its PhySphere and PhyBox classes. PhySphere utilizes the Java 3D Sphere class with Odejava's GeomSphere and Body. PhyBox employs the Java 3D Shape3D and Odejava's GeomPlane and GeomBox.

A Java 3D behavior drives the Odejava engine. In each update, new positions and orientations are calculated for the moving Odejava elements then used to translate and rotate the corresponding Java 3D elements.

CHAPTER 6

A Multitextured Landscape

This chapter's focus is on using multitexturing and a heights map to make a natural-looking 3D landscape. I describe several multitexturing approaches for making a 3D landscape look more varied and natural by using grass and stone textures, adding light and shadow with a shadow map, and supplying flowers and water with an alpha map.

The terrain is built from a heights map, which is generated using a probabilistic hill-raising algorithm.

What would a landscape be without something to wander over it? I also discuss how to make golden balls autonomously roam around the scene.

Surveying the Landscape

Multitexturing is the application of several textures to the same shape, a surprisingly versatile mechanism because it's possible to combine textures in numerous ways, especially when they have *alpha channels*. An alpha channel contains transparency information that determines the visibility of a texture's pixels. A texture with transparent (or translucent) areas lets the texture below it be seen. Several variations of this idea are used to cover a landscape with grass, stones, flowers, pools of water, and shadows.

A *heights map* is a data structure holding elevations (heights) for a landscape. The data can be obtained from existing geographical sources, or be generated using a *hill-raising* algorithm (as in this chapter). The resulting heights are used to generate a 3D scenery shape at runtime.

These techniques are demonstrated in this chapter's example, called TexLand3D, shown in Figure 6-1.

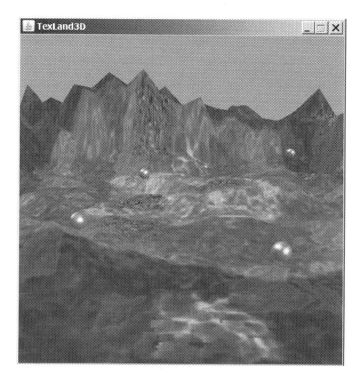

Figure 6-1. *The TexLand3D application*

The landscape is composed from a grid (or mesh) of quadrilaterals (quads) covered with a repeating grass texture that completely replaces the quads' underlying color. A partially transparent stone texture is applied on top of the grass. The grass shows through in the areas where the stone texture is transparent.

A *light map* texture is modulated with the grass and stone textures to add shadows and light without the underlying shape requiring normals or a light-enabled material. TexLand3D can load a light map from an image file, or draw one at execution time.

The texture coordinates for the grass, stone, and light map textures are generated at runtime, and the code can easily be tweaked to adjust the repetition frequency of each texture. For example, in Figure 6-1 the grass texture is repeated 16 times, the stone texture 4 times, and the light map appears 1 time.

Multitexturing is used to "splash" purple flowers and pools of water onto random areas of the floor. A *splash shape* is made from quads copied from the floor mesh and covered with a combination of a standard texture image and an *alpha map* texture. The map specifies what areas of the standard texture will be opaque, translucent, and transparent. Each splash shape is represented by a SplashShape object. Each SplashShape generates its own semirandom alpha map at runtime, which produces unique borders for each shape's flowerbed or pool. My SplashShape class owes a great deal to David Yazel's SplatShape class, and Justin Couch's AlphaDemo class (two well-respected Java 3D developers).

TexLand3D illustrates the utility of a heights map for constructing a landscape. Heights for the floor's vertices are generated using a hill-raising algorithm and stored in a 2D array of floats. This array is employed to create the multitextured floor by each SplashShape object to copy floor quads, and by roaming balls to navigate over the landscape (four of them can be seen in Figure 6-1). The balls move randomly over the surface but turn away from the landscape's edge.

Figure 6-2 shows the class diagrams for the application; only public methods are listed.

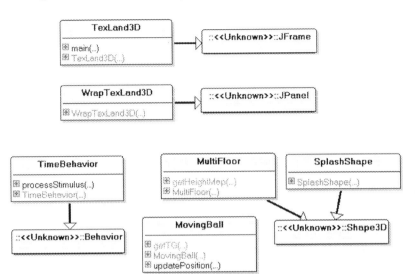

Figure 6-2. *Class diagrams for TexLand3D*

TexLand3D sets up the top-level JFrame, while WrapTexLand3D renders the 3D scene inside a JPanel. MultiFloor generates the heights map and textures the floor with grass, stones, and the light map. The splashes of flowers and water are added with SplashShape objects. The balls are represented by MovingBall objects, which are animated via periodic calls to their updatePosition() method by TimeBehavior.

Building the Scene

WrapTexLand3D constructs the scene graph shown in Figure 6-3.

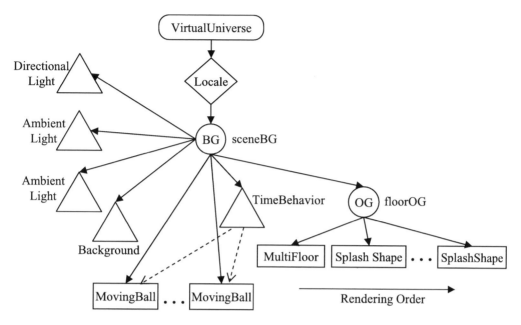

Figure 6-3. *The TexLand3D scene graph*

To make things simpler, I've hidden the details of the scene graph branches for the moving balls, the multitextured floor (MultiFloor), and the splash shapes; I'll explain them later.

The nodes at the top of the graph, the lights, and the background node are built in the same way as in previous examples, through calls from createSceneGraph():

```
// globals
private static final int BOUNDSIZE = 100;  // larger than world
private BranchGroup sceneBG;
private BoundingSphere bounds;


private void createSceneGraph()
{
  sceneBG = new BranchGroup();
  bounds = new BoundingSphere(new Point3d(0,0,0), BOUNDSIZE);

  lightScene();          // the lights
  addBackground();       // the sky
  addFloor();            // the multi-textured floor (and splashes)
  movingBalls();         // the moving balls

  sceneBG.compile();  // fix the scene
} // end of createSceneGraph()
```

addFloor() constructs the subtree on the right of Figure 6-3, starting at the OG (OrderedGroup) node. movingBalls() creates the MovingBalls branches and the TimeBehavior instance.

Creating the Floor

addFloor() builds the multitextured floor and the splash shapes that lie on top of it:

```
// global
private float[][] heights;   // heights map for the floor


private void addFloor()
{
  MultiFloor floor = new MultiFloor("grass.gif", 4,
                                     "stoneBits.gif", 2);
  heights = floor.getHeightMap();

  /* Use an ordered group  to avoid rendering conflicts
     between the floor and the splash shapes. */
  OrderedGroup floorOG = new OrderedGroup();
  floorOG.addChild(floor);

  // load the textures for the splashes
  Texture2D flowersTex = loadTexture("images/flowers.jpg");
  Texture2D waterTex = loadTexture("images/water.jpg");

  // add splashes
  for(int i=0; i < 8; i++)      // 8 splashes of flowers
    floorOG.addChild( new SplashShape(flowersTex, heights) );

  for (int i=0; i < 3; i++)     // 3 pools of water
    floorOG.addChild( new SplashShape(waterTex, heights) );

  // add all the meshes to the scene
  sceneBG.addChild( floorOG );
}  // end of addFloor()
```

The two files named in the MultiFloor constructor hold the grass and stone textures. Their contents are shown in Figures 6-4 and 6-5.

Figure 6-4. *The grass texture*   **Figure 6-5.** *The stones texture*

The stones texture has a transparent background, which allows the grass to show through when the textures are combined by MultiFloor.

The constructor's numeric arguments (4 and 2) are the number of times the textures should be repeated along the sides of the floor. There are some restrictions on what values can be used, which I explain when I discuss the MultiFloor class in "The Multitextured Floor" section.

The flowers and water textures used by the splash shapes are loaded in WrapTexLand3D rather than individually by each SplashShape object, to avoid repeated calls to Java 3D's texture loader. The textures are shown in Figures 6-6 and 6-7.

Figure 6-6. *The flowers texture*

Figure 6-7. *The water texture*

The MultiFloor and SplashShape objects are added to an OrderedGroup node so they'll be rendered in a fixed order. This avoids problems with drawing overlapping transparent geometries.

Start the Balls Moving

movingBalls() places balls randomly on the floor, and the TimeBehavior object keeps triggering updates to their positions:

```
// global
private static final int NUM_BALLS = 10;    // no. of moving balls
private static final int UPDATE_TIME = 100; // ms, for updating balls

private void movingBalls()
{
  ArrayList<MovingBall> mBalls = new ArrayList<MovingBall>();

  Texture2D ballTex = loadTexture("images/spot.gif");
  MovingBall mb;
  for (int i=0; i < NUM_BALLS; i++) {
    mb = new MovingBall(ballTex, heights);
    sceneBG.addChild( mb.getTG() );
    mBalls.add(mb);
  }

  // pass the list of balls to the behavior
  TimeBehavior ballTimer = new TimeBehavior(UPDATE_TIME, mBalls);
  ballTimer.setSchedulingBounds( bounds );
  sceneBG.addChild( ballTimer );
} // end of movingBalls()
```

TimeBehavior cycles through the MovingBalls ArrayList (mBalls) every UPDATE_TIME (100) milliseconds, calling each ball's updatePosition() method.

Moving Around the Scene

The view branch part of the scene graph isn't shown in Figure 6-3, since it's automatically created by Java 3D's SimpleUniverse class. WrapTexLand3D adds a Java 3D OrbitBehavior node to it so the user can move/rotate/zoom the camera through the scene. The behavior is set up with orbitControls() in the same way as in earlier examples.

The Multitextured Floor

MultiFloor is a subclass of Shape3D, which builds the scene graph branch shown in Figure 6-8. This corresponds to the "MultiFloor" box shown in Figure 6-3.

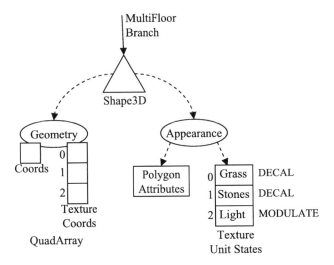

Figure 6-8. *The MultiFloor branch*

MultiFloor also generates a 2D heights map, which it uses to populate the coordinates (coords) used in the Geometry node. The heights map holds heights for a FLOOR_LEN+1 by FLOOR_LEN+1 grid of points, with each point one unit apart. FLOOR_LEN must be an even number, for reasons explained later in this section.

The heights map is defined as the following:

```
private final static int FLOOR_LEN = 20;
private float[][] heights = new float[FLOOR_LEN+1][FLOOR_LEN+1];
```

Figure 6-9 shows the heights map (*FL* stands for FLOOR_LEN).

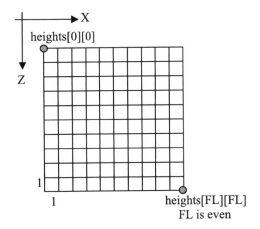

Figure 6-9. *The floor's heights map*

MultiFloor treats heights[z][x] as a height for an (x, z) coordinate. It's then an easy step to convert the heights array into the coordinates mesh shown in Figure 6-10. The height in the heights[z][x] cell becomes the coordinate (x - FLOOR_LEN/2, height, z - FLOOR_LEN/2).

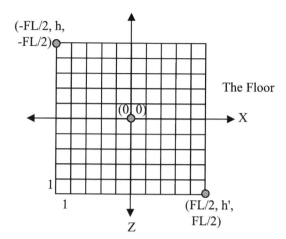

Figure 6-10. *The coordinates mesh*

The coordinates mesh is used to build a QuadArray geometry of sides FLOOR_LEN, centered at (0, 0) on the XZ plane. The requirement that the mesh is centered means that FLOOR_LEN must be even. The vertices are spaced out at 1 unit intervals along the x- and z- axes.

The Geometry node shown in Figure 6-8 contains three sets of texture coordinates, one each for the grass, stone, and light map textures. The separate coordinates allow the textures to be repeated over the mesh at different frequencies.

The textures are stored in the shape's Appearance node, inside a three-element Java 3D TextureUnitState array.

The following is the constructor for MultiFloor:

```
// globals
private final static int FLOOR_LEN = 20;

private float[][] heights;    // heights map for the floor


public MultiFloor(String texFnm1, int freq1,
                     String texFnm2, int freq2)
{
  System.out.println("floor len: " + FLOOR_LEN);
  int texLen1 = calcTextureLength(texFnm1, freq1);
  int texLen2 = calcTextureLength(texFnm2, freq2);

  heights = makeHills();
  createGeometry(texLen1, texLen2);
  createAppearance(texFnm1, texFnm2);
}
```

The texture repetition frequencies are passed to the calcTextureLength() calls. calcTexture-Length() works out the required length of the texture so it will repeat that number of times across the floor. Texture length is defined by the following equation:

```
texture length * frequency == FLOOR_LEN
```

The following is the calcTextureLength() method that uses this equation:

```
private int calcTextureLength(String texFnm, int freq)
{
  if (freq < 1)    // if 0 or negative
    freq = 1;
  else if (freq > FLOOR_LEN)  // if bigger than the floor length
    freq = FLOOR_LEN;

  return (FLOOR_LEN / freq);   // integer division
}
```

Due to calcTextureLength()'s use of integer division, the freq value should be a factor of the floor length. Since FLOOR_LEN is 20, freq should be 1, 2, 4, 5, 10, or 20.

Figures 6-11 and 6-12 show the rendering of an r.gif texture containing a single letter *R*. Figure 6-11 shows r.gif rendered with a frequency of 20, while Figure 6-12 uses a frequency of 4.

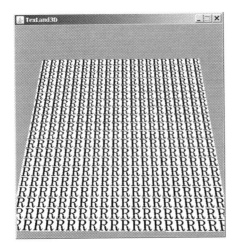

Figure 6-11. *R (freq = 20)*

Figure 6-12. *R (freq = 4)*

Heights Map Generation

makeHills() utilizes a hill-raising algorithm to produce the heights map. A cell is chosen at random inside the heights[][] array and its height is increased by a small amount (PEAK_INCR). The heights of its four neighbors on the left, right, back, and front are also increased, but by a smaller number (SIDE_INCR):

```
// hill creation constants for the heights map
private static final int NUM_HILL_INCRS = 2000;
private static final float PEAK_INCR = 0.3f;    // height incrs
private static final float SIDE_INCR = 0.25f;


private float[][] makeHills()
{
  float[][] heights = new float[FLOOR_LEN+1][FLOOR_LEN+1];
      // include heights on the front and right edges of the floor

  Random rand = new Random();
```

```
int x, z;    // index into array (x == column, z == row)
for (int i=0; i < NUM_HILL_INCRS; i++) {
  x = (int)(rand.nextDouble()*FLOOR_LEN);
  z = (int)(rand.nextDouble()*FLOOR_LEN);
  if (addHill(x, z, rand)) {
    heights[z][x] += PEAK_INCR;
    if (x > 0)
      heights[z][x-1] += SIDE_INCR;    // left
    if (x < (FLOOR_LEN-1))
      heights[z][x+1] += SIDE_INCR;    // right
    if (z > 0)
      heights[z-1][x] += SIDE_INCR;    // back
    if (z < (FLOOR_LEN-1))
      heights[z+1][x] += SIDE_INCR;    // front
  }
}
return heights;
} // end of makeHills()
```

The addHill() test in makeHills() adds a twist, by assigning probabilities to whether the heights at particular locations are increased.

In the TexLand3D landscape, I want more hills along the left side, right side, and back edge of the floor. This distribution is represented graphically by the *probability map* in Figure 6-13. The map specifies the likelihood that a given height in the heights map will be increased when selected to become a hill.

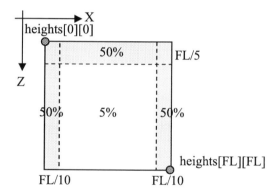

Figure 6-13. *The probability map for the heights map*

If a height cell is chosen on the left, right, or back of the heights map, there's a 50% chance that it will trigger hill-raising, while the central region only has a 5% probability of doing so.

addHill() implements the map as a series of tests of the selected heights[][] array's x- and z- cell indices and returns true if a hill should be raised at that position:

```
private boolean addHill(int x, int z, Random rand)
{
  if (z < FLOOR_LEN/5.0f)  //toward- back of floor
    return (rand.nextDouble() < 0.5);  // 50% chance of a hill

  if (x < FLOOR_LEN/10.0f)  // on the left side of the floor
    return (rand.nextDouble() < 0.5);   // 50% chance
```

```
    if ((FLOOR_LEN - x) < FLOOR_LEN/10.0f) // on the right side
      return (rand.nextDouble() < 0.5);    // 50% chance

    // other areas of the floor
    return (rand.nextDouble() < 0.05);  // 5% chance
}
```

The Floor's Geometry

As shown in Figure 6-8, the Geometry node is a QuadArray with one set of vertices and three sets of texture coordinates (one for each texture):

```
private void createGeometry(int texLen1, int texLen2)
{
  Point3f[] coords = createCoords();   // create vertices

  // create (s,t) coordinates for the three textures
  TexCoord2f[] tCoords1 = createTexCoords(coords, texLen1);
  TexCoord2f[] tCoords2 = createTexCoords(coords, texLen2);
  TexCoord2f[] tCoords3 = createTexCoords(coords, FLOOR_LEN);

  QuadArray plane = new QuadArray(coords.length,
                         GeometryArray.COORDINATES |
                         GeometryArray.TEXTURE_COORDINATE_2,
                          3, new int[]{0,1,2});

  plane.setCoordinates(0, coords);
  plane.setTextureCoordinates(0, 0, tCoords1);  // grass texture
  plane.setTextureCoordinates(1, 0, tCoords2);  // stones texture
  plane.setTextureCoordinates(2, 0, tCoords3);  // light map
  setGeometry(plane);
}  // end of createGeometry()
```

The third call to createTexCoords() is supplied with a texture length equal to FLOOR_LEN, which means that a single copy of the texture (the light map) will span the mesh.

The QuadArray() constructor doesn't include a GeometryArray.NORMALS flag, since the mesh's reflective qualities will be "faked" with the light map. However, the constructor has two arguments to specify the number of texture units it will utilize (three), and their indices. These indices are used in the calls to QuadArray.setTextureCoordinates() to assign the texture coordinates to the right texture units.

Creating the Floor's Vertices

createCoords() generates the floor's (x, y, z) coordinates by utilizing the heights map. As shown in Figures 6-9 and 6-10, the heights[][] array is treated as an (x, z) grid of heights and translated into a coordinates mesh starting at (-FLOOR_LEN/2, -FLOOR_LEN/2):

```
private Point3f[] createCoords()
{
  Point3f[] coords = new Point3f[FLOOR_LEN*FLOOR_LEN*4];
              // since each quad has 4 coords
  int i = 0;
  for(int z=0; z <= FLOOR_LEN-1; z++) {    // skip z's front row
    for(int x=0; x <= FLOOR_LEN-1; x++) {  // skip x's right column
      createTile(coords, i, x, z);
```

```
    i = i + 4;  // since 4 coords created for 1 tile
    }
  }
  return coords;
}
```

createTile() initializes four coordinates that will later form a quad (tile) in the QuadArray mesh:

```
private void createTile(Point3f[] coords, int i, int x, int z)
{
  // (xc, zc) is the (x,z) coordinate in the scene
  float xc = x - FLOOR_LEN/2;
  float zc = z - FLOOR_LEN/2;

  // points created in counter-clockwise order from bottom left
  coords[i] = new Point3f(xc, heights[z+1][x], zc+1.0f);
  coords[i+1] = new Point3f(xc+1.0f, heights[z+1][x+1], zc+1.0f);
  coords[i+2] = new Point3f(xc+1.0f, heights[z][x+1], zc);
  coords[i+3] = new Point3f(xc, heights[z][x], zc);
}  // end of createTile()
```

The x and z indices of the heights[][] array are converted into x- and z- axis values by subtracting FLOOR_LEN/2 from them.

Building the Floor's Texture Coordinates

createTexCoords() generates texture coordinates for the floor's vertices. Since the vertices are grouped in fours for each quad, the texture coordinates (*texels*) are grouped in a similar way:

```
private TexCoord2f[] createTexCoords(Point3f[] coords, int texLen)
{
  int numPoints = coords.length;
  TexCoord2f[] tcoords = new TexCoord2f[numPoints];

  TexCoord2f dummyTC = new TexCoord2f(-1,-1);   // dummy tex coord
  for(int i=0; i < numPoints; i=i+4)
    createTexTile(tcoords, i, texLen, coords, dummyTC);
                        // 4 tex coords for 1 coordinates tile
  return tcoords;
}  // end of createTexCoords()
```

The "dummy" texture coordinate, dummyTC, is used to deal with some tricky edge cases when generating the texels, which I explain later in this section.

In coords[], each group of four vertices for a quad is stored in counterclockwise order, starting from the bottom-left vertex. This same ordering is employed by createTexTile() for storing the texture coordinates in tcoords[]:

```
private void createTexTile(TexCoord2f[] tcoords, int i, int texLen,
                           Point3f[] coords, TexCoord2f dummyTC)
{
  // make the bottom-left tex coord, i
  tcoords[i] = makeTexCoord(coords[i], texLen, dummyTC);

  for (int j = 1; j < 4; j++)   // add the other three coords
    tcoords[i+j] = makeTexCoord(coords[i+j], texLen, tcoords[i]);
}  // end of createTexTile()
```

makeTexCoord() converts an (x, y, z) coordinate into an (s, t) texel based on the (x, z) value modulo the texture length, and is divided by that length. Unfortunately this causes some problems for the texels at the top and right edges of the texture:

```
private TexCoord2f makeTexCoord(Point3f coord, int texLen,
                                              TexCoord2f firstTC)
{
  float s, t;
  if (texLen > 1) {
    s = ((float)((coord.x + FLOOR_LEN/2) % texLen))/texLen;
    t = ((float)((FLOOR_LEN/2 - coord.z) % texLen))/texLen;
  }
  else {    // don't use modulo when texLen == 1
    s = ((float)(coord.x + FLOOR_LEN/2))/texLen;
    t = ((float)(FLOOR_LEN/2 - coord.z))/texLen;
  }
  if (s < firstTC.x)    // deal with right edge rounding
    s = 1.0f - s;
  if (t < firstTC.y)    // deal with top edge rounding
    t = 1.0f - t;

  return new TexCoord2f(s, t);
}  // end of makeTexCoord
```

The problem is illustrated by Figure 6-14, which shows how an R texture is mapped to the vertices covering 5*5 floor quads.

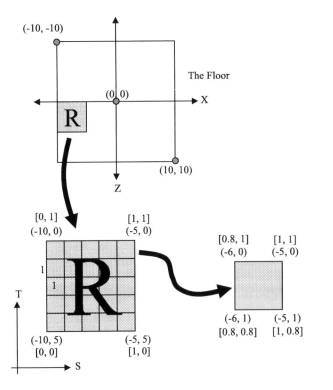

Figure 6-14. *Correctly texturing the R*

The modulo-related problems occur for mappings involving quads at the top and right edges of the texture. The single quad on the right of Figure 6-14 shows the correct texel mapping for the (x, z) coordinates (-6, 1), (-5, 1), (-5, 0), and (-6, 0). Unfortunately, makeTexCoord()'s use of modulo incorrectly maps the three coordinates, (-5, 1), (-5, 0), and (-6, 0) to [**0**, 0.8], [**0, 0**], and [0.8, **0**] respectively. The bold highlighting indicates the trouble spots: when the s or t value should be a 1, the modulo operation produces a 0.

makeTexCoord() handles this by comparing the generated texel's s and t values with the bottom left texel of the quad ([0.8, 0.8] in the example). If the generated s or t values are smaller (i.e., less than 0.8), the modulo problem has occurred. It's fixed by subtracting the offending s or t value from 1, changing the 0 to a 1.

This extra test is why createTexTile() passes the tcoords[i] texel into the makeTexCoords() calls for its three neighbors.

The Floor's Appearance

createAppearance() builds the Appearance node shown in Figure 6-8:

```
private void createAppearance(String texFnm1, String texFnm2)
{
  Appearance app = new Appearance();

  // switch off face culling
  PolygonAttributes pa = new PolygonAttributes();
  pa.setCullFace(PolygonAttributes.CULL_NONE);
  app.setPolygonAttributes(pa);

  // texture units
  TextureUnitState tus[] = new TextureUnitState[3];

  // cover the floor with the first texture
  tus[0] = loadTextureUnit(texFnm1, TextureAttributes.DECAL);

  // add second texture (it has transparent parts)
  tus[1] = loadTextureUnit(texFnm2, TextureAttributes.DECAL);

  // modulated light map
  tus[2] = loadTextureUnit("light.gif", TextureAttributes.MODULATE);
  // tus[2] = lightMapTUS();

  app.setTextureUnitState(tus);

  setAppearance(app);
}  // end of createAppearance()
```

createAppearance() loads two ground textures (the grass and stones) and combines them as decals. The second texture (the stones) has transparent parts, so both textures can be seen at runtime. The third texture, the light map, is modulated with the others so they all remain visible. The light map can either be loaded from a file or be drawn at runtime. The drawing method, lightMapTUS(), is commented out in the previous code. The light map image in light.gif is shown in Figure 6-15.

Figure 6-15. *The light map in light.gif*

Figure 6-16 shows the floor after the textures have been combined. The view is from above, with hill-raising switched off so the texturing is easier to see.

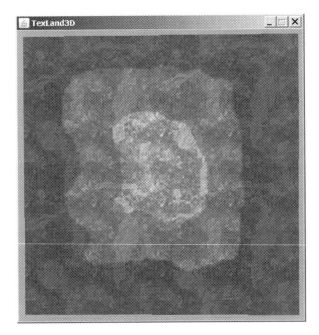

Figure 6-16. *The floor from above*

The light map modulation means that the map's darker areas add "shadows" to the ground.

Although light.gif only uses grayscales, it's possible to include colors in the map, which will tint the floor.

Making a Texture Unit

loadTextureUnit() creates a texture unit by combining a texture and texture attributes:

```
private TextureUnitState loadTextureUnit(String fnm, int texAttr)
{
  TextureLoader loader = new TextureLoader("images/"+fnm,
                         TextureLoader.GENERATE_MIPMAP, null);
  System.out.println("Loaded floor texture: images/" + fnm);

  Texture2D tex = (Texture2D) loader.getTexture();
```

```
        tex.setMinFilter(Texture2D.MULTI_LEVEL_LINEAR);

        TextureAttributes ta = new TextureAttributes();
        ta.setTextureMode(texAttr);

        TextureUnitState tus =  new TextureUnitState(tex, ta, null);
        return tus;
}  // end of loadTextureUnit()
```

Mipmaps are generated for the texture when the TextureLoader.GENERATE_MIPMAP flag is set. In mipmapping, lower resolution versions of the original texture are computed automatically. They are utilized when the texture is rendered to a smaller area, or farther away from the camera. In such cases, the original amount of texture detail isn't needed, and a lower resolution mipmap is sufficient.

Graphics Hardware Concerns

The processing required to render three texture units is handled by the graphics card. Older cards may not be able to deal with large numbers of texture units, so your code should check that the hardware is sufficient. This is done by calling Canvas3D.queryProperties() and checking the returned HashMap of graphics capabilities. The maximum number of supported texture units can be retrieved with the "textureUnitStateMax" key.

reportTextureUnitInfo() shows how queryProperties() is used. This method is located in WrapTexLand3D, where the Canvas3D object is created:

```
private void reportTextureUnitInfo(Canvas3D c3d)
/* Report the number of texture units supported by the machine's
   graphics card. Called in WrapTexLand3D. */
{
  Map c3dMap = c3d.queryProperties();

  if (!c3dMap.containsKey("textureUnitStateMax"))
    System.out.println("Texture unit state maximum not found");
  else {
    int max =((Integer)c3dMap.get("textureUnitStateMax")).intValue();
    System.out.println("Texture unit state maximum: " + max);
  }
}
```

The graphics card's behavior when the texture unit maximum is exceeded is hardware-dependent, but the extra textures will probably be rendered with TextureAttributes.REPLACE. For instance, if the maximum is 2, the light map will replace the ground textures, so only the map image is visible.

I haven't bothered using the texture unit maximum information in TexLand3D since most modern cards support at least four texture units, and TexLand3D only needs a maximum of three for a shape. I wouldn't advise this devil-may-care attitude for real games though.

Creating a Light Map at Runtime

A static light map loaded from a file is sufficient for most applications, but sometimes it's preferable to generate lighting effects at runtime, as shown in lightMapTUS().

The map's image is drawn using Java 2D, converted to a texture, then added to a TextureUnitState object, along with suitable texture attributes. lightMapTUS() builds the texture unit and delegates the drawing work to createLightMap():

```
private TextureUnitState lightMapTUS()
{
  Texture2D tex = createLightMap(); // draw light map
```

```
   TextureAttributes ta = new TextureAttributes();
   ta.setTextureMode(TextureAttributes.MODULATE); // for light

   TextureUnitState tus =  new TextureUnitState(tex, ta, null);
   return tus;
}
```

The light map texture is made from an RGB BufferedImage. Java 2D operations are utilized by manipulating the image through a Graphics2D object.

To keep the example short, createLightMap() draws a series of concentric circles filled with various shades of gray:

```
// globals
private static final int LIGHT_MAP_SIZE = 128;
   // the light map is a texture, so it's size should be a power of 2


private Texture2D createLightMap()
{
  BufferedImage img = new BufferedImage(LIGHT_MAP_SIZE,
               LIGHT_MAP_SIZE, BufferedImage.TYPE_INT_RGB);
  Graphics2D g = img.createGraphics();

  g.setRenderingHint(RenderingHints.KEY_ANTIALIASING,
                 RenderingHints.VALUE_ANTIALIAS_ON);

  g.setColor(Color.gray);
  g.fillRect(0, 0, LIGHT_MAP_SIZE, LIGHT_MAP_SIZE);

  int xCenter = LIGHT_MAP_SIZE/2;
  int yCenter = LIGHT_MAP_SIZE/2;

  int diam = LIGHT_MAP_SIZE*7/10;    // 70% of light map size
  g.setColor(Color.lightGray);
  g.fillOval(xCenter-diam/2, yCenter-diam/2, diam, diam);

  diam = LIGHT_MAP_SIZE*4/10;     // 40%
  g.setColor(Color.white);
  g.fillOval(xCenter-diam/2, yCenter-diam/2, diam, diam);

  diam = LIGHT_MAP_SIZE*2/10;     // 20%
  g.setColor(Color.lightGray);
  g.fillOval(xCenter-diam/2, yCenter-diam/2, diam, diam);

  diam = LIGHT_MAP_SIZE*15/100;   // 15%
  g.setColor(Color.gray);
  g.fillOval(xCenter-diam/2, yCenter-diam/2, diam, diam);

  g.dispose();

  // convert the buffered image into a texture
  ImageComponent2D grayImage =
            new ImageComponent2D(ImageComponent.FORMAT_RGB, img);
  Texture2D lightTex = new Texture2D(Texture.BASE_LEVEL, Texture.RGB,
                       LIGHT_MAP_SIZE, LIGHT_MAP_SIZE);
  lightTex.setImage(0, grayImage);
```

```
    return lightTex;
} // end of createLightMap()
```

After the BufferedImage has been filled, it's used to initialize a Texture2D object. Figure 6-17 shows the floor with the runtime light map viewed from above. I've switched off hill-raising to make the map easier to see.

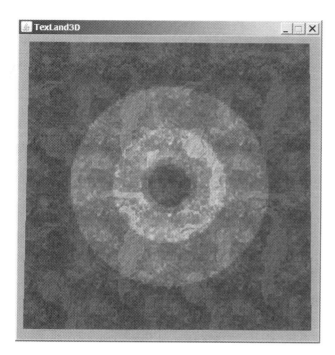

Figure 6-17. *The runtime light map*

The Splash Shape

A splash shape is represented by my SplashShape class, which combines an *alpha mask* with a texture to make the shape's boundary irregular in a random way.

An alpha mask is a texture that contains only an alpha channel (i.e., only transparency information). It can be implemented as a full RGBA image with its color channels ignored at runtime, or as a grayscale image with a single channel, which is interpreted as the alpha channel (as I do here).

The splash shape's geometry comes from the floor. A fragment of the floor's heights map is copied to make a mesh that matches that portion of the floor.

The SplashShape constructor divides up the tasks of geometry and appearance building:

```
// global
private int floorLen;   // length of floor's side


public SplashShape(Texture2D tex, float[][] heights)
{
  floorLen = heights.length-1;
```

```
    createGeometry(heights);
    makeAppearance(tex);
}
```

The result is the scene graph branch shown in Figure 6-18.

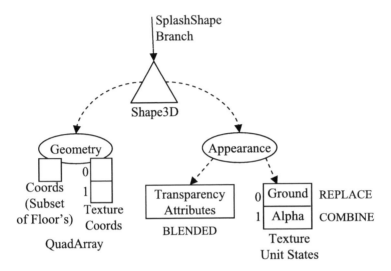

Figure 6-18. *Scene graph branch for SplashShape*

Copies of this branch appear in place of the "SplashShape" boxes in Figure 6-3.

The Splash Shape's Geometry

The splash shape's geometry is a subsection of the floor's geometry, starting at a random coordinate and extending several vertices along the x- and z- axes.

The geometry uses a QuadArray like the floor and two sets of texture coordinates, one for the ground texture (flowers, water), the other for the alpha mask. The Geometry node appears on the left side of Figure 6-18:

```
private void createGeometry(float[][] heights)
{
  // get a starting point for the splash
  Point3i startPt = getStartPt(heights);

  // create coords from a section of heights map starting at startPt
  Point3f[] coords = createCoords(startPt, heights);

  // create texture coordinates for the splash shape
  TexCoord2f[] tCoords = createTexCoords(startPt, coords);

  // make a mesh with two texture units
  QuadArray plane = new QuadArray(coords.length,
                    GeometryArray.COORDINATES |
                    GeometryArray.TEXTURE_COORDINATE_2,
                    2, new int[]{0,1});
```

```
    plane.setCoordinates(0, coords);
    plane.setTextureCoordinates(0, 0, tCoords);   // for detail texture
    plane.setTextureCoordinates(1, 0, tCoords);   // alpha mask texture
    setGeometry(plane);
}  // end of createGeometry()
```

getStartPt() obtains a starting point for the splash by randomly generated row and column indices for the floor's heights map. These are easily converted to x- and z- coordinates when needed:

```
// global
private static final int SPLASH_SIZE = 3;
    /* SplashShape copies SPLASH_SIZE*SPLASH_SIZE quads from
       the floor mesh. SPLASH_SIZE should be less than the
       floor length (which is stored in floorLen). */


private Point3i getStartPt(float[][] heights)
{
  Random rand = new Random();
  int z = (int)(rand.nextDouble()*floorLen);   // z is the row index
  int x = (int)(rand.nextDouble()*floorLen);   // x is column index

  if (z+SPLASH_SIZE > floorLen)  // if splash extends off front edge
    z = floorLen - SPLASH_SIZE;  // move back

  if (x+SPLASH_SIZE > floorLen)  // if splash extends off right edge
    x = floorLen - SPLASH_SIZE;  // move left

  return new Point3i(x, 0, z);   // don't use the y-value
}
```

The selected values are tested to see if the splash shape, which is SPLASH_SIZE units long in the x- and z- directions, extends off the map. If it does, the start point is moved back and/or to the left.

The x- and z- indices are returned in a Point3i object. This is a convenient way of packaging up the integers; the point's y-value isn't used.

The Splash Shape's Vertices

Armed with a start point and the floor's heights map, createCoords() creates a heights map for the splash shape. The map is utilized to generate the geometry's vertices, which are ordered in the same way as the floor's vertices, in groups of four, representing groups of quads:

```
private Point3f[] createCoords(Point3i startPt, float[][] heights)
{
  // copy heights from the floor's heights map
  float[][] splashHeights = getSplashHeights(startPt, heights);

  Point3f[] coords = new Point3f[SPLASH_SIZE*SPLASH_SIZE*4];
                  // since each quad in the mesh has 4 coords
  int i = 0;
  for(int z=0; z <= SPLASH_SIZE-1; z++) {     // skip z's front row
    for(int x=0; x <= SPLASH_SIZE-1; x++) {   // skip x's right column
      createTile(coords, i, x, z, startPt, splashHeights);
      i = i + 4;  // since 4 coords are needed for 1 quad
    }
```

```
    }
    return coords;
  }  // end of createCoords()
```

The splash heights map is produced by traversing the floor's heights map, starting from the splash's start point, and copying over a square of heights SPLASH_SIZE wide by SPLASH_SIZE long:

```
private float[][] getSplashHeights(Point3i startPt,
                                   float[][] heights)
{
  float[][] splashHeights = new float[SPLASH_SIZE+1][SPLASH_SIZE+1];
                // "+1" to include front and right edges

  for(int z=0; z <= SPLASH_SIZE; z++)
    for(int x=0; x <= SPLASH_SIZE; x++)
      splashHeights[z][x] = heights[startPt.z + z][startPt.x + x];

  return splashHeights;
}
```

createTile() creates coordinates for a single quad, with its top left-hand corner at (xc, zc), which is calculated by converting the splashHeights[][] indices into x- and z-coordinates:

```
private void createTile(Point3f[] coords, int i, int x, int z,
                        Point3i startPt, float[][] splashHeights)
{
  // (xc,zc) is the (x,z) coordinate in the floor mesh
  float xc = startPt.x + x - floorLen/2;
  float zc = startPt.z + z - floorLen/2;

  // points created in counter-clockwise order from bottom left
  coords[i] = new Point3f(xc, splashHeights[z+1][x], zc+1.0f);
  coords[i+1] = new Point3f(xc+1.0f,splashHeights[z+1][x+1],zc+1.0f);
  coords[i+2] = new Point3f(xc+1.0f, splashHeights[z][x+1], zc);
  coords[i+3] = new Point3f(xc, splashHeights[z][x], zc);
}
```

The Splash Shape's Texture Coordinates

The texture coordinates generation for the splash shape closely mirrors the code used in MultiFloor for generating the texture coordinates for the floor. The code is actually a bit simpler since the splash shape texture always covers the mesh, without repeating:

```
private TexCoord2f[] createTexCoords(Point3i startPt,
                                     Point3f[] coords)
{
  int numPoints = coords.length;
  TexCoord2f[] tcoords = new TexCoord2f[numPoints];

  for(int i=0; i < numPoints; i=i+4)  // 4 tex coords for 1 quad
    for (int j = 0; j < 4; j++)
      tcoords[i+j] = makeTexCoord(startPt, coords[i+j]);
  return tcoords;
}
```

The splash shape's vertices are grouped into fours for each quad in the mesh, and so the texture coordinates are similarly grouped. The points are stored in counterclockwise order, starting from the bottom left vertex.

The (x, z) parts of a vertex are converted to values between 0 and SPLASH_SIZE and divided by SPLASH_SIZE so they fall in the texel 0-1 range. The *t* value is adjusted so it increases as *z* decreases:

```
private TexCoord2f makeTexCoord(Point3i startPt, Point3f coord)
{
  float s = ((float)(coord.x - startPt.x + floorLen/2))/SPLASH_SIZE;
  float t = 1.0f -
              ((float)(coord.z - startPt.z + floorLen/2))/SPLASH_SIZE;
  return new TexCoord2f(s, t);
}
```

The Splash Shape's Appearance

makeAppearance() builds the right half of the scene branch shown in Figure 6-18:

```
private void makeAppearance(Texture2D tex)
{
  Appearance app = new Appearance();

  // the ground's texture unit
  TextureUnitState groundTUS = makeGround(tex);

  // the alpha texture unit
  TextureUnitState alphaTUS = new TextureUnitState();
  alphaTUS.setTextureAttributes( getAlphaTA() );
  alphaTUS.setTexture( getAlphaTexture() );

  // put the two texture units together
  TextureUnitState[] tus = new TextureUnitState[2];
  tus[0] = groundTUS;
  tus[1] = alphaTUS;
  app.setTextureUnitState(tus);

  // switch on transparency, and use blending
  TransparencyAttributes ta = new TransparencyAttributes();
  ta.setTransparencyMode(TransparencyAttributes.BLENDED);
  app.setTransparencyAttributes(ta);

  setAppearance(app);
} // end of makeAppearance()
```

Setting the transparency attribute is essential, otherwise the transparent parts of the alpha mask will be ignored when the textures are rendered.

Making the Ground

makeGround() loads the ground texture (either flowers or water) and its attributes into a texture unit:

```
private TextureUnitState makeGround(Texture2D tex)
{
  TextureAttributes groundTAs = new TextureAttributes();
  groundTAs.setTextureMode(TextureAttributes.REPLACE);
  groundTAs.setPerspectiveCorrectionMode(TextureAttributes.NICEST);
```

```
    TextureUnitState groundTUS = new TextureUnitState();
    groundTUS.setTextureAttributes(groundTAs);
    groundTUS.setTexture(tex);

    return groundTUS;
} // end of makeGround()
```

The TextureAttribute.REPLACE mode means that the texture replaces any underlying material color, and lighting is ignored.

Texture Attributes for the Alpha Mask

The texture attributes required for the alpha mask go beyond Java 3D's basic modes (e.g., DECAL, REPLACE, MODULATE) since it's necessary to differentiate between the alpha texture's RGBA channels.

Finer-grain channel control is available through the TextureAttributes.COMBINE mode, which permits separate texture attribute equations to be defined for the RGB and alpha channels:

```
private TextureAttributes getAlphaTA()
{
  TextureAttributes alphaTA = new TextureAttributes();

  alphaTA.setPerspectiveCorrectionMode(alphaTA.NICEST);
  alphaTA.setTextureMode(TextureAttributes.COMBINE);
        // COMBINE gives us control over the RGBA channels

  // use COMBINE_REPLACE to replace color and alpha of the geometry
  alphaTA.setCombineRgbMode(TextureAttributes.COMBINE_REPLACE);
  alphaTA.setCombineAlphaMode(TextureAttributes.COMBINE_REPLACE);

  /* the source RGB == previous texture unit (i.e. the first unit),
     and the source alpha == this texture (i.e. the alpha). */
  alphaTA.setCombineRgbSource(0,
            TextureAttributes.COMBINE_PREVIOUS_TEXTURE_UNIT_STATE);
  alphaTA.setCombineAlphaSource(0,
            TextureAttributes.COMBINE_TEXTURE_COLOR);

  /* The combined texture gets its color from the source RGB and
     its alpha from the source alpha. */
  alphaTA.setCombineRgbFunction(0,
                  TextureAttributes.COMBINE_SRC_COLOR);
  alphaTA.setCombineAlphaFunction(0,
                  TextureAttributes.COMBINE_SRC_ALPHA);

  return alphaTA;
}  // end of getAlphaTA()
```

The TextureAttribute class's setCombineXXXMode(), setCombineXXXSource(), and setCombineXXXFunction() methods are utilized to specify two equations that say how the final color of the shape is determined in terms of the ground and alpha textures. These equations can be written this way:

$$Color_{final/RGB} = Color_{tus(0)/RGB}$$

$$Color_{final/A} = Color_{alpha/RGB}$$

The final geometry color, Color$_{final}$, is divided into equations for its RGB and alpha parts (Color$_{final/RGB}$ and Color$_{final/A}$). The RGB component comes from the first texture unit (tus(0)), while the alpha comes from the color channels of the alpha texture.

The numerous combine methods in Java 3D's TextureAttributes class make it possible to define much more complex color equations than the two shown here. For instance, an equation can utilize RGB and alpha channels from several sources and combine or blend them in several ways. The TextureAttribute class documentation gives some examples, using a notation similar to mine.

A good way of gaining a better insight about color equations in Java 3D is to study the similar mechanism in OpenGL (which Java 3D borrowed).

Drawing the Alpha Mask

The alpha mask texture is generated at runtime as a BufferedImage, in much the same way as the light mask, but the image *must* be a grayscale. Why?

A look back at the color equations in the previous section shows that the *alpha* component of the geometry's color (Color$_{final/A}$) comes from the *color* part of the alpha mask (Color$_{alpha/RGB}$). For this to work, the alpha mask's color component must be a single channel, which means that the image must be a grayscale. Black will correspond to fully transparent, and white to opaque, with degrees of translucency in between.

It's also necessary to set the alpha texture's format to be Texture.ALPHA:

```
// global
private static final int ALPHA_SIZE = 64;


private Texture2D getAlphaTexture()
{
  /* the image component is defined to be a single 8-bit channel,
     which will hold a grayscale image created by alphaSplash() */
  ImageComponent2D alphaIC =
        new ImageComponent2D(ImageComponent2D.FORMAT_CHANNEL8,
                             ALPHA_SIZE, ALPHA_SIZE, true, false);

  alphaIC.set( alphaSplash() );   // generate a buffered image

  // convert the image into an alpha texture
  Texture2D tex = new Texture2D(Texture2D.BASE_LEVEL, Texture.ALPHA,
                                ALPHA_SIZE, ALPHA_SIZE);
  tex.setMagFilter(Texture.BASE_LEVEL_LINEAR);
  tex.setMinFilter(Texture.BASE_LEVEL_LINEAR);
  tex.setImage(0, alphaIC);
  return tex;
} // end of getAlphaTexture()
```

alphaSplash() must create a grayscale BufferedImage of size ALPHA_SIZE by ALPHA_SIZE due to the formats specified for the ImageComponent2D and Texture2D objects in getAlphaTexture(). However, it can use any Java 2D drawing operations it likes.

My aim is to break up the sharp rectangular border of the ground texture by utilizing the alpha mask, and to break it up in a different way for each splash shape. This is achieved by alphaSplash(), drawing a series of semirandomly positioned circles with various levels of transparency. The more opaque circles tend to be in the center of the alpha mask:

```
private BufferedImage alphaSplash()
{
  Random rand = new Random();

  // create a grayscale buffered image
  BufferedImage img = new BufferedImage(ALPHA_SIZE, ALPHA_SIZE,
                                  BufferedImage.TYPE_BYTE_GRAY);
  Graphics2D g = img.createGraphics();

  // draw into it
  g.setColor(Color.black);    // fully transparent
  g.fillRect(0, 0, ALPHA_SIZE, ALPHA_SIZE);

  int radius = 3;  // circle radius
  int offset = 8;  // offset of boxed circle from top-left of graphic
  g.setColor(new Color(0.3f, 0.3f, 0.3f)); //near transparent circles
  boxedCircles(offset, offset, ALPHA_SIZE-(offset*2), radius,
                                            100, g, rand);
  offset = 12;
  g.setColor(new Color(0.6f, 0.6f, 0.6f)); // mid-level translucent
  boxedCircles(offset, offset, ALPHA_SIZE-(offset*2), radius,
                                            80, g, rand);
  offset = 16;
  g.setColor(Color.white);    // fully opaque circles
  boxedCircles(offset, offset, ALPHA_SIZE-(offset*2), radius,
                                            50, g, rand);
  g.dispose();
  return img;
}  // end of alphaSplash()
```

boxedCircles() draws circles whose centers are somewhere within the square defined by boxedCircles() input arguments:

```
private void boxedCircles(int x, int y, int len, int radius,
                    int numCircles, Graphics2D g, Random rand)
/* Generate numCircles circles whose centers are within the square
   whose top-left is (x,y), with sides of len. A circle has a radius
   equal to the radius value.
*/
{
  int xc, yc;
  for (int i=0; i < numCircles; i++) {
    xc = x + (int)(rand.nextDouble()*len) - radius;
    yc = y + (int)(rand.nextDouble()*len) - radius;
    g.fillOval(xc, yc, radius*2, radius*2);
  }
}
```

Figure 6-19 shows some splash shapes drawn against a plain white floor viewed from above. Each shape has a different irregular border.

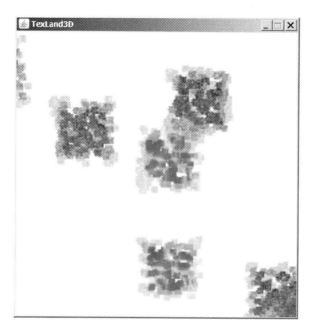

Figure 6-19. *Splash shapes on a white surface*

There's no absolute requirement that the alpha mask has to be generated at runtime. It's quite possible to load a grayscale image from a file, as in this example:

```
// in getAlphaTexture()
alphaIC.set( loadAlpha("alpha.gif") );
```

loadAlpha() is

```
private BufferedImage loadAlpha(String fnm)
{ try {
    return ImageIO.read( new File("images/" + fnm));
  }
  catch (IOException e) {
    System.out.println("Could not load alpha mask: images/" + fnm);
    return null;
  }
}
```

The file must use 8-bit grayscales, and be ALPHA_SIZE*ALPHA_SIZE large.

Moving Balls

Several textured, illuminated balls are randomly placed on the floor and then meander about aimlessly. They rotate slightly as they move and can't travel beyond the edges of the floor. When a ball encounters an edge, it turns away from it. Figure 6-20 shows a close-up of some of the balls.

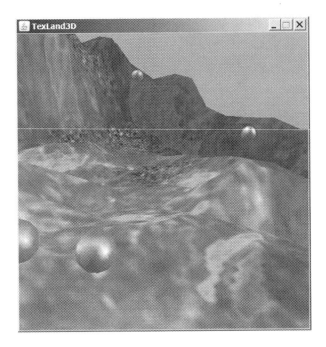

Figure 6-20. *Moving balls*

The MovingBall constructor calls makeBall() to build the scene graph branch shown in Figure 6-21. Copies of it correspond to the "MovingBall" boxes in Figure 6-3.

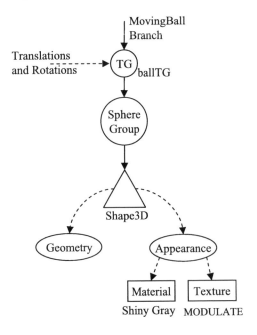

Figure 6-21. *The scene graph branch for a moving ball*

The translations and rotations applied to the ballTG TransformGroup are triggered by calls to MovingBall's updatePosition() method by TimeBehavior.

The following is the makeBall() method:

```
// globals
private static final float RADIUS = 0.25f;    // of sphere

// material colors
private static final Color3f BLACK = new Color3f(0.0f, 0.0f, 0.0f);
private static final Color3f GRAY = new Color3f(0.6f, 0.6f, 0.6f);
private static final Color3f WHITE = new Color3f(0.9f, 0.9f, 0.9f);

private TransformGroup ballTG;    // TG which the ball hangs off

// reusable object for calculations
private Transform3D t3d;  // for manipulating ballTG's transform


private void makeBall(Texture2D ballTex)
{
  Appearance app = new Appearance();

  // combine texture with material and lighting of underlying surface
  TextureAttributes ta = new TextureAttributes();
  ta.setTextureMode( TextureAttributes.MODULATE );
  app.setTextureAttributes( ta );

  // assign gray material with lighting
  Material mat= new Material(GRAY, BLACK, GRAY, WHITE, 25.0f);
     // sets ambient, emissive, diffuse, specular, shininess
  mat.setLightingEnable(true);
  app.setMaterial(mat);

  // apply texture to shape
  if (ballTex != null)
    app.setTexture(ballTex);

  // randomly position the ball on the floor
  t3d.set( genStartPosn());

  // ball's transform group can be changed (so it can move/rotate)
  ballTG = new TransformGroup(t3d);
  ballTG.setCapability(TransformGroup.ALLOW_TRANSFORM_READ);
  ballTG.setCapability(TransformGroup.ALLOW_TRANSFORM_WRITE);

  // the ball has normals for lighting, and texture support
  Sphere ball = new Sphere(RADIUS,
                      Sphere.GENERATE_NORMALS |
                      Sphere.GENERATE_TEXTURE_COORDS,
                      15, app);
  ballTG.addChild(ball);
}  // end of makeBall()
```

Positioning the Ball

A random (x, z) starting position for the ball is calculated between -floorLen/2 and floorLen/2. floorLen is obtained from the floor's heights map, which is passed to MovingBall via its constructor:

```
// global
private int floorLen;        // length of floor sides

// reusable object for calculations
private Vector3f posnVec;     // for manipulating the ball's position
private Random rand;


private Vector3f genStartPosn()
{
  float x = (float)((rand.nextDouble() * floorLen)-floorLen/2);
  float z = (float)((rand.nextDouble() * floorLen)-floorLen/2);
  float y = getHeight(x, z) + RADIUS;   // ball rests on the floor
  posnVec.set(x,y,z);
  return posnVec;
}  // end of genStartPosn()
```

getHeight() uses the floor's heights map to calculate the height at the supplied (x, z) position. The ball will usually be located somewhere between the heights map vertices, so the height is calculated as a weighted average of the (x, z) coordinate's distance from the four nearest vertices:

```
// globals
private float[][] heights;    // the floor's heights map


private float getHeight(float x, float z)
// calculate a height for the ball's (x,z) location
{
  float xLoc = x + floorLen/2;   // (xLoc,zLoc) is on the heights map
  float zLoc = z + floorLen/2;

  // split (xLoc,zLoc) coordinate into integer and fractional parts
  int xH = (int) Math.floor(xLoc);
  float xFrac = xLoc - xH;

  int zH = (int) Math.floor(zLoc);
  float zFrac = zLoc - zH;

  /* the average height is based on the (xLoc,zLoc) coord's
     distance from the four surrounding heights in the
     heights[][] array. */
  float height = ((heights[zH][xH] * (1.0f-zFrac) * (1.0f-xFrac)) +
                  (heights[zH][xH+1] * (1.0f-zFrac) * xFrac) +
                  (heights[zH+1][xH] * zFrac * (1.0f-xFrac) ) +
                  (heights[zH+1][xH+1] * zFrac * xFrac) );
  return height;
}  // end of getHeight()
```

Moving About

At periodic intervals, TimeBehavior calls MovingBall's updatePosition() method:

```
public void updatePosition()
{
  doRotateY();
  while (!moveFwd())
    doRotateY();
}
```

The ball rotates a small random amount, then moves forward. If the move isn't possible (due to the ball being at the floor's edge), it keeps turning by small random amounts until it can move.

Rotating the Ball

doRotateY() rotates the ball around its y-axis by a small random angle. The rotation is applied to the ballTG TransformGroup:

```
// globals
private final static double ROTATE_AMT = Math.PI / 18.0;
                                    // 10 degrees
// reusable objects for calculations
private Transform3D t3d, toRot;  // for ballTG's transform


private void doRotateY()
{
  ballTG.getTransform( t3d );
  toRot.rotY( rotateSlightly() );
  t3d.mul(toRot);
  ballTG.setTransform(t3d);
}


private double rotateSlightly()
// rotate between -ROTATE_AMT and ROTATE_AMT radians
{  return rand.nextDouble()*ROTATE_AMT*2 - ROTATE_AMT;  }
```

Translating the Ball

Moving the ball forward consists of three stages: first the translation is calculated, then it is tested to see if it's allowed, and then if it's OK, the move is applied to ballTG:

```
// globals
private final static float STEP = 0.1f;    // step size for moving

// reusable objects for calculations
private Vector3f posnVec, moveVec;      // for the ball's position


private boolean moveFwd()
{
  moveVec.set(0,0,STEP);
  tryMove(moveVec);  // test the move, store new position in posnVec
  if (offEdge(posnVec))
    return false;
  else {  // carry out the move, with a height change
```

```
    float heightChg = getHeight(posnVec.x, posnVec.z) +
                                    RADIUS - posnVec.y;
    moveVec.set(0, heightChg, STEP);
    doMove(moveVec);
    return true;
  }
}  // end of moveFwd()
```

The attempted move (which is stored in the posnVec global) contains the ball's new x- and z- positions, which are employed to find the floor's height at that spot. When the move is really executed, the height change between the ball's current location and the new spot is included in the move, so the ball moves up or down, following the floor.

Trying out the move involves calculating the effect of the translation, but not updating the ball's TransformGroup, ballTG:

```
// global reusable object for various calculations
private Transform3D toMove;  // for manipulating ballTG


private void tryMove(Vector3f theMove)
{
  ballTG.getTransform(t3d);
  toMove.setTranslation(theMove);
  t3d.mul(toMove);
  t3d.get(posnVec);
}
```

offEdge() checks whether the ball's intended move will take it over the floor's edge:

```
// global constant
private final static float OBS_FACTOR = 0.5f;


private boolean offEdge(Vector3f loc)
// is the ball off the edge of the floor?
{
  float r = RADIUS*OBS_FACTOR;
  return ((loc.x - r < -floorLen/2) ||    // off left edge?
          (loc.x + r > floorLen/2) ||     // off right?
          (loc.z - r < -floorLen/2) ||    // off back?
          (loc.z + r > floorLen/2));      // off front?
}
```

OBS_FACTOR is used to reduce the radius of the ball during the tests, which permits the ball to overlap the floor's edge slightly before the move is rejected.

tryMove() applies the ball translation to ballTG:

```
private void doMove(Vector3f theMove)
// translate the ball by the amount in theMove
{
  ballTG.getTransform(t3d);
  toMove.setTranslation(theMove);
  t3d.mul(toMove);
  ballTG.setTransform(t3d);
}  // end of doMove()
```

Driving the Balls

The TimeBehavior class is the Java 3D version of a timer; it wakes up every timeDelay milliseconds, and calls the updatePosition() method in all its MovingBall objects:

```
public class TimeBehavior extends Behavior
{
  private WakeupCondition timeOut;
  private ArrayList<MovingBall> mBalls;  // the moving balls

  public TimeBehavior(int timeDelay, ArrayList<MovingBall> mbs)
  { mBalls = mbs;
    timeOut = new WakeupOnElapsedTime(timeDelay);
  }

  public void initialize()
  { wakeupOn( timeOut );  }

  public void processStimulus(Enumeration criteria)
  { // ignore criteria
    for (MovingBall mBall : mBalls)    // move all the balls
      mBall.updatePosition();
    wakeupOn( timeOut );
  }

} // end of TimeBehavior class
```

More Multitexturing

The official Java 3D examples contain MultiTextureTest.java in the texture/ directory (TextureTest/ prior to Java 3D 1.4), which shows how to combine multiple textures, including the use of a light map generated at runtime.

The alpha mask technique used in my SplashShape class is borrowed from Yazel's SplatShape class and Couch's AlphaDemo class. They can be found in the Java3D-Interest mailing list archive at http://archives.java.sun.com/java3d-interest.html for May 2003 and July 2002 respectively.

Bump Mapping

Bump mapping adds lighting detail to a smooth shape, giving it a rough (or bumpy) appearance, without the shape requiring extra polygons. The bump mapping technique based on multitexturing utilizes a texture acting as a *normal map*. A normal map contains texel values for variations of the shape's surface normals. The map creates patterns of shade and light when applied to the shape.

Bump mapping in Java 3D is possible with the COMBINE_DOT3 texture mode, but it's also necessary that the graphics card supports DOT3 texturing. The demos for Java 3D 1.4 and later include a bump mapping example in the dot3/ directory. Alessandro Borges also has an example at http://planeta.terra.com.br/educacao/alessandroborges/java3d.html. Mike Jacobs wrote a JDJ article on bump mapping at http://mnjacobs.javadevelopersjournal.com/ bump_mapping_in_java3d.htm, and Joachim Diepstraten has one at http://java3d.j3d.org/ tutorials/quick_fix/dot3_bumps.html. The *Yaarq* game by Wolfgang Kienreich utilizes several texturing effects, including bump mapping (http://www.sbox.tugraz.at/home/w/wkien/#demos).

Shaders

Java 3D has supported two shading languages since version 1.4: OpenGL's GLSL (the default choice in Java 3D) and NVIDIA's Cg. Shader programs can carry out processing at the vertex level (involving their position, normals, color, texture coordinates, per vertex lighting, and others), and at the pixel level (affecting texture and pixel color). They can replicate all the multitexturing effects and can implement many other forms of texturing.

It's relatively simple to port existing GLSL and Cg shaders over to Java 3D, although your graphics card must support shader functionality. GLSL only became a core part of OpenGL with version 2.0 in 2004, so it isn't available in older (or less feature-rich) cards.

The Java 3D demos include shader examples in glsl_shader/ and cg_shader/.

Summary

This chapter described several multitexturing approaches for making a 3D landscape look more varied and natural. Grass and stone textures are combined together, light and shadow added with a shadow map, and flowers and water supplied with an alpha map. The shadow map can be fixed or created programmatically at runtime. The alpha map is produced semirandomly at execution time, rendering different borders for the flowerbeds and pools.

The landscape is built from a heights map, which is generated using a probabilistic hill-raising algorithm. The geography changes each time the program is run, but always consists of a ring of "mountains" around an inner "plain."

Golden balls autonomously roam the landscape, traveling over the ground, but never venturing beyond its borders.

CHAPTER 7

■ ■ ■

Walking Around the Models

The previous chapter was about making interesting-looking landscape. This chapter is about populating a scene with 3D models and 2D images "pretending" to be 3D. The images act as ground cover, appearing to be 3D by rotating to always face the viewer.

The user can navigate around the scene using keyboard controls. The basic approach introduced here is extended in several ways in future chapters.

This chapter also considers how to make the scene's background more realistic. We say bye-bye to the sky-blue color of earlier examples and look at three different ways of utilizingtextured backgrounds.

Populating a Scene

The techniques developed in this chapter are 3D model loading, 2D ground cover, keyboard-based movement, and creating a better background. They are demonstrated in a single example application called ObjView3D, shown in Figure 7-1.

Figure 7-1. *ObjView3D in action*

The 3D models include a penguin, a pink giant, and a helicopter, while the trees and cacti are ground cover. The following is a description of the techniques:

- *3D model loading*: Java 3D has built-in support for loading 3D modelsconstructed using the Wavefront OBJ format. ObjView3D employs a ModelLoader class that simplifies the process. Once loaded, a model can be translated, rotated, and/or scaled.

- *2D ground cover*: The scene in ObjView3D is decorated with 2D images that rest on the floor (e.g., the trees in Figure 7-1) and always stay oriented toward the viewer, giving the impression that they're 3D. This is a cheap alternative to employing real 3D models.

- *Keyboard-based movement*: I've been using the Java 3D OrbitBehavior class to change the camera's viewpoint up until now, but ObjView3D uses my KeyBehavior class instead. Key presses move the camera forward, backward, and left or right, rotate it left or right, and make it float up or down. However, the camera is prevented from descending through the floor.

- *A better background*: I look at three ways of creating a background that contains interesting detail and looks different when viewed from different places in the scene. The approaches are the following:

  1. A texture-wrapped sphere.

  2. A skybox (a Java 3D Box with textures pasted on to each face).

  3. A skybox covered with Terragen-generated textures. Terragen is a freeware photorealistic landscape renderer available at http://www.planetside.co.uk/terragen. The skybox is built from quads, which gives the programmer more control over how it's positioned.

Class Diagrams for ObjView3D

Figure 7-2 shows the class diagrams for the ObjView3D application. The class names and public methods are shown.

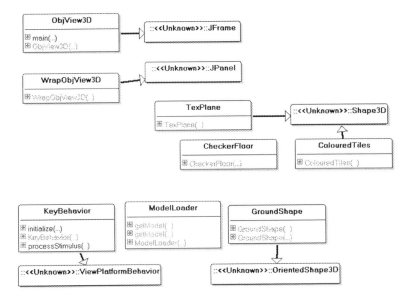

Figure 7-2. *Class diagrams for ObjView3D*

ObjView3D is the top-level JFrame for the application, utilizing WrapObjView3D to create the 3D scene inside a JPanel. This includes the lighting and the various background techniques. The skybox constructed from Terragen textures uses the TexPlane class to create its walls, floor, and ceiling.

WrapObjView3D employs ModelLoader to load the OBJ models, and GroundShape for the 2D images.

Key presses are caught by the KeyBehavior class and translated into changes to the camera's viewpoint.

The checkerboard floor is created with the CheckerFloor and ColouredTiles classes, which are unchanged from previous examples, so not described again.

A Spherical Background

addBackground() in WrapObjView3D lays a texture over the inside face of a Sphere connected to a Background node:

```
// globals
private static final String SKY_DIR = "skyBox/";
                // location of sky textures
private BranchGroup sceneBG;


private void addBackground(String fnm)
{
  Texture2D tex = loadTexture(SKY_DIR + fnm);

  Sphere sphere = new Sphere(1.0f,
                  Sphere.GENERATE_NORMALS_INWARD |
                  Sphere.GENERATE_TEXTURE_COORDS, 8);
  Appearance backApp = sphere.getAppearance();
  backApp.setTexture( tex );

  BranchGroup backBG = new BranchGroup();
  backBG.addChild(sphere);

  Background bg = new Background();
  bg.setApplicationBounds(bounds);
  bg.setGeometry(backBG);

  sceneBG.addChild(bg);
}  // end of addBackground()


private Texture2D loadTexture(String fn)
// load image from file fn as a texture
{
  TextureLoader texLoader = new TextureLoader(fn, null);
  Texture2D texture = (Texture2D) texLoader.getTexture();
  if (texture == null)
    System.out.println("Cannot load texture from " + fn);
  else {
    System.out.println("Loaded texture from " + fn);
    texture.setEnable(true);
  }
  return texture;
}  // end of loadTexture()
```

The background shape surrounds the scene, even though the Sphere's radius is set to be 1.0f. The radius isn't utilized when the shape is used as a background.

The Sphere is set to create inward normal vectors, thereby forcing the texture to appear on its inside faces—the ones visible within the scene.

The square of the number of divisions given in the Sphere constructor (8) equals the number of surfaces in the sphere. By reducing the number from 15 (the default) to 8, the cost of generating the sphere is greatly reduced without noticeably decreasing the texturing quality.

Figure 7-1 shows the spherical background in action and highlights its main weakness: the distortion of the texture when it's wrapped around the sphere. The problem can be solved by employing a skybox as the background geometry rather than a sphere.

A Skybox Background

A *skybox* is a cube made of six images that surrounds the scene. It's easily implemented by using a Java 3D Box object in the Background node. This is done in addSkyBox():

```
private void addSkyBox(String fnm)
{
  com.sun.j3d.utils.geometry.Box texCube =
      new com.sun.j3d.utils.geometry.Box(1.0f, 1.0f, 1.0f,
                Primitive.GENERATE_TEXTURE_COORDS,
                new Appearance());
            // a default appearance for the Box as a whole

  Texture2D tex = loadTexture(SKY_DIR + fnm);

  setFaceTexture(texCube, com.sun.j3d.utils.geometry.Box.FRONT, tex);
  setFaceTexture(texCube, com.sun.j3d.utils.geometry.Box.LEFT, tex);
  setFaceTexture(texCube, com.sun.j3d.utils.geometry.Box.RIGHT, tex);
  setFaceTexture(texCube, com.sun.j3d.utils.geometry.Box.BACK, tex);
  setFaceTexture(texCube, com.sun.j3d.utils.geometry.Box.TOP, tex);
  setFaceTexture(texCube, com.sun.j3d.utils.geometry.Box.BOTTOM,tex);

  BranchGroup backBG = new BranchGroup();
  backBG.addChild(texCube);

  Background bg = new Background();
  bg.setApplicationBounds(bounds);
  bg.setGeometry(backBG);

  sceneBG.addChild(bg);
} // end of addSkyBox()
```

The references to com.sun.j3d.utils.geometry.Box distinguish the class from the same-named Box class in the Swing package.

Although addSkyBox() pastes the same texture onto every face of the box, it's quite possible to stick different textures onto them.

The Box uses a default appearance (white) since each face is assigned its own Appearance node in setFaceTexture():

```
private void setFaceTexture(com.sun.j3d.utils.geometry.Box texCube,
                            int faceID, Texture2D tex)
{
  Appearance app = new Appearance();
```

```
  // make texture appear on back of face
  PolygonAttributes pa = new PolygonAttributes();
  pa.setCullFace( PolygonAttributes.CULL_FRONT);
  app.setPolygonAttributes( pa );

  if (tex != null)
    app.setTexture(tex);

  texCube.getShape(faceID).setAppearance(app);
} // end of setFaceTexture()
```

A specific cube face is obtained with Box.getShape(), which returns a Shape3D reference whose appearance can be set.

The Appearance node culls its front (outward) face, leaving its inward side to be drawn, which is the one visible to the user. Unfortunately, this means that the image is shown in reverse, but there's no simple way to display an image on a Box face with its front facing inward.

Figure 7-3 shows a shot of the scene when addSkyBox() is employed to draw a stars texture.

Figure 7-3. *A stars-filled scene*

The individual stars are visible, whereas much of the detail is distorted when the same texture is wrapped over a sphere with addBackground().

A Skybox Built with Quads

A drawback with the skybox Background node approach is that the box geometry is always in the background, which makes it difficult to have it interact with other elements in the scene. For example, the floor of the skybox is always "out of reach" of an object no matter how far it moves downward.

The approach in this section creates a skybox out of six quads connected directly to the scene graph without utilizing a Background node. This means the quads are located at specific places in the scene, and so can interact with other scenery objects.

Terragen and NConvert

This skybox version employs Terragen-generated textures. The construction of beautiful views with lakes, meadows, snow-capped mountains, and sun-streaked clouds takes just a few minutes.

Figure 7-4 shows an amateurish effort by me.

Figure 7-4. *A Terragen scene*

Links to tutorials and numerous other resources can be found at the Terragen web site. It offers several tutorials on creating a skybox from a Terragen landscape, such as the one by the Valve Developer Community at `http://developer.valvesoftware.com/wiki/ Creating_a_2D_skybox_with_Terragen`. It describes a Terragen script to automate the process, generating BMPs for the six faces. The ObjView3D directory includes a variant of that script, modified slightly for my needs.

The BMPs output by the Terragen script need to be converted into JPEGs to reduce their file size and make them readable by Java 3D's TextureLoader class. I use a command-line tool, NConvert, for the task (it's available at `http://perso.orange.fr/pierre.g/xnview/ en_nconvert.html`). The following is a typical example of how to use NConvert:

```
nconvert -quiet -out jpeg -q 90 -o skyFront.jpg sky0001.bmp
```

The Terragen BMP image, sky0001.bmp, is converted into the JPEG file skyFront.jpg, with a quality level of 90%.

From Images to Textures

The Terragen script generates six images that have to be correctly pasted on to the six quads forming the skybox. Figure 7-5 shows the box with points p1 to p8 assigned to its corners.

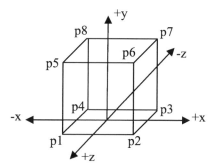

Figure 7-5. *The corners of the skybox*

The user will be located inside the box, initially facing along the -z axis. The skybox in Figure 7-5 can be opened out as shown in Figure 7-6, with images assigned to its six faces. Figure 7-6 shows the view from above.

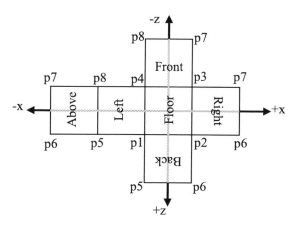

Figure 7-6. *Images assigned to the skybox faces*

The orientation of the image words ("Above", "Left", etc.) indicates the orientation of the Terragen images, so they'll match up when drawn on to the box's sides. Each image must also face inward, which means they must be assigned coordinates in an anticlockwise order starting from an image's bottom-left corner. For example, the coordinates order for the "Front" image must be p4, p3, p7, and p8.

Making the Skybox

addSceneBox() takes a length argument for the box and generates the coordinates p1 through p8 shown in Figure 7-5. The coordinates needed for a particular face are passed to a TexPlane instance, which creates a corresponding quad and textures it with the Terragen image stored in the supplied file:

```
// global
private final static double DY = 0.01;


private void addSceneBox(double wallLen)
{
  // the eight corner points
  /* base starting from front/left then anti-clockwise, at a small
     offset below the floor, DY */
  Point3d p1 = new Point3d(-wallLen/2, -DY, wallLen/2);
  Point3d p2 = new Point3d(wallLen/2, -DY, wallLen/2);
  Point3d p3 = new Point3d(wallLen/2, -DY, -wallLen/2);
  Point3d p4 = new Point3d(-wallLen/2, -DY, -wallLen/2);

  /* top starting from front/left then anti-clockwise, at height
     wallLen/4 */
  Point3d p5 = new Point3d(-wallLen/2, wallLen/4, wallLen/2);
  Point3d p6 = new Point3d(wallLen/2, wallLen/4, wallLen/2);
  Point3d p7 = new Point3d(wallLen/2, wallLen/4, -wallLen/2);
  Point3d p8 = new Point3d(-wallLen/2, wallLen/4, -wallLen/2);

  // use the six textures created with Terragen
  // floor
  sceneBG.addChild( new TexPlane(p2, p3, p4, p1,
                                 SKY_DIR+"floor.jpg"));
  // front wall
  sceneBG.addChild( new TexPlane(p4, p3, p7, p8,
                                 SKY_DIR+"skyFront.jpg"));
  // right wall
  sceneBG.addChild( new TexPlane(p3, p2, p6, p7,
                                 SKY_DIR+"skyRight.jpg"));
  // back wall
  sceneBG.addChild( new TexPlane(p2, p1, p5, p6,
                                 SKY_DIR+"skyBack.jpg"));
  // left wall
  sceneBG.addChild( new TexPlane(p1, p4, p8, p5,
                                 SKY_DIR+"skyLeft.jpg"));
  // ceiling
  sceneBG.addChild( new TexPlane(p5, p8, p7, p6,
                                 SKY_DIR+"skyAbove.jpg"));
} // end of addSceneBox()
```

The skybox is positioned a small distance below the floor (the value comes from the DY constant), so the checkerboard floor will remain visible. The height of the box is less than its breadth and width, since this reduces the heights of the mountains shown in the wall images.

Figure 7-7 shows a view from inside the scene.

Figure 7-7. *The scene with a Terragen skybox*

Texturing a Plane

TexPlane is a subclass of Shape3D which creates a single QuadArray of four vertices with a texture wrapped over it. The texture is applied without any material settings (i.e., no color or lighting effects):

```
// global
private static final int NUM_VERTS = 4;

public TexPlane(Point3d p1, Point3d p2, Point3d p3, Point3d p4,
                                           String texFnm)
{ createGeometry(p1, p2, p3, p4);

  Texture2D tex = loadTexture(texFnm);
  Appearance app = new Appearance();
  app.setTexture(tex);        // set the texture
  setAppearance(app);
} // end of TexPlane()


private void createGeometry(Point3d p1, Point3d p2,
                            Point3d p3, Point3d p4)
{
  QuadArray plane = new QuadArray(NUM_VERTS,
                       GeometryArray.COORDINATES |
                       GeometryArray.TEXTURE_COORDINATE_2 );

  // anti-clockwise from bottom left
```

```
plane.setCoordinate(0, p1);
plane.setCoordinate(1, p2);
plane.setCoordinate(2, p3);
plane.setCoordinate(3, p4);

TexCoord2f q = new TexCoord2f();
q.set(0.0f, 0.0f);
plane.setTextureCoordinate(0, 0, q);
q.set(1.0f, 0.0f);
plane.setTextureCoordinate(0, 1, q);
q.set(1.0f, 1.0f);
plane.setTextureCoordinate(0, 2, q);
q.set(0.0f, 1.0f);
plane.setTextureCoordinate(0, 3, q);

setGeometry(plane);
}  // end of createGeometry()
```

The texture coordinates are assigned in an anticlockwise order, starting at the bottom-left of the image. This matches the ordering of the points supplied to the constructor.

loadTexture() is another version of the texture loading method that I've used several times. This time it contains two extra texture operations to improve the skybox effect:

```
private Texture2D loadTexture(String fn)
// load image from file fn as a texture
{
  TextureLoader texLoader = new TextureLoader(fn, null);
  Texture2D texture = (Texture2D) texLoader.getTexture();
  if (texture == null)
    System.out.println("Cannot load texture from " + fn);
  else {
    System.out.println("Loaded texture from " + fn);

    // remove edge texels, so no seams between texture faces
    texture.setBoundaryModeS(Texture.CLAMP_TO_EDGE);
    texture.setBoundaryModeT(Texture.CLAMP_TO_EDGE);

    // smoothing for texture enlargement/shrinking
    texture.setMinFilter(Texture2D.BASE_LEVEL_LINEAR);
    texture.setMagFilter(Texture2D.BASE_LEVEL_LINEAR);
    texture.setEnable(true);
  }
  return texture;
}  // end of loadTexture()
```

The calls to the setMinFilter() and setMagFilter() smooth the image when several texture coordinates (texels) have to be reduced or enlarged, and perhaps combined, to map onto a screen pixel. Unfortunately, this combination introduces a *seam* problem at the edge of a texture: a flickering visible line that comes and goes as the viewer moves. This is solved by the two setBoundaryMode method calls since CLAMP_TO_EDGE switches off the combination operation for edge texels.

The Size of the Skybox

The skybox should be big enough to be located beyond any of the objects inside the scene, but should be positioned inside the BoundingSphere instance for the scene.

Another issue is that the camera should probably be constrained so it can't move through the sides of the skybox. In ObjView3D, the camera can't pass downward through the floor, but can travel through the walls and ceiling. Modifying the KeyBehavior class to restrict such journeys isn't difficult, as I'll show when I describe the class later.

Loading Models

Java 3D supports external model loading through its Loader interface and the Scene class. Java 3D offers two subclasses of Loader aimed at particular file formats: Lw3dLoader handles Lightwave 3D scene files, and ObjectFile processes Wavefront OBJ files. A third subclass, LoaderBase, implements the Loader interface in a generic way to encourage the building of loaders for other 3D formats through subclassing.

The Scene class uses a Loader object to extract details about a model, the most significant being its BranchGroup (usually for the purpose of adding it to the application scene).

There's a wide range of Java 3D loaders for different file formats, written by third-party developers, which I discussed in Chapter 1. In this chapter—and others—I employ the built-in OBJ loader.

For the artistically impaired (e.g., yours truly), there is a profusion of web sites that offer 3D models. A good starting point is the Google Directory on 3D models: http://directory.google.com/Top/Computers/Software/Graphics/3D/Models/. A site with many free models is 3D Cafe: http://www.3dcafe.com/.

Loading OBJ Models

Java 3D handles a subset of the full OBJ file format (as described at http://www.fileformat.info/format/wavefrontobj/). An OBJ model acceptable to Java 3D must consist of polygonal shapes made from groups of vertices. A polygon's face is defined using vertices, with the optional inclusion of normals and texture coordinates. Faces can be grouped together and different groups can be assigned materials made from ambient, diffuse, and specular colors and textures. The material information is stored in a separate MTL-formatted file (http://www.fileformat.info/format/material/). Java 3D understands a number of built-in color materials, so a shape can employ those rather than an MTL file.

Java 3D doesn't support the free-form geometry parts of the OBJ format, including free-form curves and surfaces or more advanced forms of OBJ rendering, such as interpolation and shadows.

The OBJ and MTL features understood by Java 3D are summarized in the documentation for the Java 3D ObjectFile class, where the methods for loading an OBJ file are described.

The OBJ and MTL formats are supported by all the major 3D drawing tools. Two freeware applications that I've used in the past are Blender (http://www.blender.org) and MilkShape3D (http://www.swissquake.ch/chumbalum-soft/).

An advantage of the OBJ and MTL formats is that they're text-based, so the model files can be edited without special tools. This is sometimes useful even when using 3D drawing tools. For example, the OBJ export feature of MilkShape3D produces an MTL file lacking an "illum" line for specifying the lighting type. This is easily fixed by adding

```
illum 2
```

to the file. It switches on full lighting (ambient, diffuse, and specular).

Another useful property of Java 3D's support is that each group in an OBJ model is mapped to a Java 3D Shape3D class. The vertex information becomes accessible via the shape's Geometry node component, and its material data via Appearance. This makes it quite easy to examine, and modify, a model at runtime.

Incidentally, Chapter 17 describes an OBJ model loader for JOGL, which supports a large subset of the features offered by the Java 3D loader.

The OBJ Model Loader

The constructor for my ModelLoader class creates an instance of Java 3D's ObjectFile, which is used for loading the OBJ model:

```
// globals
private ObjectFile objFileloader;

public ModelLoader()
{  objFileloader = new ObjectFile();  }
```

The ObjectFile constructor can take several flag arguments. A particularly useful one is ObjectFile.RESIZE, which forces a resize of the model so it's centered at (0, 0, 0) and its coordinates are all in the range of (-1, -1, -1) to (1, 1, 1), as in this example:

```
objFileLoader = new ObjectFile(ObjectFile.RESIZE);
```

Although it's possible to resize and reposition a model at runtime within a Java 3D application, it's better to do these things before the model is exported from the drawing package. This reduces the processing needed at runtime.

Requesting a Model

The ModelLoader.getModel() method expects a filename and an optional y-axis distance. The method returns a TransformGroup connected to the model, which moves it by the specified distance and reduces its size if it's too big:

```
public TransformGroup getModel(String fnm)
{  return getModel(fnm, 0);  }


public TransformGroup getModel(String fnm, double yMove)
// returns tg --> model
{
  // load the model
  BranchGroup modelBG = loadModel(fnm);
  if (modelBG == null)
    return null;

  double scaleFactor = getScaling(modelBG);

  // scale and move the model along the y-axis
  Transform3D t3d = new Transform3D();
  t3d.setScale(scaleFactor);
  t3d.setTranslation( new Vector3d(0,yMove,0));

  TransformGroup tg = new TransformGroup(t3d);
  tg.addChild(modelBG);
  return tg;
}  // end of getModel()
```

The y-axis translation is a commonly needed tweak; a model is often positioned a little below floor level and needs lifting up.

loadModel() uses ObjectFile.load() to load the model as a Scene object, and then extracts the BranchGroup for the model with Scene.getSceneGroup(). The BranchGroup is connected to the tg TransformGroup node, which applies the y-axis movement and scaling. The subgraph is shown in Figure 7-8.

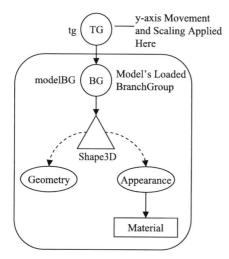

Figure 7-8. *The subgraph for the loaded model*

loadModel() is complicated by its error checking. The method returns null if there are any problems:

```
// globals
private static final String MODELS_DIR = "Models/";

private BranchGroup loadModel(String modelFnm)
// load the OBJ model stored in modelFnm
{
  String fnm = MODELS_DIR + modelFnm;
  System.out.println("Loading OBJ model from " + fnm);

  File file = new java.io.File(fnm);
  if (!file.exists()) {
    System.out.println("Could not find " + fnm);
    return null;
  }

  /* Convert the filename to a URL, so the OBJ file can find
     the MTL and image files in the Models/ subdirectory. */
  URL url = null;
  try {
    url = file.toURI().toURL();
  }
  catch(Exception e) {
    System.out.println(e);
    return null;
  }

  // read in the model from the file
```

```
    Scene scene = null;
    try {
      scene = objFileloader.load(url);
    }
    catch (FileNotFoundException e) {
      System.out.println("Could not find " + fnm);
      return null;
    }
    catch (ParsingErrorException e) {
      System.out.println("Could not parse contents of " + fnm);
      System.out.println(e);
      return null;
    }
    catch (IncorrectFormatException e) {
      System.out.println("Incorrect format in " + fnm);
      System.out.println(e);
      return null;
    }

    // return the model's BranchGroup
    if(scene != null)
      return scene.getSceneGroup();
    else
      return null;
}  // end of loadModel()
```

The ObjectFile.load() method utilized in loadModel() locates the model file using a URL, which may seem a bit strange since the file is in a local subdirectory, Models/. There's another version of ObjectFile.load() which takes a String argument for the filename, which seems more suitable. However, I found that while it could load the OBJ file, it always failed to find the MTL file associated with the model. The URL version of load() doesn't suffer from this problem.

Scaling the Model

A common mistake when loading a large model is to position it so that the camera's viewpoint is inside the model. If the back faces of the polygons aren't rendered (as is commonly the case) the user will see nothing.

getScaling() checks the model's bounding box dimensions and uniformly scales it so its new dimensions don't exceed MAX_SIZE (5) units along any axis. Since the camera starts 9 units away from the center in WrapObjView3D this makes it less likely that a large model will "disappear":

```
// global
private static final double MAX_SIZE = 5.0;
            // max size of model along any dimension


private double getScaling(BranchGroup modelBG)
// check the model's size and scale if too big
{
  double scaleFactor = 1.0;
  BoundingBox boundBox = new BoundingBox( modelBG.getBounds());

  Point3d lower = new Point3d();
  boundBox.getLower(lower);
  // System.out.println("lower: " + lower);

  Point3d upper = new Point3d();
  boundBox.getUpper(upper);
```

```
  // System.out.println("upper: " + upper);

  // calculate model scaling
  double maxDim = getMaxDimension(lower, upper);
  if (maxDim > MAX_SIZE) {
    scaleFactor = MAX_SIZE/maxDim;
    System.out.println("Applying scaling factor: " + scaleFactor);
  }

  return scaleFactor;
} // end of getScaling()
```

getMaxDimension() finds the largest side of the bounding box around the model:

```
private double getMaxDimension(Point3d lower, Point3d upper)
{
  double max = 0;
  if ((upper.x - lower.x) > max)
    max = upper.x - lower.x;
  if ((upper.y - lower.y) > max)
    max = upper.y - lower.y;
  if ((upper.z - lower.z) > max)
    max = upper.z - lower.z;
  return max;
}  // end of getMaxDimension()
```

Other Reasons for a Model Disappearing

A model may disappear because it is too big, as described previously. Other possible reasons
are that it's too small or has been drawn behind or inside another shape. For example, a model
rendered beneath the floor in ObjView3D will be hidden from view.

A first step in finding the model is to uncomment the two println()'s in getScaling(). They
report the shape's upper and lower bounding box coordinates, which will tell you where the object
is located and its size.

Positioning a Model

The ModelLoader class is used by WrapObjView3D in its addModels() method. Six OBJ models are
loaded, then translated, rotated, and scaled in various ways:

```
// global
private BranchGroup sceneBG;


private void addModels()
// in WrapObjView3D
{
  ModelLoader ml = new ModelLoader();
  Transform3D t3d = new Transform3D();

  // a large pink human
  t3d.setIdentity();    // resets t3d  (just to be safe)
  t3d.setTranslation( new Vector3d(0,0,-7));    // move
  t3d.setScale(2.5);    // enlarge
  t3d.setRotation( new AxisAngle4d(0,1,0, Math.toRadians(90)) );
            // rotate 90 degrees anticlockwise around y-axis
  TransformGroup tg1 = new TransformGroup(t3d);
```

```
    tg1.addChild( ml.getModel("humanoid.obj", 0.8) );
    sceneBG.addChild(tg1);

    // a penguin
    t3d.set( new Vector3d(-1,0,2));    // move, and resets t3d
    t3d.setScale(0.5);    // shrink
    TransformGroup tg2 = new TransformGroup(t3d);
    tg2.addChild( ml.getModel("penguin.obj") );
    sceneBG.addChild(tg2);

    // a barbell
    t3d.set( new Vector3d(7,0,-7));
    TransformGroup tg3 = new TransformGroup(t3d);
    tg3.addChild( ml.getModel("barbell.obj", 0.25) );
    sceneBG.addChild(tg3);

    // john's picture
    t3d.set( new Vector3d(2,0,5));
    t3d.setScale( new Vector3d(4,1,0.25));
        // stretch along x-axis, shrink along z-axis
    t3d.setRotation( new AxisAngle4d(1,0,0, Math.toRadians(-45)) );
            // rotate 45 degrees anticlockwise around x-axis
    TransformGroup tg4 = new TransformGroup(t3d);
    tg4.addChild( ml.getModel("longBox.obj") );
    sceneBG.addChild(tg4);

    // a helicopter
    t3d.set( new Vector3d(1,2,0));    // up into the air
    TransformGroup tg5 = new TransformGroup(t3d);
    tg5.addChild( ml.getModel("heli.obj") );
    sceneBG.addChild(tg5);

    // a colored cube
    t3d.set( new Vector3d(-3,2,-5));    // up into the air
    TransformGroup tg6 = new TransformGroup(t3d);
    tg6.addChild( ml.getModel("colorCube.obj"));
    sceneBG.addChild(tg6);
}  // end of addModels()
```

The six models illustrate different aspects of the OBJ and MTL formats:

- The large pink human (humanoid.obj) consists of a single unnamed group of vertices, colored with the "flesh" Java3D built-in material.

- The penguin (penguin.obj) utilizes a texture (specified in penguin.mtl and penguin.gif).

- The barbell (barbell.obj) is constructed from three groups of vertices representing the balls and the crossbeam. Colors for the balls are defined inside barbell.mtl.

- The box model (longBox.obj) is wrapped around with a texture of my son John (specified in longBox.mtl and john.jpg). This example shows how it's possible to create 3D "poster" shapes.

- The helicopter (heli.obj) is constructed from multiple groups, with a texture assigned to its cockpit (as defined in heli.mtl and metal.gif).

- The colored cube (colorCube.obj) is a simple OBJ model created manually by me. The faces are red or green, with the colors specified in colorCube.mtl.

Each model is positioned using similar code. A Transform3D object (t3d) is initialized with a translation vector, a scale factor, and a rotation. For example, the humanoid's position is defined using the following:

```
t3d.setIdentity();   // resets t3d
t3d.setTranslation( new Vector3d(0,0,-7));   // move
t3d.setScale(2.5);   // enlarge
t3d.setRotation( new AxisAngle4d(0,1,0, Math.toRadians(90)) );
         // rotate 90 degrees anticlockwise around y-axis
```

The Transform3D.setIdentity() call resets the matrix inside the t3d object.

Scaling is applied uniformly along all the axes. It's also possible to vary the resizing in each dimension by utilizing a vector:

```
t3d.setScale( new Vector3d(4,1,0.25));
```

The rotation component is easiest to define with an AxisAngle4d object that specifies the rotation (in radians) about a vector given as the first three arguments. The right-hand rule determines the rotation direction.

The translation, scaling, and rotation components can be added to the Transform3D object in any order. However, at runtime they're executed in the fixed sequence T-S-R (translation, scaling, rotation). This can be observed by moving the setTranslation() call for the humanoid model to after the setScale() and setRotation() calls; when the code is executed again, the model's position will be unchanged (rotated to the right at (0, 0, -7)).

It's possible to combine setIdentity() and setTranslation() into a single set() call that takes a Vector3d argument:

```
t3d.set( new Vector3d(0,0,-7));
```

This fills the Transform3D matrix with the translation and clears any rotation or scaling settings.

Once the Transform3D has been initialized, it's applied to a new TransformGroup node. The model's TransformGroup is connected to it (via a call to ModelLoader.getModel()), and the whole thing is attached to the scene graph, as in this example for the humanoid:

```
TransformGroup tg1 = new TransformGroup(t3d);
tg1.addChild( ml.getModel("humanoid.obj", 0.8) );
sceneBG.addChild(tg1);
```

Ground Cover

3D Models are complex to build and expensive to render. Often they can be replaced by 2D "fakes" that appear 3D-like. The trees and cacti in ObjView3D are instances of the GroundShape class, which illustrates the idea (see Figure 7-9).

Figure 7-9. *Cactus and tree ground cover*

A GroundShape object displays a transparent GIF drawn on the front face of a four-sided QuadArray. The center of the quad's base is at (0, 0, 0), resting on the ground. It has sides of screenSize and is always oriented toward the viewer (see Figure 7-10). The orientation is achieved by making GroundShape a subclass of OrientedShape3D and setting its axis of rotation to be the y-axis.

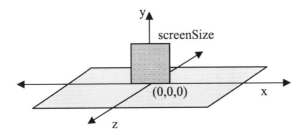

Figure 7-10. *The position of the GroundShape quad*

No matter where the user moves to, the ground shape will face him, giving the impression of 3D solidity. The drawbacks are that the shape always looks the same and the effect breaks down if the user leaves the floor and looks down on the ground shape from above.

GroundShape's geometry—a QuadArray of four vertices—is very similar to that used in TexPlane. It also uses a texture to wrap the quad, but with additional transparency attributes so the transparent parts of the GIF won't be rendered:

```
private void createAppearance(String fnm)
{
  Appearance app = new Appearance();
```

```
  // blended transparency so texture can be irregular
  TransparencyAttributes tra = new TransparencyAttributes();
  tra.setTransparencyMode( TransparencyAttributes.BLENDED );
  app.setTransparencyAttributes( tra );

  Texture2D tex = loadTexture(fnm);
  app.setTexture(tex);        // set the texture
  setAppearance(app);
} // end of createAppearance()
```

loadTexture() is a copy of the same-named method in TexPlane.

WrapObjView3D creates GroundShape instances in addGroundCover(). They're positioned at
(0, 0) on the XZ plane by default, so TransformGroups are employed to move them to the required
spots. The following code fragment creates a tree and moves it to (4, 0, 0):

```
Transform3D t3d = new Transform3D();
t3d.set( new Vector3d(4,0,0));
TransformGroup tg1 = new TransformGroup(t3d);
tg1.addChild( new GroundShape("tree1.gif", 3) );
sceneBG.addChild(tg1);
```

The numerical argument to the GroundShape constructor is a scaling factor. By default, each
shape uses a screen size of 1.

Manipulating the User's Viewpoint

WrapObjView3D calls createUserControls() to carry out two tasks:

- To position the user's initial viewpoint
- To create a KeyBehavior object that responds to keyboard input by moving the viewpoint

The createUserControls() method is defined as follows:

```
// info used to position initial viewpoint
private final static double Z_START = 9.0;


private void createUserControls()
{
  ViewingPlatform vp = su.getViewingPlatform();

  // position viewpoint
  TransformGroup targetTG = vp.getViewPlatformTransform();
  Transform3D t3d = new Transform3D();
  targetTG.getTransform(t3d);
  t3d.setTranslation( new Vector3d(0,1,Z_START));
  targetTG.setTransform(t3d);

  // set up keyboard controls to move the viewpoint
  KeyBehavior keyBeh = new KeyBehavior();
  keyBeh.setSchedulingBounds(bounds);
  vp.setViewPlatformBehavior(keyBeh);
} // end of createUserControls()
```

Positioning the User's Viewpoint

The viewpoint is positioned by adjusting the targetTG TransformGroup in the view branch part of the scene graph (shown in Figure 7-11).

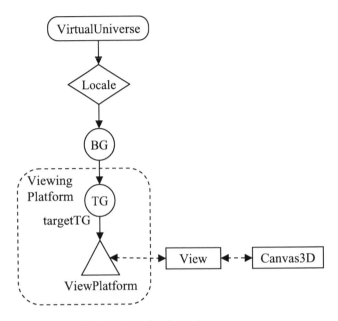

Figure 7-11. *The view branch subgraph*

You haven't seen the view branch much till now, since it's built automatically when I use the SimpleUniverse utility class to create the scene graph.

The viewpoint is represented by the ViewPlatform node in Figure 7-11 (the triangle) and is repositioned by applying transforms to the targetTG TransformGroup above it.

In createUserControls(), a targetTG reference is obtained with ViewingPlatform. getViewPlatformTransform(), and it's moved by changing its component Transform3D.

Moving the Viewpoint at Runtime

ObjView3D moves the viewpoint at runtime by attaching a KeyBehavior object to targetTG via a call to ViewingPlatform.setViewPlatformBehavior():

```
KeyBehavior keyBeh = new KeyBehavior();
keyBeh.setSchedulingBounds(bounds);
vp.setViewPlatformBehavior(keyBeh);
```

targetTG is available to methods inside KeyBehavior by having KeyBehavior inherit the Java 3D ViewPlatformBehavior class:

```
public class KeyBehavior extends ViewPlatformBehavior
{...}
```

KeyBehavior responds to arrow key presses, optionally combined with the Alt key, which move the viewpoint forward, back, left, right, and up and down, and rotate it around its y-axis. The movement and rotation operations are carried out by manipulating targetTG.

Setting Up the Key Behavior

The WakeupCondition for KeyBehavior is an AWT key press, specified in the constructor:

```
WakeupCondition keyPress =
                new WakeupOnAWTEvent( KeyEvent.KEY_PRESSED );
```

The key press is registered in initialize():

```
wakeupOn(keyPress);
```

processStimulus() checks that the wakeup criterion is an AWT event and responds to key presses:

```
public void processStimulus(Enumeration criteria)
{
  WakeupCriterion wakeup;
  AWTEvent[] event;

  while( criteria.hasMoreElements() ) {
    wakeup = (WakeupCriterion) criteria.nextElement();
    if( wakeup instanceof WakeupOnAWTEvent ) {
      event = ((WakeupOnAWTEvent)wakeup).getAWTEvent();
      for( int i = 0; i < event.length; i++ ) {
        if( event[i].getID() == KeyEvent.KEY_PRESSED )
          processKeyEvent((KeyEvent)event[i]);
      }
    }
  }
  wakeupOn( keyPress );  // re-register
} // end of processStimulus()
```

All the testing and iteration through the event[] array leads to a call to processKeyEvent(), which reacts to the key press.

Processing a Key

Key processing is divided between two methods based on whether the Alt key is being pressed:

```
private void processKeyEvent(KeyEvent eventKey)
{
  int keyCode = eventKey.getKeyCode();
  if(eventKey.isAltDown())   // key + <alt>
    altMove(keyCode);
  else
    standardMove(keyCode);
}
```

Every key has a unique key code constant—they're listed at length in Java's documentation for the KeyEvent class. Checking for modifier keys, such as Alt and Shift, can be done by testing the KeyEvent object (e.g., with isAltDown() in processKeyEvent()).

standardMove() is a multiway branch that calls doMove() or rotateY() to carry out a translation or rotation:

```
// globals
private static final double ROT_AMT = Math.PI / 36.0;    // 5 degrees
private static final double MOVE_STEP = 0.2;

// hardwired movement vectors
```

```
private static final Vector3d FWD = new Vector3d(0,0,-MOVE_STEP);
private static final Vector3d BACK = new Vector3d(0,0,MOVE_STEP);

// key names
private int forwardKey = KeyEvent.VK_UP;
private int backKey = KeyEvent.VK_DOWN;
private int leftKey = KeyEvent.VK_LEFT;
private int rightKey = KeyEvent.VK_RIGHT;


private void standardMove(int keycode)
{
  if(keycode == forwardKey)
    doMove(FWD);
  else if(keycode == backKey)
    doMove(BACK);
  else if(keycode == leftKey)
    rotateY(ROT_AMT);
  else if(keycode == rightKey)
    rotateY(-ROT_AMT);
} // end of standardMove()
```

altMove() employs a similar coding structure to move the viewer up or down, left or right:

```
// global movement vectors
private static final Vector3d LEFT = new Vector3d(-MOVE_STEP,0,0);
private static final Vector3d RIGHT = new Vector3d(MOVE_STEP,0,0);
private static final Vector3d UP = new Vector3d(0,MOVE_STEP,0);
private static final Vector3d DOWN = new Vector3d(0,-MOVE_STEP,0);

private void altMove(int keycode)
{
  if(keycode == forwardKey) {
    upMoves++;
    doMove(UP);
  }
  else if(keycode == backKey) {
    if (upMoves > 0) {  // don't drop below start height
      upMoves--;
      doMove(DOWN);
    }
  }
  else if(keycode == leftKey)
    doMove(LEFT);
  else if(keycode == rightKey)
    doMove(RIGHT);
}  // end of altMove()
```

altMove() shows how it's possible to constrain camera movement: it stops the camera moving below its starting position by keeping a record of its vertical movement in upMoves.

Rotating

rotateY() applies a y-axis rotation to targetTG:

```
// globals for repeated calculations
private Transform3D t3d = new Transform3D();
private Transform3D toRot = new Transform3D();
```

```
private void rotateY(double radians)
{
  targetTG.getTransform(t3d);
      // targetTG is the ViewPlatform's TransformGroup
  toRot.rotY(radians);
  t3d.mul(toRot);
  targetTG.setTransform(t3d);
} // end of rotateY()
```

t3d and toRot are globals to avoid the overhead of temporary object creation every time that rotateY() is called.

toRot is initialized with the required rotation, overwriting any previous value. It's then multiplied to targetTG's current rotation, which "adds" it to the viewpoint's orientation without affecting its translation component.

Translating

doMove() works in a similar way to rotateY() but "adds" a translation to the viewpoint's current position:

```
// globals for repeated calculations
private Transform3D t3d = new Transform3D();
private Transform3D toMove = new Transform3D();


private void doMove(Vector3d theMove)
{ targetTG.getTransform(t3d);
  toMove.setTranslation(theMove);
  t3d.mul(toMove);
  targetTG.setTransform(t3d);
}
```

The translation vector is stored in the toMove Transform3D object then multiplied to the Transform3D instance for targetTG.

Summary

This chapter examined several ways of enhancing a 3D scene.

I presented three techniques for making backgrounds: using a textured sphere, a skybox built from a box, and a skybox utilizing quads. The latter method allows the floor and skyline to be constructed from images exported from Terragen, a freeware photorealistic landscape (and sky) renderer.

The scene was decorated with Wavefront OBJ models and "fake 3D" trees and bushes, which are actually 2D images that always stay orientated toward the viewer.

I left Java 3D's OrbitBehavior class behind and implemented a simple behavior for processing key presses and moving the camera in response. I use variants of this KeyBehavior class in several future chapters.

CHAPTER 8

■ ■ ■

More Backgrounds and Overlays

In Chapter 7, I described several ways of making detailed backgrounds that look different when viewed from different places in the scene. The techniques all utilize textures wrapped over 3D geometries connected to the scene graph.

This chapter considers a different approach: the background is represented by a standard BufferedImage, which is drawn separately from the rest of the scene graph. This means that a large variety of image processing techniques become available for modifying the graphic at runtime.

The approach uses *mixed mode rendering*, where most of the scene is built using a scene graph, but the background is created outside the scene graph structure.

Mixed mode rendering also makes it very easy to create *overlays*, semitransparent areas onscreen where text or graphics can be drawn in the foreground without obscuring the gameplay beyond. I describe how to draw overlays composed from text and images.

There are three examples in this chapter:

1. A scene made up of three "planets" (textured spheres) with a static background of stars. This shows the basic technique for background creation with mixed mode rendering.

2. The same three planets scene, but with a rotating background of stars. The background image is rotated by a separate thread, using an affine transformation. This illustrates how to manipulate the background at runtime.

3. A variant of the 3D model application, ObjView3D, from Chapter 7. When the user turns left or right, the background is shifted by a small amount as well. Overlays are part of this example.

Retained, Immediate, and Mixed Modes

I've being using Java 3D's *retained mode* in all my 3D examples up until now. The scene is constructed by adding nodes to a scene graph, and the responsibility for rendering, and optimizing, the scene is left to Java 3D.

Immediate mode discards the scene graph, placing all the scene creation and rendering tasks into the hands of the programmer. To be precise, only the content branch part of the scene graph is jettisoned in immediate mode; the view branch is still present, to manage Java 3D's interface with the enclosing Java application or applet.

The middle path is to keep the scene graph for most 3D elements, but to build a few visual components outside the graph when necessary. This *mixed mode* approach is employed in this chapter to implement backgrounds and overlays.

The immediate and mixed modes are utilized in the same way, by subclassing Canvas3D. Canvas3D has four methods that are called at specific times during each rendering cycle:

- *preRender()*: Called after the canvas has been cleared but before any rendering has been done for the current frame.

- *renderField()*: Carries out scene rendering. For a desktop application, the screen is the "field." However, there may be multiple fields in more exotic configurations (e.g., there are two fields for stereoscopic displays).

- *postRender()*: Called after all the rendering has been completed for the current frame but before the buffer containing the frame has been made visible to the user.

- *postSwap()*: Called after the frame has been made visible.

A background image is drawn into the frame by preRender(). The image is added to the frame *before* any retained mode rendering and so appears at the back of the scene.

An overlay image is drawn into the frame by postRender(). Since the picture is added to the frame *after* the retained mode rendering, it appears at the front of the scene.

The Earth, Moon, and Mars

Figure 8-1 shows the Planets3D application, with a stars image as the background.

Figure 8-1. *Three planets and stars*

Mouse and control key combinations permit the camera to be translated and rotated through the scene (by utilizing Java 3D's OrbitBehavior). Unfortunately, no matter how much the camera is moved or turned, the stars background never changes.

Class diagrams for Planet3D are given in Figure 8-2, with only the public methods listed.

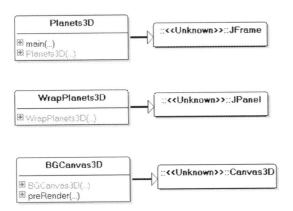

Figure 8-2. *Class diagrams for Planets3D*

Figure 8-3 shows the content branch part of the scene graph constructed by WrapPlanets3D.

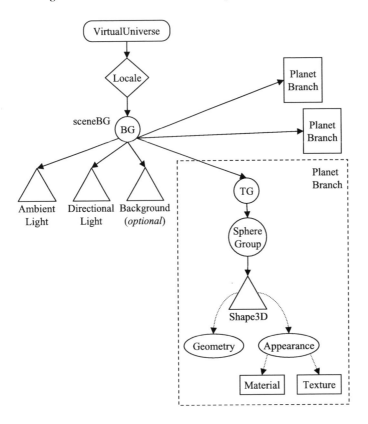

Figure 8-3. *The content branch for Planets3D*

Each "planet" is a Java 3D Sphere, with a blended material and texture appearance, located at a fixed position in the scene. The planets don't rotate.

The OrbitBehavior is attached to the viewing platform in the scene graph's view branch, so is not shown in Figure 8-3.

The Background node is an optional component. It'll become useful when the background image is smaller than the canvas, a scenario I discuss in the "Some Variations on a Theme" section of this chapter.

Building the Scene

The WrapPlanets3D()constructor creates the 3D canvas in the standard way and attaches a SimpleUniverse to it:

```
// globals
private static final int PWIDTH = 512;    // size of panel
private static final int PHEIGHT = 512;

private SimpleUniverse su;


public WrapPlanets3D(String backFnm)
// A panel holding a 3D canvas
{
  setLayout( new BorderLayout() );
  setOpaque( false );
  setPreferredSize( new Dimension(PWIDTH, PHEIGHT));

  GraphicsConfiguration config =
      SimpleUniverse.getPreferredConfiguration();

  // Canvas3D canvas3D = new Canvas3D(config);
  BGCanvas3D canvas3D = new BGCanvas3D(config, backFnm);

  add("Center", canvas3D);
  canvas3D.setFocusable(true);    // give focus to the canvas
  canvas3D.requestFocus();

  su = new SimpleUniverse(canvas3D);
  createSceneGraph();
  initUserPosition();        // set user's viewpoint
  orbitControls(canvas3D);   // controls for moving the viewpoint

  su.addBranchGraph( sceneBG );
} // end of WrapPlanets3D()
```

The usual Canvas3D object has been replaced by a BGCanvas3D instance, which takes the background image filename (backFnm) as an argument. Since BGCanvas3D is a subclass of Canvas3D, it can be used in the same way as Canvas3D.

The panel holding the canvas is set to be 512×512 pixels. The background image must have (at least) these dimensions in order to fill the canvas.

createSceneGraph() constructs the lights, the background node, and the planets:

```
//globals
private static final int BOUNDSIZE = 100;  // larger than world

private BranchGroup sceneBG;
```

```
private BoundingSphere bounds;    // for environment nodes


private void createSceneGraph()
{
  sceneBG = new BranchGroup();
  bounds = new BoundingSphere(new Point3d(0,0,0), BOUNDSIZE);

  lightScene();        // add the light
  addBackground();     // add the sky (optional)

  // add planets
  addPlanet("earth.jpg", 3.0f, new Vector3f(-2,0,0));
  addPlanet("moon.jpg", 0.8f, new Vector3f(4,-1,0));
  addPlanet("mars.jpg", 2.0f, new Vector3f(2,3,-15));

  sceneBG.compile();   // fix the scene
} // end of createSceneGraph()
```

The lighting consists of a single ambient light and a single directional light.

The background color is sky blue and isn't really needed in this example since the background image fills the canvas. However, it'll become useful later in the "Some Variations on a Theme" section:

```
private void addBackground()
{ Background back = new Background();
  back.setApplicationBounds( bounds );
  back.setColor(0.17f, 0.65f, 0.92f);      // sky color
  sceneBG.addChild( back );
}  // end of addBackground()
```

addPlanet() builds the scene graph branch labeled as Planet Branch in Figure 8-3. A Sphere instance is created with a blended material and texture appearance and positioned in the scene using a TransformGroup:

```
// globals
private static final Color3f BLACK = new Color3f(0.0f, 0.0f, 0.0f);
private static final Color3f GRAY = new Color3f(0.6f, 0.6f, 0.6f);
private static final Color3f WHITE = new Color3f(0.9f, 0.9f, 0.9f);


private void addPlanet(String texFnm, float radius, Vector3f posVec)
{
  Appearance app = new Appearance();

  // combine texture with material and lighting of underlying surface
  TextureAttributes ta = new TextureAttributes();
  ta.setTextureMode( TextureAttributes.MODULATE );
  app.setTextureAttributes( ta );

  // a gray material with lighting
  Material mat = new Material(GRAY, BLACK, GRAY, WHITE, 25.0f);
     // sets ambient, emissive, diffuse, specular, shininess
  mat.setLightingEnable(true);
  app.setMaterial(mat);

  // apply texture to shape
  Texture2D texture = loadTexture("images/" + texFnm);
```

```
  if (texture != null)
    app.setTexture(texture);

  // make the sphere with normals for lighting, and texture support
  Sphere globe = new Sphere(radius,
                      Sphere.GENERATE_NORMALS |
                      Sphere.GENERATE_TEXTURE_COORDS,
                      15, app);   // mesh division is 15

  // position the sphere
  Transform3D t3d = new Transform3D();
  t3d.set(posVec);
  TransformGroup tg = new TransformGroup(t3d);
  tg.addChild(globe);

  sceneBG.addChild(tg);
} // end of addPlanet()
```

The gray material is enabled for lighting, so the ambient and directional light will affect the sphere's coloration.

Java 3D's Sphere class supports the automatic generation of normals and texture coordinates. *Normals* are required for the lighting effects, and *texture coordinates* are utilized to wrap the texture around the sphere. Similar support is offered by the other Java 3D geometry classes: Box, Cone, and Cylinder.

The divisions argument for Sphere() is used by the sphere's tessellation; increasing the number of divisions makes the sphere smoother, but at the cost of increased rendering time.

The texture is loaded from the images/ subdirectory. The image used for the earth is shown in Figure 8-4.

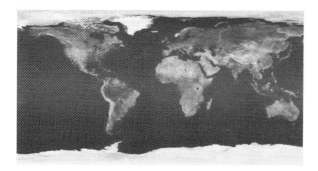

Figure 8-4. *The earth texture (Source: NASA/JPL-Caltech)*

The Background

The BGCanvas class extends Canvas3D in order to redefine preRender() (which does nothing in Canvas3D).

The constructor loads the specified background image:

```
// globals
private BufferedImage backIm;    // the background image
private J3DGraphics2D render2D;  // for 2D rendering into 3D canvas


public BGCanvas3D(GraphicsConfiguration gc, String backFnm)
{ super(gc);
  backIm = loadImage(backFnm);
  render2D = this.getGraphics2D();
}
```

The canvas is configured by calling super() with the GraphicsConfiguration object.

render2D is a J3DGraphics2D object, which provides several methods for carrying out 2D rendering on a 3D canvas.

loadImage() attempts to load a picture from the images/ subdirectory:

```
private BufferedImage loadImage(String fnm)
{
  BufferedImage im = null;
  try {
    im = ImageIO.read( getClass().getResource("images/" + fnm));
    System.out.println("Loaded Background: images/" + fnm);
  }
  catch(Exception e)
  { System.out.println("Could not load background: images/" + fnm); }

  return im;
}  // end of loadImage()
```

preRender() is called in every cycle prior to the scene graph's rendering. It draws the image using J3DGraphics2D.drawAndFlushImage():

```
public void preRender()
{  render2D.drawAndFlushImage(backIm, 0, 0, this);  }
```

The second and third arguments are the (x, y) coordinate in the canvas where the top-left corner of the image is positioned.

Some Variations on a Theme

If Planets3D is called with sun.gif as the background image, the scene is displayed as shown in Figure 8-5.

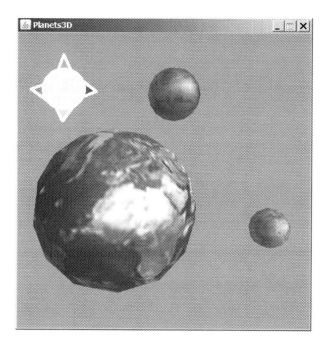

Figure 8-5. *Planets with a sunny background*

The sun is a transparent GIF, shown in Figure 8-6.

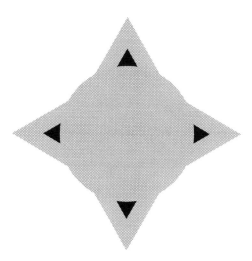

Figure 8-6. *The sun*

The blue background in Figure 8-5 is generated by the Background node, which highlights a rather surprising rendering order. Although the call to preRender() precedes scene graph rendering, the scene graph's Background node is placed behind the preRender() image.

This ordering offers the possibility of optimizing background generation, since it's no longer necessary for the background picture to be the same size as the 3D canvas; any "gaps" can be filled with the color supplied by a Background node.

Figure 8-7 shows the contents of galaxy.jpg.

Figure 8-7. *The galaxy (Source: NASA/JPL-Caltech)*

This image is part of the scene in Figure 8-8.

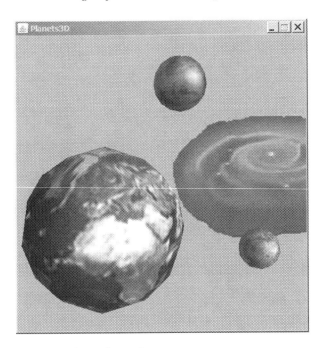

Figure 8-8. *Planets in a galaxy*

The easiest way of creating a black background is to not add a Background node to the scene at all; black is the default background color. The call to addBackground() can be commented out in WrapPlanets3D.

Figure 8-8 also shows that I've repositioned the image. I changed the (x, y) coordinates supplied to drawAndFlushImage() in preRender():

```
public void preRender()
{  render2D.drawAndFlushImage(backIm, 150, 100, this);  }
```

Spinning the Background

A major benefit of rendering the background using a subclass of Canvas3D is that the image is a BufferedImage rather than a Java 3D Background node. This makes it easier to apply Java 2D effects to the image at runtime, such as rotation, fading, scaling, and various color adjustments.

In this section, I describe how to rotate the background image. Figure 8-9 shows two screenshots of the SpinPlanets3D application taken a few seconds apart.

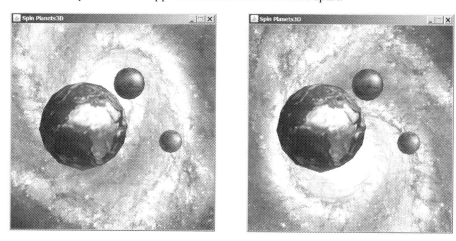

Figure 8-9. *The whirlpool of space (Source: NASA/JPL-Caltech)*

The background image is rotated around its center by 2 degrees in a clockwise direction every 200 ms. The image is drawn onto the canvas so its center is located at the canvas's center.

The class diagrams for SpinPlanets3D are shown in Figure 8-10; only the public methods are listed.

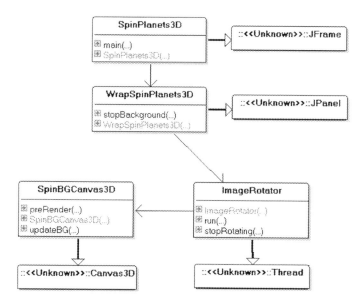

Figure 8-10. *Class diagrams for SpinPlanets3D*

SpinPlanets3D creates the top-level JFrame and uses WrapSpinPlanets3D to create the scene graph. The ImageRotator thread loads the background image and applies the rotation operation at 200 ms intervals. ImageRotator updates SpinBGCanvas3D's image by calling updateBG().

SpinBGCanvas3D's preRender() is called by Java3D's rendering thread to draw the background.

The scene graph built by WrapSpinPlanets3D is virtually identical to the one made by Wrap-Planets3D in Figure 8-3. It's a little simpler since no Background node is added to the graph. Black is a fine substitute when the background image has transparent elements or is too small to fill the canvas.

Building the Scene and Terminating

WrapSpinPlanets3D's constructor is similar to the constructor in WrapPlanets3D:

```
// globals
private static final int PWIDTH = 512;    // size of panel
private static final int PHEIGHT = 512;

private ImageRotator imRotator; // for rotating the background image


public WrapSpinPlanets3D(String backFnm)
{
  setLayout( new BorderLayout() );
  setOpaque( false );
  setPreferredSize( new Dimension(PWIDTH, PHEIGHT));

  GraphicsConfiguration config =
        SimpleUniverse.getPreferredConfiguration();
  SpinBGCanvas3D canvas3D =
        new SpinBGCanvas3D(config, PWIDTH, PHEIGHT);
  add("Center", canvas3D);
  canvas3D.setFocusable(true);      // give focus to the canvas
  canvas3D.requestFocus();

  imRotator = new ImageRotator(backFnm, canvas3D);

  su = new SimpleUniverse(canvas3D);
  createSceneGraph();
  initUserPosition();         // set user's viewpoint
  orbitControls(canvas3D);    // controls for moving the viewpoint
  su.addBranchGraph( sceneBG );

  imRotator.start();    // start the background rotating
} // end of WrapSpinPlanets3D()
```

The ImageRotator thread, imRotator, rotates the background visual and passes the result to SpinBGCanvas3D for rendering. Therefore, its constructor requires the image's filename and a SpinBGCanvas3D reference as arguments. The thread is started once the scene has been constructed.

The thread is terminated when the application is about to finish. A WindowListener in SpinPlanets3D is triggered by a window-closing event and calls WrapSpinPlanets3D's stopBackground():

```
public void stopBackground()
{  imRotator.stopRotating();  }
```

Rotating the Image

The ImageRotator constructor loads the image and stores the graphics configuration to speed up the rotation operations applied later:

```
// globals
private static final int ROT_AMT = 2;    // rotation, in degrees

private SpinBGCanvas3D canvas3D;
private BufferedImage backIm;
private GraphicsConfiguration gc;
private int currAngle;


public ImageRotator(String backFnm, SpinBGCanvas3D c3d)
{
  canvas3D = c3d;

  backIm = loadBGImage(backFnm);
  canvas3D.updateBG(backIm);
     // initially use the unrotated image as the background
  currAngle = ROT_AMT;

  /* get GraphicsConfiguration so images can be copied
     easily and efficiently */
  GraphicsEnvironment ge =
       GraphicsEnvironment.getLocalGraphicsEnvironment();
  gc = ge.getDefaultScreenDevice().getDefaultConfiguration();
} // end of ImageRotator()
```

The original image, stored in backIm, is passed to the canvas by calling SpinBGCanvas3D.updateBG(). This gives the canvas something to draw at startup.

A while loop in run() rotates the picture, passes the result to the canvas, and sleeps for a short time before repeating:

```
// globals
private static final int DELAY = 200;    // ms (update interval)

private boolean isRunning;

public void run()
{
  isRunning = true;
  BufferedImage rotIm;

  while(isRunning) {
    rotIm = getRotatedImage(backIm, currAngle);
    canvas3D.updateBG(rotIm);  // pass image to canvas

    currAngle += ROT_AMT;
    if (currAngle > 360)   // reset after one complete rotation
      currAngle -= 360;

    try {
      Thread.sleep(DELAY);       // wait a while
    }
    catch (Exception ex) {}
  }
} // end of run()
```

The rotation angle in currAngle is incremented in ROT_AMT steps, modulo 360.

Manipulating the Image

When getRotatedImage() is given a BufferedImage and an integer angle, it creates a new Buffered-
Image rotated by that number of degrees in a clockwise direction. The image's center is used as the
center of rotation:

```
private BufferedImage getRotatedImage(BufferedImage src, int angle)
{
  if (src == null)
    return null;

  int transparency = src.getColorModel().getTransparency();
  BufferedImage dest =  gc.createCompatibleImage(
                   src.getWidth(), src.getHeight(), transparency);
  Graphics2D g2d = dest.createGraphics();

  AffineTransform origAT = g2d.getTransform();
                                    // save original transform

  // rotate the coord. system of the dest. image around its center
  AffineTransform rot = new AffineTransform();
  rot.rotate( Math.toRadians(angle), src.getWidth()/2,
                               src.getHeight()/2);
  g2d.transform(rot);

  g2d.drawImage(src, 0, 0, null);    // copy in the image

  g2d.setTransform(origAT);      // restore original transform
  g2d.dispose();

  return dest;
} // end of getRotatedImage()
```

Rotation and Clipping

A tricky aspect of getRotatedImage() is that the affine transformation employs the original image
as a clipping rectangle. If the rotation takes the picture outside those bounds, it'll be clipped, as
illustrated by Figure 8-11.

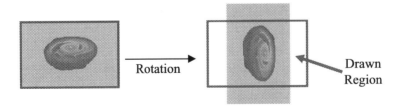

Figure 8-11. *A rotation that clips the image*

In Figure 8-11, the top and bottom parts of the rotated image are clipped. Also, the two vertical
white gaps in the drawn region will be rendered transparent if the original picture has an alpha
channel, or in black if the image is opaque.

The simplest way to avoid clipping important parts of the image is to give the image a large enough border so that the significant visuals reside within the drawn region. If the picture is square, all its important details should lie within a "rotation" circle defined by the dimensions of the square. This idea is shown in Figure 8-12.

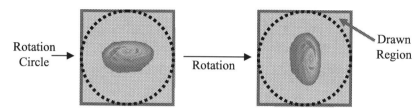

Figure 8-12. *Details inside the rotation circle will not be clipped.*

Visuals within the rotation circle won't be clipped when a rotation is applied around the image's center.

Avoiding Gaps in the Rotated Image

Another issue with the rotation operation is how large the picture should be so there are no gaps in the rotated version (e.g., how do you avoid the gaps in Figure 8-11?). A square is a good shape for a centrally rotated image, but how big should the square be to always fill the canvas no matter what the rotation?

When a square image of size len is rotated around its center, it'll mark out a rotation circle defined by the length of its diagonal, as shown on the left side of Figure 8-13.

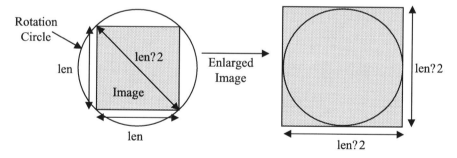

Figure 8-13. *Enlarging an image to fit a rotation circle*

When the image is rotated inside a canvas with the same len-by-len dimensions, gaps will appear. The only way to avoid this problem is to enlarge the picture so its length is equal to the diameter of the rotation circle, which is $\sqrt{(len^2 + len^2)}$, or len$\sqrt{2}$.

For instance, an image the same size as a 512×512 canvas will need to be enlarged to at least $512\sqrt{2}$ by $512\sqrt{2}$ (724×724 pixels) to avoid any gaps when rotated around the center of that canvas.

The drawback of this enlargement is the large increase in image size (it doubles), which makes the rotation calculation more time-consuming.

This is the case for the whirlpool image shown in Figure 8-9. Its dimensions are 725×726 pixels, and is 175KB in size. SpinPlanets3D responds very sluggishly to mouse movements due to the processing required to rotate the large image every 200 ms.

The speed problem can be resolved by utilizing a smaller background image and filling the gaps with a Background node color. In fact, for SpinPlanets3D, no Background node is needed at all, since the default black background is suitable as a stand-in for deep space.

Figure 8-14 shows the scene with galaxy.jpg as the background picture (439×440 pixels; 8.2KB), and there's only a very slight delay when responding to mouse movements. The small file size is due to the image containing large areas of blue and black, which can be readily compressed.

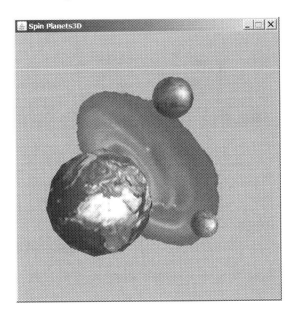

Figure 8-14. *Planets in a spinning galaxy*

Figure 8-15 shows the scene with sun.gif (167×180 pixels; 1.5KB); there's no discernable delay in the application when the user moves the mouse.

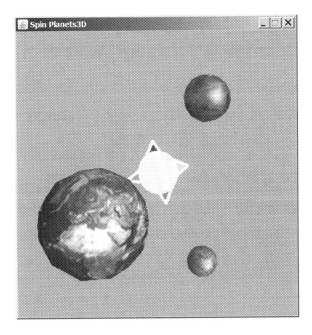

Figure 8-15. *Planets with a spinning sun*

Terminating the Thread

The loop inside run() in ImageRotator continues while isRunning is true. The thread is stopped by
setting isRunning to false with stopRotating():

```
public void stopRotating()
{   isRunning = false; }
```

stopRotating() is called from stopBackground() in WrapSpinPlanets3D, which is called from
SpinPlanets3D when the frame's close box is clicked.

Drawing the Background Image

SpinBGCanvas3D draws the background image using preRender() in a similar way to previously.
However, the details are a little more complicated due to the issue of shared data between multiple
threads.

preRender() is called by Java 3D's rendering thread when it needs to update the scene (for
example, when the camera position has moved). Complications arise because there's also an
ImageRotator thread ticking away, updating the background image every 200 ms.

Since the picture is manipulated by two threads, SpinBGCanvas3D must contain synchronization code to enforce mutual exclusion when both threads want to access the image concurrently.

The SpinBGCanvas3D constructor saves the canvas's dimensions and creates a J3DGraphics2D
object for 2D drawing:

```
// globals
private BufferedImage backIm = null;    // the background image
private J3DGraphics2D render2D;
                        // for 2D rendering into the 3D canvas
private int panelWidth, panelHeight;   // of drawing area


public SpinBGCanvas3D(GraphicsConfiguration gc,
                        int pWidth, int pHeight)
{ super(gc);
  panelWidth = pWidth;
  panelHeight = pHeight;
  render2D = this.getGraphics2D();
} // end of SpinBGCanvas3D()
```

The image reference, backIm, which is initially null, is updated with updateBG(), called from
ImageRotator:

```
public void updateBG(BufferedImage im)
{   setBGImage(im);
    drawBackground();
}

private synchronized void setBGImage(BufferedImage im)
{   backIm = im;   }
```

After backIm has been updated, drawBackground() draws the image:

```
private synchronized void drawBackground()
{
  if (backIm == null)    // no image to draw
    return;
  int xc = (panelWidth - backIm.getWidth())/2;
  int yc = (panelHeight - backIm.getHeight())/2;
  render2D.drawAndFlushImage(backIm, xc, yc, this);
}
```

drawBackground() positions the center of the image at the center of the canvas.

The synchronization keywords used in setBGImage() and drawBackground() seem unnecessary until we consider the Java 3D thread. It calls preRender() whenever it needs to redraw the scene. preRender() delegates this task to drawBackground():

```
public void preRender()
{  drawBackground();  }
```

I don't want the rendering thread to call drawBackground() when the image is being updated in setBGImage(), or when the image is already being drawn by ImageRotator calling drawBackground(). These mutual exclusion cases are handled by adding the synchronization keyword to setBGImage() and drawBackground().

The Model Viewer with a Shifting Background and Overlays

SpinPlanets3D is an example of an application where the background changes independently of other scene activity; the background rotates no matter what the user does inside the 3D space.

A more common type of application is one where the background changes depending on the user's movements in the scene. For instance, as the user rotates *left*, the background rotates to the *right*, in a manner similar to how we see the real world.

The ObjView3D example in this section implements this kind of background manipulation. It's a modified version of the model viewer described in Chapter 7.

Figure 8-16 shows two screenshots of ObjVIew3D, the second taken after the user has moved to a different part of the scene.

Figure 8-16. *Moving in ObjView3D*

As the user moves left and right, the background shifts in the opposite direction (right and left). If the user pirouettes on the spot, the background will disappear off one side of the canvas and eventually reappear at the other side.

This version of ObjView3D also includes the two overlays at the bottom of the screen, as shown in Figure 8-17.

Figure 8-17. *The overlays in ObjView3D*

On the left is the text "Moves: 374" and on the right a translucent image containing the title of the application. The number in the "Moves" message is incremented each time the background is shifted.

The class diagrams for this version of ObjView3D are given in Figure 8-18. Only the public methods are shown.

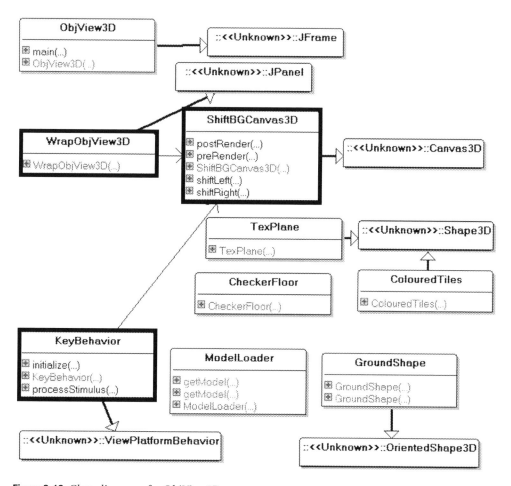

Figure 8-18. *Class diagrams for ObjView3D*

The application is complicated, but most of it is the same as in Chapter 7, with all the changes localized in the three classes with the thick borders. The following are the main differences:

- ShiftBGCanvas3D is new. It shifts the background and manages the overlays.

- WrapObjView3D, which sets up the 3D world, now utilizes ShiftBGCanvas3D rather than Canvas3D. It passes a ShiftBGCanvas3D reference to KeyBehavior. Only a single 3D model is loaded (the "humanoid") to simplify the scene.

- KeyBehavior contains extra code to communicate with ShiftBGCanvas3D. It asks it to move the background left or right.

I won't talk about the unchanged parts of ObjView3D; if you're not familiar with those classes, please look back at Chapter 7.

Setting up the Canvas

The WrapObjView3D constructor employs ShiftBGCanvas3D in almost the same way as the standard Canvas3D:

```
// globals
private static final int PWIDTH = 512;    // size of panel
private static final int PHEIGHT = 512;

private ShiftBGCanvas3D canvas3D;


public WrapObjView3D()
// construct the 3D canvas
{
  setLayout( new BorderLayout() );
  setOpaque( false );
  setPreferredSize( new Dimension(PWIDTH, PHEIGHT));

  GraphicsConfiguration config =
        SimpleUniverse.getPreferredConfiguration();
  canvas3D = new ShiftBGCanvas3D(config, PWIDTH, PHEIGHT);
  add("Center", canvas3D);

  canvas3D.setFocusable(true);
  canvas3D.requestFocus();
  su = new SimpleUniverse(canvas3D);

  // depth-sort transparent objects on a per-geometry basis
  View view = su.getViewer().getView();
  view.setTransparencySortingPolicy(View.TRANSPARENCY_SORT_GEOMETRY);

  createSceneGraph();
  createUserControls();

  su.addBranchGraph( sceneBG );
} // end of WrapObjView3D()
```

The dimensions of the panel are passed to ShiftBGCanvas3D to help it with the positioning of the background image.

The ShiftBGCanvas3D variable, canvas3D, is global so it can be easily passed to the KeyBehavior instance created in createUserControls():

```
KeyBehavior keyBeh = new KeyBehavior(canvas3D);
```

Modifying the Key Behavior

KeyBehavior calls two public methods in ShiftBGCanvas3D: shiftLeft() and shiftRight().

When the camera moves or turns left/right, the background is moved right/left with shiftRight()/shiftLeft().

Rotation is handled by KeyBehavior's standardMove() method:

```
// globals
private AmmoManager ammoMan;
private ShiftBGCanvas3D canvas3D;


private void standardMove(int keycode)
/* Make viewer moves forward or backward;
   rotate left or right. */
{
  if(keycode == forwardKey)
    doMove(FWD);
  else if(keycode == backKey)
    doMove(BACK);
  else if(keycode == leftKey) {
    rotateY(ROT_AMT);
    canvas3D.shiftRight(10);
  }
  else if(keycode == rightKey) {
    rotateY(-ROT_AMT);
    canvas3D.shiftLeft(10);
  }
} // end of standardMove()
```

The new code is highlighted in bold. I experimented with various shift values until the background seemed to move realistically.

KeyBehavior deals with camera translation in altMove():

```
private void altMove(int keycode)
// moves viewer up or down, left or right
{
  if(keycode == forwardKey) {
    upMoves++;
    doMove(UP);
  }
  else if(keycode == backKey) {
    if (upMoves > 0) {  // don't drop below start height
      upMoves--;
      doMove(DOWN);
    }
  }
  else if(keycode == leftKey) {
    doMove(LEFT);
```

```
      canvas3D.shiftRight(1);
    }
    else if(keycode == rightKey) {
      doMove(RIGHT);
      canvas3D.shiftLeft(1);
    }
}  // end of altMove()
```

Both turning and translation are handled by shifting the background. The only difference is that a rotation left or right triggers a larger shift (by 10 units) than a translation (1 unit). This difference reflects the fact that when a person turns, the view in front of him changes more drastically than if he only moves laterally.

A Canvas with a Background and Overlays

ShiftBGCanvas3D overrides Canvas3D's preRender() *and* postRender() methods.

The preRender() method draws a background that is moved left or right depending on the camera position. postRender() draws a "Moves: <no>" text message and a translucent title image in the foreground.

The ShiftBGCanvas3D constructor loads the background and title images and creates a drawing surface for the background and foreground visuals:

```
// globals
private static final String BACK_IM = "night.gif";
private static final String TITLE_IM = "title.png";

private BufferedImage drawIm, backIm, titleIm;
private Graphics2D drawg2d;   // for drawing into drawIm
private J3DGraphics2D render2D;   // for 2D rendering into 3D canvas

private int panelWidth, panelHeight;  // size of drawing area
private int imWidth;        // width of background image
private int xc;  // current x-axis position for drawing the BG image

// for displaying messages
private Font msgsFont;
private int moveNum = 0;


public ShiftBGCanvas3D(GraphicsConfiguration gc,
                              int pWidth, int pHeight)
{ super(gc);
  panelWidth = pWidth;
  panelHeight = pHeight;

  /* create a drawing surface with support for an alpha channel,
     and a graphic context for drawing into it */
  drawIm = new BufferedImage(panelWidth, panelHeight,
                                  BufferedImage.TYPE_4BYTE_ABGR);
  drawg2d = drawIm.createGraphics();

  render2D = this.getGraphics2D();

  backIm = loadImage(BACK_IM);   // load background image
  xc = 0; // x-axis drawing position for BG image
  if (backIm != null) {
```

```
      imWidth = backIm.getWidth();
      if (imWidth < panelWidth)
        System.out.println("WARNING: background image is too narrow");
    }

    titleIm = loadImage(TITLE_IM);    // load title image

    // create message font
    msgsFont = new Font("SansSerif", Font.BOLD, 24);
  } // end of ShiftBGCanvas3D()
```

The drawing surface is a BufferedImage called drawIm, and its associated graphics context is called drawg2d.

The background will often be composed from *two* copies of the background picture, and these images need to be combined into a single visual before being rendered by drawAndFlushImage() in preRender(). The drawing surface is used for this composition.

The foreground consists of two overlays: the "Moves" text and the translucent title. They're combined into a single image in postRender() by writing them onto the drawing surface and calling drawAndFlushImage().

These composition tasks could be assigned to two separate drawing surfaces—one for the background, one for the foreground—but it's straightforward to reuse the same surface.

The drawIm BufferedImage is of type BufferedImage.TYPE_4BYTE_ABGR, which includes an alpha channel. This means that transparent or translucent images will be rendered correctly.

Efficiency is another reason for using BufferedImage.TYPE_4BYTE_ABGR. If OpenGL is the underlying graphics API, drawIm can be rendered without drawAndFlushImage() having to make a copy of it.

backIm contains the basic background image, a sunset, shown in Figure 8-19.

Figure 8-19. *The ObjView3D background*

I've widened the image so it's longer than the canvas width. The code in preRender() assumes that the image is at least the width of the canvas, and the constructor prints a warning if this is not so. This assumption means that, at most, two copies of the image will be needed to completely span the width of the canvas.

The translucent image in titleIm is loaded from a PNG file and is shown in Figure 8-20.

Figure 8-20. *The translucent title*

Drawing the Background

The background is moved left and right by KeyBehavior calling ShiftBGCanvas3D's shiftLeft() and shiftRight() methods:

```
// globals
private int xc = 0;

private int moveNum = 0;


public void shiftLeft(int amt)
// shift the background left by amt
{ xc -= amt;
  moveNum++;
}

public void shiftRight(int amt)
// shift the background right by amt
{ xc += amt;
  moveNum++;
}
```

The global xc variable stores the x-coordinate of the left edge of the backIm image. It starts at 0 and is decremented and incremented by shiftLeft() and shiftRight(). The moveNum counter records the number of times that the image has been shifted.

preRender() uses the current value of xc to decide where to position backIm in the canvas and whether another copy needs to be drawn in order to fully span the canvas:

```
public void preRender()
// draw the background
{
  if (backIm == null)    // no background image to draw
    return;

  clearSurface();

  // adjust x coord to be within the bounds of the image width
  if (xc >= imWidth)
    xc -= imWidth;
  else if (xc <= -imWidth)
    xc += imWidth;

  if (xc > 0) {      // background starts on the right
    drawg2d.drawImage(backIm, xc-imWidth, 0, null);    // draw lhs
    if (xc < panelWidth)      // start of BG is on-screen
      drawg2d.drawImage(backIm, xc, 0, null);    // draw rhs
  }
  else {  // xc <= 0, background starts on the left
    drawg2d.drawImage(backIm, xc, 0, null);    // draw lhs
    int endBG = xc + imWidth;
    if (endBG < panelWidth)    // end of BG is on-screen
      drawg2d.drawImage(backIm, endBG, 0, null);    // draw rhs
  }

  render2D.drawAndFlushImage(drawIm, 0, 0, this);
}  // end of preRender()
```

The drawing surface is cleared prior to the creation of a new background using a technique suggested by mokopa in the Java 3D forum at http://www.javagaming.org/forums/index.php?topic=7320.0. clearSurface() contains the implementation:

```
private void clearSurface()
{
  drawg2d.setComposite(
        AlphaComposite.getInstance(AlphaComposite.CLEAR, 0.0f));
  drawg2d.fillRect(0,0, panelWidth, panelHeight);
  drawg2d.setComposite(
        AlphaComposite.getInstance(AlphaComposite.SRC_OVER, 1.0f));
  drawg2d.setColor(Color.BLACK);
}  // end of clearSurface()
```

The alpha composition rule is set to AlphaComposite.CLEAR with full transparency. As a consequence, the filled rectangle will set the alpha and RGB channels in the image to 0 for all the pixels. This deletes whatever was in the drawing surface, making it fully transparent.

Then the alpha composition is changed to fully opaque AlphaComposite.SRC_OVER. Any subsequent drawings will be written onto the surface without being influenced by the surface's transparency.

Back in preRender(), xc is adjusted to be within the range -imWidth to imWidth. These extremes are the x-axis values where the image is completely off the canvas on the left and right sides and so can be redrawn at the xc=0 position.

The if-test breaks the drawing task into two parts.

If xc is greater than 0, the left edge of backIm may be in the middle of the canvas, as illustrated by Figure 8-21.

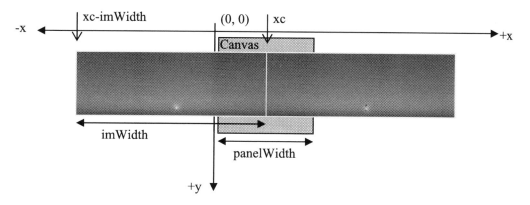

Figure 8-21. *The background when xc > 0*

This requires a second copy of backIm to be drawn on the left, so the full width of the canvas is covered. Figure 8-21 shows gray areas above and below the background pictures in order to clarify the position of the images; none of the canvas is visible in the application.

The Figure 8-21 situation is implemented using this code fragment:

```
if (xc > 0) {     // background starts on the right
  drawg2d.drawImage(backIm, xc-imWidth, 0, null);    // draw lhs
  if (xc < panelWidth)      // start of BG is on-screen
    drawg2d.drawImage(backIm, xc, 0, null);   // draw rhs
}
```

Two copies of backIm are drawn into the drawIm BufferedImage via the drawg2d graphics context. However, the right-hand backIm is only drawn if xc is on the canvas (i.e., less than the panel width).

This code could be optimized by drawing subregions of the images into drawIm. There's really no need to draw the parts of the picture located off the sides of the canvas.

The other drawing case is when xc is less than or equal to 0, which means that backIm's left edge starts off the left side of the canvas. This situation is shown graphically in Figure 8-22.

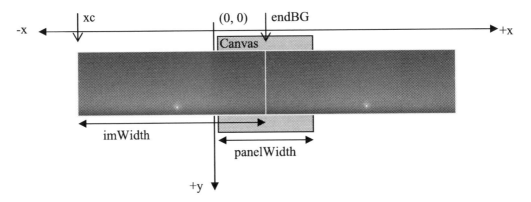

Figure 8-22. *The background when xc <= 0*

This requires a second copy of backIm to be drawn on the right, so the canvas is fully covered. Figure 8-22 is implemented using this code fragment:

```
// xc <= 0, background starts on the left
drawg2d.drawImage(backIm, xc, 0, null);    // draw lhs
int endBG = xc + imWidth;
if (endBG < panelWidth)    // end of BG is on-screen
  drawg2d.drawImage(backIm, endBG, 0, null);    // draw rhs
```

Once again two copies of backIm are drawn via the drawg2d graphics context into the drawIm BufferedImage. But the right-hand backIm is only drawn if endBG (xc+imWidth) is on the canvas (i.e., less than the panel width).

The Deep Blue Sea

The scene graph for ObjView3D includes a Background node displaying dark blue. The relevant method in WrapObjView3D is the following:

```
private void addBackground()
// the deep blue sea
{ Background back = new Background();
  back.setApplicationBounds( bounds );
  back.setColor(0, 0, 0.639f);    // dark blue
  sceneBG.addChild( back );
} // end of addBackground()
```

This means that the background image doesn't need to extend the full depth of the canvas, as shown by Figure 8-23.

Figure 8-23. *The view from the checkerboard's edge*

Where the image ends, the dark-blue Background node takes over, giving the impression of ocean extending to the horizon. It means that the background image can be shorter than the height of the canvas, making the picture smaller, and therefore less time-consuming to manipulate.

Adding Overlays

Overlays can be implemented as part of the scene graph by pasting a texture representing the overlay onto a quad positioned just in front of the user's viewpoint.

The drawback with this approach is that the overlay quad may overlap or obscure objects in the scene when the user moves very close to them. This problem can't occur with overlays generated in postRender() since they're drawn onto the canvas after scene graph rendering has been completed:

```
public void postRender()
// draw the text message and the title image in the foreground
{
  clearSurface();

  // draw the title image, with hardwired positioning
  drawg2d.drawImage(titleIm, panelWidth-195, panelHeight-60, null);

   // draw the firing info.
  drawg2d.setFont(msgsFont);
  drawg2d.setColor(Color.red);
  drawg2d.drawString("Moves: " + moveNum, 10, panelHeight-10);

  render2D.drawAndFlushImage(drawIm, 0, 0, this);
}  // end of postRender()
```

postRender() uses the same drawing surface (drawIm and drawg2d) as preRender(), so starts by wiping it clean. The text message and the translucent title are drawn onto the surface, and the resulting drawIm image is placed onto the canvas.

Summary

This chapter looked at how Java 3D's mixed mode rendering can be utilized to create backgrounds and overlays (text/graphics always in the foreground). Most of a scene is built using Java 3D's scene graph API as usual, but the background and overlays are drawn directly onto the canvas.

One advantage is that it's possible to apply a range of image manipulation techniques, such as rotations and translations, which allow the background and/or overlays to change at runtime. In one example, the background rotates automatically, while in another its position is linked to the camera's movements.

PART 2

Nonstandard Input Devices

CHAPTER 9

Webcam Snaps

Over the next few chapters, I look at using nonstandard input devices, including the game pad (in Chapters 11 and 12) and the P5 data glove (in Chapter 14), but I start with the webcam in this chapter and the next. (Chapter 13 is a sort of interlude, where I look at 3D sound generation using the JOAL API; JOAL is employed in the subsequent data glove chapter.)

The webcam is perhaps surprisingly a great "building block" for creating unusual input devices. The trick is to use it to deliver images (e.g., the user's hand or face) to the application, which extracts information from those images to act as the input.

I explain the image processing aspects of this approach in Chapter 10 when I code an "arm-waving" device. It allows me to navigate around a 3D scene using nothing but my hand (no keyboard or mouse is required).

This chapter concentrates on how to generate the webcam snaps used in the image processing stage. I examine and compare two ways of capturing images from a webcam: with TWAIN (Technology Without an Interesting Name), and JMF (Java Media Framework). The aim is to grab images as quickly as possible, then display them in rapid succession in a JPanel. The panel output includes the number of pictures displayed so far and the average time to take a snap—information that'll help me judge the two technologies.

The crucial difference, which we'll see with timing tests, is that JMF is 150 to 200 times faster at taking a snap than similar code using TWAIN. For that reason, I'll be using JMF-based image grabbing in Chapter 10.

Webcam Snaps with TWAIN

The TWAIN specification defines an API for obtaining images from scanners and digital cameras (http://www.twain.org/). There are implementations for Windows and the Mac, but UNIX/Linux isn't supported due to TWAIN's requirement that the capture device offer a dialog box that exposes its features. SANE (Scanner Access Now Easy) is a popular image acquisition API for UNIX/Linux, described at http://www.sane-project.org/.

I'm using Morena 6.3.2.2, a commercial Java interface for TWAIN (it also supports SANE); a 30-day evaluation copy is available at http://www.gnome.sk/Twain/jtp.html. Another good commercial product, JTwain (http://asprise.com/product/jtwain/), offers a similar 30-day evaluation version. A free alternative, also called JTwain, was developed by Jeff Friesen in a series of articles at java.net (http://today.java.net/pub/a/today/2004/11/18/twain.html).

The Windows installation of Morena involves three JAR files (morena.jar, morena_windows.jar, and morena_license.jar). They should be added to Java's classpath or copied into <JAVA_HOME>\jre\lib\ext and <JRE_HOME>\lib\ext.

TWAIN offers a simple abstraction for image acquisition based on a *source* (the capture device) and a *source manager*, which handles the interactions between the application and the source. As a consequence, the two most important Morena classes are TwainSource and TwainManager.

The main stages in a TWAIN-enabled application are quite simple:

1. Use TwainManager to select a source (a TwainSource object).
2. Get/set the source's capabilities.
3. Acquire images from the source.
4. Close down the source and manager, and exit.

Displaying Pictures Using TWAIN

The ShowPics application uses TWAIN to grab pictures from the webcam and displays them in a JPanel. The application is shown running in Figure 9-1.

Figure 9-1. *ShowPics in action*

The text in Figure 9-1 is "Pic 26. 3.80 secs." The time is an average for how long ShowPics takes to snap a picture. (The JMF version of this application produces a picture every 20 to 25 ms on average.)

The class diagrams for the program, with only the public methods visible, are shown in Figure 9-2.

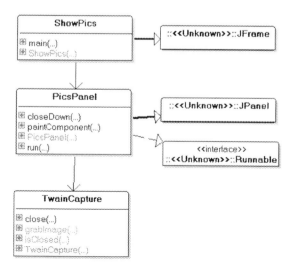

Figure 9-2. *Class diagrams for ShowPics*

PicsPanel is threaded so it can keep repeatedly calling grabImage() in the TwainCapture while the separate GUI thread draws the grabbed images into the JPanel.

The only thing of note in ShowPics (the top-level JFrame) is that clicking its close box triggers a call to closeDown() in PicsPanel. This in turn calls close() in TwainCapture to close the link with the webcam.

Snapping a Picture Again and Again and ...

PicsPanel's run() method is a loop dedicated to calling grabImage() and to calculating the average time to take a snap:

```
// globals
private static final int DELAY = 1000;   // ms

private BufferedImage image = null;
private TwainCapture camera;
private boolean running;

// used for the average ms snap time info
private int imageCount = 0;
private long totalTime = 0;


public void run()
/* take a picture every DELAY ms */
{
  camera = new TwainCapture(SIZE);
     // must link to Twain device in same thread that uses it

  long duration;
  BufferedImage im = null;
  running = true;

  while (running) {
    long startTime = System.currentTimeMillis();
    im = camera.grabImage();    // take a snap
    duration = System.currentTimeMillis() - startTime;

    if (im == null)
      System.out.println("Problem loading image " + (imageCount+1));
    else {
      image = im;    // only update image if im contains something
      imageCount++;
      totalTime += duration;
      repaint();
    }

    if (duration < DELAY) {
      try {
        Thread.sleep(DELAY-duration); // wait until DELAY has passed
      }
      catch (Exception ex) {}
    }
  }

  // saveSnap(image, SAVE_FNM);    // save last image
  camera.close();    // close down the camera
} // end of run()
```

Each iteration of the loop is meant to take DELAY milliseconds. The time to take a snap is stored in duration and used to modify the loop's sleep period. If the snap duration exceeds the DELAY time, the loop doesn't sleep at all.

The DELAY value used in run() is 1,000 ms (1 second), which I chose by examining the statistics output to the screen when the program is executing. A delay of 1 second makes the webcam "movie" run at 1 frame/second (1 FPS) or slower, which is inadequate for movie emulation.

Morena requires that the TWAIN source be manipulated from a single thread, which includes the initialization of the device, grabbing pictures, and closing the link at the end. If this rule isn't followed, the application usually crashes and often causes Windows to start acting strangely. Consequently, all interactions with the TWAIN device are localized inside run().

Terminating the Application

The single-threaded requirement affects the way that the application is closed. When the user presses the close box in the JFrame, closeDown() is called in PicsPanel:

```
public void closeDown()
{
  running = false;
  while (!camera.isClosed()) {
    try {
      Thread.sleep(DELAY);  // wait a while
    }
    catch (Exception ex) {}
  }
}
```

closeDown() sets running to false, then waits for the camera to close. When running is false, the loop in run() will eventually finish, and TwainCapture.closed() will be called just before run() exits. closed() sets a boolean to true inside TwainCapture, which allows TwainCapture.isClosed() to return true. Only then will closedDown() return, permitting the application to terminate.

This approach means that the program's GUI will "freeze" for 1 to 2 seconds when the close box is clicked, since closeDown() blocks the GUI thread while it waits.

The more usual way of coding termination behavior is to put a call to TwainCapture.close() inside closeDown(). Although this enables the application to exit quickly, it also frequently crashes the JRE and makes Windows unresponsive. This is a consequence of manipulating the TWAIN source in the GUI thread rather than in the PicsPanel thread.

Painting the Panel

The paintComponent() method draws the webcam picture in the panel and writes some statistics near the bottom:

```
public void paintComponent(Graphics g)
{
  super.paintComponent(g);
  g.drawImage(image, 0, 0, this);    // draw the snap

  // write statistics
  g.setColor(Color.blue);
  g.setFont(msgFont);
  if (imageCount > 0) {
    double avgGrabTime = (double) totalTime / (imageCount*1000);
    g.drawString("Pic " + imageCount + "   " +
                 df.format(avgGrabTime) + " secs",
```

```
                     5, SIZE-10);  // bottom left
  }
  else  // no image yet
    g.drawString("Loading...", 5, SIZE-10);
} // end of paintComponent()
```

The panel has fixed dimensions (SIZE * SIZE), which explains the use of SIZE in the draw-String() calls. There's no need to scale the image in paintComponent(), since grabImage() in TwainCapture does it.

paintComponent() is called when the application is first made visible, which occurs before any images have been retrieved from the source device. In that case, paintComponent() draws the string "Loading..." at the bottom left of the panel.

Saving a Snap

It's very simple to save a snap to a file by using the ImageIO.write() method:

```
private void saveSnap(BufferedImage im, String fnm)
// Save image as JPG
{
  System.out.println("Saving image");
  try {
    ImageIO.write(im, "jpg", new File(fnm));
  }
  catch(IOException e)
  { System.out.println("Could not save image");  }
}
```

saveSnap() is called with the current BufferedImage and a filename.

The TWAIN Capture Device

The TwainCapture constructor carries out the first two steps in using a TWAIN device:

1. Use TwainManager to select a source (a TwainSource object).

2. Get/set the source's capabilities.

```
// globals
private int size;        // x/y- dimensions of final BufferedImage
private double scaleFactor;  // snap --> returned image scaling

private TwainSource source;
private MediaTracker imageTracker;
private boolean closedDevice;


public TwainCapture(int sz)
{
  size = sz;
  scaleFactor = 0;    // dummy initial value

  source = null;
  imageTracker = new MediaTracker( new JPanel() );
  closedDevice = true;    // since device is not available yet

  source = chooseSource();
```

```
    // source = defaultSource();  // simpler alternative
    System.out.println("Using source " + source);

    // hide the TWAIN source user interface
    source.setVisible(false);
    closedDevice = false;
}  // end of TwainCapture()
```

The chooseSource() method selects a suitable source device and TwainSource.setVisible(false) ensures that its features dialog box won't be displayed.

The MediaTracker object created in the constructor is used later to monitor the image acquisition in grabImage().

chooseSource() selects a TWAIN source based on whether it has a controllable GUI, which means that the setVisible() call in the constructor will have an effect:

```
private TwainSource chooseSource()
{
  TwainSource src = null;
  try {
    if (!TwainManager.isAvailable()) {
      System.out.println("Twain not available");
      close();
      System.exit(1);
    }

    TwainSource[] srcs = TwainManager.listSources();
    System.out.println("No. of Twain Sources: " + srcs.length);
    if (srcs.length == 0) {     // no sources
      close();
      System.exit(1);
    }

    int guiIdx = -1;    // index position of GUI controllable device
    for (int i=0; i < srcs.length; i++) {
      System.out.println("" + (i+1) + ". Testing " + srcs[i]);
      if (srcs[i].getUIControllable()) {
        guiIdx = i;
        System.out.println("  UI is controllable");
      }
    }
    if (guiIdx == -1) {  // no source is GUI controllable
      System.out.println("No controllable source GUIs");
      close();
      System.exit(1);
    }
    else
      src = srcs[guiIdx];
  }
  catch (TwainException e)
  { System.out.println(e);
    close();
    System.exit(1);
  }

  if (src == null) {
    close();
    System.exit(1);
  }

  return src;
}  // end of chooseSource()
```

The core actions of the method are to call TwainManager.listSources() and examine each of the TwainSource objects in the returned array.

chooseSource() is considerably lengthened by the need to handle errors. It's important to always close the source manager before exiting or the OS may be affected; that task is carried out by close():

```
synchronized public void close()
{ try {
    TwainManager.close();
  }
  catch (TwainException e)
  { System.out.println(e); }
  closedDevice = true;
}
```

close() and grabImage() are synchronized so that it's impossible to close the source while an image is being snapped. In fact, this behavior is already impossible due to the coding style used in PicsPanel's run(), but I've left the synchronization in place as an extra safeguard.

An Alternative Way to Choose a Source

On a machine with a single capture device, which allows its features dialog box to be made invisible, the generality of chooseSource() is overkill. defaultSource() selects a source by retrieving the default one:

```
private TwainSource defaultSource()
// use the default TWAIN source
{
  TwainSource src = null;
  try {
    src = TwainManager.getDefaultSource();
  }
  catch (TwainException e)
  { System.out.println(e);
    close();
    System.exit(1);
  }
  return src;
}
```

This method can be called in the constructor instead of chooseSource():

```
source = defaultSource();
```

Grabbing an Image

Taking a snap is a matter of passing the TWAIN source object to Toolkit.createSource() and waiting for the image to be fully loaded:

```
synchronized public BufferedImage grabImage()
{
  if (closedDevice)
    return null;

  Image im = Toolkit.getDefaultToolkit().createImage(source);
  imageTracker.addImage(im, 0);
  try {
```

```
    imageTracker.waitForID(0);
  }
  catch (InterruptedException e) {
    return null;
  }
  if (imageTracker.isErrorID(0))
    return null;

  return makeBIM(im);
}
```

To make it easier for the snap to be manipulated, it's converted to a BufferedImage before being returned:

```
private BufferedImage makeBIM(Image im)
{
  BufferedImage copy = new BufferedImage(size, size,
                            BufferedImage.TYPE_INT_RGB);

  // create a graphics context
  Graphics2D g2d = copy.createGraphics();

  // image --> resized BufferedImage
  setScale(g2d, im);
  g2d.drawImage(im,0,0,null);
  g2d.dispose();
  return copy;
}  // end of makeBIM()
```

There are numerous ways of formatting a BufferedImage, and makeBIM() utilizes the TYPE_INT_RGB format that assumes there's no alpha component in the image. An alternative is to employ TYPE_3BYTE_BGR, which supports dynamic texturing in OpenGL v.1.2 (and above) and Direct3D. TYPE_3BYTE_BGR would be a good idea if the image was going to be used as a texture in Java 3D.

setScale() resizes the image by modifying the graphics context's scale factor:

```
private void setScale(Graphics2D g2d, Image im)
{
  if (scaleFactor == 0.0) {  // scale not yet set
    int width = im.getWidth(null);       // get the image's dimensions
    int height = im.getHeight(null);
    if (width > height)
      scaleFactor = ((double) size) / width;
    else
      scaleFactor = ((double) size) / height;
  }
  g2d.scale(scaleFactor, scaleFactor);  // scale the context
}
```

When setScale() is called the first time, it calculates a scale factor that will fit the image into the JPanel's dimensions (size * size). Later calls use that value to resize all the grabbed images.

TWAIN Timing Tests

Although the TWAIN approach works, its speed is somewhat less than spectacular. It takes several seconds for the device to be initialized (2 to 5 seconds). The time seems longer when TwainManager.listSources() is used instead of TwainManager.getDefaultSource(), but it's hard to judge since I only have two TWAIN devices attached to my machine.

The first call to TwainCapture.grabImage() takes several seconds (2 to 5 seconds) to retrieve the first image after the initialization has finished. This means there's a possible 10-second wait before the first image appears in the JPanel.

Subsequent calls to grabImage() gradually become faster, reaching a gallop at a snap every 2 to 3 seconds.

A slow frame rate may not necessarily be a bad thing, since it depends on the requirements of the application. For instance, the need to reduce network bandwidth usage may make a reduced frame rate acceptable. Nevertheless, it would be better to use a technology where fast snap speeds were at least possible.

The rate set in PicsPanel's run() is one picture every 1,000 ms (1 second), which is very optimistic. Since a snap really takes 2 to 3 seconds, the sleep code in run()'s loop never has an opportunity to be executed.

Webcam Snaps with JMF

I revisit the application in this section, replacing TWAIN with JMF, more specifically the JMF Performance Pack for Windows v.2.1.1e (`http://java.sun.com/products/java-media/jmf/`). The overall class structure is much the same as before, as Figure 9-3 indicates.

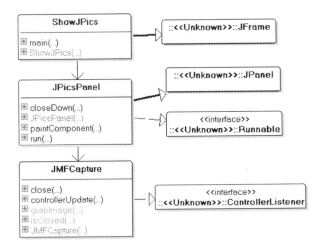

Figure 9-3. *Class diagrams for ShowJPics*

The class names have been changed (to protect the innocent), but ShowJPics is actually identical to ShowPics.

PicsJPanel is threaded in the same way as PicsPanel since it repeatedly calls grabImage() in the JMFCapture object.

JMFCapture contains the JMF code for accessing the capture device, but externally it looks just like TwainCapture, offering the same method prototypes.

Again Taking Pictures Again and Again

The run() method in JPicsPanel is similar to the one in PicsPanel:

```
// globals
private static final int DELAY = 40;   //ms

private JMFCapture camera;


public void run()
/* take a picture every DELAY ms */
{
  camera = new JMFCapture(SIZE);

  long duration;
  BufferedImage im = null;
  running = true;

  while (running) {
    long startTime = System.currentTimeMillis();
    im = camera.grabImage();  // take a snap
    duration = System.currentTimeMillis() - startTime;

    if (im == null)
      System.out.println("Problem loading image " + (imageCount+1));
    else {
      image = im;   // only update image if im contains something
      imageCount++;
      totalTime += duration;
      repaint();
    }

    if (duration < DELAY) {
      try {
        Thread.sleep(DELAY-duration);  //wait until DELAY time passed
      }
      catch (Exception ex) {}
    }
  }

  // saveSnap(image, SAVE_FNM);    // save last image
  camera.close();      // close down the camera
}  // end of run()
```

One reason for the similarity is that the JMF source is manipulated solely from the panel's thread in the same way as the TWAIN source in PicsPanel. This makes JPicsPanel's closeDown() method identical to the one in PicsPanel:

```
public void closeDown()
{
  running = false;
  while (!camera.isClosed()) {
    try {
      Thread.sleep(DELAY);
    }
    catch (Exception ex) {}
  }
}
```

This has the same disadvantage as the coding in PicsPanel: when the user clicks the close box, the application "freezes" for 1 to 2 seconds while closeDown() waits for the run() loop to terminate and JMFCapture.close() to finish. The more obvious approach of calling JMFCapture.close() directly from closeDown() will cause the OS to start behaving badly.

An important change is the value of DELAY: 40 ms, compared to 1 second in PicsPanel. Timing tests show that the JMF can capture an image every 30 ms on average. The remaining 10 ms gives the run() loop time to sleep while the panel is being redrawn.

The Capture Device with JMF

The steps in taking a snap with JMF are more involved than in TWAIN:

1. Get a media locator for the specified capture device.

2. Create a player for the device, putting it into the *realized* state. A player in the realized state knows how to render its data, so it can provide rendering components and controls when asked.

3. Create a frame grabber for the player.

4. Wait until the player is in the started state.

5. Initialize a BufferToImage object.

6. Start grabbing frames and converting them to images.

7. Close the player to finish.

The code corresponding to stages 1 through 5 is commented here in the JMFCapture constructor:

```
// globals
private static final String CAP_DEVICE =
            "vfw:Microsoft WDM Image Capture (Win32):0";
            // common name in WinXP

private int size;        // x/y- dimensions of final BufferedImage

private Player p;
private FrameGrabbingControl fg;
private boolean closedDevice;


public JMFCapture(int sz)
{
  size = sz;
  closedDevice = true;   // since device is not available yet

  // link player to capture device
  try {
    MediaLocator ml = findMedia(CAP_DEVICE);  // stage 1

    p = Manager.createRealizedPlayer(ml);      // stage 2
    System.out.println("Created player");
  }
  catch (Exception e) {
    System.out.println("Failed to create player");
    System.exit(0);
  }
```

```
    p.addControllerListener(this);

    // create the frame grabber (stage 3)
    fg = (FrameGrabbingControl) p.getControl(
            "javax.media.control.FrameGrabbingControl");
    if (fg == null) {
      System.out.println("Frame grabber could not be created");
      System.exit(0);
    }

    // wait until the player has started (stage 4)
    System.out.println("Starting the player...");
    p.start();
    if (!waitForStart()) {
      System.err.println("Failed to start the player.");
      System.exit(0);
    }

  waitForBufferToImage();   // stage 5
}  // end of JMFCapture()
```

findMedia() calls CaptureDeviceManager.getDeviceList() to get information on the capture devices registered with JMF, then cycles through it looking for the named device:

```
// globals
private static final String CAP_LOCATOR = "vfw://0";


private MediaLocator findMedia(String requireDeviceName)
{
  Vector devices = CaptureDeviceManager.getDeviceList(null);

  if (devices == null) {
    System.out.println("Devices list is null");
    System.exit(0);
  }
  if (devices.size() == 0) {
    System.out.println("No devices found");
    System.exit(0);
  }

  for (int i = 0; i < devices.size(); i++) {
    CaptureDeviceInfo devInfo =
          (CaptureDeviceInfo) devices.elementAt(i);
    String devName = devInfo.getName();
    if (devName.equals(requireDeviceName)) {   // found device
      System.out.println("Found device: " + requireDeviceName);
      return devInfo.getLocator();   // this method may not work
    }
  }

  System.out.println("Device " + requireDeviceName + " not found");
  System.out.println("Using default media locator: " + CAP_LOCATOR);
  return new MediaLocator(CAP_LOCATOR);
}  // end of findMedia()
```

If the desired device is found, a MediaLocator object is created with
CaptureDeviceInfo.getLocator(); a media locator is similar to a URL but for media devices.
If the device isn't found, the code uses the default locator string, "vfw://0".

There are a few issues with this approach, one being the choice of device name to pass to
findMedia(). Windows XP and 2000 almost always name their capture device vfw:Microsoft WDM
Image Capture (Win32):0. Another common name is vfw:Logitech USB Video Camera:0 for
Logitech devices; Windows 98 employs vfw:Microsoft WDM Image Capture:0.

Another problem is that a device must be registered with JMF before it can be manipulated by the
API. Registration is carried out with JMF's Registry Editor in the Capture Devices tab (see Figure 9-4).

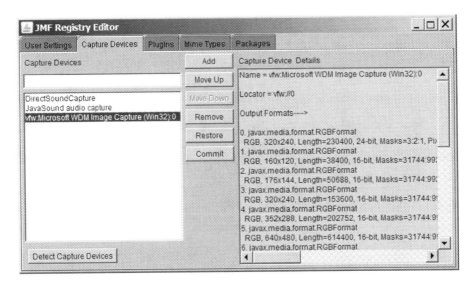

Figure 9-4. *Registering capture devices in JMF*

Pressing the Detect Capture Devices button generates the device's name, the media locator
URL, and the supported image formats. This information is also available by clicking the device
name in the left-hand list.

Unfortunately, there's no way to trigger this registration process from within a user program.
However, if the webcam is present when JMF is installed, it will be registered automatically as part
of the installation process.

Waiting for a BufferToImage

I was surprised to discover that the initialization phase may need several attempts to create a
BufferToImage object.

waitForBufferToImage() calls hasBufferToImage() repeatedly until it returns true; usually two
to three tries are necessary. hasBufferToImage() takes a snap then checks whether the resulting
Buffer object really contains something:

```
// globals
private double scaleFactor;  // snap --> final image scaling
private BufferToImage bufferToImage = null;
```

```
private boolean hasBufferToImage()
{
  Buffer buf = fg.grabFrame();      // take a snap
  if (buf == null) {
    System.out.println("No grabbed frame");
    return false;
  }

  // there is a buffer, but check if it's empty or not
  VideoFormat vf = (VideoFormat) buf.getFormat();
  if (vf == null) {
    System.out.println("No video format");
    return false;
  }

  System.out.println("Video format: " + vf);
  int width = vf.getSize().width;      // the image's dimensions
  int height = vf.getSize().height;
  if (width > height)
    scaleFactor = ((double) size) / width;
  else
    scaleFactor = ((double) size) / height;

  // initialize bufferToImage with the video format info.
  bufferToImage = new BufferToImage(vf);
  return true;
}  // end of hasBufferToImage()
```

Aside from FrameGrabbingControl.grabFrame() returning null, it may return a Buffer object with no internal video information. Only when there's an actual VideoFormat object can a BufferToImage object be created. It's then also possible to extract the format's size in order to calculate a scale factor for later snaps.

Grabbing an Image

grabImage() captures a snap as a Buffer object by calling FrameGrabbingControl.grabFrame(), converts it to an image, and then to a BufferedImage:

```
synchronized public BufferedImage grabImage()
{
  if (closedDevice)
    return null;

  // grab the current frame as a buffer object
  Buffer buf = fg.grabFrame();
  if (buf == null) {
    System.out.println("No grabbed buffer");
    return null;
  }

  // convert buffer to image
  Image im = bufferToImage.createImage(buf);
  if (im == null) {
    System.out.println("No grabbed image");
    return null;
  }
```

```
    return makeBIM(im);  // image --> BufferedImage
} // end of grabImage()
```

makeBIM() is similar to the same-named method in TwainCapture.

Closing the Capture Device

close() calls Player.close() to terminate the link to the capture device:

```
synchronized public void close()
{  p.close();
   closedDevice = true;
}
```

close() and grabImage() are synchronized so that it's impossible to close the player while a frame is being snapped. In fact, JPicsPanel already makes this impossible since close() is only called when run()'s snapping loop has finished. But I've left the synchronization in place just so I can feel a little safer; I did the same thing in TwainCapture.

Comparing TWAIN and JMF Capture

TWAIN isn't capable of generating sequences of captured images at high frame rates. It manages only one new frame every 3.5 seconds, compared to JMF's one image every 20 ms.

Both approaches are slow to start, taking several seconds to finish their initialization phase, but TWAIN also takes an age to obtain the first snap.

TWAIN is a Windows/Mac protocol, but JMF wins for portability since it also supports UNIX/Linux.

Morena 6, the Java TWAIN API I employed, is commercial software, while JMF is free. However, there is a freeware Java wrapper for TWAIN, described at http://today.java.net/pub/a/today/2004/11/18/twain.html.

TWAIN doesn't need a separate registration process in order to find capture devices at runtime. JMF applications depend on the JMF registry knowing about devices, which requires the user to manually add new devices via the editor.

The TWAIN API is simpler to use than JMF because it focuses on image grabbing, while JMF supports time-based multimedia. However, there are numerous JMF examples that explain these features, including the collection at Sun's JMF web site (http://java.sun.com/products/java-media/jmf/2.1.1/solutions/). A good book on JMF that also has several chapters on Java 3D is *Java Media APIs: Cross-Platform Imaging, Media, and Visualization* by Alejandro Terrazas, John Ostuni, and Michael Barlow (Sams, 2002). One of its longer examples is a 3D chat room that combines Java 3D and JMF.

On balance, I'll be using JMF rather than TWAIN to deliver images to my arm-waving application in the Chapter 10. JMF is fast enough for my needs, portable, and free.

QTJ

Another way of implementing capture is to use QuickTime for Java (QTJ). QTJ provides an object-based Java layer over the QuickTime API, making it possible to play QuickTime movies, edit and create them, capture audio and video, and perform 2D and 3D animations. QuickTime is available for the Mac and Windows. Details about QTJ's installation, documentation, and examples can be found at http://developer.apple.com/quicktime/qtjava/.

Chris Adamson talks about video and audio capture in Chapter 6 of his book *QuickTime for Java: A Developer's Notebook* (O'Reilly, 2005). He's somewhat hampered by the fact that QTJ doesn't support an onscreen component for its SequenceGrabber class; SequenceGrabber offers a grabPict() method, but there's no efficient way of getting that image on to the screen (Adamson mentions a 1-frame/second drawing rate).

A solution was found by Jochen Broz after the book's publication and posted to the quicktime-java mailing list (`http://lists.apple.com/archives/QuickTime-java/2005/Nov/msg00036.html`). He bypasses the inefficiencies of grabPict() and generates a BufferedImage directly from the SequenceGrabber frame. Adamson explains the details in a note at `http://www.oreillynet.com/mac/blog/2005/11/capturing_to_the_screen_with_q.html` and reports tests showing frame rates of 32 FPS, which is a frame captured every 30 ms or so; that's slower than JMF but still reasonable for many applications.

Other Uses for Webcam Snaps

Chapter 10 uses the JMFCapture class to take webcam snaps of a user's arm. They're analyzed and converted into commands for navigating around a 3D scene.

Chapter 28.85, "Waving a Magic Wand," at my Killer Game Programming in Java web site at `http://fivedots.coe.psu.ac.th/~ad/jg/` utilizes JMFCapture to take snaps of me waving a magic wand in front of the webcam. The application uses positional data extracted from the grabbed images to move an onscreen picture of a wand in a corresponding manner. The onscreen wand also shoots magic bolts.

Another application of this chapter's frame-grabbing technique is to paste images in rapid succession on to a Java 3D "movie screen." This is the subject of two articles I wrote for O'Reilly's web site. The first article uses JMF (`http://www.onjava.com/pub/a/onjava/2005/06/01/kgpjava.html`), the other employs QTJ (`http://www.onjava.com/pub/a/onjava/2005/06/01/kgpjava_part2.html`). The articles can also be found as Chapters 28.3 and 28.5 at my Killer Game Programming in Java site.

Webcams can be employed as robot eyes. In the article "Futurama: Using Java Technology to Build Robots That Can See, Hear, Speak, and Move," Steve Meloan describes the robotics work of Simon Ritter, a technology evangelist at Sun (`http://java.sun.com/developer/technicalArticles/Programming/robotics/`). The robots utilize LEGO Mindstorms running leJOS, an open source 14 KB JRE available from `http://lejos.sourceforge.net/`. The mix of Java technologies includes speech recognition, synthesis, and image processing. For instance, a PC takes webcam snaps of a ball, the images are analyzed, and the resulting data guides the robot to the ball.

Ritter initially used a TWAIN interface, much like the approach in this chapter, but found it slow (he averaged 1.5 frames/second). He then moved to JMF, but used a slightly different technique than I've outlined. The capture device is accessed through a CaptureDeviceManager and MediaLocator object, but a PushBufferStream is connected to the device to make it act as a data source. A call to PushBufferStream.read() returns immediately with a Buffer object containing a captured image.

The drawback with this *push* technology is that read() returns the first picture from a stream of images generated by the camera, a stream that may start to be filled as soon as the camera is switched on. That means that read() may retrieve an image that's several seconds out of date. My JMF code utilizes *pull* technology, which snaps an image only when requested, so ensures that it's current.

The leJOS site is a good place to start finding out about Java LEGO robotics. leJOS was updated at the end of 2006 to support LEGO NXT, the exciting next generation of LEGO Mindstorms launched in September 2006.

Summary

This chapter compared two approaches for capturing images from a webcam: TWAIN (the Technology Without an Interesting Name), and JMF (Java Media Framework). My primary interest is speed, and JMF wins easily by being able to take a picture every 20 ms or so, nearly 200 times faster than similar code using TWAIN.

The JMF-based image capturing class, JMFCapture, is at the heart of the next chapter, which implements an "arm-waving" device for navigating through a 3D scene.

CHAPTER 10

■ ■ ■

Navigating a 3D Scene by Waving Your Arm

In this chapter, I explain how to navigate through a Java 3D world containing a checkerboard floor, a stormy background, a giant humanoid, and assorted ground cover, all mostly borrowed from the example in Chapter 7. The novelty here is that the navigation is achieved by the user moving and rotating his left arm; no keyboard or mouse manipulation is required. This "magic" is made possible by the user wearing a wrist strap containing three colored bands (blue, yellow, and red). Pictures of the strap are generated using the JMFCapture class from Chapter 9; a basic form of pattern recognition then finds the largest visible colored band on the strap. This information is converted into navigational commands for moving the camera around the world.

Using the Wrist Strap

The *wrist strap*, a rather fancy name for a sheet of paper with three colored rectangles printed on it, will be used for exploring the Java 3D scene shown in Figure 10-1.

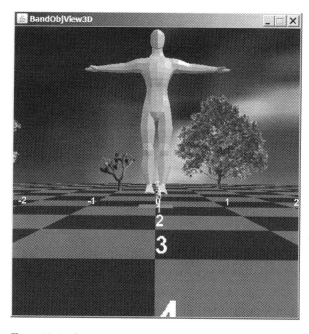

Figure 10-1. *The 3D world*

The wrist strap is shown in Figure 10-2.

Figure 10-2. *The wrist strap (blue, yellow, red)*

The strap is taped around the user's left wrist, as shown in Figure 10-3.

The blue band is the lower half of the visible strap, yellow is at the top, and red is hidden on the other side of the user's arm.

Figure 10-3. *Wrist strap in place*

A web camera is positioned close to the user on his left side and takes pictures of the wrist strap (Figure 10-3 is such a snap). A new picture is processed every 0.1 seconds on average.

The largest visible band and its position in the image are converted into navigation commands inside the 3D scene. The yellow band triggers forward movement, the blue band turns the user's viewpoint to the right and the red band turns it to the left. The rotations match the way the user's arm needs to turn so that the colored band is in front of the camera.

If the center of the band in the current image is far enough to the right, compared to the center of the band in the previously snapped image, forward motion is stopped. This corresponds to the user moving his arm backward.

Figure 10-4 shows the user from a short distance away. The webcam is on the left of the monitor, partially hidden by the user's left arm.

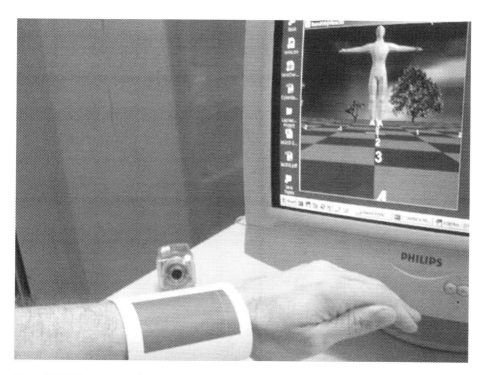

Figure 10-4. *The arm-waving user*

Image Processing

The application utilizes a simple form of pattern recognition, which can be divided into three broad steps: segmentation, feature extraction, and classification, as illustrated by Figure 10-5.

Figure 10-5. *Pattern-matching steps*

Segmentation involves finding interesting regions (also called *blobs*) within an image. A *membership function* is applied to each pixel to allocate it to a particular blob. The size of the blobs are increased by combining/merging smaller blobs together (a process called *blob-growing*). This is time-consuming since it may require multiple passes over the blobs. In the interest of processing speed and coding simplicity, my code doesn't combine blobs. *Feature extraction* measures the blobs in various ways, which may include counting the number of member pixels, the color spread, or the closeness of a blob to a prescribed shape. The resulting feature vectors are used to match blobs with higher-level objects (e.g., a blob is really a car), or to trigger actions (e.g., sound an alarm because a blob has a bomb-like shape).

The feature extraction and *classification* in my code is quite simple: a blob's (x, y) center is found, and the blob's color determined. This data is used to generate navigation commands for moving and rotating the camera in the 3D scene.

Image Processing Issues

Image processing is a complicated art whose success greatly depends on the design of the imaging task. In this case, processing is simplified by positioning the camera just a few inches from the user's wrist and only having to identify rectangular blobs of simple colors.

One complication is the background: the user's hand, arm, shirt, and head (as shown in Figure 10-3). For example, in early tests a red blob kept being detected even when the wrist strap's yellow band was right in front of the camera. This was triggered by the user's red shirt, which occupied a comparatively large part of the image.

Another problem is the lighting environment. Overhead lights can cause "leeching out" of color, caused by excessive reflection. This makes it more difficult to find the color bands.

Different webcams generate slightly different images. For instance, the camera attached to my second test machine produces a slightly greener image. This makes green a bad choice for a band color, since so much of the background has a similar hue.

Dealing with the Issues

Most image processing applications support a configuration/testing stage so the hardware and software parameters can be tweaked; I employ a similar strategy here.

In the next section, I describe the FindBands application, which analyzes webcam images without affecting a Java 3D scene. FindBands acts as a test rig for the image processing classes utilized in this chapter's main example, BandObjView3D. BandObjView3D converts the wrist strap data into navigational commands for exploring a 3D scene, and is described in the "Arm Navigation" section later in this chapter.

Finding the Bands

The FindBands application carries out the same image processing as BandObjView3D, but reports more about it. Figure 10-6 shows the FindBands window.

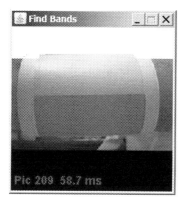

Figure 10-6. *FindBands in action*

FindBands doesn't use Java 3D; instead the images taken from the webcam are processed and displayed in rapid succession in the application window. Each image will usually have a large block of white pixels at the top; white indicates that the original pixels were *not* added to any blobs. The pixels in the white block that retain their color were added to blobs.

Figure 10-6 shows that blobs were created for parts of the red band in the wrist strap, a chunk of the yellow band, and parts of the user's left arm.

An important optimization in FindBands (and BandObjView3D) is that processing stops as soon as a large enough blob is created. The blob for the yellow band in Figure 10-6 grew to the necessary size (800 pixels) to stop the analysis, halting somewhere in the top part of the yellow band. The rest of the image wasn't examined, as indicated by the lack of white pixels.

This approach is obviously a little dangerous, since it may mean that larger blobs located farther down the image will be ignored. This problem can be alleviated to some degree by adjusting the large blob size constant; making the constant bigger means that more of the image will be examined.

The text in dark blue at the bottom of Figure 10-6 reads "Pic 209 58.7 ms." The second number is the average processing time for all the webcam images. In my tests, the average was always within the range of 50 to 80 ms, including 20 to 30 ms for grabbing the image from the camera (as noted in Chapter 9). This indicates that the actual analysis only takes around 40 ms. The first number in the text string is the total number of images displayed so far.

FindBands also prints translation and rotation command strings to standard output, such as the following:

```
    :
turn right
turn right
turn right
  forwards
  forwards
  forwards
No large blob
No large blob
  forwards
```

```
forwards
forwards
  :
```

Each line indicates how the large blob in the webcam image is classified (yellow is "forward," blue is "turn right," and red is "turn left").

The "No large blob" string means that no suitably large blob was found in the image. This failure is also observable in the FindBands window, which will render the image almost completely white; "No large blob" means that processing will continue right to the end of the picture.

FindBands Class Diagrams

The class diagrams for the FindBands application are given in Figure 10-7; only the public methods are shown.

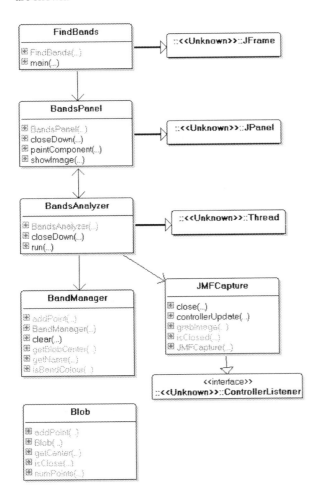

Figure 10-7. *FindBands class diagrams*

The FindBands and BandsPanel classes implement the application window and its drawing pane. Image processing is handled by BandsAnalyzer, which uses the JMFCapture class from Chapter 9 to take snaps (the class is unchanged from there, so I won't be discussing it again).

A BandManager object is created for each color band in the wrist strap (three altogether for red, yellow, and blue). Each BandManager stores a collection of Blob objects, one Blob object for each blob of color found in the image.

Image Processing Overview

All the image processing tasks in FindBands are carried out by BandsAnalyzer, which repeatedly takes a snap, analyzes it, and displays the result in BandsPanel.

Figure 10-8 shows the main stages in the processing of a single image:

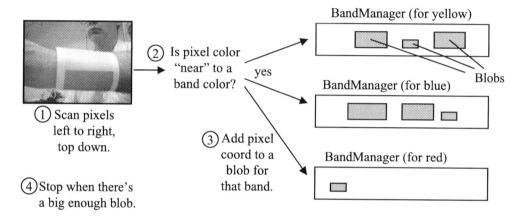

Figure 10-8. *Image processing in FindBands*

The image is examined in a left-to-right, top-down manner, a pixel at a time. If the pixel's color is close enough to one of the band colors, the pixel's coordinates are passed to the relevant BandManager object for that band. The Blob objects already stored in the BandManager are examined to see if any of them are near to the pixel's coordinate, in which case the coordinate is added to the closest blob. If no neighborhood blob is found, a new one is created, starting with the pixel coordinate.

Figure 10-8 corresponds to the "segmentation" stage in Figure 10-5. When a blob grows to a sufficiently large size, segmentation stops, and the blob is passed to the feature extraction stage. Only a single feature is calculated: the average center point for the blob. The center and the blob's color are used to generate translation and rotation command strings during the classification stage.

The Bands Analyzer

The analysis begins by creating three BandManager objects for the three band colors:

```
// globals
private static final int NUM_BANDS = 3;   // no. of bands colors

private static final Color BAND1 = new Color(205, 16, 80);   // red
private static final Color BAND2 = new Color(200, 200, 85); //yellow
private static final Color BAND3 = new Color(50, 150, 200);  // blue
```

```
private BandManager bandMans[];     // band managers for the bands


// in the constructor...
bandMans = new BandManager[NUM_BANDS];

// initialize the band managers; there should be NUM_BANDS of them
bandMans[0] = new BandManager("red1", BAND1);
bandMans[1] = new BandManager("yellow", BAND2);
bandMans[2] = new BandManager("blue", BAND3);
```

An obvious question is how did I decide on the values for the band colors, BAND1, BAND2, and BAND3? It was mostly a matter of trial and error, guided by a need for colors that are very different from each other and from the image background.

Green was tried and rejected since one of my webcams makes the background look slightly greenish, which confuses the analysis. Red is also problematic, since my skin appears quite red in some webcam pictures. This seems to be due to the fluorescent lights in my office, because the problem doesn't arise when the images are generated in natural light.

The RGB values for each band color come from examining a webcam snap (such as Figure 10-3) in a photo application (e.g., Adobe Photoshop, GIMP). Several values were measured at different places in a band to calculate an average.

I examined a webcam image so that environmental factors, such as camera quality and lighting conditions, were factored into the numbers. The downside is that when FindBands is employed with a different camera or on a different machine, the color constants usually need to be adjusted.

The Analysis Loop

BandAnalyzer performs its analysis in a loop in its run() method, processing a new webcam image in each iteration:

```
// globals
private static final int SNAP_INTERVAL = 120;
                            // ms; the time between snaps


private JMFCapture camera;   // JMF webcam object
private int imSize;          // size of captured image
private BandsPanel bandsPanel;
       // for displaying the snapped (and modified) images
private boolean running;


public void run()
{
  camera = new JMFCapture(imSize);    // initialize the webcam
  System.out.println("**Camera Ready**");

  long duration;
  BufferedImage im = null;
  running = true;

  while (running) {
    long startTime = System.currentTimeMillis();
    im = camera.grabImage();  // take a snap
    analyzeImage(im);         // analyze the image
    applyBigBlob();         // convert blob info to trans/rot cmds
```

```
      duration = System.currentTimeMillis() - startTime;

      if (im == null)
        System.out.println("Problem loading image");
      else
        bandsPanel.showImage(im, duration);   // show image in JPanel

      if (duration < SNAP_INTERVAL) {
        try {
          Thread.sleep(SNAP_INTERVAL-duration);
          // wait until interval has passed
        }
        catch (Exception ex) {}
      }
    }
  camera.close();      // close down the camera
}  // end of run()
```

The loop uses a JMFCapture object to take a picture every SNAP_INTERVAL ms. analyzeImage() implements the segmentation illustrated in Figure 10-8. applyBigBlob() uses the large blob (if it exists) to generate a translation or rotation command string.

The resulting image, which will have been modified by analyzeImage(), is displayed by bandsPanel (the JPanel) via a call to BandsPanel.showImage().

My value for SNAP_INTERVAL is based on the average processing time reported by FindBands (as shown in Figure 10-6). SNAP_INTERVAL is set at 120 ms to let the BandsAnalyzer thread sleep for a while at the end of each iteration (about 50 ms); this gives Java some time to render the image to the screen.

Analyzing an Image

analyzeImage()implements the segmentation shown in Figure 10-8:

```
// constant
private static final int WHITE = 0xffffff;   // white pixel color


private void analyzeImage(BufferedImage im)
{
  if (im == null) {
    System.out.println("Input image is null");
    return;
  }

  reset();    // reset the bands analyzer

  // extract pixels from the image into an array
  int imWidth = im.getWidth();
  int imHeight = im.getHeight();
  int [] pixels = new int[imWidth * imHeight];
  im.getRGB(0, 0, imWidth, imHeight, pixels, 0, imWidth);

  int xc = 0;      // store the current pixel coordinates
  int yc = 0;
  int bandId;      // id of band manager
  boolean madeBigBlob = false;
```

```
  // examine the pixels
  int i = 0;
  while((i < pixels.length) && (!madeBigBlob)) {
    bandId = isBandColour(pixels[i]);
    if (bandId != -1)    // pixel color is a band color
      madeBigBlob = addPointToBand(bandId, xc, yc);
    else       // pixel color isn't a band color
      pixels[i] = WHITE;   // clear the pixel to white

    // move to next coordinate in image
    xc++;
    if (xc == imWidth) {     // at end of row
      xc = 0;    // start next row
      yc++;
    }
    i++;
  }

  // update the image with the new pixels data
  im.setRGB(0, 0, imWidth, imHeight, pixels, 0, imWidth);
}  // end of analyzeImage()
```

The image is manipulated as a pixel array by calling BufferedImage.getRGB(). This makes it very simple to iterate over the pixels, using (xc, yc) to store the coordinates of the current pixel.

Each pixel is compared to the band colors with isBandColour():

```
private int isBandColour(int pixel)
{
  // extract RGB components from the current pixel as integers
  int redVal = (pixel>>16)&255;
  int greenVal = (pixel>>8)&255;
  int blueVal = pixel&255;

  for(int i=0; i < NUM_BANDS; i++)
    if (bandMans[i].isBandColour(redVal, greenVal, blueVal))
      return i;
  return -1;
}  // end of isBandColour()
```

The bit manipulation at the start of isBandColour() relies on the pixel using the ARGB format. This format is specified when JMFCapture creates a snap using the BufferedImage.TYPE_INT_RGB constant.

Each pixel is a 32-bit word, with 8 bits for each color component. The extracted RGB colors will have integer values between 0 and 255, with 255 meaning full-on.

The returned value from isBandColour() is the index of the relevant band manager in the bandMans[] array, or -1 if the pixel isn't close enough to any of the band colors.

Back in analyzeImage(), a pixel is added to a blob via the band manager for the matched color. Otherwise the pixel is switched to white to indicate its uselessness:

```
if (bandId != -1)    // pixel color is a band color
  madeBigBlob = addPointToBand(bandId, xc, yc);
else       // pixel color isn't a band color
  pixels[i] = WHITE;   // clear the pixel to white
```

addPointToBand() asks the relevant BandManager to store the pixel in a blob:

```
// globals for band manager and blob indices
private int bandIdx, blobIdx;


private boolean addPointToBand(int bandId, int x, int y)
{
  boolean madeBigBlob = false;

  if ((bandId < 0) || (bandId >= NUM_BANDS))
    System.out.println("Band ID out of range: " + bandId);
  else {
    int blobId = bandMans[bandId].addPoint(x,y);
    if (blobId != -1) {    // made a large-enough blob
      madeBigBlob = true;
      bandIdx = bandId;    // store indices for large blob
      blobIdx = blobId;
    }
  }
  return madeBigBlob;
}  // end of addPointToBand()
```

If the resulting blob has become large enough to halt the processing, BandManager.addPoint() returns its index and the indices of the band manager and blob are recorded in bandIdx and blobIdx. These indices allow the blob to be quickly accessed later by applyBigBlob().

Using the Large Blob

If analyzeImage() has found a large blob, the two global indices, bandIdx and blobIdx, will have values. These are utilized in applyBigBlob() to extract the relevant band and blob features, and then to generate translation and rotation command strings:

```
// global
private Point prevCenterPt = null;
        // center of blob in previous image


private void applyBigBlob()
{
  if (bandIdx != -1) {  // there is a large blob
    BandManager bm = bandMans[bandIdx];
    Point pt = bm.getBlobCenter(blobIdx);    // blob's center pt

    if (prevCenterPt != null) {    // there is a previous center point
      rotateView( bm.getName() );
      translateView(pt, prevCenterPt);
    }
    prevCenterPt = pt;  // save for next analysis
  }
  else
    System.out.println("No large blob");
}  // end of applyBigBlob()
```

The previous image's blob center (prevCenterPt) is compared with the current center in translateView() in order to determine a translation.

From Color to Rotation

The color name is mapped to a left (or right) rotation string. In BandObjView3D, this method will call navigation code in the Java 3D scene, but here it just prints a string:

```
private void rotateView(String bmName)
{
  if (bmName.equals("red1"))
    System.out.println("turn left");
  else if (bmName.equals("blue"))
    System.out.println("turn right");
}
```

From Points to Translation

The x-axis difference between the current center point and the one for the previous image is used to generate a translation string:

```
// globals
// min. distance for blob center to move to trigger a translation
private static final int MIN_MOVE_DIST = 10;

private boolean movingFwd;


private void translateView(Point currPt, Point prevPt)
{
  int xChg = currPt.x - prevPt.x;

  if (xChg < -MIN_MOVE_DIST)
    movingFwd = true;
  else if (xChg > (MIN_MOVE_DIST*2))
    // stopping requires more of a change
    movingFwd = false;

  if (movingFwd)
    System.out.println("  forwards");
}  // end of translateView()
```

When the user starts traveling forward in the 3D world, he will keep going until he requests a stop. This is implemented by setting a movingFwd boolean to true when the wrist strap is moved forward. It's only set to false when the strap is moved backward by a large amount. The value for MIN_MOVE_DIST was arrived at by a process of trial and error and will need to be adjusted depending on the distance of the camera from the user's arm.

In this code, the movingFwd boolean only triggers a System.out.println() call, but in BandsObjView3D it will translate the user's viewing position.

One tricky aspect of the mapping is the assumption that the movement of a blob to the left in the image means that the user has moved his arm forward. This is not the case for some webcams that flip their images; in that case, a leftward movement occurs when the user moves his arm backward. This is easily corrected by switching the if-tests in translateView().

I don't use the y coordinates of the center points, partly because I don't need to, and also because deliberate vertical change is hard to differentiate from random arm movement.

The Band Manager

A BandManager object manages all the blobs created for a given band color. It offers isBandColour() to check whether a pixel is close to the band manager's color. addPoint() adds a pixel coordinate to a blob and reports whether a large enough blob has been made. BandManager also has methods to return the band color and a given blob's center point.

BandManager is initialized with a name and the color it represents and creates an empty ArrayList for future Blob objects:

```
// globals
private String bandName;

// RGB components for this band manager's color
private int redCol, greenCol, blueCol;

private ArrayList<Blob> blobs;
private int currBlobIdx;  // index of last blob that was updated


public BandManager(String nm, Color c)
{
  bandName = nm;

  redCol = c.getRed();
  greenCol = c.getGreen();
  blueCol = c.getBlue();

  blobs = new ArrayList<Blob>();
  currBlobIdx = -1;
}  // end of BandManager()
```

isBandColour() calculates the Euclidean distance between the pixel's color and the band color, and tests whether it is less than a certain amount:

```
// max distance*distance to the band color
private static final int MAX_DIST2 = 5000;


public boolean isBandColour(int r, int g, int b)
/* is (r,g,b) close enough to the band color? */
{
  int redDiff = r - redCol;
  int greenDiff = g - greenCol;
  int blueDiff = b - blueCol;

  return (((redDiff * redDiff) +
          (greenDiff * greenDiff) +
          (blueDiff * blueDiff)) < MAX_DIST2);
}  // end of isBlobColour()
```

isBandColour() actually calculates the *square* of the distance between the colors, skipping the expensive square root operation.

The MAX_DIST2 value was decided on by experimentation: the square root of MAX_DIST2 is around 71, or about 24 for each color component (a component's value can range between 0 and 255).

Adding a pixel to a blob involves first cycling though the existing blobs to check whether the pixel is close to one of them. findCloseBlob() returns the index of the blob, or -1 if nothing suitable is found. The index is employed in a Blob.addPoint() call to add the pixel's coordinates to the right blob:

```
// globals
private int currBlobIdx;  // index of last blob that was updated

public int addPoint(int x, int y)
{
  int largeIdx = -1;   // index of Blob with enough points

  int blobIndex = findCloseBlob(x,y);
  if (blobIndex != -1) {   // found a blob close to (x,y)
    Blob b = blobs.get(blobIndex);
    boolean isLarge = b.addPoint(x,y);
    currBlobIdx = blobIndex;
    if (isLarge)   // created a large enough blob
      largeIdx = blobIndex;
  }
  else {   // no close blob, so create a new one
    Blob b = new Blob();
    b.addPoint(x,y);
    blobs.add(b);
    currBlobIdx = blobs.size() - 1;
  }
  return largeIdx;
}  // end of addPoint()
```

currBlobIdx is used to record the ArrayList index position of the blob that was just updated.

If the blob has grown sufficiently large, addPoint() returns its index, causing BandAnalyzer to cut short any further image processing.

findCloseBlob() first checks whether the blob that was previously updated can be updated again, before it falls back to cycling through the blobs. The hope is that successive pixels in an image often end up joining the same blob:

```
private int findCloseBlob(int x, int y)
/* find a blob that's close to (x,y) */
{
  Blob blob;

  // try current blob first
  if (currBlobIdx != -1) {
    blob = blobs.get(currBlobIdx);
    if (blob.isClose(x,y))
      return currBlobIdx;
  }

  // otherwise try the others
  for(int i=0; i < blobs.size(); i++) {
    if (i != currBlobIdx) {
      blob = blobs.get(i);
      if (blob.isClose(x,y))
        return i;
    }
  }
  return -1;   // didn't find a close blob
}  // end of findCloseBlob()
```

Representing a Blob

A blob is a collection of pixel coordinates that are close to each other in the image and have a similar color.

A blob facilitates feature extraction by collecting related image data together in one place. FindBands only utilizes a single blob *feature*, the blob's center, which is calculated by dividing the sums of the blob's x and y coordinates by the number of those coordinates:

```
// globals
private ArrayList<Point> points;
private int numPoints;
private int xSum, ySum;    // sums of (x,y) coords


public Blob()
{  points = new ArrayList<Points>();
   numPoints = 0;
   xSum = 0; ySum = 0;
} // end of Blob()
```

A pixel's proximity to a blob is determined by isClose():

```
// constant
private static final int PROXIMITY = 4;


public boolean isClose(int x, int y)
/* is (x,y) close to a point in the blob? */
{
  Point p;
  for(int i=0; i < numPoints; i++) {
    p = points.get(i);
    if ((Math.abs(x - p.x) < PROXIMITY) &&
        (Math.abs(y - p.y) < PROXIMITY))
      return true;
  }
  return false;
}  // end of isClose()
```

PROXIMITY is another "magic" number, decided on by testing. The larger the value, the easier it is for a point to join the blob.

Adding a pixel coordinate to the blob involves adding a Point object to the blob's ArrayList. addPoint() also checks whether the blob has enough points to be classified as large:

```
// no. of points necessary to make a large blob
private static final int LARGE_BLOB_SIZE = 800;


public boolean addPoint(int x, int y)
/* add (x,y) to the blob's points, and report if the
   blob is now 'large' */
{
  points.add( new Point(x,y) );
  numPoints++;
  xSum += x; ySum += y;
  return (numPoints > LARGE_BLOB_SIZE);
}  // end of addPoint()
```

Increasing the LARGE_BLOB_SIZE value will lengthen the image processing time, since more points will need to be added to the blobs before one grows sufficiently large. A larger LARGE_BLOB_SIZE makes it less certain that a blob will attain the necessary size, increasing the chance of the image classification failing. However, if a blob is found, it's more likely to be the largest one in the image.

Arm Navigation

The main purpose of FindBands is to help test the image processing part of the code without Java 3D complicating things. FindBands reports details about the analysis that can be used to fine-tune the hardware, environment, and software. When everything is working satisfactorily, the move to BandObjView3D is relatively simple.

BandObjView3D is a combination of the ObjView3D example from Chapter 7 and FindBands. This is evident in its class diagrams, shown in Figure 10-9. To reduce clutter, I've left out private methods and data and superclasses and interfaces.

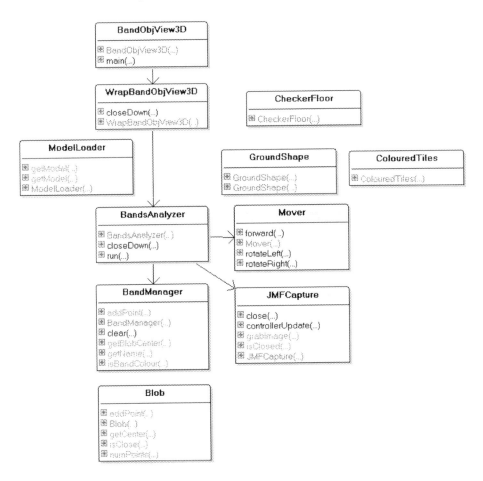

Figure 10-9. *Class diagrams for BandObjView3D*

BandObjView3D is the application JFrame and does little more than create the WrapBandObjView3D JPanel for rendering the 3D scene.

WrapBandObjView3D is similar to WrapObjView3D in ObjView3D: it creates a checkerboard floor with a red center square and labeled XZ axes, using the CheckerFloor and ColouredTiles classes.

A humanoid model and ground shapes are standing on the floor; the model is loaded by the ModelLoader class, and the ground shapes are loaded with GroundShape. The lighting and background are also done by WrapBandObjView3D.

WrapBandObjView3D employs a new Mover class to affect the user's viewpoint; in WrapObjView3D, movement is achieved with my KeyBehavior class.

BandsAnalyzer performs almost the same image analysis as in FindBands, using BandManager, Blob, and JMFCapture unchanged. BandsAnalyzer differs in that it calls translation and rotation methods in Mover rather than rendering images to a JPanel and printing command strings to standard output.

I won't discuss BandManager, Blob, and JMFCapture again, since they're the same as before. I'll also skip most of the 3D scene creation code in WrapBandObjView3D, since it's been borrowed without modification from ObjView3D in Chapter 7.

I'll concentrate on explaining two features: how Mover affects the user's 3D viewpoint, and how BandsAnalyzer communicates with Mover.

Creating the 3D Scene

WrapBandObjView3D contains the following lines in its constructor:

```
// global
private BandsAnalyzer ba;    // to analyze the user's arm movements


// in the constructor...
createSceneGraph();
Mover mover = createMover();
su.addBranchGraph(sceneBG);

ba = new BandsAnalyzer(mover);
ba.start();    // start responding to user arm movements
```

createSceneGraph() initializes most parts of the 3D scene, including its lighting, sky, floor, and the floating sphere.

createMover() creates a Mover object:

```
private Mover createMover()
{
  ViewingPlatform vp = su.getViewingPlatform();
  TransformGroup targetTG = vp.getViewPlatformTransform();
        // viewer transform group

  return new Mover(targetTG);
     /* Mover translates/rotates the user's viewpoint
        depending on the user's arm movements */
}  // end of createMover()
```

The targetTG reference passed to Mover is the user's viewing platform TransformGroup (TG), a node in the view branch part of the application's scene graph (see Figure 10-10). targetTG controls the movement of the user's viewpoint around the 3D scene.

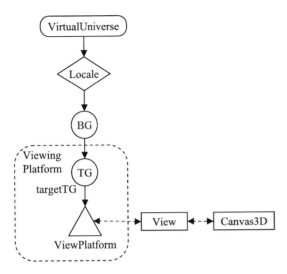

Figure 10-10. *The view branch graph*

KeyBehavior in the original ObjView3D application uses targetTG as well, but gains access to it by being a subclass of Java 3D's ViewPlatformBehavior.

Back in WrapBandObjView3D's constructor, the Mover reference is passed to BandsAnalyzer. This allows BandsAnalyzer to call Mover's translation and rotation methods, which affect the targetTG node.

Moving the User's Viewpoint

Mover only permits the viewpoint to move forward and to rotate left or right. The meaning of *forward* depends on the viewpoint's current orientation.

The constructor specifies a starting position for the viewpoint by calling doMove():

```
// global
private TransformGroup targetTG;   // the viewpoint TG

public Mover(TransformGroup vTG)
{ targetTG = vTG;
  doMove( new Vector3d(0, 0.5, 5.0) );   // starting position
}
```

doMove() multiplies the translation vector to the Transform3D component of the viewpoint. This "adds" the translation to the viewpoint position:

```
// globals for repeated calculations
private Transform3D t3d = new Transform3D();
private Transform3D toMove = new Transform3D();


private void doMove(Vector3d theMove)
{ targetTG.getTransform(t3d);
  toMove.setTranslation(theMove);
  t3d.mul(toMove);
  targetTG.setTransform(t3d);
} // end of doMove()
```

The initial default position of the user's viewpoint is at (0, 0, 0), with forward being along the negative z-axis. The call to doMove() moves the viewpoint to (0, 0.5, 5) and keeps it facing along the negative z-axis.

Translating

The public face of moving forward is the forward() method, which is called by BandsAnalyzer:

```
// forward movement constants
private static final double MOVE_STEP = 0.2;
private static final Vector3d FWD = new Vector3d(0,0,-MOVE_STEP);

public void forward()
{   doMove(FWD);   }
```

The translation is along the negative z-axis, which always means *forward*, even after the viewpoint has been rotated.

Rotating

The public face of rotation is represented by two methods:

```
private static final double ROT_AMT = Math.PI / 36.0;    // 5 degrees

public void rotateLeft()
{   rotateY(ROT_AMT);   }

public void rotateRight()
{   rotateY(-ROT_AMT);   }
```

rotateY() multiplies the rotation (in radians) to the Transform3D component of the viewpoint TransformGroup, which effectively "adds" the rotation to the old orientation:

```
// global for repeated calculations
private Transform3D toRot = new Transform3D();

private void rotateY(double radians)
{ targetTG.getTransform(t3d);
  toRot.rotY(radians);
  t3d.mul(toRot);
  targetTG.setTransform(t3d);
}
```

From Analysis to Action

The BandsAnalyzer class is largely unchanged from its FindBands version, since the image processing involving BandManager, Blob, and JMFCapture is the same. However, rotateView() and translateView() are different:

```
// global
private Mover mover;      // for moving the 3D viewpoint (camera)


private void rotateView(String bmName)
// blob color --> rotation
{
  if (bmName.equals("red1"))
```

```
      mover.rotateLeft();
    else if (bmName.equals("blue"))
      mover.rotateRight();
}

private void translateView(Point currPt, Point prevPt)
/* The change in the x values of the current center point
   (currPt) and the previous center point (prevPt) triggers
   a viewpoint translation forward.
*/
{ int xChg = currPt.x - prevPt.x;

  if (xChg < -MIN_MOVE_DIST)
    movingFwd = true;
  else if (xChg > (MIN_MOVE_DIST*2))
    movingFwd = false;

  if (movingFwd)
    mover.forward();
}  // end of translateView()
```

The changes involve replacing the System.out.println() calls in the FindBands versions by calls to Mover.

Other Approaches

Another example of this approach can be found in the online Chapter 28.85, "Waving a Magic Wand," at my Killer Game Programming in Java web site (http://fivedots.coe.psu.ac.th/~ad/jg). The user waves a magic wand in front of the webcam, and an onscreen wand moves in a corresponding manner and emits magic bolts as an added bonus. The image processing employs a variant of the BandsAnalyzer class and captures images using JMFCapture.

I've implemented my own very simple image-processing operations in these examples, based around region (blob) building. The code uses basic Java 2D features for accessing the internals of a BufferedImage (e.g., BufferedImage.getRGB()). More serious programming probably calls for more advanced APIs, focusing specifically on image analysis.

JAI

Java Advanced Imaging (JAI) offers extended image processing capabilities beyond those found in Java 2D (https://jai.dev.java.net/). For example, geometric operations include translation, rotation, scaling, shearing, and transposition and warping. Pixel-based operations utilize lookup tables and rescaling equations but can be applied to multiple sources, then combined to get a single outcome. Modifications can be restricted to regions in the source, statistical operations are available (e.g., mean and median), and frequency domains can be employed.

Sun offers an online book on JAI (dating from 1999) at http://java.sun.com/products/java-media/jai/forDevelopers/jai1_0_1guide-unc/JAITOC.fm.html. Image analysis is covered in Chapter 9.

ImageJ

For complex image processing, I like ImageJ (`http://rsb.info.nih.gov/ij/`), which can be utilized either as a stand-alone application or as an image processing library.

ImageJ supports standard image processing functions, such as contrast manipulation, sharpening, smoothing, edge detection, and median filtering. It also offers geometric transformations, such as scaling, rotation, and flips.

Its analysis capabilities include the calculation of area and pixel value statistics for user-defined selections, and it can create density histograms and line profile plots.

ImageJ can be easily extended with macros and plug-ins; there are hundreds available at the ImageJ web site.

Image Processing Books

Two books on image processing, using Java as an implementation language include *Digital Image Processing: A Practical Introduction Using Java* by Nick Efford (Addison Wesley, 2000) and *Image Processing in Java* by Douglas A. Lyon (Prentice Hall, 1999).

Both texts use the standard Java libraries (e.g., Java 2D); they don't utilize JAI or ImageJ.

Summary

The JMFCapture class of Chapter 9 for grabbing pictures from a webcam is the basis of the two image processing examples described in this chapter.

The FindBands application demonstrates a basic form of pattern recognition (segmentation, feature extraction, and classification) that finds the largest visible colored band on a wrist strap.

FindBands acts as a test rig for the image processing classes (BandsAnalyzer, BandManager, and Blob) utilized in BandObjView3D (the chapter's second example). BandObjView3D converts wrist strap movements into navigational commands for exploring the Java 3D world described in Chapter 7.

CHAPTER 11

Building a Gamepad Controller with JInput

Playing PC games with a keyboard and mouse can sometimes feel like playing tennis in a tuxedo—entirely possible but not quite right. Wouldn't it be so much cooler to pull out that gamepad, joystick, or steering wheel, plug it in, and play games the way that nature intended? It's not that difficult, as the next two chapters will show. I start by giving some background on JInput (https://jinput.dev.java.net/), an open source API for game controller discovery and polled input.

I explain how to program with JInput by describing three small applications that display information about the input devices attached to your PC. I also develop a GamePadController class that offers a simplified interface to my gamepad. GamePadController is utilized in two examples: a Swing application called GamePadViewer in this chapter, and a revised version of Arms3D (the articulated arms example from Chapter 4) in the next chapter.

Arms3D illustrates how a gamepad can enhance the user's playing experience, replacing a confusing mix of keys with more intuitive buttons and sticks. The gamepad also allows multiple inputs to be processed at once, so that different parts of the grabber's arms can rotate and move at the same time.

JInput

JInput is a cross-platform API for the discovery and polling of input devices, ranging from the familiar (keyboard, mouse) to more fun varieties (joysticks, gamepads).

The range of supported devices depends on the underlying OS. On Windows, JInput employs DirectInput; on Linux it relies on /dev/input/event* device nodes, and there's a Mac OS X version as well. Posts to the JInput forum at Java Games Forums (http://www.javagaming.org/forums/index.php?board=27.0) suggest that JInput runs well on Windows and Linux but is less fully implemented on OS X. I've only tested my code on Windows and would welcome comments by readers using other platforms.

JInput first appeared in 2003, as part of a collection of open source technologies (JOGL, JOAL, JInput) initiated by the Game Technologies Group at Sun Microsystems. JInput was developed by members of the JSR 134 expert group (a group concerned with Java gaming).

I'm using the May 2006 Windows version (the most recent as of January 2007), which I downloaded as jinput_windows_20060514.zip from https://jinput.dev.java.net/. It came from the Win32 folder under the Documents & Files menu item.

Recent JInput releases differ from the popular version 1.1 from 2004. In particular, the old Axis class has been renamed to Component, and the component Identifier classes have been reorganized and expanded. Unfortunately, this means that older JInput examples, notably those in the excellent tutorial by Robert Schuster at https://freefodder.dev.java.net/tutorial/jinputTutorialOne.html, won't work without some modifications.

If you're looking for up-to-the-minute information, visit the JInput forum at `http://www.javagaming.org/forums/index.php?board=27.0`. The current JInput maintainer is an active member and helped me considerably while I was writing the first draft of this chapter.

The Gamepad and Windows

A lot of heartaches can be avoided by choosing your game-playing device with care. There are two points to look out for: first, the device should definitely support the OS that you're using. This usually isn't an issue with Windows, but you may need to do some research for Linux or Mac OS X. The other good idea, based on comments in the JInput forum, is to choose a device that uses a USB connector.

My gamepad is of Chinese origin, without a brand name. Top and front views of the device are shown in Figures 11-1 and 11-2.

Figure 11-1. *Top view of the gamepad*   **Figure 11-2.** *Front view of the gamepad*

It offers a direction pad (D-Pad) on the left, two analog sticks in the center, and 12 buttons. The ANALOG button located between the sticks in Figure 11-1 switches the sticks on and off. Functionally, the device is very similar to the popular Logitech Dual Action Gamepad.

Eagle-eyed readers may note that there only seem to be ten buttons (excluding the ANALOG button). The other two are built into the analog sticks, which can be pressed down to act as buttons.

When Windows detects a new input device it either installs one of its own device drivers or requests one from you. After this process is finished, it's important to calibrate and test the device. This is done through the Game Controllers application accessible through the Control Panel in Windows XP.

Figure 11-3 shows part of the Game Controllers main window.

Figure 11-3. *Part of the game controllers window*

Figure 11-3 gives the first indication of how Windows "sees" the gamepad: as a USB Vibration Joystick, which isn't particularly informative. More details are available via the Properties button, which leads to testing and calibration windows for the device.

It's important that the gamepad be calibrated so that Windows correctly interprets its inputs. Poor calibration will manifest itself at the JInput level as values that are incorrectly rounded or have the wrong sign.

Part of the Game Controllers Function Test window is shown in Figure 11-4.

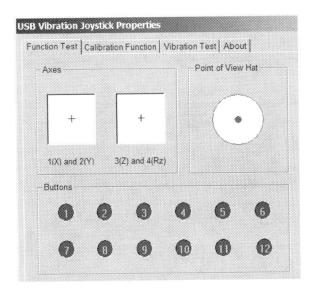

Figure 11-4. *Testing the gamepad*

When the ANALOG button is on, the gamepad's two analog sticks affect the crosshairs inside the axes squares; the D-Pad draws an arrow inside the right-hand circle; and button presses light up the radio boxes. When the ANALOG button is off, stick movement is ignored, and the D-Pad affects the crosshair in the left-hand square.

When the analog sticks are active, the crosshairs can be moved anywhere in their boxes. The position of each crosshair is specified using two axes: the x- and y- axes of the left stick are labeled as X and Y, while the corresponding axes for the right stick are called Z and Rz.

For the D-Pad, it's only possible to draw an arrow in eight compass positions around the edge of the circle. The test window calls the D-Pad a *point of view hat* (POV hat), terminology that I'll employ from now on.

This gamepad also has a vibration, or *rumbler*, feature, which is testable via a separate Vibration Test window. Rumbling can be switched on for the left or right sides of the pad, or both sides at once.

After you've finished calibration and testing, you can be confident that the gamepad is recognized by the OS, and you'll also have a good idea about your gamepad's input capabilities. My no-name gamepad has two analog sticks, a POV hat, 12 buttons, and rumbler capability.

Another important check is to find out whether DirectX can see your device, since JInput uses DirectX under Windows. An easy way of doing this is with the dxdiag utility, Windows' DirectX diagnostic tool, which can be started via Windows' Run menu item. Figure 11-5 shows part of its Input tab, which reports what devices can be communicated with by DirectInput.

DirectInput Devices					
Device Name	Status	Controller ID	Vendor ID	Product ID	Force Feedback Driver
Mouse	Attached	n/a	n/a	n/a	n/a
Keyboard	Attached	n/a	n/a	n/a	n/a
USB Vibration Joystick	Attached	0	0x0079	0x0006	C:\WINDOWS\USB Vibration\7906\EZFRD32.dll

Figure 11-5. *Part of the dxdiag input tab*

My gamepad is listed, so both Windows and DirectX are happy. Now it's time to try JInput.

Installing and Testing JInput

As I mentioned earlier, I downloaded jinput_windows_20060514.zip from
`https://jinput.dev.java.net/`. It came from the Win32 folder under the Documents & Files menu
item. It contains three files: jinput-windows.jar (the high-level Java part of the API), jinput-dx8.dll,
and jinput-raw.dll (the OS-level parts).

I extracted the files and placed them in their own folder in a convenient location; I chose
d:\jinput\bin (see Figure 11-6).

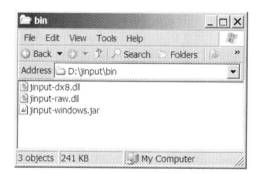

Figure 11-6. *JInput libraries folder*

Two other essential downloads from `https://jinput.dev.java.net/` are the API documentation and the tests JAR, both available from the Core folder under the Documents & Files menu item.

The tests JAR, jinput-tests-20060514.jar, contains three test applications, ControllerReadTest,
ControllerTextTest, and RumbleTest. Calling them can be a bit tricky since the java command line
must include classpath and library path settings for the JInput software in d:\jinput\bin and must
correctly name the required application inside the tests JAR.

The applications are called like so:

```
java -cp d:\jinput\bin\jinput-windows.jar;.
    -Djava.library.path="d:\jinput\bin"
        net.java.games.input.test.ControllerReadTest

java -cp d:\jinput\bin\jinput-windows.jar;.
    -Djava.library.path="d:\jinput\bin"
        net.java.games.input.test.ControllerTextTest

java -cp d:\jinput\bin\jinput-windows.jar;.
    -Djava.library.path="d:\jinput\bin"
        net.java.games.input.test.RumbleTest
```

Of course, the directory paths will depend on where you placed the JInput library files.

Typing these long lines is rather tiring, so I packaged the command line inside runTest.bat. It contains the following:

```
java -cp d:\jinput\bin\jinput-windows.jar;.
    -Djava.library.path="d:\jinput\bin"
        net.java.games.input.test.%1
```

This means that the program calls become these:

```
runTest ControllerReadTest
```

```
runTest ControllerTextTest
```

```
runTest RumbleTest
```

Examining the Input Devices

ControllerReadTest opens a window for each input device (controller) it detects and reports the current status of the components. A component is a *widget* on the device that generates input, such as a button, stick axis, or hat key.

On my machine, ControllerReadTest opens three subwindows—for the keyboard, the mouse, and the gamepad. Figure 11-7 shows the window for the gamepad.

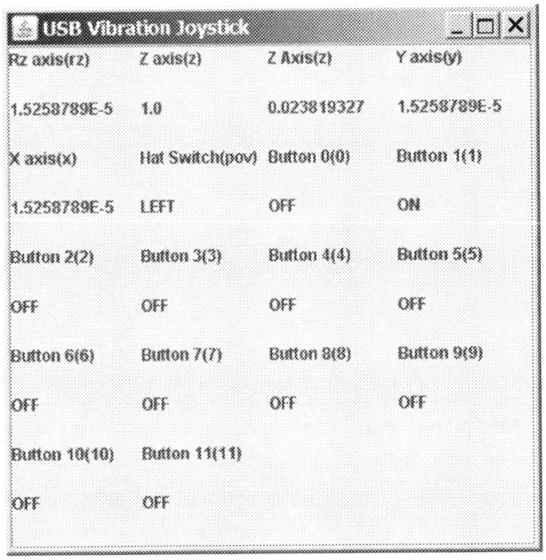

Rz axis(rz)	Z axis(z)	Z Axis(z)	Y axis(y)
1.5258789E-5	1.0	0.023819327	1.5258789E-5
X axis(x)	Hat Switch(pov)	Button 0(0)	Button 1(1)
1.5258789E-5	LEFT	OFF	ON
Button 2(2)	Button 3(3)	Button 4(4)	Button 5(5)
OFF	OFF	OFF	OFF
Button 6(6)	Button 7(7)	Button 8(8)	Button 9(9)
OFF	OFF	OFF	OFF
Button 10(10)	Button 11(11)		
OFF	OFF		

Figure 11-7. *The gamepad window in ControllerReadTest*

The window is updated as I press the sticks, hat, and buttons. Each component *name* in the window is followed by a component *identifier* in brackets. Below each name is the component's current *status*. For example, the POV hat appears in row 3, column 2 of the window, and is given the name Hat Switch, the identifier POV, and has the status LEFT.

The use of identifiers isn't always consistent; a close look at Figure 11-7 shows that the z identifier is used in row 1, column 2, and in row 1, column 3.

Even worse, the gamepad itself may be physically labeled in a different way. For instance, my gamepad has the numbers 1 through 12 printed next to its buttons, but Figure 11-7 shows that these are referred to with the identifiers 0 through 11 by JInput.

When the image in Figure 11-7 was generated, I was pressing the POV hat on the left side, holding down the button labeled "2," and pushing the right-hand stick directly to the right. That's shown as a LEFT value for "Hat Switch" (pov), ON for "Button 1" (1), and a 1.0 value for the "Z axis" (z) components.

Experimenting with the sticks, hat, and buttons inside ControllerReadTest is a great way of finding out what information is delivered by JInput. The window also reveals the somewhat arcane mapping between the gamepad's physical labeling and the names and identifiers assigned to the components internally.

The mystery of the two uses of the z identifier in row 1, column 2, and row 1, column 3 was solved by testing the gamepad. When the ANALOG button is switched on, the z identifier in row 1, column 3 responds in the same way as the x-axis for the left stick (row 3, column 1), so it is superfluous. The z identifier in row 1, column 2 is used with the right-hand stick, so is what I need in my code.

Figure 11-8 illustrates the value ranges generated by the left and right sticks. The left stick produces floats between 1.0 and -1.0 for the x- and y- axes, and the right stick produces similar values for the z- and rz- axes. (The axis names come from the sticks' component identifiers).

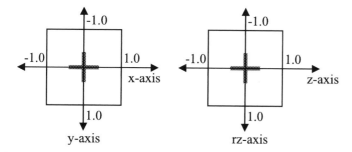

Figure 11-8. *Axes values for the left and right analog sticks*

One surprising aspect of Figure 11-8 is that the y- and rz- axes are reversed from their usual orientations. Also, when a stick isn't being used, the axes' values are *close* to 0.0f, but not exactly zero (as shown in Figure 11-7).

Hat positions are reported as float constants, as summarized by Figure 11-9.

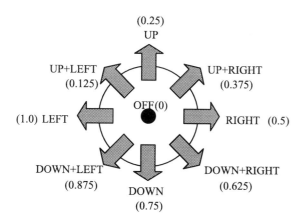

Figure 11-9. *Hat constants*

The hat consists of four buttons positioned on its left, right, top and bottom. They correspond to the constants LEFT, RIGHT, UP, and DOWN; the other constants are generated by holding down adjacent buttons. For example, DOWN+LEFT is reported when the LEFT and DOWN buttons are pressed at the same time.

The float values for these constants are given in the Component.POV class documentation.

The Other JInput Test Applications

Aside from ControllerReadTest, there are two other test applications in jinput-tests-20060514.jar: ControllerTextTest and RumblerTest.

ControllerTextTest writes details about every device to standard output: it's a very long list, since it includes information about every key on the keyboard. Consequently, it's a good idea to redirect the output into a text file:

```
runTest ControllerTextTest > devices.txt
```

The following are the details supplied about my gamepad:

```
USB Vibration Joystick
Type: Stick
Component Count: 18
Component 0: Rz axis
    Identifier: rz
    ComponentType: Absolute Analog
Component 1: Z axis
    Identifier: z
    ComponentType: Absolute Analog
Component 2: Z Axis
    Identifier: z
    ComponentType: Absolute Analog
Component 3: Y axis
    Identifier: y
    ComponentType: Absolute Analog
Component 4: X axis
    Identifier: x
    ComponentType: Absolute Analog
Component 5: Hat Switch
    Identifier: pov
    ComponentType: Absolute Digital
Component 6: Button 0
    Identifier: 0
    ComponentType: Absolute Digital
Component 7: Button 1
    Identifier: 1
    ComponentType: Absolute Digital
Component 8: Button 2
    Identifier: 2
    ComponentType: Absolute Digital
Component 9: Button 3
    Identifier: 3
    ComponentType: Absolute Digital
Component 10: Button 4
    Identifier: 4
    ComponentType: Absolute Digital
```

```
Component 11: Button 5
    Identifier: 5
    ComponentType: Absolute Digital
Component 12: Button 6
    Identifier: 6
    ComponentType: Absolute Digital
Component 13: Button 7
    Identifier: 7
    ComponentType: Absolute Digital
Component 14: Button 8
    Identifier: 8
    ComponentType: Absolute Digital
Component 15: Button 9
    Identifier: 9
    ComponentType: Absolute Digital
Component 16: Button 10
    Identifier: 10
    ComponentType: Absolute Digital
Component 17: Button 11
    Identifier: 11
    ComponentType: Absolute Digital
```

The first two lines give the device name and type. Rather strangely, JInput believes the gamepad is a joystick (a *stick*), which is actually quite common. Each component has an index number—for instance, the x-axis is component 4. The component names and identifiers are the same as those shown by ControllerReadTest in Figure 11-7.

I explain the ComponentType information in the "Examining a Component" section.

The RumbleTest application checks every device to see if it can generate force feedback.

For my gamepad, it reports "Found 5 rumblers," and progresses to test each one. It's rather hard to tell the differences between them, but the first rumbler setting seems to activate the left rumbler, the second setting controls the right rumbler, and the other three trigger both rumblers together.

Three JInput Applications

I cover the basics of JInput programming by describing three applications:

- *ListControllers*: It prints a list of all the detected input devices (controllers).

- *ControllerDetails*: It outputs a list of all of the components that form part of a specified controller.

- *TestController*: This displays the numbers generated by a given component as the user manipulates it.

These examples all read input from the command line and report to standard output, which allows me to put off the issue of integrating Swing and JInput until later in the chapter.

The compilation and execution of these programs is carried out with the help of two batch files that add in the necessary classpath and library path settings. compileJI.bat contains the following:

```
javac -classpath d:\jinput\bin\jinput-windows.jar;. %1
```

runJI.bat holds the following:

```
java -cp d:\jinput\bin\jinput-windows.jar;.
    -Djava.library.path="d:\jinput\bin" %1 %2 %3
```

The %1, %2, and %3 arguments allow at most three arguments to the java call. The following examples only use one argument when calling compileJI.bat and runJI.bat:

```
compileJI ListControllers.java
runJI ListControllers
```

Listing the Controllers

On my test machine, ListControllers produces the following output:

```
> runJI ListControllers
Executing ListControllers with JInput...
JInput version: 2.0.0-b01
0. Mouse, Mouse
1. Keyboard, Keyboard
2. USB Vibration Joystick, Stick
```

Each controller is assigned an index number, and the controller's name and type are listed. A controller's index number will be used as input to ControllerDetails and TestController later on, so it's worth noting that the gamepad is controller number 2.

ListControllers main() method obtains an array of controllers and prints their names and types:

```
public static void main(String[] args)
{
  System.out.println("JInput version: " + Version.getVersion());

  ControllerEnvironment ce =
        ControllerEnvironment.getDefaultEnvironment();
  Controller[] cs = ce.getControllers();

  // print the name and type of each controller
  for (int i = 0; i < cs.length; i++)
    System.out.println(i + ". " +
        cs[i].getName() + ", " + cs[i].getType() );
} // end of main()
```

It uses JInput's ControllerEnvironment class to ask the OS about its input devices, which are retrieved as an array of Controller objects.

Viewing Controller Details

The ControllerDetails application prints components and rumblers information for a specified controller. The data can be written to a text file or sent to the screen.

ControllerDetails is based on a similar application by Robert Schuster in his JInput tutorial at https://freefodder.dev.java.net/tutorial/jinputTutorialOne.html.

ListControllers labels the gamepad as controller number 2, so its information is obtained like so:

```
> runJI ControllerDetails 2
Executing ControllerDetails with JInput...
Details for: USB Vibration Joystick, Stick, Unknown
Components: (18)
0. Rz axis, rz, absolute, analog, 0.0
```

```
 1. Z axis, z, absolute, analog, 0.0
 2. Z Axis, z, absolute, analog, 0.0
 3. Y axis, y, absolute, analog, 0.0
 4. X axis, x, absolute, analog, 0.0
 5. Hat Switch, pov, absolute, digital, 0.0
 6. Button 0, 0, absolute, digital, 0.0
 7. Button 1, 1, absolute, digital, 0.0
 8. Button 2, 2, absolute, digital, 0.0
 9. Button 3, 3, absolute, digital, 0.0
10. Button 4, 4, absolute, digital, 0.0
11. Button 5, 5, absolute, digital, 0.0
12. Button 6, 6, absolute, digital, 0.0
13. Button 7, 7, absolute, digital, 0.0
14. Button 8, 8, absolute, digital, 0.0
15. Button 9, 9, absolute, digital, 0.0
16. Button 10, 10, absolute, digital, 0.0
17. Button 11, 11, absolute, digital, 0.0
Rumblers: (5)
0. null on axis; no name
1. null on axis; no name
2. null on axis; no name
3. null on axis; no name
4. null on axis; no name
No subcontrollers
```

The "Details for:" line gives the name and type of the controller and its port type. The port type should be Usb, but is shown as Unknown (due to restrictions in DirectX).

The 18 components consist of five axes, a hat, and 12 buttons, which confirms the information that I gathered from Windows and JInput's ControllerReadTest.

Each component has an index that I'll need later for TestController. For instance, the y-axis is component index 3.

The rumbler information is rather sparse, since there's no identifier or name for any of the rumblers.

I explain the data that is listed for each component in the "My Gamepad's Components" section.

Information can also be sent to a file. For example, details on the mouse can be stored in mouseDevice.txt by calling this:

```
runJI ControllerDetails 0 mouseDevice.txt
```

The file will contain the following:

```
Details for: Mouse, Mouse, Unknown
Components: (6)
0. X-axis, x, relative, analog, 0.0
1. Y-axis, y, relative, analog, 0.0
2. Wheel, z, relative, analog, 0.0
3. Button 0, Left, absolute, digital, 0.0
4. Button 1, Right, absolute, digital, 0.0
5. Button 2, Middle, absolute, digital, 0.0
No Rumblers
No subcontrollers
```

ControllerDetails' main() method obtains an array of controllers in the same way as
ListControllers and examines one of them:

```
public static void main(String[] args)
{
  if (args.length < 1)
    System.out.println("Usage: ControllerDetails <index> [<fnm>]");
  else {
    ControllerEnvironment ce =
          ControllerEnvironment.getDefaultEnvironment();
    Controller[] cs = ce.getControllers();
    if (cs.length == 0) {
      System.out.println("No controllers found");
      System.exit(0);
    }

    int index = extractIndex(args[0], cs.length);
            // get controller index from the command line

    PrintStream ps = getPrintStream(args);
    printDetails(cs[index], ps);  // print details for the controller
    ps.close();
  }
} // end of main()
```

extractIndex() parses the command-line argument to extract the index integer and checks that
it's valid (i.e., between 0 and cs.length-1).

getPrintStream() links a PrintStream to the file named on the command line; if no filename is
supplied, it uses System.out (stdout) instead.

printDetails() reports on the specified controller's components and rumblers. If it finds any
subcontrollers, it recursively visits them and reports their details:

```
private static void printDetails(Controller c, PrintStream ps)
{
  ps.println("Details for: " + c.getName() + ", " +
              c.getType() + ", " + c.getPortType() );

  printComponents(c.getComponents(), ps);
  printRumblers(c.getRumblers(), ps);

  // print details about any subcontrollers
  Controller[] subCtrls = c.getControllers();
  if (subCtrls.length == 0)
    ps.println("No subcontrollers");
  else {
    ps.println("No. of subcontrollers: " + subCtrls.length);
    // recursively visit each subcontroller
    for (int i = 0; i < subCtrls.length; i++) {
      ps.println("---------------");
      ps.println("Subcontroller: " + i);
      printDetails( subCtrls[i], ps);
    }
  }
} // end of printDetails()
```

The use of the static keyword for the printDetails() method has no bearing on JInput. I used
static methods in ControllerDetails and TestController simply to avoid having to define classes.

Examining a Component

A *component* can be many things: a button, a slider, a dial. However, every component has a name and type (called, rather misleadingly, an *identifier*) and generates a value when manipulated. A component has three attributes: relative (or absolute), analog (or digital), and a dead zone setting:

> *Relative/absolute*: A relative component returns a value relative to the previously output value. For example, a relative positional component will return the distance moved since it was last polled. An absolute component produces a value that doesn't depend on the previous value. The attribute is tested with Component.isRelative().

> *Analog/digital*: An analog component can have more than two values. For instance, a gamepad x-axis component can return three different values corresponding to being pressed on the left, the right, or not at all. A digital component only has two possible values, which is suitable for boolean devices such as buttons. This attribute is tested with Component.isAnalog().

> *Dead* zone: The dead zone value, mainly for joystick devices, specifies a threshold before the component switches from 0.0f (representing Off) to an On value. This mechanism means that slight changes in joystick position can be ignored.

printComponents() in ControllerDetails is defined as the following:

```
private static void printComponents(
                         Component[] comps, PrintStream ps)
{ if (comps.length == 0)
    ps.println("No Components");
  else {
    ps.println("Components: (" + comps.length + ")");
    for (int i = 0; i < comps.length; i++)
      ps.println( i + ". " +
          comps[i].getName() + ", " +
          getIdentifierName(comps[i]) + ", " +
          (comps[i].isRelative() ? "relative" : "absolute") + ", " +
          (comps[i].isAnalog() ? "analog" : "digital") + ", " +
           comps[i].getDeadZone());
  }
} // end of printComponents()
```

getIdentifierName() augments the Component.getIdentifier() method:

```
private static String getIdentifierName(Component comp)
{
  Component.Identifier id = comp.getIdentifier();
  if (id == Component.Identifier.Button.UNKNOWN)
    return "button";    // an unknown button
  else if(id == Component.Identifier.Key.UNKNOWN)
    return "key";    // an unknown key
  else
    return id.getName();
}
```

If the component's identifier is Component.Identifier.Button.UNKNOWN or Component. Identifier.Key.UNKNOWN, the returned string is set to "button" or "key" depending on the identifier type, which is more informative than just returning an "unknown" string.

The presence of rumblers is reported by printRumblers():

```
private static void printRumblers(Rumbler[] rumblers, PrintStream ps)
{
  if (rumblers.length == 0)
    ps.println("No Rumblers");
  else {
    ps.println("Rumblers: (" + rumblers.length + ")");
    Component.Identifier rumblerID;
    for (int i=0; i < rumblers.length; i++) {
      rumblerID = rumblers[i].getAxisIdentifier();
      ps.print(i + ". " + rumblers[i].getAxisName() + " on axis; ");
      if (rumblerID == null)
        ps.println("no name");
      else
        ps.println("name: " + rumblerID.getName() );
    }
  }
} // end of printRumblers()
```

A rumbler may have a name and identifier. There's also a Rumbler.rumble() method to make the component vibrate. The setting can range between 0.0f and 1.0f, with 1.0f meaning full-on.

My Gamepad's Components

Here's the component output from ControllerDetails for my gamepad once again:

```
0. Rz axis, rz, absolute, analog, 0.0
1. Z axis, z, absolute, analog, 0.0
2. Z Axis, z, absolute, analog, 0.0
3. Y axis, y, absolute, analog, 0.0
4. X axis, x, absolute, analog, 0.0
5. Hat Switch, pov, absolute, digital, 0.0
6. Button 0, 0, absolute, digital, 0.0
7. Button 1, 1, absolute, digital, 0.0
8. Button 2, 2, absolute, digital, 0.0
9. Button 3, 3, absolute, digital, 0.0
10. Button 4, 4, absolute, digital, 0.0
11. Button 5, 5, absolute, digital, 0.0
12. Button 6, 6, absolute, digital, 0.0
13. Button 7, 7, absolute, digital, 0.0
14. Button 8, 8, absolute, digital, 0.0
15. Button 9, 9, absolute, digital, 0.0
16. Button 10, 10, absolute, digital, 0.0
17. Button 11, 11, absolute, digital, 0.0
```

The list shows that all the components return absolute values. The 0.0s at the end of every line indicate that none of the components use dead zones, which is a little problematic for the analog sticks. It probably means that they'll be unlikely to return 0 when switched off.

The next step is to test the various components to get an idea of the values they return when activated. For example, what numbers do the buttons deliver when pressed and released? What floats are generated when the hat buttons are clicked? What values are returned when an analog stick is moved around? These questions are answered by the TestController application in the next subsection.

Testing a Controller

TestController displays the numbers generated by a component when it's manipulated. The program is called with controller and component index arguments, as in the following example:

```
runJI TestController 2 0
```

The 2 denotes the gamepad, and the 0 is for the right-hand analog stick's vertical axis (rz-axis). The controller index value comes from the output of ListControllers, and the component index from ControllerDetails.

When a component is "pressed," a value is printed to the screen. Keeping the component pressed doesn't generate multiple outputs, and releasing a component doesn't trigger an output either. These design decisions mean that the screen isn't swamped with numbers.

In the next example, I moved the right-hand analog stick up and down several times (i.e., along the rz-axis); I terminated the program by typing **ctrl-c**:

```
> runJI TestController 2 0
Executing TestController with JInput...
No. of controllers: 3
Polling controller: USB Vibration Joystick, Stick
No. of components: 18
Component: Rz axis
1.0; -0.8110323; -1.0; -0.9448844; -1.0; -1.0; -0.92126346;
1.0; 0.9763485; 0.36220336; 1.0; 0.46456087; 1.0; -0.4016022;
-1.0; Failed to poll device: Device is released
Controller no longer valid
Terminate batch job (Y/N)? y
>
```

The ctrl-c generates a rather messy series of diagnostic messages, starting with "Failed to poll device." Also, the abnormal termination of the batch file requires the user to type **y** to return to the DOS prompt.

The -1.0 values are printed when I push the stick fully down, and the 1.0s appear when I push it up. This output matches the numbers obtained from JInput's ControllerReadTest application (shown in Figure 11-7).

The output is complicated by intermediate values reported when the stick is moved slowly from its center (near to 0) toward an edge (where it reports +/-1.0).

TestController shares a lot of code with my earlier examples:

```java
public static void main(String[] args)
{
  if (args.length < 2) {
    System.out.println("Usage: TestController <index>
                                    <component index>");
    System.exit(0);
  }

  // get a controller using the first index value
  Controller c = getController(args[0]);

  // get a component using the second index value
  Component component = getComponent(args[1], c);

  pollComponent(c, component);    // keep polling the component
} // end of main()
```

The component polling is carried out in pollComponent():

```
// global constant
private static final int DELAY = 40;   // ms  (polling interval)
private static final float EPSILON = 0.0001f;
                        // to deal with values near to 0.0


private static void pollComponent(Controller c, Component component)
{
  float prevValue = 0.0f;
  float currValue;

  int i = 1;    // used to format the output
  while (true) {
    try {
      Thread.sleep(DELAY);       // wait a while
    }
    catch (Exception ex) {}

    c.poll(); // update the controller's components
    currValue = component.getPollData();  // get current value
    if (currValue != prevValue) {  // the value has changed
      if (Math.abs(currValue) > EPSILON) {
        // only show values not near to 0.0f
        System.out.print(currValue + "; ");
        i++;
      }
      prevValue = currValue;
    }

    if (i%10 == 0) {    // after several outputs, put in a newline
      System.out.println();
      i = 1;
    }
  }
} // end of pollComponent()
```

The method repeatedly polls the specified component, sleeping for DELAY ms (40 ms) between each one. The interval has to be short in order to catch rapid presses.

The polling is done in two steps: first Controller.poll() makes the controller update its components' values, then the new component value is retrieved by Component.getPollData().

To cut down the volume of data, a new value is only displayed if it's different from the previous one. Also, I don't show component *releases* (i.e., when the user stops pressing a button, the hat, or stick), which would appear as 0s, or values close to 0.0f.

A Gamepad Controller

My GamePadController class makes the accessing of the gamepad's sticks, hat, buttons, and rumbler simpler. It's utilized in the Swing example in the next section and the Arms3D application in the next chapter.

It's surprisingly difficult to write a general-purpose gamepad controller due to the wide variety of components that a gamepad might possess—buttons, sticks, hats, D-Pads, and rumblers. Consequently, I haven't written a one-size-fits-all class that tries to support every possible combination of components. Instead, GamePadController manages a device with 12 buttons, two analog sticks, a hat, and a rumbler. In other words, GamePadController is aimed at my gamepad. This keeps the class simple, while illustrating how JInput processing can be hidden.

Figure 11-10 shows the class diagram for GamePadController, with only its public methods listed.

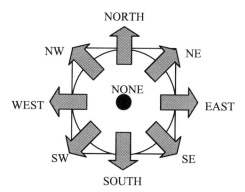

Figure 11-10. *Class diagram for GamePadController*

GamePadController simplifies the interface to the components by returning the stick and hat positions as compass directions. getXYStickDir() returns a compass value for the left stick (which manages the x- and y- axes), getZRZStickDir() returns a compass direction for the right stick (it deals with the z- and rz axes), and getHatDir() does the same for the hat.

The possible compass values are shown in Figure 11-11.

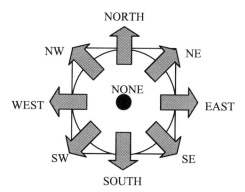

Figure 11-11. *Compass directions for the sticks and hat*

This compass approach hides the numerical details of the stick axes and offers a single way of thinking about the sticks and POV hat. A drawback is that the compass view restricts the values a stick can return; for example, it's not possible to get a position halfway between SW and SOUTH.

A button is checked with isButtonPressed(), or all the button settings can be retrieved in an array (getButtons()). The On and Off settings are represented by booleans.

The rumbler is switched on and off with setRumbler() and its current status retrieved with isRumblerOn(). GamePadController only offers access to a single rumbler, and the choice of which one is hard-wired into the class.

The poll() method updates all the component values.

Initializing the Controller

GamePadController() obtains a list of controllers, then searches through it for the gamepad. If a controller is found, its components are searched to find the indices of the sticks axes, the POV hat, the buttons, and a rumbler:

```
// globals
private Controller controller;   // for the gamepad


public GamePadController()
{
  // get the controllers
  ControllerEnvironment ce =
      ControllerEnvironment.getDefaultEnvironment();
  Controller[] cs = ce.getControllers();
  if (cs.length == 0) {
    System.out.println("No controllers found");
    System.exit(0);
  }
  else
    System.out.println("Num. controllers: " + cs.length);


  // get the gamepad controller
  controller = findGamePad(cs);
  System.out.println("Game controller: " +
                  controller.getName() + ", " +
                  controller.getType());

  // collect indices for the required gamepad components
  findCompIndices(controller);

  findRumblers(controller);
} // end of GamePadController()
```

findGamePad() loops through the controllers array looking for a gamepad:

```
private Controller findGamePad(Controller[] cs)
{
  Controller.Type type;
  int index = 0;
  while(index < cs.length) {
    type = cs[index].getType();
    if ((type == Controller.Type.GAMEPAD) ||
        (type == Controller.Type.STICK))
      break;
    index++;
  }
  if (index == cs.length) {
    System.out.println("No game pad found");
    System.exit(0);
  }
  else
    System.out.println("Game pad index: " + i);

  return cs[index];
} // end of findGamePad()
```

The only unusual aspect of this method is that it checks whether the controller type is a GAMEPAD or a STICK (i.e., a joystick). This extra test is due to the output generated by ControllerDetails, which lists my gamepad as a joystick.

Checking the Components

findCompIndices() records the indices of the sticks axes, the POV hat, and the buttons in xAxisIdx, yAxisIdx, zAxisIdx, rzAxisIdx, povIdx, and the buttonsIdx[].

Storing the indices means that a particular component can be quickly accessed later, without needing to search through the game controller's components information every time:

```
// globals
private Component[] comps;   // holds the components

// comps[] indices for specific components
private int xAxisIdx, yAxisIdx, zAxisIdx, rzAxisIdx;
                         // indices for the analog sticks axes
private int povIdx;          // index for the POV hat


private void findCompIndices(Controller controller)
{
  comps = controller.getComponents();
  if (comps.length == 0) {
    System.out.println("No Components found");
    System.exit(0);
  }
  else
    System.out.println("Num. Components: " + comps.length);

  // get indices for sticks axes: (x,y) and (z,rz)
  xAxisIdx = findCompIndex(comps,
                Component.Identifier.Axis.X, "x-axis");
  yAxisIdx = findCompIndex(comps,
                Component.Identifier.Axis.Y, "y-axis");

  zAxisIdx = findCompIndex(comps,
                Component.Identifier.Axis.Z, "z-axis");
  rzAxisIdx = findCompIndex(comps,
                Component.Identifier.Axis.RZ, "rz-axis");

  // get POV hat index
  povIdx = findCompIndex(comps,
                Component.Identifier.Axis.POV, "POV hat");

  findButtons(comps);
}  // end of findCompIndices()
```

findCompIndices() delegates the index searches to findCompIndex() for the axes and POV hat, and to findButtons() for the buttons:

```
private int findCompIndex(Component[] comps,
                        Component.Identifier id, String nm)
{
  Component c;
  for(int i=0; i < comps.length; i++) {
    c = comps[i];
```

```
    if ((c.getIdentifier() == id) && !c.isRelative()) {
      System.out.println("Found " + c.getName() + "; index: " + i);
      return i;
    }
  }

  System.out.println("No " + nm + " component found");
  return -1;
}  // end of findCompIndex()
```

findCompIndex() searches through comps[] for the supplied component ID, returning the corresponding array index, or -1 if the identifier can't be found. The component must also be absolute.

findButtons() performs a similar search through comps[], collecting the indices for a maximum of NUM_BUTTONS buttons, which it stores in buttonsIdx[]:

```
// globals
public static final int NUM_BUTTONS = 12;
private int buttonsIdx[];    // indices for the buttons


private void findButtons(Component[] comps)
{
  buttonsIdx = new int[NUM_BUTTONS];
  int numButtons = 0;
  Component c;

  for(int i=0; i < comps.length; i++) {
    c = comps[i];
    if (isButton(c)) {     // deal with a button
      if (numButtons == NUM_BUTTONS)    // already enough buttons
        System.out.println("Found an extra button; index: " +
                                           i + ". Ignoring it");

      else {
        buttonsIdx[numButtons] = i;  // store button index
        System.out.println("Found " + c.getName() + "; index: " + i);
        numButtons++;
      }
    }
  }

  // fill empty spots in buttonsIdx[] with -1's
  if (numButtons < NUM_BUTTONS) {
    System.out.println("Too few buttons (" + numButtons +
                       "); expecting " + NUM_BUTTONS);
    while (numButtons < NUM_BUTTONS) {
      buttonsIdx[numButtons] = -1;
      numButtons++;
    }
  }
}  // end of findButtons()
```

findButtons() ignores extra buttons, and if there aren't enough it fills the empty spots in buttonsIdx[] with -1s.

isButton() returns true if the supplied component is a button. The component needs to be digital and absolute, and its identifier class name must end with "Button" (i.e., it must be Component.Identifier.Button):

```
private boolean isButton(Component c)
{
  if (!c.isAnalog() && !c.isRelative()) {  // digital & absolute
    String className = c.getIdentifier().getClass().getName();
    if (className.endsWith("Button"))
      return true;
  }
  return false;
}  // end of isButton()
```

I use the class name to identify the button since Component.Identifier.Button defines numerous button identifiers, and I don't want to check the component against each one.

Finding the Rumblers

The rumblers are accessed using Controller.getRumblers(), and one is chosen to be the rumbler offered by the class:

```
// globals
private Rumbler[] rumblers;
private int rumblerIdx;       // index for the rumbler being used


private void findRumblers(Controller controller)
{
  // get the gamepad's rumblers
  rumblers = controller.getRumblers();
  if (rumblers.length == 0) {
    System.out.println("No Rumblers found");
    rumblerIdx = -1;
  }
  else {
    System.out.println("Rumblers found: " + rumblers.length);
    rumblerIdx = rumblers.length-1;    // use last rumbler
  }
}  // end of findRumblers()
```

findRumblers() stores the index of the last rumbler in the rumblers array. There's no particular reason for this choice, except that in my gamepad it vibrates the left and right sides of the gamepad together.

Polling the Device

An application will utilize the GamePadController by calling its poll() method to update the component's values and then one or more of its get methods to retrieve the new values.

GamePadController's poll() method calls poll() in the controller:

```
public void poll()
{  controller.poll();  }
```

Reading the Stick Axes

The two sticks return axes values as floats between -1.0 and 1.0 (see Figure 11-8). GamePadController simplifies this interface by returning compass directions (as shown in Figure 11-11).

The left analog stick manages the x- and y- axes, while the right stick deals with the z- and rz- axes. GamePadController's public stick methods call getCompassDir() with the relevant component indices for the axes:

```
public int getXYStickDir()
// return the (x,y) analog stick compass direction
{
  if ((xAxisIdx == -1) || (yAxisIdx == -1)) {
    System.out.println("(x,y) axis data unavailable");
    return NONE;
  }
  else
    return getCompassDir(xAxisIdx, yAxisIdx);
} // end of getXYStickDir()


public int getZRZStickDir()
// return the (z,rz) analog stick compass direction
{
  if ((zAxisIdx == -1) || (rzAxisIdx == -1)) {
    System.out.println("(z,rz) axis data unavailable");
    return NONE;
  }
  else
    return getCompassDir(zAxisIdx, rzAxisIdx);
} // end of getXYStickDir()
```

getCompassDir() retrieves the floats for the required axes and converts them into a compass heading:

```
// global public stick and hat compass positions
public static final int NUM_COMPASS_DIRS = 9;

public static final int NW = 0;
public static final int NORTH = 1;
public static final int NE = 2;
public static final int WEST = 3;
public static final int NONE = 4;   // default value
public static final int EAST = 5;
public static final int SW = 6;
public static final int SOUTH = 7;
public static final int SE = 8;


private int getCompassDir(int xA, int yA)
{
  float xCoord = comps[xA].getPollData();
  float yCoord = comps[yA].getPollData();

  int xc = Math.round(xCoord);
  int yc = Math.round(yCoord);

  if ((yc == -1) && (xc == -1))    // (y,x)
    return NW;
```

```
    else if ((yc == -1) && (xc == 0))
      return NORTH;
    else if ((yc == -1) && (xc == 1))
      return NE;
    else if ((yc == 0) && (xc == -1))
      return WEST;
    else if ((yc == 0) && (xc == 0))
      return NONE;
    else if ((yc == 0) && (xc == 1))
      return EAST;
    else if ((yc == 1) && (xc == -1))
      return SW;
    else if ((yc == 1) && (xc == 0))
      return SOUTH;
    else if ((yc == 1) && (xc == 1))
      return SE;
    else {
      System.out.println("Unknown (x,y): (" + xc + "," + yc + ")");
      return NONE;
    }
}  // end of getCompassDir()
```

The axes values are retrieved by using their index positions and Component.getPollData():

```
float xCoord = comps[xA].getPollData();
float yCoord = comps[yA].getPollData();
```

They're rounded to integers (either 0 or 1), and a series of if-tests determine which compass setting should be returned. The rounding shows that position information is lost, but with the aim of simplifying the interface.

The compass constants in GamePadController are public so they can be utilized in other classes that use the compass data.

Reading the POV Hat

The polling of the hat returns a float corresponding to different combinations of key presses (see Figure 11-9). getHatDir() maps this to the same compass directions as used by the sticks:

```
public int getHatDir()
{
  if (povIdx == -1) {
    System.out.println("POV hat data unavailable");
    return NONE;
  }
  else {
    float povDir = comps[povIdx].getPollData();
    if (povDir == POV.CENTER)  // 0.0f
      return NONE;
    else if (povDir == POV.DOWN)  // 0.75f
      return SOUTH;
    else if (povDir == POV.DOWN_LEFT)  // 0.875f
      return SW;
    else if (povDir == POV.DOWN_RIGHT)  // 0.625f
      return SE;
```

```
      else if (povDir == POV.LEFT)  // 1.0f
        return WEST;
      else if (povDir == POV.RIGHT)  // 0.5f
        return EAST;
      else if (povDir == POV.UP)  // 0.25f
        return NORTH;
      else if (povDir == POV.UP_LEFT)  // 0.125f
        return NW;
      else if (povDir == POV.UP_RIGHT)  // 0.375f
        return NE;
      else  { // assume center
        System.out.println("POV hat value out of range: " + povDir);
        return NONE;
      }
    }
  }
}  // end of getHatDir()
```

Reading the Buttons

getButtons() returns all the button values in a single array, each value represented by a boolean:

```
public boolean[] getButtons()
{
  boolean[] buttons = new boolean[NUM_BUTTONS];
  float value;
  for(int i=0; i < NUM_BUTTONS; i++) {
    value = comps[ buttonsIdx[i] ].getPollData();
    buttons[i] = ((value == 0.0f) ? false : true);
  }
  return buttons;
}  // end of getButtons()
```

A JInput button value (a float) is read by selecting the relevant component using its index and calling getPollData():

```
value = comps[ buttonsIdx[i] ].getPollData();
```

A single button is accessed with isButtonPressed():

```
public boolean isButtonPressed(int pos)
{
  if ((pos < 1) || (pos > NUM_BUTTONS)) {
    System.out.println("Button position out of range (1-" +
                                    NUM_BUTTONS + "): " + pos);
    return false;
  }

  float value = comps[ buttonsIdx[pos-1] ].getPollData();
        // array range is 0-NUM_BUTTONS-1
  return ((value == 0.0f) ? false : true);
} // end of isButtonPressed()
```

The supplied button position (pos) is expected to be in the range 1 to NUM_BUTTONS.

Using the Rumbler

The rumbler is switched on or off with setRumbler():

```
// global
private boolean rumblerOn = false;    // is rumbler on or off?


public void setRumbler(boolean switchOn)
{
  if (rumblerIdx != -1) {
    if (switchOn)
      rumblers[rumblerIdx].rumble(0.8f);  // almost full on
    else  // switch off
      rumblers[rumblerIdx].rumble(0.0f);
    rumblerOn = switchOn;     // record rumbler's new status
  }
}  // end of setRumbler()
```

The rumbler vibrates with a value of 0.8f; the maximum value (1.0f) seems a bit too "violent" for my gamepad.

The rumbler's current status is retrieved with isRumblerOn(), which returns the rumblerOn value:

```
public boolean isRumblerOn()
{  return rumblerOn;  }
```

Other Approaches

GamePadController is designed for a gamepad with two analog sticks, a POV hat, 12 buttons, and a rumbler. Its interface is simpler to use than JInput directly, but it can't deal with other gamepad configurations. As you might expect, there are other ways of packaging up JInput.

Xj3D (http://www.xj3d.org/) is a toolkit for building X3D-based applications that uses JInput to support input devices such as data gloves, joysticks, tracking devices, and gamepads. (X3D is the ISO standard for real-time 3D graphics, a successor to VRML, but with extras such as humanoid animation and NURBS.)

Xj3D devices are accessible via a variety of classes (e.g., GamepadDevice, JoystickDevice, TrackerDevice, WheelDevice, and MouseDevice), each of which maintains a game state class (e.g., GamepadState, JoystickState, WheelState). GamepadState supports several buttons, two sticks, a slider, and a D-Pad. The documentation for these classes can be found at http://www.xj3d.org/javadoc/.

The Lightweight Java Game Library (LWJGL), (http://lwjgl.org/) utilizes JInput with a wrapper for manipulating component axes and buttons. The LWJGL tutorials page has an article on how to use it: http://lwjgl.org/wiki/doku.php/lwjgl/tutorials/input/basiccontroller.

Swing and JInput

My GamePadViewer application is shown in Figure 11-12.

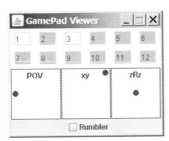

Figure 11-12. *The GamePadViewer application*

It's meant to emulate the Function Test window in the Game Controllers control panel in Windows (see Figure 11-4). The buttons are displayed as two rows of text fields, with yellow denoting that the numbered button is being pressed. The three boxes in the center are for the POV hat and the left and right analog sticks. The dot's position in each box indicates the current hat/stick position.

The check box at the bottom of the window can be selected/deselected in order to switch the rumbler on/off.

Figure 11-12 shows the situation when the buttons 1 and 3 are pressed, the left-hand POV hat button is held down, and the left stick is pushed to the top right. The rumbler is currently inactive.

Figure 11-13 shows GamePadViewer's class diagrams, with only the public methods visible.

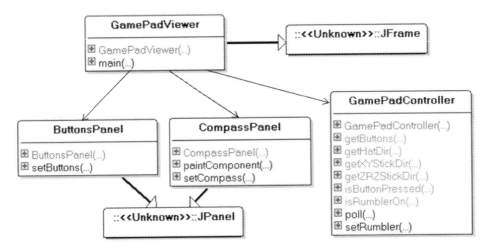

Figure 11-13. *Class diagrams for GamePadViewer*

The GamePadViewer class is the top-level JFrame, which constructs its GUI from a ButtonsPanel for the buttons, and three instances of CompassPanel for the POV hat and two sticks. The rumbler is managed by GamePadViewer.

GamePadViewer periodically polls GamePadController and gathers data about the hat, sticks, and buttons. It passes that data to the GUI objects via ButtonsPanel.setButtons() and CompassPanel.setCompass(), which update their GUI elements.

GamePadViewer monitors the rumbler check box itself and calls GamePadController. setRumbler() when necessary.

Constructing the Application

The GamePadViewer constructor creates the GUI and initiates polling of the gamepad by calling startPolling():

```
// globals
private GamePadController gpController;
private Timer pollTimer;    // timer which triggers the polling


public GamePadViewer()
{
  super("GamePad Viewer");

  gpController = new GamePadController();

  makeGUI();

  addWindowListener( new WindowAdapter() {
    public void windowClosing(WindowEvent e)
    { pollTimer.stop();    // stop the timer
      System.exit(0);
    }
  });

  pack();
  setResizable(false);
  setVisible(true);

  startPolling();
} // end of GamePadViewer()
```

startPolling() uses a timer (pollTimer) to schedule the polling, which needs to be stopped when the application exits.

The GUI is conventional Swing code so won't be described in detail here. GamePadViewer utilizes the ButtonsPanel class to manage the button text fields, and three instances of CompassPanel for the POV hat and sticks:

```
// globals for the GUI
private CompassPanel xyPanel, zrzPanel, hatPanel;
    // shows the two analog sticks and POV hat
private ButtonsPanel buttonsPanel;
private JCheckBox rumblerCheck;


private void makeGUI()
{
```

```
Container c = getContentPane();
c.setLayout(new BoxLayout(c, BoxLayout.Y_AXIS));
                  // vertical box layout
buttonsPanel = new ButtonsPanel();
c.add(buttonsPanel);

JPanel p = new JPanel();
p.setLayout(new BoxLayout(p, BoxLayout.X_AXIS));
                  // three CompassPanels in a row
hatPanel = new CompassPanel("POV");
p.add(hatPanel);

xyPanel = new CompassPanel("xy");
p.add(xyPanel);

zrzPanel = new CompassPanel("zRz");
p.add(zrzPanel);

c.add(p);

// rumbler check box
rumblerCheck = new JCheckBox("Rumbler");
rumblerCheck.addItemListener(new ItemListener() {
  public void itemStateChanged(ItemEvent ie)
  {
    if (ie.getStateChange() == ItemEvent.SELECTED)
      gpController.setRumbler(true);  // switch on
    else  // deselected
      gpController.setRumbler(false);  // switch off
  }
});
c.add(rumblerCheck);
}  // end of makeGUI()
```

Selecting the rumbler check box triggers calls to GamePadController.setRumbler().

Polling the Gamepad

startPolling() creates an ActionListener object that polls the gamepad and updates the GUI. It also starts a timer that activates the object every DELAY ms:

```
// global
private static final int DELAY = 40;    // ms (polling interval)
      // needs to be fast to catch fast button pressing!

private void startPolling()
{
  ActionListener pollPerformer = new ActionListener() {
    public void actionPerformed(ActionEvent e)
    {
      gpController.poll();

      // update the GUI:
      // get POV hat compass direction
      int compassDir = gpController.getHatDir();
      hatPanel.setCompass( compassDir );
```

```
        // get compass directions for the two analog sticks
        compassDir = gpController.getXYStickDir();
        xyPanel.setCompass( compassDir );

        compassDir = gpController.getZRZStickDir();
        zrzPanel.setCompass( compassDir );

        // get button settings
        boolean[] buttons = gpController.getButtons();
        buttonsPanel.setButtons(buttons);
    }
  }; // end of ActionListener

  pollTimer = new Timer(DELAY, pollPerformer);
  pollTimer.start();
} // end of startPolling()
```

startPolling() illustrates the standard technique for integrating JInput polling and Swing GUI updates. The tricky issue is that changes to the GUI must be performed from the event-dispatching thread. startPolling() does this by employing javax.swing.Timer, which schedules its ActionListener argument in that thread.

It's important that the ActionListener code executes quickly, since the GUI can't respond to user actions while the code is being run.

A CompassPanel.setCompass() call stores the compass direction in the CompassPanel object and triggers a repaint. The black dot's position in the panel is determined by looking up an array of (x, y) coordinates, using the compass heading as an index.

ButtonsPanel.setButtons() cycles through the supplied boolean array and changes the backgrounds of its text fields accordingly: yellow means On, gray is Off.

Alternatives to JInput

JXInput (http://www.hardcode.de/jxinput/) is a cross-platform API for using the mouse, the keyboard, and other input devices. However, nonstandard devices, such as gamepads, are only supported on Windows because of JXInput's use of DirectInput.

For each device, JXInput can manage up to six axes (three positional and three rotational), two sliders, four hats, and 128 buttons. It supports callbacks and events and has a Java 3D InputDevice implementation.

JXInput was developed in late 2002 by Joerg Plewe and Stefan Pfafferott, as part of their very entertaining *FlyingGuns* Java 3D game (http://www.flyingguns.com/).

The Joystick Driver for Java (http://sourceforge.net/projects/javajoystick/) isn't just for joysticks, but any input device with 2–6 degrees of freedom (which includes gamepads). There's a listener class, JoystickListener, with callbacks for when a button or axis changes, and it's also possible to use polling. JavaJoystick is implemented on Windows and Linux. It dates from 2001 and hasn't been updated since 2003.

Summary

After introducing my gamepad to Windows XP, I made it accessible to Java with JInput, a cross-platform API for the discovery and polling of input devices.

I wrote three small JInput applications that display information about the input devices attached to my PC. I also developed a GamePadController class that offers a simplified interface to my gamepad and then employed it in a Swing application called GamePadViewer.

GamePadController makes an appearance in the next chapter as well, when I connect my gamepad to the articulated arms example from Chapter 4, making the arms much easier to use.

CHAPTER 12

■■■

Gamepad Grabbers

Back in Chapter 4, I developed an example involving two multijointed arms with fingers (*grabbers*). One drawback of the coding was the bewildering mix of key combinations needed to translate and rotate the arms. This chapter connects a gamepad to the grabbers, making them much easier to control, mainly because of the intuitive mapping of the grabbers' operations to the pad's analog sticks, hat, and buttons. For example, the left stick controls the x- and y-axis rotations of the left arm, and the right stick handles the right arm.

    This chapter also discusses sound production, obstacles, collision detection, a technique for integrating different input sources into the application, and how to attach a shape to the camera's viewpoint so it moves when the camera moves.

Example Overview

This chapter's techniques are illustrated in a single application, called ArmsPad3D, which is shown in Figure 12-1.

Figure 12-1. *The ArmsPad3D application*

The grabbers are visible at the sides of the window in Figure 12-1. The 3D models on the checkerboard floor come from OBJ files for a cow, a pig, and a teapot, loaded using the ModelLoader class from the ObjView3D example in Chapter 7. The trees are ground shapes created with the GroundShape class from the same example.

The following are the novel elements of the application:

- *Sound*: The application includes a SoundsPlayer class that can play music continuously in the background and short sound clips when the grabbers hit obstacles.

- *Obstacles*: The obstacles are rendered as translucent white boxes standing on the floor. The scene's 3D models and ground shapes are surrounded with them (as shown in Figure 12-1). The grabbers can't move through the obstacles.

- *Collision detection*: The original grabbers example in Chapter 4 detects collisions with the help of Java 3D wake-up criteria and a behavior. In this chapter I use a simpler mechanism, a *try-it-and-see* approach, which stops the grabber arms from passing through each other or the floor, or from traveling into the obstacles. Also, when a collision is detected, the gamepad's rumbler is switched on to give the user some feedback.

- *Gamepad input*: The grabbers are controllable via the gamepad. Apart from simplifying the user interface, the gamepad also makes it easier for the application to process multiple inputs at the same time. For instance, the grabbers' base can rotate and move forward while the arms are turning.

- *Multiple input sources*: The grabbers are actually controlled via operations sent from the gamepad *or* the keyboard. The data is converted into GrabberOp objects, which lets the grabbers execute without having to know the source of their operations. This coding approach makes it easy to plug other forms of input devices (such as a mouse) into the application in the future.

- *Linking the grabbers and the camera*: The grabbers are connected to the camera, so the arms translate and rotate in unison with it. This only requires minor adjustments to the grabber classes from Chapter 4. Most are size changes to the grabber's component cylinders and boxes. Since the arms are closer to the camera viewpoint, they look better if they're a bit smaller.

The class diagrams for ArmsPad3D in Figure 12-2 are shaded to indicate the amount of class reuse from previous examples. Class names only are shown to reduce the diagram's complexity.

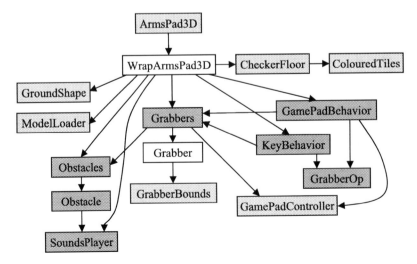

Figure 12-2. *Class diagrams for ArmsPad3D*

The dark boxes in Figure 12-2 are new classes, which I explain later in this chapter (i.e., SoundsPlayer, Obstacles, Obstacle, KeyBehavior, GamePadBehavior, GrabberOp, and Grabbers). The light boxes are for classes unchanged from previous examples, which I won't be looking at again. The two boxes with mottled texturing (WrapArmsPad3D and Grabber) have a few new features that I'll describe, but most of their code is the same as before.

ArmsPad3D creates the usual JFrame, which utilizes WrapArmsPad3D to render the 3D scene inside a JPanel. Much of WrapArmsPad3D's functionality is familiar from ObjView3D (Chapter 7), using CheckerFloor and ColouredTiles to create the checkerboard floor, GroundShape for the 2D tree billboards, and ModelLoader for the 3D models.

The obstacles are managed by an Obstacles instance, which stores a list of Obstacle objects. SoundsPlayer plays background music and sound clips.

The grabbers are represented by a Grabbers instance, which delegates arm manipulation to two Grabber instances, and collision detection to two GrabberBounds objects. There was a Grabbers class in the Arms3D example of Chapter 4, but I've changed it so substantially that it qualifies as "new."

Keyboard and gamepad input arrive via the KeyBehavior and GamePadBehavior classes, which send operations to Grabbers in the form of GrabberOp instances. GamePadBehavior periodically polls the gamepad via a GamePadController instance.

The classes unchanged from previous examples are the following:

- CheckerFloor and ColouredTiles were first used in Chapter 4.

- GroundShape and ModelLoader were introduced in Chapter 7.

- GrabberBounds is from Chapter 4.

- GamePadController was explained in Chapter 11.

I reuse code from Chapters 4, 7, and 11, so it's a good idea if you read those chapters before this one.

Playing Sounds

A SoundsPlayer object acts as a storehouse (jukebox) for sounds, and a sound is played by supplying its name to the SoundsPlayer.

SoundsPlayer is utilized in two ways in ArmsPad3D: to continuously play a MIDI sequence as background music while the application is running, and to play sound clips (short WAV files) when the grabbers hit obstacles.

Java comes with an extensive Java Sound API that supports the recording, playback, and synthesis of sampled audio, such as WAV files and MIDI. But its power isn't needed here, since basic playback is possible with the much simpler AudioClip class. AudioClip is sufficient for this application's needs, with one limitation that can be coded around.

SoundsPlayer stores the MIDI and WAV files as AudioClip objects in a HashMap (the objects' keys are their filenames). The HashMap is called soundsMap because it maps filenames to sounds. SoundsPlayer also stores the running time of the clips in a separate HashMap, called soundLensMap:

```
private HashMap<String, AudioClip> soundsMap;
private HashMap<String, Integer> soundLensMap;
```

The running time is utilized by the Obstacle class, as I explain when I get to that code. AudioClip's limitation is that it doesn't offer a method for accessing a clip's running time, so I supply the value as part of SoundsPlayer's load() method:

```
// global
private final static String SOUND_DIR = "Sounds/";


public boolean load(String fnm, int soundLen)
/* Load the sound file and store it as an AudioClip
   in the hash map. Store its length in the soundLens map.
*/
{
  if (soundsMap.get(fnm) != null) {
    System.out.println(SOUND_DIR + fnm + " already loaded");
    return true;
  }

  AudioClip audioClip = Applet.newAudioClip(
              getClass().getResource(SOUND_DIR + fnm) );
  if (audioClip == null) {
    System.out.println("Problem loading " +  SOUND_DIR + fnm);
    return false;
  }

  System.out.println("Loaded " +  SOUND_DIR + fnm);
  soundsMap.put(fnm, audioClip);
  soundLensMap.put(fnm, soundLen);
  return true;
}  // end of load()
```

The clip is loaded with Applet.newAudioClip(), then stored in the soundsMap HashMap.

A sound's running time can be discovered with the help of any decent audio editing tool. On Windows, I use WavePad (http://nch.com.au/wavepad/), which offers a great mix of features and is free.

I only need the running time for the sound clips, so the MIDI file is loaded with the single argument version of load():

```
public boolean load(String fnm)
{  return load(fnm, -1);  }
```

AudioClips can be played once with AudioClip.play() or repeatedly with loop(), or stopped with stop(). These method calls are wrapped up in SoundsPlayer methods that search the soundsMap HashMap for the specified AudioClip, as in this method for playing a sound:

```
public void play(String fnm)
// retrieve the relevant AudioClip, and start it playing
{
  AudioClip audioClip = (AudioClip) soundsMap.get(fnm);
  if (audioClip == null) {
    System.out.println("Could not find " +  SOUND_DIR + fnm);
    return;
  }
  audioClip.play();
}  // end of play()
```

Background Music with SoundsPlayer

The SoundsPlayer object is created in WrapArmsPad3D, which also loads and starts the MIDI sequence:

```
// globals in WrapArmsPad3D
private static final String BG_MUSIC = "Mission_Impossible_TV.mid";
private SoundsPlayer soundsPlayer;


// in the WrapArmsPad3D constructor
soundsPlayer = new SoundsPlayer();
soundsPlayer.load(BG_MUSIC);    // load the background MIDI sequence
soundsPlayer.playLoop(BG_MUSIC);  // play it continuously
```

This code snippet should start the pulse-pounding theme from the 1960s TV show *Mission Impossible*.

Unfortunately, a bug in (some versions of) Java SE 5 and 6 means that nothing may be heard. This is due to a problem with the creation of the MIDI transmitter for playing the sound, a bug that's also present in the Java Sound API. There's a report, No. 6483856, in Sun's bug database at http://bugs.sun.com/bugdatabase/view_bug.do?bug_id=6483856. Please vote for it to be fixed.

A key benefit of the MIDI format is that it represents musical data in an extremely efficient way, leading to drastic reductions in file sizes compared to sampled audio (such as WAV files). For instance, files containing high-quality stereo require about 10MB per minute of sound, while a typical MIDI sequence may need less than 10KB.

Even so, other music formats could be used for the background music. One of AudioClip's great strengths is the large number of formats it supports: Windows WAV files, Sun Audio (AU files), Mac AIFF files, different kinds of MIDI (type 0 and type 1), and RMF (Rich Music Format). Data can be 8- or 16-bit, mono or stereo, with sample rates between 8,000Hz and 48,000Hz.

Another helpful feature of AudioClip is that different clips can play at the same time, letting the sounds be layered together. However, only a single copy of a clip can be playing at once. This can be too restrictive for some sound effects, such as explosions, where it's common practice to play several instances of a sound so they overlap. The standard trick is to create multiple copies of the required audio and load the files as separate AudioClip objects; these "different" objects can be played simultaneously.

Obstacle Noises with SoundsPlayer

WrapArmsPad3D loads its 3D models and ground shapes by reusing the ModelLoader and GroundShape classes from Chapter 7. At the same time, the obstacles and collision noises are created. The following code fragment from addModels() loads the cow model, its obstacle box, and a cow.wav clip:

```
// from addModels() in WrapArmsPad3D
// a cow model
t3d.setTranslation( new Vector3d(-2,0,-4));   // move
t3d.setScale(0.7); // shrink
TransformGroup tg1 = new TransformGroup(t3d);
tg1.addChild( ml.getModel("cow.obj", 1.3) );
sceneBG.addChild(tg1);

soundsPlayer.load("cow.wav", 1500);
obstacles.add("cow.wav", -1.75,-4, 2.55,1.6,1);
                // (x, z) location and dimensions of the obstacle
```

SoundsPlayer.load()'s numerical argument is the 1500 ms running time of cow.wav (1.5 secs).

The WAV filename is passed to Obstacles.add() so the sound can be played later. The numerical arguments in the add() call define the obstacle's position. It rests on the floor centered at the specified (x, z) location (i.e., (-1.75, 4)), with the supplied x-, y-, and z-axis dimensions (2.55 by 1.6 by 1.0).

Managing Obstacles

The Obstacles class is mostly just a wrapper around an ArrayList of Obstacle objects. It can create a new Obstacle object and add it to the list, and it offers several intersection methods.

Obstacles also stores a reference to the SoundsPlayer object and the Java 3D BranchGroup for the scene, sceneBG. It passes these references to each Obstacle instance so the obstacle can play a sound and attach a semitransparent box to the scene.

Obstacles' constructor creates the ArrayList and stores the references:

```
// globals
private BranchGroup sceneBG;
private SoundsPlayer soundsPlayer;
private ArrayList<Obstacle> obs;


public Obstacles(BranchGroup sceneBG, SoundsPlayer sp)
{
  this.sceneBG = sceneBG;
  soundsPlayer = sp;
  obs = new ArrayList<Obstacle>();
} // end of Obstacles()
```

The add() method adds an Obstacle instance to the list:

```
public void add(String sndfnm, double x, double z,
                     double xLen, double yLen, double zLen)
{  obs.add( new Obstacle(sceneBG, soundsPlayer, sndfnm,
                   x, z, xLen, yLen, zLen) );  }
```

The long sequence of input arguments specifies the obstacle's (x, z) position on the floor and the lengths of its sides.

A typical intersection method cycles through the ArrayList, testing a supplied Bounds object against each Obstacle:

```
public boolean intersect(Bounds b)
{
  Obstacle ob;
  for(int i=0; i < obs.size(); i++) {
    ob = obs.get(i);
    if (ob.intersect(b))
      return true;
  }
  return false;
} // end of intersect()
```

Making an Obstacle

An obstacle is composed from two things: a Java 3D bounding box for detecting collisions with the grabbers, and a semitransparent Java 3D box shape located in the same space in the scene. Figure 12-3 shows a close-up of the box around the cow model (with the pig in the background).

Figure 12-3. *The cow inside an Obstacle box*

The main purpose of the visible box is to help test and debug the application. It could be removed without affecting the collision detection functionality.

Obstacle's dual nature can be seen in its constructor:

```
// globals
private SoundsPlayer soundsPlayer;
private String soundFnm;  public Obstacle(BranchGroup sceneBG, SoundsPlayer sp,
          String sndfnm, double x, double z,
          double xLen, double yLen, double zLen)
{
  soundsPlayer = sp;
  soundFnm = sndfnm;

  makeBoundBox(x, z, xLen, yLen, zLen);
  if (sceneBG != null)
    addVisibleBox(sceneBG, x, z, xLen, yLen, zLen);
} // end of Obstacle()
```

makeBoundBox() handles the creation of the bounding box, while the visible box is made by addVisibleBox(). This latter call should be commented out to make the obstacle invisible.

The (x, z) input arguments are used to center the box; no y value is given since the code always rests the obstacle on the ground. The xLen, yLen, and zLen triple are the lengths of the box's sides.

Making the Boxes

The bounding box is created with the help of Java 3D's BoundingBox class. There are also bounds classes for spheres and more general polyhedra:

```
// globals
private BoundingBox boundBox;


private void makeBoundBox(double x, double z,
                double xLen, double yLen, double zLen)
{
  Point3d lower = new Point3d(x-xLen/2, 0, z-zLen/2);
  Point3d upper = new Point3d(x+xLen/2, yLen, z+zLen/2);
  boundBox = new BoundingBox(lower, upper);
} // end of makeBoundBox
```

Making the visible box takes a bit more work but utilizes Java 3D's Box class for the geometric aspects. It occupies the same space as the bounding box: centered at (x, z) on the XZ plane, with sides of xLen, yLen, and zLen. Its appearance is a default white, but translucent:

```
private void addVisibleBox(BranchGroup sceneBG, double x, double z,
                double xLen, double yLen, double zLen)
{
  Appearance app = new Appearance();     // default white color

  // switch off face culling
  PolygonAttributes pa = new PolygonAttributes();
  pa.setCullFace(PolygonAttributes.CULL_NONE);
  app.setPolygonAttributes(pa);

  // semi-transparent appearance
  TransparencyAttributes ta = new TransparencyAttributes();
  ta.setTransparencyMode( TransparencyAttributes.BLENDED );
  ta.setTransparency(0.7f);     // 1.0f is totally transparent
  app.setTransparencyAttributes(ta);

  Box obsBox = new Box( (float)xLen/2, (float)yLen/2,
                                (float)zLen/2, app);
  // fix box position
  Transform3D t3d = new Transform3D();
  t3d.setTranslation( new Vector3d(x, yLen/2+0.01, z) );
                    // bit above ground

  TransformGroup tg = new TransformGroup();
  tg.setTransform(t3d);
  tg.addChild(obsBox);

  sceneBG.addChild(tg);
} // end of addVisibleBox()
```

Face culling is switched off so the user can see the inside walls of a box when they look inside an obstacle.

The box is positioned a bit above the floor so that its rendering won't interact with the box's base. It's attached to the scene via the sceneBG BranchGroup.

Collision Detection

Obstacle contains two versions of an intersect() method: one for Bounds input, one for a point. The methods are quite similar; here's the Bounds version:

```
public boolean intersect(Bounds b)
/* If b intersects with the bounding box for this object
   then play a sound. */
{
  boolean isIntersecting = boundBox.intersect(b);
  if (isIntersecting)
    playSound();
  return isIntersecting;
} // end of intersect()
```

There's a very tricky aspect to playing a collision sound; what do you do when multiple collisions occur in rapid succession?

Rapid player movement is achieved by the user holding down a key or a button on the gamepad. When a collision occurs, the user will take a few milliseconds to release the key/button, and in that time the collision will be detected multiple times.

If each collision triggers sound output, the result is a rapid noisy stutter caused by the clip restarting repeatedly. It's restarted due to AudioClip's restriction that multiple instances of the same clip can't be played concurrently.

This stutter may not be a drawback for some applications, but it should be avoided in ArmsPad3D. If there's still a collision after the sound's end, it can be played again then.

Another aspect of sound playing is that it shouldn't "freeze" the rest of the application; a sound effect may last for 1 to 2 seconds, which is much too long for the grabbers to be unresponsive.

The simplest solution is to use a thread to play the sound, but this may be seriously inefficient. The issue is that each time the sound needs to be played, a new thread is created, with the associated overheads of thread creation and subsequent termination.

A better solution is to keep reusing a single *worker* thread, which only needs to be created once and is repeatedly employed to play all the sounds.

This technique is known as *thread pooling*; a collection of worker threads is reused to process tasks as they arrive at the pool. In our application, the pool only needs a single thread, which executes the sound-playing tasks in sequence.

Since J2SE 5.0, the creation of thread pools has been very simple, achieved with one of the static factory methods in Executors (a class in the java.util.concurrent package). We need Executors.newSingleThreadExecutor(), which creates a pool holding a single worker thread (an *executor*) who carries out the tasks one at a time.

The thread pool, called soundExecutor, is created in the Obstacle constructor:

```
// global
private ExecutorService soundExecutor;

// in the Obstacle constructor
soundExecutor = Executors.newSingleThreadExecutor();
```

The playSound() method sends a task to the pool in the form of a Runnable object:

```
// globals
private String soundFnm;
private SoundsPlayer soundsPlayer;
private boolean isSoundPlaying = false;
```

```
private void playSound()
{
  if ((soundFnm != null) && !isSoundPlaying) {
    soundExecutor.execute( new Runnable() {
      public void run()
      {
        isSoundPlaying = true;
        int sndLen = soundsPlayer.getLength(soundFnm);
        if (sndLen == -1)
          sndLen = 1000;    // reasonable waiting time (1 sec)
        soundsPlayer.play(soundFnm);
        try {
          Thread.sleep(sndLen);    // wait for sound to finish
        }
        catch(InterruptedException ex) {}
        isSoundPlaying = false;
      }
    });
  }
} // end of playSound()
```

playSound() gets the worker thread to play the collision sound, thereby allowing the rest of the application to continue executing.

Unfortunately, there's still a difficulty, which is solved with the isSoundPlaying boolean in playSound(). Although the worker thread created with Executors.newSingleThreadExecutor() is guaranteed to execute its tasks sequentially, there's no limit on how many tasks can be added to the pool's queue. The collision detection code may be executed several times before the user releases the navigation key moving the grabbers. In that time, several tasks will be added to the pool's queue and subsequently played. This means that a single collision will result in the collision sound being played multiple times.

This behavior is prevented with the isSoundPlaying boolean. It lets playSound() ignore new sound playing requests if the sound is already playing; the call returns without adding a new task to the pool's queue.

This approach introduces a new question: how long should the boolean be set to true while the sound plays to its end? Since the AudioClip class has no running time method, one must be set up inside SoundsPlayer. The retrieved time is used to make the thread sleep for as long as the sound is playing, after which the boolean is set back to false. If there isn't a time available, the thread "wings it" by sleeping for a second.

Even isSoundPlaying isn't a rock-solid solution to the problem of multiple sound-playing tasks. There's a very short interval between the if-test at the start of playSound() and the setting of isSoundPlaying at the beginning of the task. This might be enough time for a second call to playSound() to get past the test and create a second task. But it's quite unlikely, and the only (nonserious) consequence is that the sound will play an extra time.

Sending Input to the Grabbers

Movement requests are sent to the grabbers either from the keyboard or the gamepad. Instead of having the grabbers deal with their data directly, the information is converted into GrabberOp instances. This enforces a clean separation between the input sources (the keyboard and gamepad) and the input's processing in Grabbers. The Grabbers code becomes much less convoluted, and it's straightforward to add new input sources, such as the mouse or a data glove.

The keyboard, the gamepad, and the grabbers are connected in addGrabbers() in WrapArmsPad3D. The relevant code fragment is shown here:

```
// in addGrabbers() in WrapArmsPad3D

GamePadController gamePad = new GamePadController();

Grabbers grabbers = new Grabbers(. . .);
   // Grabbers input arguments will be explained later

// set up gamepad behavior to catch gamepad input
GamePadBehavior gamePadBeh = new GamePadBehavior(grabbers, gamePad);
gamePadBeh.setSchedulingBounds(bounds);
sceneBG.addChild(gamePadBeh);

// set up keyboard controls to catch keyp resses
KeyBehavior keyBeh = new KeyBehavior(grabbers);
keyBeh.setSchedulingBounds(bounds);
sceneBG.addChild(keyBeh);
```

KeyBehavior sends key presses to the grabbers as GrabberOp instances, while GamePadBehavior does the same for gamepad input.

Processing Keyboard Input

The version of KeyBehavior in ArmsPad3D differs from other KeyBehaviors explained earlier (e.g., KeyBehavior in ObjView3D). They contain methods that convert the keyboard data into translations and rotations applied to TransformGroups. This KeyBehavior class passes the data to a GrabberOp instance to initialize it, then sends the GrabberOp object to Grabbers for processing:

```
// global
private Grabbers grabbers;


public void processStimulus(Enumeration criteria)
{
  WakeupCriterion wakeup;
  AWTEvent[] event;
  GrabberOp gop;

  while( criteria.hasMoreElements() ) {
    wakeup = (WakeupCriterion) criteria.nextElement();
    if( wakeup instanceof WakeupOnAWTEvent ) {
      event = ((WakeupOnAWTEvent)wakeup).getAWTEvent();
      for( int i = 0; i < event.length; i++ ) {
        if( event[i].getID() == KeyEvent.KEY_PRESSED ) {
          gop = new GrabberOp( (KeyEvent)event[i] );
                    // make a GrabberOp
          if (!gop.isOp(GrabberOp.NONE))
            grabbers.processOp(gop);
              // send it to Grabbers for processing
        }
      }
    }
  }
  wakeupOn( keyPress );
} // end of processStimulus()
```

The call to GrabberOp.isOp() tests if the generated operation is a no-op (one that does nothing), in which case processOp() isn't called.

Building a Grabber Operation for a Key Press

GrabberOp represents a grabber operation using four integer variables:

- *opVal*: Holds the grabber operation name (as an integer)
- *partVal*: Holds the integer name for the grabber part being used by this operation
- *jointVal*: Holds the integer name of the joint being used by this operation
- *rotVal*: Holds the rotation direction (positive or negative) for joint operations

These integer variables are defined as globals in the GrabberOp class:

```
private int opVal, partVal, jointVal, rotVal;
```

Their values come from a very large set of public integer constants. They're public so they can be used by other classes (e.g., Grabbers and Grabber).

A GrabberOp object is created either from keystrokes (sent by KeyBehavior) or from gamepad input (sent by GamePadBehavior), so there are three constructors: a default, simple version; one for key input; and one for gamepad input. I explain the key-based constructor and its related methods here, and return to the gamepad methods after explaining GamePadBehavior.

The key-based constructor calls set() methods, which examine the input to decide how to assign values to opVal, partVal, jointVal, and rotVal:

```
// globals
// better names for the translation/rotation keys
// for translating the grabbers
private final static int forwardKey = KeyEvent.VK_UP;
private final static int backKey = KeyEvent.VK_DOWN;
private final static int leftKey = KeyEvent.VK_LEFT;
private final static int rightKey = KeyEvent.VK_RIGHT;


public GrabberOp()
{ // default values
  opVal = NONE;
  partVal = NO_PART;
  jointVal = NOT_JOINT;
  rotVal = NO_ROT;
} // end of GrabberOp();


public GrabberOp(KeyEvent eventKey)
// create a GrabberOp from keystrokes (sent by KeyBehavior)
{
  this();   // assign default values

  // the shift and alt keys are used as modifiers
  int keyCode = eventKey.getKeyCode();
  boolean isShift = eventKey.isShiftDown();
  boolean isAlt = eventKey.isAltDown();

  if((keyCode == forwardKey) || (keyCode == backKey) ||
     (keyCode == leftKey) || (keyCode == rightKey))
```

```
      setBaseOp(keyCode, isAlt);
   else {  // grabbers
     if (isShift)    // right grabber
       setRightGrabberOp(keyCode, isAlt);
     else  // left grabber
       setLeftGrabberOp(keyCode, isAlt);
   }
}  // end of GrabberOp() the keyboard
```

The grabbers respond to the arrow keys and x, y, z, and f, which can be combined with the Shift and Alt keys to affect their meaning. The pressed keys are identified at the start of the GrabberOp() constructor.

The grabbers consist of three parts: the base and the left and right arms. The base can translate and rotate, while each arm has x-, y-, and z-axis joints and fingers that can open and close. Based on the keys, setBaseOp(), setLeftGrabber(), or setRightGrabber() are called in order to assign values to the GrabberOp state variables (opVal, partVal, jointVal, and rotVal).

setBaseOp() gives a flavor of the coding of these set methods:

```
private void setBaseOp(int keycode, boolean isAlt)
/* Make grabbers move forward or backward;
   rotate left or right */
{
  partVal = BASE;
  if(isAlt) {    // key + <alt>
    if(keycode == forwardKey)
      opVal = BASE_UP;
    else if(keycode == backKey)
      opVal = BASE_DOWN;
    else if(keycode == leftKey)
      opVal = BASE_LEFT;
    else if(keycode == rightKey)
      opVal = BASE_RIGHT;
  }
  else {  // just <key>
    if(keycode == forwardKey)
      opVal = BASE_FWD;
    else if(keycode == backKey)
      opVal = BASE_BACK;
    else if(keycode == leftKey)
      opVal = BASE_ROT_LEFT;
    else if(keycode == rightKey)
      opVal = BASE_ROT_RIGHT;
  }
} // end of setBaseOp()
```

For example, if the up arrow (forwardKey) and Alt keys are pressed together, the resulting GrabberOp operation will specify that the grabbers' base be lifted up. The values assigned to the state variables are the following:

- opVal == BASE_UP
- partVal == BASE
- jointVal == NONE
- rotVal == NONE

jointVal and rotVal are unaffected since they refer to the arm joints, which aren't used in base-related operations.

Each of the four state variables has its own get, set, and is-test methods, which makes it simple to query the GrabberOp states. For example, opVal is accessed with the following:

```
public int getOp()
{   return opVal;   }

public boolean isOp(int op)
{   return opVal == op;   }

public void setOp(int op)
{   opVal = op;   }   // no checking of op
```

Processing Gamepad Input

GamePadBehavior periodically polls the gamepad controller and converts the component settings into new GrabberOp objects. These are passed to the Grabbers object for processing.

The constructor creates an ArrayList to hold the GrabberOp objects and initializes the time-based wake-up condition:

```
// globals
private static final int DELAY = 75;    // ms (polling interval)

private Grabbers grabbers;
private ArrayList<GrabberOp> gops;
                // storage for the created GrabberOps
private GamePadController gamePad;
private WakeupCondition wakeUpCond;


public GamePadBehavior(Grabbers gs, GamePadController gp)
{
  grabbers = gs;
  gamePad = gp;

  gops = new ArrayList<GrabberOp>();
  wakeUpCond = new WakeupOnElapsedTime(DELAY);
} // end of GamePadBehavior()
```

processStimulus() is called every DELAY milliseconds, polls GamePadController to refresh its state information, then examines the left and right sticks, the hat, and the buttons. The resulting list of GrabberOp objects sent over to Grabbers for processing:

```
public void processStimulus(Enumeration criteria)
{
  gops.clear();       // empty the GrabberOps list

  gamePad.poll();     // update the gamepad's components

  /* create GrabberOps for the gamepad components:
        left/right sticks, a hat, and buttons
  */
  processLeftStick( gamePad.getXYStickDir() );
  processRightStick( gamePad.getZRZStickDir() );
  processHat( gamePad.getHatDir() );
  processButtons( gamePad.getButtons() );
```

```
  // send the GrabberOps to Grabbers
  for(int i=0; i < gops.size(); i++)
    grabbers.processOp( gops.get(i) );

  wakeupOn(wakeUpCond);          // make sure we are notified again
} // end of processStimulus()
```

The process methods in GamePadBehavior test for the various possible states of the gamepad components and build GrabberOp objects in response. All the methods are quite similar; for example, processLeftStick() converts the eight compass directions of the left stick into GrabberOp objects:

```
private void processLeftStick(int dir)
{
  if ((dir == GamePadController.NORTH) ||
      (dir == GamePadController.SOUTH) ||
      (dir == GamePadController.EAST) ||
      (dir == GamePadController.WEST))
      gops.add( new GrabberOp(GamePadController.LEFT_STICK, dir) );
  else if (dir == GamePadController.NE) {
    gops.add( new GrabberOp(GamePadController.LEFT_STICK,
                        GamePadController.NORTH) );
    gops.add( new GrabberOp(GamePadController.LEFT_STICK,
                        GamePadController.EAST) );
  }
  else if (dir == GamePadController.NW) {
    gops.add( new GrabberOp(GamePadController.LEFT_STICK,
                        GamePadController.NORTH) );
    gops.add( new GrabberOp(GamePadController.LEFT_STICK,
                        GamePadController.WEST) );
  }
  else if (dir == GamePadController.SE) {
    gops.add( new GrabberOp(GamePadController.LEFT_STICK,
                        GamePadController.SOUTH) );
    gops.add( new GrabberOp(GamePadController.LEFT_STICK,
                        GamePadController.EAST) );
  }
  else if (dir == GamePadController.SW) {
    gops.add( new GrabberOp(GamePadController.LEFT_STICK,
                        GamePadController.SOUTH) );
    gops.add( new GrabberOp(GamePadController.LEFT_STICK,
                        GamePadController.WEST) );
  }
}  // end of processLeftStick()
```

The diagonal directions are converted into two operations each, which means that only the GamePadController constants NORTH, SOUTH, EAST, and WEST need to be processed over in GrabberOp.

The translation is complicated by the large range of input types and output operations. The two sticks and hat can be assigned eight different compass directions each, and there are 12 buttons. There are 24 different grabber operations. The complexity is reduced by using public constants rather than a bevy of anonymous numbers and booleans.

Building a Grabber Operation for the Gamepad

The GrabberOp constructor for the gamepad must map all the possible input types to GrabberOp operations. It does this by dividing the input into four groups: data from the left stick, the right stick, the hat, and the buttons:

```
public GrabberOp(int gamePadComponent, int val)
// create a GrabberOp from the gamepad input
{
  this();

  // input may be from left or right stick, hat, or buttons
  if (gamePadComponent == GamePadController.LEFT_STICK)
    setLeftStick(val);
  else if (gamePadComponent == GamePadController.RIGHT_STICK)
    setRightStick(val);
  else if (gamePadComponent == GamePadController.HAT)
    setHat(val);
  else if (gamePadComponent == GamePadController.BUTTONS)
    setButton(val);
  else
    System.out.println("Do not recognize gamepad component: " +
                           gamePadComponent);
}  // end of GrabberOp() for the gamepad
```

The "set" operations for gamepad input have the same structure as the keyboard-based ones I described previously: a series of if-tests decide what values to assign to opVal, partVal, jointVal, and rotVal. setLeftStick() is a typical method (it creates a GrabberOp object for affecting the grabber's left arm):

```
private void setLeftStick(int dir)
/* Deal with input from the gamepad's left stick.
   The left stick maps to the left grabber. */
{
  partVal = LEFT_GRABBER;

  if (dir == GamePadController.NORTH) {    // y up
    opVal = LEFT_Y_POS;
    jointVal = Y_JOINT;  rotVal = POS;
  }
  else if (dir == GamePadController.SOUTH) {   // y down
    opVal = LEFT_Y_NEG;
    jointVal = Y_JOINT;  rotVal = NEG;
  }
  else if (dir == GamePadController.EAST) {  // x right
    opVal = LEFT_X_NEG;
    jointVal = X_JOINT;  rotVal = NEG;
  }
  else if (dir == GamePadController.WEST) {  // x left
    opVal = LEFT_X_POS;
    jointVal = X_JOINT;  rotVal = POS;
  }
}  // end of setLeftStick()
```

Each arm has four joints (x-, y-, z-, and the fingers), and each joint can be rotated in a positive or negative direction. For instance, if the user presses the left stick upward (which is denoted by GamePadController.NORTH), the arm's y-axis joint should be rotated in a positive direction to move it up. The GrabberOp states are set to the following:

- opVal == LEFT_Y_POS
- partVal == LEFT_GRABBER
- jointVal == Y_JOINT
- rotVal == POS

It may seem that opVal contains all the necessary information (left, y, pos), which is needlessly duplicated by partVal, jointVal, and rotVal. The duplication is useful because the part, joint, and rotation information become easier to access from Grabbers and Grabber. The alternative would be additional code to extract the component attributes from opVal.

The Grabbers

The grabbers consist of a base and left and right arms, just as they did in Chapter 4. However, the base can be translated *and* rotated (the old version could only be translated). Also, the grabbers are attached to the camera viewpoint, so they move in unison with it. This is achieved by using a PlatformGeometry instance, so the base is moved by affecting the viewpoint's targetTG TransformGroup. Movement commands may come from the keyboard or the gamepad, arriving as GrabberOp objects.

Collision processing is more elaborate. An operation is tried out, and if the resulting base or arm positions intersect with each other, the obstacles, or the floor, the operation is undone. This *try-it-and-see* technique is employed before the scene is rendered, so a move followed by an undo won't be displayed. The user only notices that the grabbers don't move. This is quite different from the approach in Chapter 4, where the collision is detected after the offending operation has been rendered. A behavior is triggered that executes a reverse operation to undo the move. To the user, this looks like the base or arm "bouncing" back from its move.

A collision with an obstacle triggers the playing of a sound in the Obstacle object and the gamepad rumbles.

Connecting the Grabbers to the Camera

The grabbers are attached to the camera viewpoint in addGrabbers() in WrapArmsPad3D. The following is the relevant code fragment:

```
// in addGrabbers() in WrapArmsPad3D...

// get targetTG, the TG for the camera viewpoint
ViewingPlatform vp = su.getViewingPlatform();
TransformGroup targetTG = vp.getViewPlatformTransform();

// create the grabbers
Vector3d posnVec = new Vector3d(0, -0.5, -0.9);
Grabbers grabbers = new Grabbers(posnVec, 0.4f,
                         targetTG, obstacles, gamePad);
  // supply grabbers position and each arm's x-axis offset

// add grabbers to the viewpoint
PlatformGeometry pg = new PlatformGeometry();
pg.addChild( grabbers.getTG() );
vp.setPlatformGeometry(pg);
```

The PlatformGeometry object is essentially a BranchGroup attached to the targetTG TransformGroup which moves the camera viewpoint. Figure 12-4 shows the view branch subgraph.

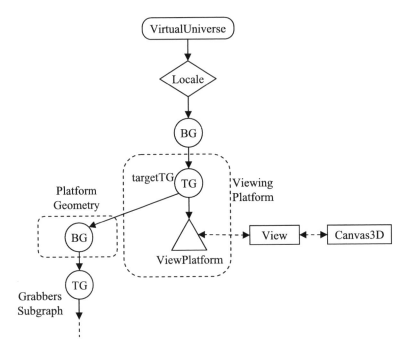

Figure 12-4. *The view branch subgraph*

A reference to targetTG is passed into Grabbers since the grabbers move by changing the camera viewpoint. Grabbers also receives a position vector (posnVec), which is used to place it a little way in front of (and below) the viewpoint. I decided on (0, -0.5, -0.9) by experimentation.

Constructing the Grabbers

The scene graph for the grabbers is a TransformGroup (grabbersTG) parent with two Grabber subgraphs for the left and right arms:

```
// globals
// scene graph elements
private TransformGroup targetTG;
          // the ViewPlatform's transform group
private TransformGroup grabbersTG;
private Grabber leftGrabber, rightGrabber;

private Obstacles obs;    // for collision detection
private GamePadController gamePad;    // used to switch on rumbling


public Grabbers(Vector3d posnVec, float grabOffset,
                TransformGroup targetTG,
                Obstacles obs, GamePadController gp)
{
  this.targetTG = targetTG;
  this.obs = obs;
  gamePad = gp;
```

```
Texture2D tex = loadTexture(TEX_FNM);  // used by both grabbers

  // position the grabbers
  t3d.set(posnVec);
  grabbersTG = new TransformGroup(t3d);

  // add the left grabber
  leftGrabber = new Grabber("left", tex, -grabOffset);
  grabbersTG.addChild( leftGrabber.getBaseTG() );

  // add the right grabber
  rightGrabber = new Grabber("right", tex, grabOffset);
  grabbersTG.addChild( rightGrabber.getBaseTG() );
}  // end of Grabbers()


public TransformGroup getTG()
// called by WrapArms3D
{  return grabbersTG;  }
```

Processing an Operation

processOp() tries out the requested GrabberOp operation in doOp(). A resulting collision causes the operation to be undone, and Grabbers notifies the user by rumbling the gamepad:

```
synchronized public void processOp(GrabberOp gop)
{
  if (doOp(gop))
    if (isColliding()) {
      rumblePad();
      undoOp(gop);
    }
} // end of processOp()
```

processOp() is synchronized since it can be called by two behaviors (KeyBehavior and GamePadBehavior) that may be running concurrently. Without the synchronization, there's a chance that processOp() could be called by both behaviors at the same time, which would most likely cause the grabbers' state to become inconsistent.

The try-it-and-see approach puts the control logic in one class, called from processOp(). By comparison, the behavior triggering employed in Chapter 4 spreads the collision processing over several classes and connects it with rather opaque event handling.

Doing an Operation

An operation may either affect the grabbers base or one of the arms:

```
private boolean doOp(GrabberOp gop)
{
  if (gop.isOp(GrabberOp.NONE))
    return false;

  boolean done = false;
  if (gop.isPart(GrabberOp.BASE))
    done = affectBase(gop);
  else if (gop.isPart(GrabberOp.LEFT_GRABBER))
    done = leftGrabber.rotate(gop);
```

```
    else if (gop.isPart(GrabberOp.RIGHT_GRABBER))
      done = rightGrabber.rotate(gop);
    return done;
}  // end of doOp()
```

The code uses GrabberOp.isPart() to examine the partVal state in the GrabberOp instance. The processing for the arms is carried out by the Grabber instances, but base operations are left to Grabbers.

The base can be translated or rotated, and the choice comes down to an examination of the opVal state in the GrabberOp object:

```
// globals
// used when rotating the base
private static final double ROT_AMT = Math.PI / 36.0; // 5 degrees
private static final double MOVE_STEP = 0.2;

// hardwired movement vectors used when translating the base
private static final Vector3d FWD = new Vector3d(0,0,-MOVE_STEP);
private static final Vector3d BACK = new Vector3d(0,0,MOVE_STEP);
private static final Vector3d LEFT = new Vector3d(-MOVE_STEP,0,0);
private static final Vector3d RIGHT = new Vector3d(MOVE_STEP,0,0);
private static final Vector3d UP = new Vector3d(0,MOVE_STEP,0);
private static final Vector3d DOWN = new Vector3d(0,-MOVE_STEP,0);

private int upMoves = 0;


private boolean affectBase(GrabberOp gop)
{
  if (gop.isOp(GrabberOp.BASE_FWD))
    doMove(FWD);
  else if (gop.isOp(GrabberOp.BASE_BACK))
    doMove(BACK);
  else if (gop.isOp(GrabberOp.BASE_ROT_LEFT))
    rotateY(ROT_AMT);
  else if (gop.isOp(GrabberOp.BASE_ROT_RIGHT))
    rotateY(-ROT_AMT);
  else if (gop.isOp(GrabberOp.BASE_UP)) {
    upMoves++;
    doMove(UP);
  }
  else if (gop.isOp(GrabberOp.BASE_DOWN)) {
    if (upMoves > 0) {  // don't drop below start height
      upMoves--;
      doMove(DOWN);
    }
    else
      return false;    // since doing nothing
  }
  else if (gop.isOp(GrabberOp.BASE_LEFT))
    doMove(LEFT);
  else if (gop.isOp(GrabberOp.BASE_RIGHT))
    doMove(RIGHT);

  return true;
}  // end of affectBase()
```

This code should look familiar from previous chapters. doMove() and rotateY() apply translations and rotations to the targetTG TransformGroup, thereby moving the camera viewpoint and the grabbers attached to it:

```
// globals
// used for repeated calcs
private Transform3D t3d = new Transform3D();
private Transform3D toMove = new Transform3D();
private Transform3D toRot = new Transform3D();


private void doMove(Vector3d theMove)
// move targetTG by the amount in theMove
{
  targetTG.getTransform(t3d);
  toMove.setTranslation(theMove);
  t3d.mul(toMove);
  targetTG.setTransform(t3d);
} // end of doMove()


private void rotateY(double radians)
// rotate about the y-axis of targetTG by radians
{ targetTG.getTransform(t3d);
  toRot.rotY(radians);
  t3d.mul(toRot);
  targetTG.setTransform(t3d);
} // end of rotateY()
```

Detecting a Collision

After the operation has affected the grabbers' TransformGroups, it's time to see if a collision has occurred. isColliding() deals with the following cases:

- The arms may be touching each other

- The left or right arm might be touching an obstacle

- The left or right arm might be touching the ground

These cases are translated into five if-tests in isColliding():

```
// globals
private Grabber leftGrabber, rightGrabber;
private Obstacles obs;


private boolean isColliding()
{
  BoundingSphere[] bs = rightGrabber.getArmBounds();
  if (leftGrabber.touches(bs))    // arms touching each other?
    return true;

  // check the right arm against the obstacles
  if (obs.intersects(bs))
    return true;

  // check the left arm against obstacles
```

```
  bs = leftGrabber.getArmBounds();
  if (obs.intersects(bs))
    return true;

  // are either arms touching the ground?
  if (leftGrabber.touchingGround())
    return true;

  if (rightGrabber.touchingGround())
    return true;

  return false;
}  // end of isColliding()
```

The Grabber methods, getArmBounds(), touches(), and touchingGround() are the same as in Chapter 4. The Obstacles method, intersects(), was described earlier.

Undoing an Operation

If a collision is detected, the operation (the GrabberOp object, gop) has to be reversed. This is easy to do in this application since the operation is either a translation or a rotation.

There are three cases to consider: whether the original operation was applied to the base, the left arm, or the right arm. A base operation is reversed inside Grabbers, while GrabberOp and the relevant Grabber instance deals with the reversal of an arm rotation:

```
private void undoOp(GrabberOp gop)
{
  if (gop.isPart(GrabberOp.BASE))  // is a base op
    undoBase(gop);
  else {
    GrabberOp revGOP = gop.reverse();  // reverse the rotation op
    if (revGOP.isPart(GrabberOp.LEFT_GRABBER))
      leftGrabber.rotate(revGOP);
    else  // must be right grabber
      rightGrabber.rotate(revGOP);
  }
}  // end of undoOp()
```

undoBase() checks the opVal state in the original GrabberOp and then carries out the reverse translation or rotation:

```
private void undoBase(GrabberOp baseGOP)
{
  switch (baseGOP.getOp()) {
    case GrabberOp.NONE: break;       // do nothing

    case GrabberOp.BASE_FWD: doMove(BACK); break;
    case GrabberOp.BASE_BACK: doMove(FWD); break;
    case GrabberOp.BASE_LEFT: doMove(RIGHT); break;
    case GrabberOp.BASE_RIGHT: doMove(LEFT); break;
    case GrabberOp.BASE_ROT_LEFT: rotateY(-ROT_AMT); break;
    case GrabberOp.BASE_ROT_RIGHT: rotateY(ROT_AMT); break;
    case GrabberOp.BASE_UP: doMove(DOWN); break;
    case GrabberOp.BASE_DOWN: doMove(UP); break;

    default: System.out.println("Not a base grabber op"); break;
  }
} // end of undoBase()
```

All the arm operations are joint rotations, so reversing one is just a matter of reversing the rotation direction, positive to negative, and vice versa. This is done by GrabberOp.reverse(), which generates a new GrabberOp instance; it's a copy of the original except for the rotation direction:

```
// in the GrabberOp class
public GrabberOp reverse()
{
  // copy the op, part, and joint values for this object
  GrabberOp gop = new GrabberOp();
  gop.setOp(opVal);
  gop.setPart(partVal);
  gop.setJoint(jointVal);

  // reverse the rotation (if possible)
  if (rotVal == NO_ROT) {
    System.out.println("Cannot reverse since no rotation found");
    gop.setRotation(rotVal);
  }
  else if (rotVal == POS)
    gop.setRotation(NEG);
  else    // must be NEG
    gop.setRotation(POS);

  return gop;
}  // end of reverse()
```

Once the reversed GrabberOp object has been generated, it can be processed by the Grabber instance in the same way as other operations.

Alerting the User

processOp() calls rumblePad() when it detects a collision, causing the gamepad to rumble for a short time. This is somewhat trickier to implement correctly than it may at first seem.

The rumbler is turned on and off by two separate calls to GamePadController.setRumbler(), which means that Grabbers must wait for a short time between the calls to give the pad time to rumble. Having Grabbers go to sleep is unacceptable, since it would prevent the grabbers from responding to other user input. The answer is to use a worker thread in a thread pool (as when playing a sound in Obstacle). The pool, called rumblerExecutor, is created in the Grabbers constructor:

```
// global
private ExecutorService rumblerExecutor;

// in the Grabbers constructor
rumblerExecutor = Executors.newSingleThreadExecutor();
```

Another issue is how to deal with rapid multiple calls to setRumbler(), caused when the user holds down a key (or button) that triggers a collision.

This can be avoided by employing another idea from the sound-playing code in Obstacle: a boolean, called isRumbling, prevents a new task from being added to the pool's queue until the existing task has finished executing:

```
// globals
private GamePadController gamePad;
private boolean isRumbling = false;


private void rumblePad()
```

```
/* Play the rumbler for 0.5 secs if it's not already
   rumbling, and ignore other rumbler requests until
   the current task has finished. */
{
  if (!isRumbling) {
    rumblerExecutor.execute( new Runnable() {
      public void run()
      {
        isRumbling = true;
        gamePad.setRumbler(true);
        try {
          sleep(500);    // wait for 0.5 secs
        }
        catch(InterruptedException ex) {}
        gamePad.setRumbler(false);
        isRumbling = false;
      }
    });
} // end of rumblePad()
```

The Grabber Arms

The Grabber class is essentially the same one that's in Arms3D in Chapter 4. A grabber arm can turn left or right or up or down, and spin around its long axis; its two fingers can open and close. All these operations are implemented as joint rotations: there are three joints at the start of the arm for the x-, y-, and z- axes and a joint for each finger.

There are three areas where the Grabber class in this chapter is different from the one in Arms3D:

- *Arm size*: Due to the proximity to the camera, the dimensions of the arm and fingers have been reduced to roughly a quarter of the size of the originals.

- *Input data*: The rotate() method processes a GrabberOp input argument rather than a collection of integers. The code is changed to examine the GrabberOp values, but the same rotations are carried out.

- *Collision detection*: Grabber no longer needs to create a list of "collision" joints since Grabbers no longer creates wake-up criteria using those joints. However, the collision *checking* methods, getArmBounds(), touches(), and touchingGround() are unchanged because they utilize the GrabberBounds object, which is the same as in Arms3D.

Summary

This chapter brought Java 3D and JInput together, showing how input from a gamepad can control articulated arms in a 3D scene.

The example reused many elements from earlier chapters, including the checkerboard floor, the background, the arms, the model loader, the ground shapes, and the gamepad controller.

The new techniques included obstacles, a try-it-and-see form of collision detection, a technique for integrating different input sources into the application (the gamepad and keyboard), a sound player, and how to attach the grabbers to the camera's viewpoint so they move together.

CHAPTER 13

3D Sound with JOAL

This chapter interrupts the discussion of nonstandard input devices programming so we can look at JOAL (https://joal.dev.java.net/), a Java wrapper around OpenAL. OpenAL, the Open Audio Library, is a cross-platform API for programming 2D and 3D audio (http://www.openal.org/).

JOAL (and OpenAL) is introduced through a JOALSoundMan class that simplifies the creation of spatial 3D sound effects, and its use is demonstrated with a few simple nongraphical examples. In Chapter 14, JOALSoundMan is utilized to add 3D sound to Java 3D, and it crops up again in Chapter 17, managing the audio effects in my JOGL code.

Why JOAL and Java 3D?

In Chapter 1, I mentioned that Java 3D supports 2D and 3D sound. The API includes three sound-related classes: BackgroundSound for ambient sound (sound that's audible everywhere in the scene); PointSound for a sound source located at a particular spot; and ConeSound for a point source aimed in a specific direction.

PointSound and ConeSound are *spatial* sound classes, since their volume and the audio mix coming from the left and right speakers depends on the sound's location in relation to the listener (which is usually the camera's viewpoint). Another factor is the relative velocities of the sound source and listener if they're moving.

The bad news is that PointSound and ConeSound contain some nasty bugs, which led to their demotion to optional parts of Java 3D starting with version 1.3.2. Also, the Java 3D development team wanted the classes reimplemented so they didn't rely on the Headspace audio engine, third-party software not maintained by Sun. They hoped to persuade a kindly Java 3D community member to do this work, using JOAL.

The end's almost in sight; in July 2006, David Grace posted JoalMixer to the org.jdesktop.j3d.audioengines.joal branch of the j3d-incubator project (https://j3d-incubator.dev.java.net/). It includes revised PointSound, ConeSound, and BackgroundSound classes, built with JOAL.

Unfortunately, JoalMixer arrived too late for the Java 3D 1.5 release, and can only be utilized at the moment by recompiling the Java 3D sources. For gallant users interested in this approach, there are detailed instructions in the java.net Java 3D forum thread on spatialized audio at http://forums.java.net/jive/thread.jspa?threadID=4638&start=0&tstart=105.

I decided *not* to be gallant and roll my own JOAL code instead (a JOALSoundMan class). It offers ambient and point sounds, and is reusable across Java, Java 3D, and JOGL applications, without requiring any recompilation of those APIs.

Background on OpenAL and JOAL

JOAL is a thin layer of Java over OpenAL, so its 2D and 3D audio features are really those of OpenAL. For that reason, I talk about OpenAL first, and then JOAL.

OpenAL supports the construction of a sound application containing a collection of audio sources located in 3D space, heard by a single listener. The space doesn't need a graphical representation in the application.

The main OpenAL entities are the buffer, the source, and the listener:

- A *buffer* stores sound information, typically a sound clip loaded from a WAV file. There may be many buffers in a program.

- A *source* is a point in the 3D space that emits a sound in all directions. A source isn't the audio sample, but the location where the sample is played. Each source must refer to a buffer to have a sound to play. It's possible to connect several sources to the same buffer.

- An application has a single *listener*, which represents the user in the scene. Listener properties (position, and perhaps velocity) are combined with the properties of each source (position, velocity, etc.) to determine how the source's audio is heard.

OpenAL is available on a wide range of platforms, including Windows, Mac OS X, Linux, the PlayStation 2, and Xbox. The API is hardware-independent but utilizes hardware support if the underlying sound card has it. There's a growing list of commercial games employing OpenAL, including *Doom 3*, *Unreal Tournament 2004*, and *Battlefield 2*, and it has a wide following in the open source games world (see the list at http://www.openal.org/titles.html).

OpenAL is currently maintained by Creative Labs, perhaps best known for its Sound Blaster line of audio cards.

The Windows version of OpenAL (and JOAL) supports Creative Lab's EAX and EFX (Environmental Audio eXtensions and EFfects eXtensions) technologies. EAX offers reverberations and low-pass filtering effects, while EFX adds filtering at the OpenAL source level. EAX and EFX require sound card support, so they aren't widely available.

OpenAL's main web site is at http://www.openal.org/, which includes various ports of the library and documentation. You don't need the software since we're using JOAL, but the OpenAL 1.1 Programmer's Guide and Specification (at http://www.openal.org/documentation.html) are worth a read.

An excellent series of OpenAL programming articles can be found at DevMaster.net (http://www.devmaster.net/articles.php?catID=6), and there are more links at http://www.openal.org/links.html. Although these tutorials are written in C for OpenAL, JOAL methods and OpenAL functions are so similar that the information is still helpful.

There are two official OpenAL mailing lists archived at http://opensource.creative.com/pipermail/openal/ and http://opensource.creative.com/pipermail/openal-devel/. There's a Nabble forum for OpenAL at http://www.nabble.com/OpenAL-f14243.html.

What About JOAL?

I'm not using OpenAL directly, but rather the Java wrapper, JOAL. All the necessary JOAL software can be found at https://joal.dev.java.net/, so there's no need to download the OpenAL libraries. I'll explain the installation details in the next section.

The DevMaster.net OpenAL tutorials have been "translated" into JOGL (at https://joal-demos.dev.java.net/) except for one on Ogg Vorbis streaming. Starfire Research also has some brief but good JOAL examples, starting at http://www.starfireresearch.com/services/java/docs/joal.html.

The main JOAL forum is at `http://www.javagaming.org/forums/index.php?board=26.0`. There's also a JOAL list at the lwjgl.org site, `http://lwjgl.org/forum/index.php?board=10.0`. The focus is on the Lightweight Java Game Library (LWJGL), but there's plenty of general information as well. If these forums don't answer your questions, you should consider searching through the OpenAL lists that I mentioned.

Installing JOAL

The current Windows version of JOAL as of January 2007 is release build 1.1.0, dated December 22, 2006, at `https://joal.dev.java.net/`, via the Documents & Files menu. The file (joal-1.1.0-windows-i586.zip) contains two JAR files, joal.jar and gluegen-rt.jar, and two DLLs, joal-native.dll and gluegen-rt.dll. Other useful downloads are the API documentation (joal-1.1.0-docs.zip) and the source code for the demos (joal-demos-src.zip).

joal.jar and gluegen-rt.jar should be copied into <JAVA_HOME>\jre\lib\ext and <JRE_HOME>\lib\ext. On my WinXP test machine, they're the directories c:\Program Files\Java\jdk1.6.0\jre\lib\ext and c:\Program Files\Java\jre1.6.0\lib\ext.

joal-native.dll and gluegen-rt.dll should be placed in a directory of your choice (I chose d:\joal).

Figure 13-1 shows the two DLLs in my d:\joal directory.

Figure 13-1. *The two DLLs needed for JOAL*

These DLLs are needed at runtime, so every call to java.exe requires a command-line option to supply the path to the libraries. For instance, to run the JOAL application, JoalExample1.java needs the following:

```
java -Djava.library.path="d:\joal" JoalExample1
```

I'm lazy, so I use a DOS batch file instead:

```
runJoal JoalExample1
```

runJoal.bat contains the following:

```
@echo off
echo Executing %1 with JOAL...
java -Djava.library.path="d:\joal" %1 %2
echo Finished.
```

The %1 and %2 arguments allow at most two command-line arguments to be passed to the java.exe call. The corresponding shell scripts for runJoal.bat on OS X/UNIX are very similar.

Managing JOAL Sounds

Most JOAL applications look the same: there's an initialization phase, then the buffers, their sources, and the listener are created. During the program's execution, the sources and/or listener are moved around, causing the sound output to change. At termination, the source and buffers are deleted.

I decided to package up these stages into a JOALSoundMan class in order to hide the repetitive manipulation of the low-level buffers, sources, and listener data structures.

JOALSoundMan has three groups of public methods:

1. *General*: JOALSoundMan() initializes JOAL and creates a listener located at (0, 0, 0), facing along the negative z-axis. cleanUp() deletes any source and buffer data structures created during the application's execution.

2. *Buffer and source*: load() loads a specified WAV file and creates a buffer for it. The buffer is then associated with a new source located at the origin. A second version of load() includes an (x, y, z) coordinate for positioning the source. Every source is assigned a name that is used to refer to it in other methods. setPos() changes the position of a named source. play() plays the named source. pause() pauses the source, and stop() stops it.

3. *Listener*: moveListener() moves the listener by a specified x- and z- step. setListenerPos() moves the listener to the new (x, 0, z) coordinate. It's not possible to change the listener's y-axis position, a restriction that simplifies the coding.

   setListenerOri() changes the listener's orientation to the specified number of degrees in the anticlockwise direction around the y-axis. turnListener() turns the listener a specified number of degrees around its y-axis, starting from its present orientation. There's no way to rotate the listener around the x- or z- axes. getX(), getY(), and getAngle() return the listener's current position and y-axis angle.

I explain these methods in more detail in the following sections.

Initializing JOAL

The JOALSoundMan constructor creates two HashMaps, initializes OpenAL, and creates the listener:

```
// global stores for the sounds
private HashMap<String, int[]> buffersMap;   // (name, buffer) pairs
private HashMap<String, int[]> sourcesMap;   // (name, source) pairs


public JOALSoundMan()
{
  buffersMap = new HashMap<String, int[]>();
  sourcesMap = new HashMap<String, int[]>();

  initOpenAL();
  initListener();
} // end of JOALSoundMan()
```

JOALSoundMan assumes that every sound will have its own JOAL buffer and source. The two HashMaps store them, indexed by the sound's name.

initOpenAL() sets up a link to OpenAL via the ALut library (so named to remind OpenGL programmers of GLUT):

```
// globals
private AL al;  // to access OpenAL


private void initOpenAL()
{
  try {
    ALut.alutInit();     // creates an OpenAL context
    al = ALFactory.getAL();   // used to access OpenAL
    al.alGetError();          // clears any error bits

    // System.out.println("JOAL version: " + Version.getVersion());
  }
  catch (ALException e) {
    e.printStackTrace();
    System.exit(1);
  }
} // end of initOpenAL()
```

The System.out.println() call to display JOAL's version is commented out in initOpenAL() since the Version class isn't present in JOAL 1.1.0, although it was available in the previous beta releases.

Initializing the Listener

JOALSoundMan.initListener() places the listener at the origin, looking along the negative z-axis. Figure 13-2 illustrates the setup: the triangle is the listener, with its apex pointing toward a "look at" point. The view is from above, looking down onto the XZ plane.

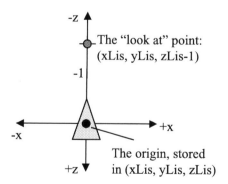

Figure 13-2. *The listener's orientation*

setListener() stores the listener's position in the globals xLis, yLis, and zLis. The "look at" point is one unit along the negative z-axis, at (xLis, yLis, zLis-1):

```
// global listener info
private float xLis, yLis, zLis;    // current position
private float[] oriLis;   // orientation
```

```
private void initListener()
// position and orientate the listener
{
  xLis = 0.0f; yLis  = 0.0f; zLis = 0.0f;
  al.alListener3f(AL.AL_POSITION, xLis, yLis, zLis);
                        // position the listener at the origin

  al.alListener3i(AL.AL_VELOCITY, 0, 0, 0);    // no velocity

  oriLis = new float[] {xLis, yLis, zLis-1.0f,  0.0f, 1.0f, 0.0f};
     /* the first 3 elements are the "look at" point,
         the second 3 are the "up direction" */
  al.alListenerfv(AL.AL_ORIENTATION, oriLis, 0);
} // end of initListener()
```

The listener properties are set with calls to AL.alListenerXX() methods, where XX denotes the data type assigned to the property. The first argument of the method is the property being affected.

The listener's orientation is defined in terms of the "look at" point and a vector for the "up" direction. In initListener(), "up" is the y-axis. Both values are stored in a global oriLis[] array, and assigned to the AL.AL_ORIENTATION property.

It's worth noting that oriLis[0], oriLis[1], and oriLis[2] are the "look at" point's x-, y-, and z- values. The x- and z- values will be changed later as the listener moves around.

The location of the listener's ears becomes important when the listener or sources move, since they dictate the volume and distribution of sound emitted by the speakers. The location of the ears, and even their number, isn't defined by the OpenAL specification; the details are left to the implementation.

A listener in a standard PC environment with stereo speakers, or headphones, has two ears mapped to the speakers (headphones) as shown in Figure 13-3.

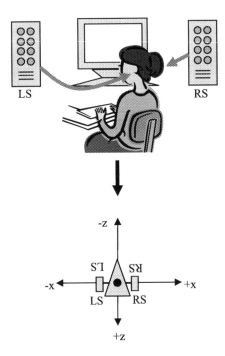

Figure 13-3. *The listener's ears*

LS is the left speaker; *RS* the right one.

By default in OpenAL the listener starts at the origin and faces along the negative z-axis, so that the listener's left and right ears are mapped to the left and right speakers. This means that most of the code in setListener() is unnecessary, since it duplicates the default position and orientation employed in JOAL. I included it just to be on the safe side.

JOAL Clean Up

Before the JOAL application terminates, it should stop playing sounds and delete any buffers and sources:

```
public void cleanUp()
{
  Set<String> keys = sourcesMap.keySet();
  Iterator<String> iter = keys.iterator();

  String nm;
  int[] buffer, source;
  while(iter.hasNext()){
    nm = iter.next();

    source = sourcesMap.get(nm);
    System.out.println("Stopping " + nm);
    al.alSourceStop(source[0]);
    al.alDeleteSources(1, source, 0);

    buffer = buffersMap.get(nm);
    al.alDeleteBuffers(1, buffer, 0);
  }

  ALut.alutExit();
} // end of cleanUp()
```

The names associated with the sources are converted into an Iterator, which loops through the buffer and source HashMaps using Al.alDeleteBuffers() and Al.alDeleteSources() to delete the entries. Playing sounds are stopped with Al.alSourceStop().

The ALut.alutExit() method shuts down OpenAL and closes the output device.

Loading a Sound

A sound is loaded by first being converted into a JOAL buffer. Then the buffer is linked to a JOAL source, and the source is placed at a particular location in the scene. The buffer and source references are stored in global HashMaps, using the sound's name as the key:

```
public boolean load(String nm, boolean toLoop)
{
  if (sourcesMap.get(nm) != null) {
    System.out.println(nm + " already loaded");
    return true;
  }

  int[] buffer = initBuffer(nm);
  if (buffer == null)
    return false;

  int[] source = initSource(nm, buffer, toLoop);
```

```
  if (source == null) {
    al.alDeleteBuffers(1, buffer, 0);
              // no need for the buffer anymore
    return false;
  }

  if (toLoop)
    System.out.println("Looping source created for " + nm);
  else
    System.out.println("Source created for " + nm);

  buffersMap.put(nm, buffer);
  sourcesMap.put(nm, source);
  return true;
} // end of loadSource()
```

Buffer creation is handled by initBuffer(), while initSource() creates the source.

The toLoop boolean is used in initSource() to specify whether the source should play its sound repeatedly.

Making a Buffer

The WAV file is loaded into several data arrays, then the buffer is initialized with those arrays:

```
// global
private final static String SOUND_DIR = "Sounds/";
          // where the WAV files are stored

private int[] initBuffer(String nm)
{
  // create arrays for holding various WAV file info
  int[] format = new int[1];
  ByteBuffer[] data = new ByteBuffer[1];
  int[] size = new int[1];
  int[] freq = new int[1];
  int[] loop = new int[1];

  // load WAV file into the data arrays
  String fnm = SOUND_DIR + nm + ".wav";
  try {
    ALut.alutLoadWAVFile(fnm, format, data, size, freq, loop);
  }
  catch(ALException e) {
    System.out.println("Error loading WAV file: " + fnm);
    return null;
  }
  // System.out.println("Sound size = " + size[0]);
  // System.out.println("Sound freq = " + freq[0]);


  // create an empty buffer to hold the sound data
  int[] buffer = new int[1];
  al.alGenBuffers(1, buffer, 0);
  if (al.alGetError() != AL.AL_NO_ERROR) {
    System.out.println("Could not create a buffer for " + nm);
    return null;
  }
```

```
  // store data in the buffer
  al.alBufferData(buffer[0], format[0], data[0], size[0], freq[0]);

  // ALut.alutUnloadWAV(format[0], data[0], size[0], freq[0]);
            // not in API anymore
  return buffer;
} // end of initBuffer()
```

ALut only offers ALut.alutLoadWAVFile() at present, so a buffer is restricted to being a stereo or mono WAV file.

The size[] and freq[] data arrays contain information on the size and frequency of the loaded file. The commented-out println()s show how to access it:

```
// System.out.println("Sound size = " + size[0]);
// System.out.println("Sound freq = " + freq[0]);
```

An empty buffer is created with AL.alGenBuffers(), then filled with the data from the arrays with Al.alBufferData().

Earlier versions of JOAL used ALut.alutUnloadWAV() to release the WAV file. The call is no longer required and has been removed from the API.

initBuffer()'s result is an array holding a reference to the buffer, or null.

Making a Source

The source is positioned at (0, 0, 0), and linked to the buffer that was just created. The source may play repeatedly, depending on the toLoop argument:

```
private int[] initSource(String nm, int[] buf, boolean toLoop)
{
  // create a source (a point in space that emits a sound)
  int[] source = new int[1];
  al.alGenSources(1, source, 0);
  if (al.alGetError() != AL.AL_NO_ERROR) {
    System.out.println("Error creating source for " + nm);
    return null;
  }

  // configure the source
  al.alSourcei(source[0], AL.AL_BUFFER, buf[0]);  // bind buffer
  al.alSourcef(source[0], AL.AL_PITCH, 1.0f);
  al.alSourcef(source[0], AL.AL_GAIN, 1.0f);
  al.alSource3f(source[0], AL.AL_POSITION, 0.0f, 0.0f, 0.0f);
                  // position the source at the origin
  al.alSource3i(source[0], AL.AL_VELOCITY, 0, 0, 0);  // no velocity
  if (toLoop)
    al.alSourcei(source[0], AL.AL_LOOPING, AL.AL_TRUE);  // looping
  else
    al.alSourcei(source[0], AL.AL_LOOPING, AL.AL_FALSE); //play once

  if (al.alGetError() != AL.AL_NO_ERROR) {
    System.out.println("Error configuring source for " + nm);
    return null;
  }

  return source;
} // end of initSource()
```

An empty source is created with AL.alGenSources(), and its various attributes are set via calls to AL.alSourceXX(). The most important is the AL.AL_BUFFER attribute, which links the source to the buffer.

initSource() returns an array holding the source reference, or null.

Figure 13-4 shows the source located at the origin, as viewed from above.

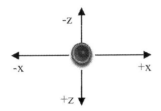

Figure 13-4. *A source in 3D space*

The point source emits sound in every direction.

Positioning a Source

A source is easily moved by changing the (x, y, z) coordinate in its AL.AL_POSITION attribute. setPos() does the task:

```
// globals
private HashMap<String, int[]> sourcesMap;


public boolean setPos(String nm, float x, float y, float z)
// move the nm sound to (x,y,z)
{
  int[] source = (int[]) sourcesMap.get(nm);
  if (source == null) {
    System.out.println("No source found for " + nm);
    return false;
  }

  al.alSource3f(source[0], AL.AL_POSITION, x, y, z);
  return true;
} // end of setPos()
```

setPos(), and the other source-related methods, use the sound's name as a key into sourcesMap. The retrieved source has its position adjusted.

Positioning a source is such a common task that JOALSoundMan offers a variant of load(), which employs setPos():

```
public boolean load(String nm, float x, float y, float z, boolean toLoop)
{
  if (load(nm, toLoop))
    return setPos(nm, x, y, z);
  else
    return false;
}
```

Playing, Stopping, and Pausing a Source

A source can be played, stopped, and paused with AL.alSourcePlay(), AL.alSourceStop(), and AL.alSourcePause(). The JOALSoundMan methods for playing, stopping, and pausing a source are all similar; they use the sound's name to find the source, then call the relevant AL method. This programming style is illustrated by the JOALSoundMan.play() method:

```
public boolean play(String nm)
{
  int[] source = (int[]) sourcesMap.get(nm);
  if (source == null) {
    System.out.println("No source found for " + nm);
    return false;
  }

  System.out.println("Playing " + nm);
  al.alSourcePlay(source[0]);
  return true;
} // end of play()
```

Calling play() on a stopped source will restart it but resume a paused source.

Moving the Listener

It's useful to be able to move the listener in different ways—either with an (x, z) step added to the listener's current position, or by supplying it with an entirely new (x, z) location. Neither approach changes the listener's y-axis position (at 0).

moveListener() performs the step-based move by utilizing the positional method, setListenerPos(), to do most of the work:

```
// globals
private float xLis, yLis, zLis;    // listener's current position


public void moveListener(float xStep, float zStep)
// move the listener by a (x,z) step
{
  float x = xLis + xStep;
  float z = zLis + zStep;
  setListenerPos(x, z);
} // end of moveListener()
```

Changing the listener's position also requires an update to its orientation. The trick is to calculate the x- and z-axis offsets of the listener's move and apply them to the "look at" point. This is illustrated in Figure 13-5.

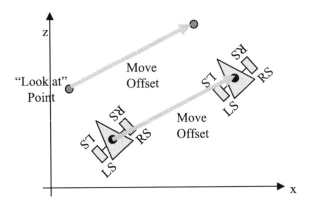

Figure 13-5. *Moving the listener and its "look at" point*

The following is the moveListener() method:

```
public void setListenerPos(float xNew, float zNew)
// position the listener at (xNew,zNew)
{
  float xOffset = xNew-xLis;
  float zOffset = zNew-zLis;

  xLis = xNew;  zLis = zNew;
  al.alListener3f(AL.AL_POSITION, xLis, yLis, zLis);

  /* keep the listener facing the same direction by
     moving the "look at" point by the (x,z) offset */
  oriLis[0] += xOffset;
  oriLis[2] += zOffset;
    // no change needed to y-coord in oriLis[1]
  al.alListenerfv(AL.AL_ORIENTATION, oriLis, 0);
}  // end of setListenerPos()
```

There's no need to manipulate y-axis values, since the listener only moves over the XZ plane.

Turning the Listener

Turning the listener is complicated by having to turn the "look at" point as well. However, the calculations are simplified by only permitting the listener to rotate around the y-axis.

Figure 13-6 shows what happens when the listener rotates by angleLis degrees.

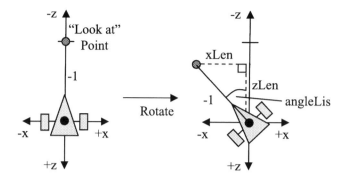

Figure 13-6. *Rotating the listener and the "look at" point*

xLen and zLen are added to the listener's position to get the new "look at" point. This approach is implemented by turnListener(), which utilizes setListenerOri() to do most of the work:

```
// globals
private float xLis, yLis, zLis;    // current position
private float[] oriLis;   // orientation
private int angleLis = 0;


public void turnListener(int degrees)
// turn the listener anticlockwise by the amount stored in degrees
{  setListenerOri( angleLis+degrees ); }


public void setListenerOri(int ang)
/* Set the listener's orientation to be ang degrees
   in the anticlockwise direction around the y-axis. */
{
  angleLis = ang;
  double angle = Math.toRadians(angleLis);
  float xLen = -1.0f * (float) Math.sin(angle);
  float zLen = -1.0f * (float) Math.cos(angle);

  /* face in the (xLen, zLen) direction by adding the
     values to the listener position */
  oriLis[0] = xLis+xLen; oriLis[2] = zLis+zLen;
  al.alListenerfv(AL.AL_ORIENTATION, oriLis, 0);
}  // end of setListenerOri()
```

angleLis is a global storing the listener's total rotation away from its starting direction along the negative z-axis. The user supplies an angle change which is added to angleLis.

turnListener() rotates the listener by the specified number of degrees from its current orientation, while setListenerOri() measures the angle from the listener's initial position. These methods allow the listener to rotate in two ways, either relative to its current orientation, or from its initial position.

Using JOALSoundMan

In the rest of this chapter, I go through several small examples showing how JOALSoundMan can move a source and translate and rotate the listener. None of these use 3D (or 2D) graphics, although the last one utilizes a simple GUI.

I also use JOALSoundMan in a Java 3D example in the next chapter, and with JOGL in Chapter 17.

Moving a Source

In MovingSource.java, a source is placed at (0, 0, 0), at the same spot as the listener (which by default starts at the origin and faces along the negative z-axis). Gradually the source is moved along the negative z-axis, away from the listener, causing the repeating sound to fade away. Figure 13-7 shows the situation diagrammatically.

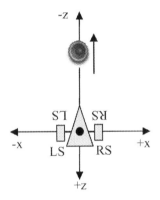

Figure 13-7. *Moving the source*

The following is the complete MovingSource.java program:

```
public class MovingSource
{
  public static void main(String[] args)
  {
    if (args.length != 1) {
      System.out.println("Usage: runJOAL MovingSource <WAV name>");
      System.exit(1);
    }
    String soundName = args[0];

    JOALSoundMan soundMan = new JOALSoundMan();
    // the listener is at (0,0,0) facing along the negative z-axis

    if (!soundMan.load(soundName, true))
      System.exit(1);
    // default position for sound is (0,0,0)
    soundMan.play(soundName);

    // move the sound along the negative z-axis
    float step = 0.1f;
    float zPos = 0.0f;
```

```
  for(int i=0; i < 50; i++) {
    zPos -= step;
    soundMan.setPos(soundName, 0, 0, zPos);
    try {
      Thread.sleep(250);    // sleep for 0.25 secs
    }
    catch(InterruptedException ex) {}
  }

  // soundMan.stop(soundName);
  soundMan.cleanUp();
}  // end of main()

} // end of MovingSource class
```

MovingSource must be supplied with the name of a WAV file (e.g., FancyPants.wav):

```
> runJOAL MovingListener FancyPants
```

JOALSoundMan.load() loads the sound from the Sounds/ subdirectory and positions the source at the origin. JOALSoundMan.play() starts it playing, and the while loop gradually moves it with repeated calls to JOALSoundMan.setPos().

After the loop finishes, the sound could be stopped with JOALSoundMan.stop(), but JOALSoundMan.cleanUp() does that anyway.

Moving the Listener

Another way of making a source fade away is to leave it alone and move the listener instead. This is demonstrated by MovingListener.java, which starts with the same configuration as MovingSource.java (the source and listener both at the origin) but incrementally shifts the listener along the z-axis. This is shown in Figure 13-8.

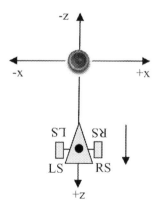

Figure 13-8. *Moving the listener*

The following is the main() method for MovingListener.java:

```
public static void main(String[] args)
{
  if (args.length != 1) {
```

```
    System.out.println("Usage: runJOAL MovingListener <WAV name>");
    System.exit(1);
  }
  String soundName = args[0];

  JOALSoundMan soundMan = new JOALSoundMan();
  // the listener is at (0,0,0) facing along the negative z-axis

  if (!soundMan.load(soundName, true))
    System.exit(1);
  // default position for sound is (0,0,0)
  soundMan.play(soundName);

  // move the listener along the z-axis
  for(int i=0; i < 50; i++) {
    soundMan.moveListener(0, 0.1f);
    try {
      Thread.sleep(250);    // sleep for 0.25 secs
    }
    catch(InterruptedException ex) {}
  }
  soundMan.cleanUp();
} // end of main()
```

The only difference from MovingSource.java is that the listener is translated in 0.1 steps along the z-axis by calling JOALSoundMan.moveListener().

Moving the Listener Between Sources

MovingListener2.java translates the listener away from one source toward another; Figure 13-9 shows most of the details.

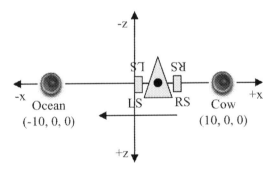

Figure 13-9. *Moving the listener between sources*

The "cow" source repeatedly moos at (10, 0, 0), and the listener starts at the same spot. It then travels incrementally along the x-axis toward (-10, 0, 0) where an "ocean" source is playing.

The mooing will initially be the loudest sound coming from the speakers, but will slowly fade away, being replaced by the increasingly louder "ocean." The orientation of the listener means that both ears receive the same amount of sound, so the fade-out of the cow and fade-in of the ocean are the same for both speakers.

The following is the main() method of MovingListener2.java:

```java
public static void main(String[] args)
{
  JOALSoundMan soundMan = new JOALSoundMan();

  float xPos = 10.0f;
  soundMan.moveListener(xPos, 0);
  // the listener is at (xPos,0,0) facing along the negative z-axis

  // cow at (xPos,0,0)
  if (!soundMan.load("cow", xPos,0,0, true))
    System.exit(1);
  soundMan.play("cow");

  // ocean at (-xPos,0,0)
  if (!soundMan.load("ocean", -xPos,0,0, true))
    System.exit(1);
  soundMan.play("ocean");

  // move the listener from cow to ocean
  float xStep = (2.0f * xPos)/40.0f;
  for(int i=0; i < 40; i++) {
    soundMan.moveListener(-xStep, 0);
    try {
      Thread.sleep(250);    // sleep for 0.25 secs
    }
    catch(InterruptedException ex) {}
  }
  soundMan.cleanUp();
}  // end of main()
```

Turning the Listener

This example examines how the listener's orientation affects the speakers' output.

As shown in Figure 13-10, the listener begins by facing along the negative z-axis as usual, but positioned at (1, 0, 0). The FancyPants sound plays repeatedly off to its right. Then the listener is slowly rotated in an anticlockwise direction in a full circle.

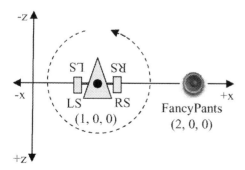

Figure 13-10. *Rotating the listener*

The effect on the audio is more interesting than previously because the balance of sound changes between the left and right ears (the left and right speakers).

FancyPants is initially loudest for the right ear/speaker (when the listener's angle is 0). As the listener turns, the volume decreases in the right ear and increases in the left, until at 90 degrees the sound is the same from both speakers. As the listener continues turning toward 180 degrees, the sound in the right ear decreases almost to nothing and becomes louder in the left ear. At 180 degrees, the left ear is nearest to the source and the sound is at its loudest there. Thereafter, the volume starts increasing again in the right ear. At 270 degrees, the listener is facing the source, and the sound has the same volume from both speakers once again. After that, the left speaker gets quieter until the listener returns to its starting orientation at 360 degrees.

The following is the main() function of TurningListener.java:

```
public static void main(String[] args)
{
  if (args.length != 1) {
    System.out.println("Usage: runJOAL TurningListener <WAV name>");
    System.exit(1);
  }
  String soundName = args[0];

  JOALSoundMan soundMan = new JOALSoundMan();
  // the listener is at (0,0,0) facing along the negative z-axis
  soundMan.moveListener(1,0);    // now at (1,0,0)

  if (!soundMan.load(soundName, 2,0,0, true))    // at (2,0,0)
    System.exit(1);
  soundMan.play(soundName);

  // rotate listener anticlockwise
  for(int i=0; i < 60; i++) {
    soundMan.turnListener(6);  // 6 degrees each time
    try {
      Thread.sleep(250);   // sleep for 0.25 secs
    }
    catch(InterruptedException ex) {}
  }
  soundMan.cleanUp();
} // end of main()
```

The only new coding feature here is the call to JOALSoundMan.turnListener() inside the loop.

JOAL and Swing

There's nothing preventing JOAL from being used in Java applications with GUIs. The SingleSource.java example utilizes Swing buttons to play, suspend, and stop a JOAL source. Figure 13-11 shows the GUI.

Figure 13-11. *The SingleSource application*

The SingleSource() constructor loads the source with JOALSoundMan and sets up the GUI:

```
// globals
private JOALSoundMan soundMan;
private String soundName;


public SingleSource(String nm)
{
  super("Single Static Source");

  soundMan = new JOALSoundMan();
  soundName = nm;

  if (!soundMan.load(soundName, true))
    System.exit(1);

  buildGUI();

  addWindowListener( new WindowAdapter() {
    public void windowClosing(WindowEvent e)
    { soundMan.cleanUp();
      System.exit(0);
    }
  });

  pack();
  setResizable(false);    // fixed size display
  setVisible(true);
}  // end of SingleSource()
```

The window-closing event is caught so that JOALSoundMan.cleanUp() can be called before termination.

buildGUI() sets up three buttons, whose action listeners are the class itself. When any of the buttons are pressed, SingleSource's actionPerformed() method is called:

```
// globals
private JButton playButton, stopButton, pauseButton;


public void actionPerformed(ActionEvent e)
{
  if (e.getSource() == playButton)
    soundMan.play(soundName);
  else if (e.getSource() == stopButton)
    soundMan.stop(soundName);
  else if (e.getSource() == pauseButton)
    soundMan.pause(soundName);
}  // end of actionPerformed
```

The relevant play(), stop(), or sound() method is called in JOALSoundMan.

Other Source Types

As I mentioned earlier, Java 3D includes three sound-related classes: BackgroundSound for ambient sound; PointSound for a sound source located at a particular place in the scene; and ConeSound for a point source aimed in a specific direction. All of these can be implemented using JOAL, as David Grace's JoalMixer illustrates (a subproject available at https://j3d-incubator.dev.java.net/).

JOALSoundMan creates point sound sources; so how much work is needed for it to support ambient and cone sounds?

Ambient Sounds

For ambient sounds, JOALSoundMan can utilize an OpenAL "feature": stereo WAV files will not be played positionally. This means that calls to JOALSoundMan.setPos() for a stereo source will have no effect on the sound coming from the speakers. This can be tested by calling the MovingListener.java example with a stereo WAV file:

```
> runJOAL MovingListener FancyPantsS
```

FancyPantsS.wav is a stereo version of the mono FancyPants.wav, which I created using the WavePad audio editing tool (http://www.nch.com.au/wavepad/).

Another way of playing sounds ambiently is to use Java's own sound classes (e.g., AudioClip), or perhaps the SoundsPlayer class I developed in Chapter 12, since they don't use positional effects.

A third approach is to "connect" the source to the listener, so that it moves as the listener does. Then the source's volume and speaker distribution will stay the same no matter where the listener moves to.

The AL.AL_SOURCE_RELATIVE attribute changes the source's position to be *relative* to the listener, as shown in the following code fragment:

```
al.alSourcei(source[0], AL.AL_SOURCE_RELATIVE, AL.AL_TRUE);
al.alSource3f(source[0], AL.AL_POSITION, 0.0f, 0.0f, 0.0f);
```

The source will always be at the same spot as the listener.

Cone Sounds

A cone sound is a point source with four additional parameters. A typical cone is shown in Figure 13-12.

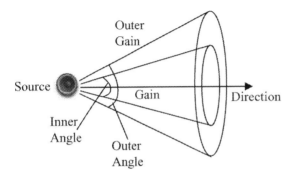

Figure 13-12. *A cone sound*

Two cones are defined in terms of inner and outer angles around a central direction vector. The inner cone plays the sound using the AL.AL_GAIN volume setting (often 1.0f), but the volume tails off in the outer cone, decreasing to the AL.AL_CONE_OUTER_GAIN value (typically 0.0f) at the outer cone's edges.

The following code snippet shows how the source's attributes are set:

```
al.alSourcef(source[0], AL.AL_CONE_INNER_ANGLE, innerAngle);
al.alSourcef(source[0], AL.AL_CONE_OUTER_ANGLE, outerAngle);
al.alSourcef(source[0], AL.AL_GAIN, 1.0f);
al.alSourcef(source[0], AL.AL_CONE_OUTER_GAIN, 0.0f);
al.alSource3f(source[0], AL.AL_DIRECTION, x, y, z);
```

innerAngle and outerAngle are specified in degrees (e.g., 30.0f and 45.0f). The (x, y, z) direction should be a vector, such as (0, 0, 1) to make the cone point along the z-axis.

Summary

This chapter discussed JOAL, a Java wrapper around OpenAL for programming with 2D and 3D audio.

I developed a JOALSoundMan class that hides the low-level details of buffer, source, and listener creation, and I demonstrated its use with several simple examples.

JOALSoundMan will appear again in the next chapter when I employ it to add 3D sound to a Java 3D example, and in Chapter 17 when it does something similar for a JOGL program.

■ ■ ■

CHAPTER 14

The P5 Glove

If you've been keeping count, the nonstandard devices that I've looked at so far are the webcam (for watching your arm waving) and the gamepad, both of which are common add-on devices for the PC. This chapter travels a less popular path, tentatively entering the exciting world of virtual reality (VR) gaming. *Tentative* because VR gear (e.g., data gloves, stereoscopic goggles, and even full-body suits) can be rather expensive and complex. Fortunately, I'm using the low-priced, simple-to-use P5 virtual reality glove, so it's full steam ahead into a bargain-basement version of *Minority Report*.

Hyperbole aside, this chapter explains how to communicate with the P5 glove using Java, and how to implement wrapper classes that hide most of the interfacing details. The chapter's main focus is on developing a variant of the Java 3D example from Chapter 7 (a scene full of 3D models). This time the camera moves forward and backward and turns left or right based only on glove movements; no key presses are necessary.

I utilize my JOAL sound manager class from the previous chapter to put a musical cow into the scene; the music's intensity and speaker mix varies depending on the user's proximity to the cow. Perhaps mercifully, the music can be paused by the user clenching his fist or pressing a button on the glove. Another fist-clench, or button-press, resumes the audio accompaniment.

Another aspect of this chapter is the approach taken to integrate a less well-known device into Java. Before any coding began, the device was tested and configured using OS tools and software supplied by the vendor. Configuration details were also obtained from a simple GUI application with no 3D visuals, making the transition to the full 3D example easier. The wrapper classes were designed to hide and simplify as much of the glove's basic API as possible.

Introducing the P5 Glove

The P5 virtual reality glove (Figure 14-1) is an inexpensive data glove suitable for gaming and 3D virtual environments.

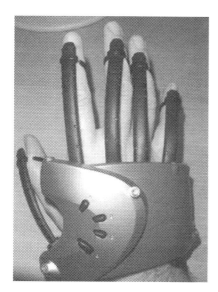

Figure 14-1. *The P5 virtual reality glove*

The user moves his hand in front of a receptor *tower* (shown on the right of Figure 14-2), which contains two infrared sensors. They detect the visible LEDs on the glove (there are eight altogether) and convert them into an (x, y, z) position for the glove and an orientation in terms of pitch, yaw, and roll.

Figure 14-2. *The glove and the receptor tower*

The glove is plugged into the tower, which is connected to the PC's USB port.

The glove also has bend sensors in its fingers and four buttons on the top. The P5 is an amazing piece of hardware, but its driver software is less impressive. Fortunately, the P5 has a very active hacker and hobbyist community, which has done a great job of supplying replacements. It is also a great source of help and advice.

Carl Kenner's site (http://www.geocities.com/carl_a_kenner/p5glove.html) has links to P5 drivers for Windows, Linux, and the Mac and other wonderful stuff such as P5 music and games. I downloaded Kenner's Dual Mode Driver Beta 3 for Windows. It is *dual mode* since it supplies position data in either relative or absolute terms. A *relative* position is an offset from the last glove position, while an *absolute* position is relative to a fixed origin in space.

Compared to the P5's official software, Kenner's driver offers improved data filtering, better accuracy, better access to finger and LED information, and many other goodies. Most importantly for my needs, it has a Java API. (Other languages are supported as well, including Delphi, Visual Basic, C, and Visual C++.)

Two other great sources of glove information are the P5 glove mini wiki at http://scratchpad.wikia.com/wiki/P5_Glove and the p5glove Yahoo group at http://groups.yahoo.com/group/p5glove/.

I haven't mentioned a company web site because the P5's manufacturers, Essential Reality, sadly went out of business in the middle of 2004. As a consequence, it's possible to find brand-new P5 gloves for sale for around US$50 on eBay and at various resellers; Essential Reality was offering them for US$150. Professional data gloves cost far more. The P5 wiki has a page of links to potential purchasing sources, http://p5glove.pbwiki.com/Purchase/, and it's a popular topic in the p5glove Yahoo group.

Using Kenner's Java API

Kenner's Dual Mode Driver for Windows (stored in A_DualModeDriverBeta3.zip) can be downloaded from the Files section of Yahoo's p5glove group at http://groups.yahoo.com/group/p5glove/. Linux and Mac drivers can also be found there, along with many other goodies.

The Java programming-related files in A_DualModeDriverBeta3.zip are P5DLL.dll, and CP5DLL.java in the subdirectory include/com/essentialreality/.

It's easiest to work with a CP5DLL JAR file created like so:

```
javac -d . CP5DLL.java    // create the com.essentialreality package

jar cvf CP5DLL.jar com    // roll the package up into a JAR
```

The resulting JAR file, CP5DLL.jar, should be copied into <JAVA_HOME>\jre\lib\ext and <JRE_HOME>\lib\ext. On my Windows XP test machine, they're the directories c:\Program Files\Java\jdk1.6.0\jre\lib\ext and c:\Program Files\Java\jre1.6.0\lib\ext.

The DLL, P5DLL.dll, can be placed in a directory of your choice. I chose c:\Program Files\P5 Glove, the directory created by Essential Reality's P5 installer.

Every call to java.exe requires a command-line option to supply the path to the DLL's location. For instance, to run the P5 application, P5Example.java needs the following:

```
java -Djava.library.path="c:\Program Files\P5 Glove" P5Example
```

As in other examples, I use a DOS batch file to reduce typing tedium:

```
runP5 P5Example
```

runP5.bat contains the following:

```
@echo off
echo Executing P5 code
java -Djava.library.path="c:\Program Files\P5 Glove" %1
echo Finished.
```

The CP5DLL class consists of numerous public constants, variables, and methods, and three inner classes: P5Data, P5Info, and P5State (as illustrated by Figure 14-3). P5Data can be ignored since it's only included for backward-compatibility; its functionality has been superseded by P5Info and P5State.

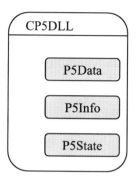

Figure 14-3. *The CP5DLL classes*

The 40-plus public methods in the top-level CP5DLL class are used to initialize and configure the glove (or gloves) connected to the PC. For example, it's possible to adjust the amount of data filtering.

The 40-plus public variables in P5State expose the glove's current position, rotation, button values, LEDs, and much more. There's an update() method that should be called whenever the values need to be refreshed.

Most of the 25-plus public variables in P5Info hold device details, such as the manufacturer name and the version numbers. As with P5State, there's an update() method that initializes the values.

The documentation for Kenner's Java API is rather sparse; for instance, there's no Java example in the distribution. The best place for finding out about the API is the p5glove Yahoo group (http://groups.yahoo.com/group/p5glove/), which has a searchable interface; Kenner is an active member.

The only Java example I could find is the amusing Robot Glove application by Eric Lundquist (http://www.robotgroup.net/index.cgi/RobotGlove). Inputs from the P5 glove are converted into commands sent to a Lynxmotion robot arm via the Java Communications API; as your hand moves, so does the robot.

Examining the Glove's Data

The ShowGlove application described in this section allows the different kinds of glove data to be examined easily.

Later, in the "A Specialized Glove Class" section of this chapter, I use this program to decide how to map glove *gestures* (particular positions or orientations of the glove) to camera movement actions in HandView3D.

It's fairly easy to come up with suitable gestures; for instance, turning left is triggered by rolling the glove to the left. But how *far* should the glove be rolled before it "counts" as a camera turn? Is a 20-degree roll enough? Or 40 degrees? The numerical details can be worked out by looking at the values reported by ShowGlove as different glove gestures are tried out.

What ShowGlove Displays

The ShowGlove GUI is shown in Figure 14-4.

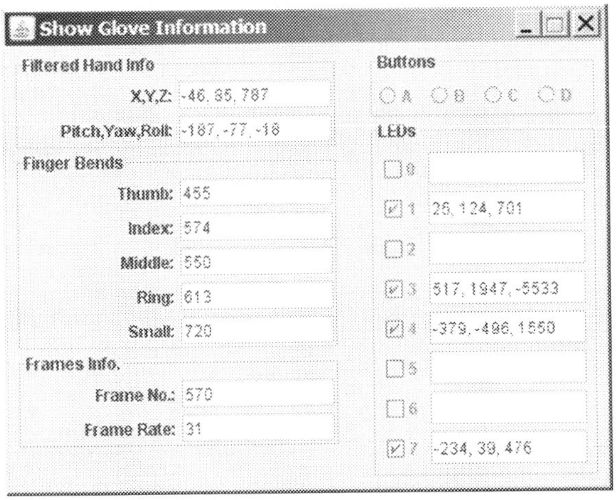

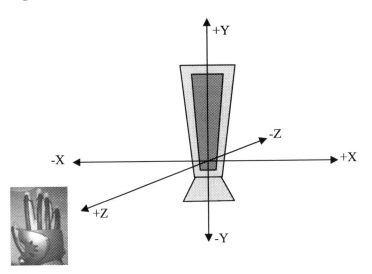

Figure 14-4. *The ShowGlove GUI*

Filtered versions of the glove's position and orientation are shown in the Filtered Hand Info panel. The P5 filters smooth out "jumps" in the data caused by the tower failing to detect some of the LEDs. The reported numbers are averages of the current position/rotation *and* the ten previous values. This filtering strategy can be adjusted via methods in CP5DLL.

The (x, y, z) numbers are absolute values relative to coordinate axes shown in Figure 14-5. The origin is centered near the base of the tower.

Figure 14-5. *Coordinate axes for the glove*

The glove's orientation is given in terms of pitch, yaw, and roll, which are illustrated in Figure 14-6.

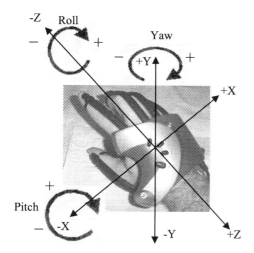

Figure 14-6. *Pitch, yaw, and roll for the glove*

Pitch is the rotation about the x-axis; *yaw* acts around the y-axis; and *roll* uses the z-axis. A positive pitch rotates the hand upward; a positive yaw turns it to the right; and a positive roll turns the top of the hand to face right.

The fingers' bend data depends on the glove's calibration settings. (The P5 is calibrated via its Windows control panel, which comes as part of its installation software.) On my glove, outstretched fingers typically show a value of around 1000, while bent fingers register around 400.

There are four buttons on the top face of the glove, labeled *A*, *B*, *C*, and *D*. These are mapped to the same-named radio buttons in the ShowGlove GUI. When a button is pressed, the radio button is selected, the exception being the D button. When D is pressed, the glove automatically switches off, so the button's change isn't detected by CP5DLL and not shown by ShowGlove.

There are eight LEDs on the glove, numbered as shown in Figure 14-7.

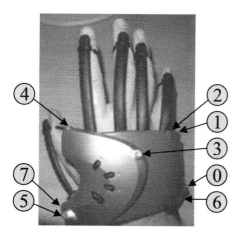

Figure 14-7. *LEDs on the glove*

Those numbers are used as labels in the LEDs panel in ShowGlove.

The reliability of the position and orientation data depends on the LEDs being visible to the tower. One of the problems is that the user's fingers may block LEDs on the front edge of the glove (e.g., LEDs 1, 2, and 4) from being seen. The simplest solution is for the user to keep his fingers bent and to bend his wrist so that the top of his hand is aimed slightly toward the tower. Hand positioning is one of the hidden training issues with the P5 glove, analogous to the training needed when first using a mouse.

Another trick for making the top of the user's hand more visible is to place the tower on a box, so it's slightly higher than the hand.

ShowGlove Overview

The class diagrams for ShowGlove are given in Figure 14-8. Only the public methods are shown.

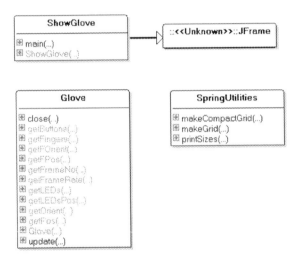

Figure 14-8. *Class diagrams for ShowGlove*

The ShowGlove class creates the GUI and polls the glove every GLOVE_DELAY ms (200 ms) to gather data to populate the GUI's various text fields, radio buttons, and check boxes. The polling phase calls update() in the Glove class followed by its get methods.

The Glove class is a *wrapper* (a facade) around Kenner's CP5DLL class, hiding the glove's initialization, data collection, and closedown at the end of the application.

The SpringUtilities class comes from the J2SE 1.4.2 tutorial; it contains utility methods for manipulating the SpringLayout class. SpringLayout permits components to be positioned in a grid formation without each cell having to be the same size (as is the case with GridLayout). I use SpringLayout for the LEDs panel (see Figure 14-4) since the check boxes column needs much less horizontal space than the text fields in the adjacent column.

I won't describe the GUI creation code in ShowGlove; it's quite standard and not relevant to how the glove is accessed.

Initializing and Terminating the Glove

The ShowGlove constructor creates a Glove instance and sets up a window listener that closes down the P5 glove when the JFrame is closed:

```
// global variables
private Glove glove;

// for glove polling
private Timer pollTimer;    // timer which triggers the polling
private DecimalFormat df;


public ShowGlove()
{
  super("Show Glove Information");

  glove = new Glove();
  initGUI();

  addWindowListener( new WindowAdapter() {
    public void windowClosing(WindowEvent e)
    { glove.close();
      pollTimer.stop();   // stop the timer
      System.exit(0);
    }
  });

  pack();
  setResizable(false);
  setVisible(true);

  df = new DecimalFormat("0");    // no decimal places
  startPolling();
}  // end of ShowGlove()
```

The windowClosing() method also stops the polling timer.

Polling the Glove

startPolling() sets up a timer to be activated every GLOVE_DELAY ms. The timer triggers an update of the glove's data and refreshes the GUI:

```
// time delay between glove polling
private static final int GLOVE_DELAY = 200;   // ms


private void startPolling()
{
  ActionListener pollPerformer = new ActionListener() {
    public void actionPerformed(ActionEvent e)
    {
      glove.update();  // call update() before showing the data
      showHandInfo();
      showFingersInfo();
      showFramesInfo();
```

```
      showButtonsInfo();
      showLEDsInfo();
    }
  };

  pollTimer = new Timer(GLOVE_DELAY, pollPerformer);
  pollTimer.start();
}  // end of startPolling()
```

The GUI must be updated in the event-dispatching thread; so a javax.swing Timer is utilized that executes the action handler (pollPerformer) in that thread.

After the call to Glove.update(), the show methods (e.g., showHandInfo()) call Glove's get methods. The following is the code for showHandInfo():

```
// global GUI variable - it displays the filtered glove
    position (X,Y,Z) and the filtered Pitch,Yaw,Roll. */
private JTextField handInfo[];


private void showHandInfo()
// show the filtered (x,y,z) and (pitch,yaw,roll)
{ showVals(handInfo[0], glove.getFPos());
  showVals(handInfo[1], glove.getFOrient());
}

private void showVals(JTextField tf, float vals[])
{ tf.setText( df.format(vals[0]) + ", " +
              df.format(vals[1]) + ", " +
              df.format(vals[2]) );   }
```

The Glove.getFPos() and Glove.getFOrient() methods return the filtered position and orientation as three-element arrays. Their data is formatted and written to the two text fields in the Filtered Hand Info panel (see Figure 14-4).

The Glove

The Glove class is a facade for Kenner's CP5DLL class; it initializes the glove, closes it down, and offers a small set of get methods. These supply the following:

- The glove's (x, y, z) position, both filtered and raw data
- The glove's pitch, yaw, and roll, both filtered and raw data
- Finger bend amounts
- Button presses
- Visible LEDs and their values
- The current frame number and frame rate

A typical usage pattern for the Glove class is to call its update() method followed by one or more get methods.

The P5 glove's default configuration is utilized, except that the z-axis is reversed, so the positive z-axis is pointing outward toward the user (as shown in Figure 14-5). Normally, the negative z-axis is pointing outward. Also, the P5's mouse mode is switched off, which stops glove movements and finger bends from being interpreted as mouse moves and button presses.

The Glove() constructor creates a CP5DLL instance and initializes it:

```
// links to the P5 glove(s)
private CP5DLL gloves;
private CP5DLL.P5State gloveState;


public Glove()
{
  gloves = new CP5DLL();

  // initialize the glove
  if (!gloves.P5_Init()) {
    System.out.println("P5 Initialization failed");
    System.exit(1);
  }

  gloves.P5_SetForwardZ(-1);   // so positive Z is toward the user
  gloves.P5_SetMouseState(-1, false);   // disable mouse mode

  // make sure there's only one glove
  int numGloves = gloves.P5_GetCount();
  if (numGloves > 1) {
    System.out.println("Too many gloves detected: " + numGloves);
    System.exit(1);
  }

  printGloveInfo();
  gloveState = gloves.state[0];   // store a ref to the glove state
} // end of Glove()
```

The CP5DLL instance, gloves, can potentially access multiple gloves, a feature I don't need. So a reference to the state of the single glove is stored in gloveState; it's used subsequently to update and access the glove's data.

printGloveInfo() employs the CP5DLL.P5Info class to print out details about the device. A code fragment shows the general approach:

```
CP5DLL.P5Info gloveInfo = gloves.info[0];
System.out.println(
        "Vendor ID: " + gloveInfo.vendorID +
        "; Product ID: " + gloveInfo.productID +
        "; Version: " + gloveInfo.version);
```

Updating and Accessing the Glove

Glove's update() method calls the update() method in CP5DLL.P5State:

```
public void update()
{ gloveState.update(); }
```

The get methods in Glove read the public variables exposed by CP5DLL.P5State. For instance, getFPos() and getFOrient() return the filtered position and orientation data from CP5DLL.P5State:

```
public float[] getFPos()
// filtered (x,y,z) position
{ return new float[]{gloveState.filterPos[0],
                     gloveState.filterPos[1],
                     gloveState.filterPos[2]};  }
```

```
public float[] getFOrient()
// filtered (pitch,yaw,roll)
{ return new float[] {gloveState.filterPitch,
                      gloveState.filterYaw,
                      gloveState.filterRoll};  }
```

This coding approach has the drawback of creating new objects whenever the get methods are called. However, it relieves the user of the need to pass arrays into the methods and is the same coding style as used in Kenner's API.

Closing Down

Glove's close() method restores the mouse mode setting and closes the connection to the P5:

```
public void close()
{ gloves.P5_RestoreMouse(-1);
  gloves.P5_Close();
}
```

Unfortunately, the call to restore the mouse mode has no effect on my Windows XP test machine. It's necessary to go to the P5 glove control panel to switch the mode back on.

A Specialized Glove Class

The Glove class is a general-purpose wrapper for Kenner's CP5DLL class and so is still fairly complicated. The HandView3D application uses the P5 in more specific ways, principally for navigation and a limited number of actions (such as music pausing and resuming). This more limited "palette" allows me to develop a simpler wrapper for the CP5DLL class called FPSGlove.

The class diagram for FPSGlove is given in Figure 14-9, showing only its public methods.

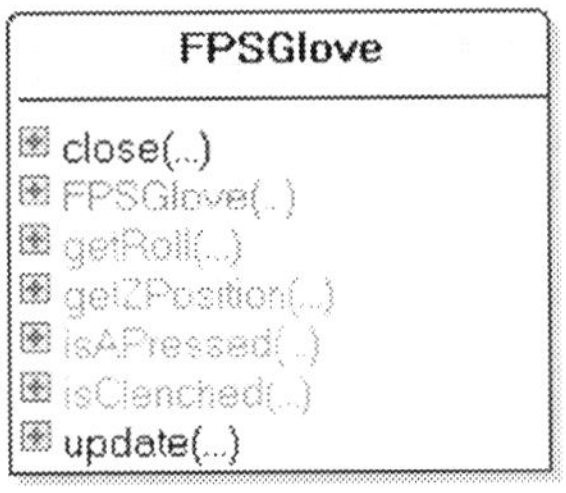

```
        FPSGlove
▩ close(...)
▩ FPSGlove(..)
▩ getRoll(...)
▩ getZPosition(...)
▩ isAPressed(..)
▩ isClenched(..)
▩ update(...)
```

Figure 14-9. *Class diagram for FPSGlove*

The following are FPSGlove's new methods:

- getZPosition() returns a constant representing the z-axis position of the glove relative to the tower. The constant can be NEAR, FAR, or MIDDLE.

- getRoll() returns a constant representing the roll orientation of the glove. The constant can be ROLL_LEFT, ROLL_RIGHT, or LEVEL.

- isClenched() returns true if the user's fingers are bent enough to classify as a clenched fist.

- isAPressed() returns true if the *A* button on the glove has been pressed.

This new glove wrapper class only accesses the CP5DLL data needed by HandView3D, so is smaller than the Glove class. I've also simplified the class's interface, returning constants and booleans instead of arrays of floats.

Initializing the Glove

The FPSGlove() constructor is almost identical to the one in Glove. It initializes the link to the glove and stores the glove state for future use:

```
// links to the P5 glove(s)
private CP5DLL gloves;
private CP5DLL.P5State gloveState;


public FPSGlove()
{
  gloves = new CP5DLL();

  // initialize the glove
  if (!gloves.P5_Init()) {
    System.out.println("P5 Initialization failed");
    System.exit(1);
  }

  gloves.P5_SetForwardZ(-1);     // so positive Z is toward the user
  gloves.P5_SetMouseState(-1, false);  // disable mouse mode

  // make sure there's only one glove
  int numGloves = gloves.P5_GetCount();
  if (numGloves > 1) {
    System.out.println("Too many gloves detected: " + numGloves);
    System.exit(1);
  }

  gloveState = gloves.state[0];  // store a ref to the glove state
} // end of FPSGlove()
```

Updating and Closing

The update() and close() methods are unchanged from the Glove class:

```
public void update()
{ gloveState.update(); }


public void close()
{ gloves.P5_RestoreMouse(-1);   // restore mouse mode (does not work)
  gloves.P5_Close();
}
```

Getting the Position

getZPosition() examines the filtered z-axis location of the glove and returns one of the position constants NEAR, FAR, or MIDDLE.

The idea is that HandView3D will move the camera forward when the value is NEAR (i.e., near to the tower), move the camera back when the value is FAR (far from the tower), and not adjust the camera at all when the value is MIDDLE.

After some experimentation with ShowGlove, I decided that NEAR should start at less than 500 units from the tower, while FAR should start at more than 900. Therefore, the MIDDLE region is between 500 and 900 units, which is a comfortable distance to rest my arm on the computer desk and not have the camera move. By default a glove unit is roughly 0.5 millimeters:

```
// public z-axis position constants (for closeness to tower)
public final static int NEAR = 0;
public final static int FAR = 1;
public final static int MIDDLE = 2;

// position constraints
private final static int NEAR_MIN = 500;
                          // how near to the tower before it counts
private final static int FAR_MIN = 900;   // how far back


public int getZPosition()
{
  float zPos = gloveState.filterPos[2];    // filtered z-axis pos
  if (zPos < NEAR_MIN)    // near to the tower
    return NEAR;
  else if (zPos > FAR_MIN)  // far from the tower
    return FAR;
  else
    return MIDDLE;
}  // end of getZPosition()
```

The NEAR, FAR, and MIDDLE constants are public so they can be utilized by other classes.

On a Roll

getRoll() examines the filtered roll value supplied by the P5 and returns one of the constants ROLL_LEFT, ROLL_RIGHT, or LEVEL. HandView3D uses these constants to turn the camera left, right, or not at all.

Once again, I've used threshold values for triggering the rotation. When the glove is rotated more than 80 degrees to the right, ROLL_RIGHT is returned. When the glove is less than -40 degrees to the left, ROLL_LEFT is the result. Between -40 and 80, the glove is assumed to be unrotated and returns LEVEL.

The greater threshold for rolling right is due to the way that I rest my right hand on the desk, rotated right by about 30 degrees. I don't want a rotation to occur when my hand is in that position:

```
// public roll orientation constants
public final static int ROLL_LEFT = 3;
public final static int ROLL_RIGHT = 4;
public final static int LEVEL = 5;

// rotation constraints
private final static int RIGHT_ROLL_MIN = 80;
              // how far to roll right before it counts
private final static int LEFT_ROLL_MIN = -40;  // roll left
```

```
public int getRoll()
{
  float roll = gloveState.filterRoll;    // the glove's roll
  if (roll < LEFT_ROLL_MIN)    // rolled left
    return ROLL_LEFT;
  else if (roll > RIGHT_ROLL_MIN)  // rolled right
    return ROLL_RIGHT;
  else
    return LEVEL;
}  // end of getRoll()
```

Clenching My Fist

When I clench my fist, I want the music playing in HandView3D to pause (or resume if it's already paused).

The data supplied by ShowGlove shows that clenching usually causes the thumb bend value to decrease to around 800, the little finger to around 500, and the other fingers to about 350. In other words, my glove doesn't generate particularly low bending values for the thumb and little finger.

As a consequence, I've coded isClenched() to return true if at least FINGERS_BENT fingers (three, including the thumb) are bent to have values less than or equal to BEND_MIN (500):

```
// finger bend constraints
private final static int FINGERS_BENT = 3;
          // the minimum no. of fingers that need to be bent

private final static int BEND_MIN = 500;
          /* how far a finger must bend to count
             (a smaller value means more bend) */


public boolean isClenched()
{
  short[] fingerBends = gloveState.fingerAbsolute;

  boolean isClenched = false;
  int bentCount = 0;
  for(int i=0; i < fingerBends.length; i++) {
    if (fingerBends[i] <= BEND_MIN)  // bent enough to count
      bentCount++;
  }
  return (bentCount >= FINGERS_BENT);
}  // end of isClenched()
```

Pressing the *A* Button

isAPressed() returns true if the glove button labeled *A* is pressed:

```
public boolean isAPressed()
{ boolean[] buttonPresses = gloveState.button;
  return buttonPresses[0];  // the "A" button
}
```

HandView3D utilizes isAPressed() as another way of toggling the music on and off.

One issue is that a button press will only be recorded in gloveState if the button is depressed when update() is called. This won't be a problem if the update() calls occur frequently (e.g., every 100 ms or more often), since a button press takes several tenths of a second to be carried out.

A Test Rig for FPSGlove

The MotionTest application explained in this section is a test rig for the FPSGlove class.

One of my aims is to assess the threshold values used in FPSGlove for detecting the glove's position and orientation. MotionTest is also used to check the initialization, update/get cycle, and termination phases of FPSGlove.

MotionTest has a deliberately simple user interface, so I don't need to worry about Swing or Java 3D. It prints an *N* or *F* when the glove is near or far from the receptor tower; an *L* or *R* if the glove is rolled to the left or right; and a * if the glove is clenched.

A typical execution is shown here:

```
> runP5 MotionTest
Executing P5 code: MotionTest ...
N N N N N N N N N N N N N N N N L N L
N L N L N L N L N L N L N L N L N L N L
F L F L F L F L F L F L F L F L F L F L
F L F L F L F L F L L L F F F * * * * *
* * * * * * * * N * N * N * N * N * N *
N * N *
```

The glove starts near the tower, then is rotated left. It stays rotated left as it's moved farther away from the tower. The user clenches his fist when the glove is level and a middling distance from the tower; then the glove is moved nearer to the tower again.

The MotionTest constructor initializes FPSGlove, enters an update/get cycle, and terminates when the *A* button is pressed. Between each update/get iteration, it sleeps for GLOVE_DELAY ms:

```
// delay between glove polling
private static final int GLOVE_DELAY = 100;   // ms

private int i = 1;   // used for formatting the text output


public MotionTest()
{
  FPSGlove glove = new FPSGlove();

  while(!glove.isAPressed()) {
    glove.update();   // update the glove settings

    // show position, roll, hand clenching
    showZPosition(glove);
    showRoll(glove);
    if (glove.isClenched()) {
      System.out.print("* ");
      i++;
    }
```

```
      if (i > 20) {    // lots of info printed, so add a newline
        i = 1;
        System.out.println();
      }

      try {   // sleep a bit
        Thread.sleep(GLOVE_DELAY);
      }
      catch(InterruptedException e) {}
    }

  glove.close();
}  // end of MotionTest()
```

After an update, the current position, roll, and firing status are all retrieved. This means that several letters may be printed during a single update/get iteration. For example, if the glove is near to the tower, rotated left, and the fingers are bent, then *N*, *L*, and * will be printed.

The z-axis position is reported as *N* (near to the tower), or *F* (far). showZPosition() utilizes FPSGlove.getZPosition():

```
private void showZPosition(FPSGlove glove)
{
  int handPos = glove.getZPosition();
  switch(handPos) {
    case FPSGlove.NEAR: System.out.print("N "); i++; break;
    case FPSGlove.FAR: System.out.print("F "); i++; break;
    case FPSGlove.MIDDLE: break;
    default: System.out.print("?? "); i++; break;  //shouldn't happen
  }
}  // end of showZPosition()
```

showRoll() prints an *L* (the glove is rolled left) or *R* (rolled right). It employs FPSGlove.getRoll():

```
private void showRoll(FPSGlove glove)
{
  int handOrient = glove.getRoll();
  switch(handOrient) {
    case FPSGlove.ROLL_LEFT: System.out.print("L "); i++; break;
    case FPSGlove.ROLL_RIGHT: System.out.print("R "); i++; break;
    case FPSGlove.LEVEL: break;
    default: System.out.print("?? "); i++; break;  //shouldn't happen
  }
}  // end of showRoll()
```

Visiting the Musical Cow

Having developed and tested the FPSGlove wrapper class, it's time to use it to connect the P5 to a Java 3D scene. The resulting application, called HandView3D, is shown in Figure 14-10.

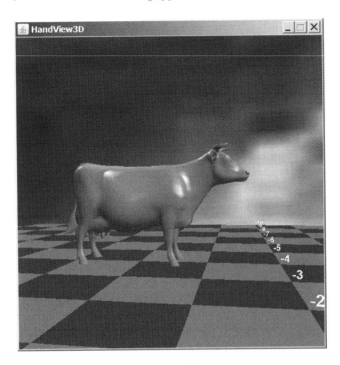

Figure 14-10. *The HandView3D application*

The 3D scene is a familiar one: a checkerboard floor, a background, and lights. The cow is new, as is the music, spatially located under the cow and playing repeatedly.

The user can travel through the scene by moving his or her glove forward, backward, left, and right. As the camera's position changes in relation to the cow, the music varies in intensity and the speaker mix is adjusted.

If the music lover clenches his fist, the music is paused until he clenches it again. The music can also be toggled on and off by pressing the *A* button on the glove.

Figure 14-2 shows the user navigating around the scene.

Figure 14-11 gives the class diagrams for HandView3D, showing only the public methods.

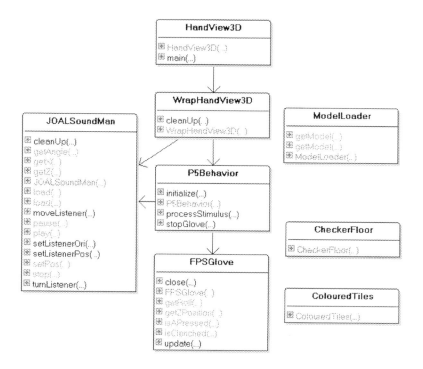

Figure 14-11. *Class diagrams for HandView3D*

HandView3D creates a JFrame holding a WrapHandView3D JPanel where the scene is rendered. HandView3D andWrapHandView3D are very similar to the ObjView3D and WrapObjView3D classes in Chapter 7. The ModelLoader, CheckFloor, and ColouredTiles classes are unchanged.

JOALSoundMan (from Chapter 13) manages the 3D sound; FPSGlove is from the previous section.

All that's really new is P5Behavior and several methods in WrapHandView3D that create the behavior, utilize JOALSoundMan, and close down the glove and sound production at termination time. I'll describe those in detail now.

The Glove Behavior

P5Behavior is a class implementing a time-driven Java3D behavior triggered every DELAY ms:

```java
public class P5Behavior extends ViewPlatformBehavior
{
  private static final int DELAY = 75;   // ms  (polling interval)
  // more constants go here

  private WakeupCondition wakeUpCond;
  private FPSGlove glove;

  // sound-related
  private JOALSoundMan soundMan;
  private String soundNm;    // name of the JOAL source
```

```
// more globals go here

public GamePadBehavior(JOALSoundMan sm, String nm)
{
  soundMan = sm;
  soundNm = nm;

  glove = new FPSGlove();
  wakeUpCond = new WakeupOnElapsedTime(DELAY);
} // end of GamePadBehavior()

public void initialize()
{  wakeupOn(wakeUpCond);  }

// more methods go here
} // end of P5Behavior
```

P5Behavior extends ViewPlatformBehavior so the scene graph's ViewPlatform's transform group, called targetTG, is available. P5Behavior adjusts the player's camera position by applying translations and rotations to targetTG.

A reference to JOALSoundManager is required so the listener can be translated and rotated in unison with the camera. JOALSoundManager also switches the cow's music on and off, which requires its name, soundNm.

Polling the Glove

When processStimulus() is triggered, it updates the glove's state with a call to FPSGlove.update(), then reads the current data to possibly translate and turn the camera and toggle the cow's music on and off:

```
public void processStimulus(Enumeration criteria)
{
  glove.update();  // update the glove settings

  // possibly translate, turn, and toggle the sound
  translate();
  turn();
  toggleSound();

  wakeupOn(wakeUpCond);       // make sure we are notified again
} // end of processStimulus()
```

The next scene graph frame is rendered only when processStimulus() has finished, so all the camera changes will appear in the scene at the same time.

Translating the Camera

The z-axis position can be either FPSGlove.NEAR, FPSGlove.FAR, or FPSGlove.MIDDLE. The first two make the camera move forward or backward:

```
// globals
private static final double MOVE_STEP = 0.2;

// hardwired movement vectors
private static final Vector3d FWD = new Vector3d(0,0,-MOVE_STEP);
private static final Vector3d BACK = new Vector3d(0,0,MOVE_STEP);
```

```
private void translate()
{
  int handPos = glove.getZPosition();
  switch(handPos) {
    case FPSGlove.NEAR: doMove(FWD); break;
    case FPSGlove.FAR: doMove(BACK); break;
    case FPSGlove.MIDDLE: break;   // do nothing
    default: System.out.println("pos?"); break;   // shouldn't happen
  }
}  // end of translate()
```

doMove() applies a translation to the targetTG TransformGroup and to the JOAL listener:

```
// globals for repeated calcs
private Transform3D t3d = new Transform3D();
private Transform3D toMove = new Transform3D();
private Vector3d trans = new Vector3d();


private void doMove(Vector3d theMove)
{
  targetTG.getTransform(t3d);
  toMove.setTranslation(theMove);
  t3d.mul(toMove);
  targetTG.setTransform(t3d);

  // reposition the JOAL listener
  t3d.get(trans);
  soundMan.setListenerPos((float)trans.x, (float)trans.z);
} // end of doMove()
```

P5Behavior doesn't support translations left, right, up, or down. They wouldn't be hard to add by mapping horizontal and vertical glove movements to camera moves.

Turning the Camera

The roll constant can be either FPSGlove.ROLL_LEFT, FPSGlove.ROLL_RIGHT, or FPSGlove.LEVEL. The first two trigger a camera rotation around the y-axis:

```
// global
private static final double ROT_AMT = Math.PI / 36.0;    // 5 degrees


private void turn()
{
  int handOrient = glove.getRoll();
  switch(handOrient) {
    case FPSGlove.ROLL_LEFT: rotateY(ROT_AMT); break;    // turn left
    case FPSGlove.ROLL_RIGHT: rotateY(-ROT_AMT); break; // turn right
    case FPSGlove.LEVEL: break;   // do nothing
    default: System.out.println("rot?"); break;   // shouldn't happen
  }
}  // end of turn()
```

rotateY() applies a rotation to the targetTG TransformGroup and to the JOAL listener:

```
// global for repeated calcs
private Transform3D toRot = new Transform3D();
```

```
private void rotateY(double radians)
{
  targetTG.getTransform(t3d);
  toRot.rotY(radians);
  t3d.mul(toRot);
  targetTG.setTransform(t3d);

  // rotate the JOAL listener
  soundMan.turnListener((int) Math.toDegrees(radians));
} // end of rotateY()
```

Toggling the Sound

When the user clenches his fist or presses the *A* button, the cow music is paused (if it's currently playing) or resumed (if it's paused).

The simple implementation (and the *wrong* one) would be to call FPSGlove.isClenched() and FPSGlove.isAPressed() and check whether either is true in order to toggle the sound. This code fragment does this:

```
// global
private boolean soundPlaying = true;


private void toggleSound()
// this is WRONG
{
  if (glove.isClenched()||glove.isAPressed()) {
    if (soundPlaying)   // play --> paused
      soundMan.pause(soundNm);
    else  // paused --> resumed
      soundMan.play(soundNm);
    soundPlaying = !soundPlaying;
  }
}  // end of toggleSound() -- WRONG
```

The code is incorrect because toggleSound() is called every time that processStimulus() is called (every 75 ms). Unfortunately, a user can't clench and unclench his fist in that short an interval or easily press and release a button. This means that a playing sound would be paused on one call to processStimulus(), but the next call (75 ms later) would very likely detect that the hand is still closed (or the button still pressed) and resume the music. In other words, the music would resume just 75 ms after being paused.

The solution is to impose a *minimum time interval* between soundPlaying changes. For example, a user can probably clench and unclench his hand in a second. Therefore, a modification to the soundPlaying state shouldn't be allowed until at least a second after it is last changed.

A counter is the simplest way of coding the time interval. It's started after a state change and incremented each time that processStimulus() is woken up. Another state change is only permitted after the counter has reached a certain value. This approach is used in the correct version of toggleSound():

```
// globals
private static final int TOGGLE_MAX = 14;
      // toggle count at which soundPlaying can be toggled

private boolean soundPlaying = true;
private int toggleCounter = 0;
```

```
private void toggleSound()
// this is CORRECT
{
  if (toggleCounter < TOGGLE_MAX)
    toggleCounter++;

  if ((glove.isClenched()||glove.isAPressed()) &&
      (toggleCounter == TOGGLE_MAX)) {
    toggleCounter = 0;   // reset

    if (soundPlaying)    // play --> paused
      soundMan.pause(soundNm);
    else   // paused --> resumed
      soundMan.play(soundNm);
    soundPlaying = !soundPlaying;
  }
}  // end of toggleSound() -- CORRECT
```

The music is toggled on/off if the glove is clenched or button *A* is pressed, but only if toggleCounter has reached TOGGLE_MAX. This imposes an interval between state changes equal to TOGGLE_MAX*DELAY, which is about 1 second (14×75 ms).

Adding a Musical Cow

WrapHandView3D adds a cow to the scene with the help of ModelLoader from Chapter 7. JOALSoundMan positions a sound at the same spot and starts it playing:

```
// in WrapHandView3D
// globals
private static final String COW_SND = "spacemusic";
private BranchGroup sceneBG;


private void addCow()
{
  ModelLoader ml = new ModelLoader();
  Transform3D t3d = new Transform3D();

  // a cow model
  t3d.setTranslation( new Vector3d(-2,0,-4));   // move
  t3d.setScale(0.7); // shrink
  TransformGroup tg1 = new TransformGroup(t3d);
  tg1.addChild( ml.getModel("cow.obj", 1.3) );
  sceneBG.addChild(tg1);

  if (!soundMan.load(COW_SND, -2, 0, -4, true))
    System.out.println("Could not load " + COW_SND);
  else
    soundMan.play(COW_SND);
}  // end of addCow()
```

Both the model and music are placed at (-2, 0, 4). The music is set to play repeatedly.

Initializing the Viewpoint

WrapHandView3D positions the camera and JOAL listener at the same spot and connects the P5 behavior object to the camera's viewpoint:

```
// globals
private final static double Z_START = 9.0;

private P5Behavior p5Beh;
    // moves/rotates the viewpoint with P5 glove input


private void createUserControls()
{
  ViewingPlatform vp = su.getViewingPlatform();

  // position viewpoint
  TransformGroup targetTG = vp.getViewPlatformTransform();
  Transform3D t3d = new Transform3D();
  targetTG.getTransform(t3d);
  t3d.setTranslation( new Vector3d(0,1,Z_START));
  targetTG.setTransform(t3d);

  // position JOAL listener at same spot as camera
  soundMan.moveListener(0, (float)Z_START);

  // set up P5 glove controls to move the viewpoint
  p5Beh = new P5Behavior(soundMan, COW_SND);
  p5Beh.setSchedulingBounds(bounds);
  vp.setViewPlatformBehavior(p5Beh);
} // end of createUserControls()
```

The viewpoint and listener start at the same (x, z) coordinate, (0, Z_START).

P5Behavior is given a reference to the JOALSoundMan and the name of the cow music, so it can move the listener and viewpoint together and pause/resume the music.

Cleaning Up

When the user presses HandView3D's close box, there's some cleaning up needed before termination. Good housekeeping dictates that the JOAL sources and buffers (managed by JOALSoundMan) should be deleted and that the P5 glove link should be closed.

HandView3D calls cleanUp() in WrapHandView3D when a window-closing event is detected:

```
// in WrapHandView3D
// globals
private P5Behavior p5Beh;
private JOALSoundMan soundMan;

public void cleanUp()
{ p5Beh.stopGlove();
  soundMan.cleanUp();
}
```

cleanUp() calls stopGlove() in P5Behavior:

```
// in P5Behavior
// global
private FPSGlove glove;
```

```
public void stopGlove()
{ glove.close();
  setEnable(false);
}
```

The call to setEnable() switches off the behavior so it can't be triggered again.

The P5 Glove and JInput

If you've been reading these chapters in order, you may be wondering if JInput could be utilized with the P5 glove. (JInput is a Java API for the discovery and polling of input devices described in Chapters 11 and 12.)

When the P5 is plugged in to the PC's USB port, DirectInput sees it as a USB device, as shown by dxdiag in Figure 14-12.

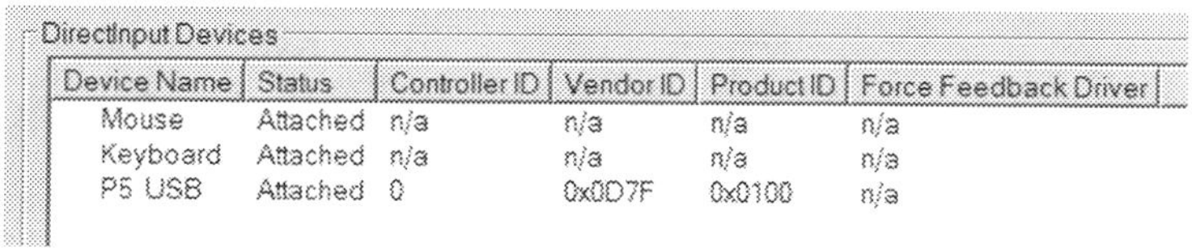

Device Name	Status	Controller ID	Vendor ID	Product ID	Force Feedback Driver
Mouse	Attached	n/a	n/a	n/a	n/a
Keyboard	Attached	n/a	n/a	n/a	n/a
P5 USB	Attached	0	0x0D7F	0x0100	n/a

DirectInput Devices

Figure 14-12. *Part of the dxdiag input tab*

The ListControllers application from Chapter 11 supplies slightly more information:

```
> runJI ListControllers
Executing ListControllers with JInput...
JInput version: 2.0.0-b01
0. Mouse, Mouse
1. Keyboard, Keyboard
2. P5  USB, Stick
```

The P5 controller is classified as a joystick.

Details about the controller are available by calling ControllerDetails (also from Chapter 11):

```
> runJI ControllerDetails 2
Executing ControllerDetails with JInput...
Details for: P5  USB, Stick, Unknown
No Components
No Rumblers
No subcontrollers
```

This output shows that the P5 is barely sending any information to DirectX, which means that JInput can't observe its components. This isn't really surprising since the P5 relies on generic USB support in Windows rather than employing a DirectInput driver.

JInput is capable of "seeing" all of the P5's components but requires someone to write a JInput plug-in for the glove. According to JInput experts, most of the code needed for such a plug-in is already available in Kenner's API.

Summary

This chapter looked at how to utilize the P5 data glove. Its ability to deliver hand position and movement data to an application makes it an interesting and fun input device.

The ShowGlove program lets me examine the data sent by the glove, including its (x, y, z) position, pitch, yaw, roll, finger bends, and button presses. This information helped me design an FPSGlove class for converting the raw glove data into a form suitable for the main example, HandView3D.

HandView3D combines the P5 (via the FPSGlove class), Java 3D, and 3D sound from JOAL to create a scene with a musical cow. Navigation is possible by moving the glove, and the music's intensity and speaker mix varies depending on the user's proximity to the cow.

This chapter illustrates common strategies for utilizing less well-known hardware. There was a testing and configuration stage using OS and vendor tools. Configuration details for the glove were also obtained from a simple GUI application before embarking on the more complex Java 3D example. Help was obtained from informed sources (in this case the p5Glove Yahoo forum). The wrapper classes (Glove and FPSGlove) simplified Carl Kenner's API by focusing on the needs of the applications.

PART 3

■■■

JOGL

CHAPTER 15

Two JOGL Programming Frameworks

This chapter introduces JOGL (`https://jogl.dev.java.net/`), a Java wrapper for the 3D (and 2D) graphics library OpenGL (`http://www.opengl.org/`). I'll implement a simple example, a rotating multicolored cube, using two programming frameworks, one employing *callbacks*, the other utilizing *active rendering*. One way that I compare them is by seeing how well they handle different frame rates for the cube's animation.

The next chapter explores JOGL features in more detail when I develop an application containing many of the elements you've already seen coded in Java 3D, including a checkerboard floor, a rotating textured sphere, a skybox, a billboard, overlays, and keyboard navigation. Chapter 17 examines how to load OBJ models, implement collision detection, and play 3D sound.

What Is JOGL?

JOGL is one of the open-source technologies initiated by the Game Technology Group at Sun Microsystems back in 2003 (the others are JInput and JOAL, which I cover in Chapters 11 through 14). JOGL provides full access to the APIs in the OpenGL 2.0 specification, as well as vendor extensions, and can be combined with AWT and Swing components. It supports both of the main shader languages, GLSL and Nvidia's Cg.

JOGL has the same focus as OpenGL on 2D and 3D rendering. It doesn't include support for gaming elements such as sound or input devices, which are nicely dealt with by JOAL and JInput.

Most features of the popular OpenGL GLU and GLUT libraries are present in JOGL. GLU (the OpenGL Utility Library) includes support for rendering spheres, cylinders, disks, camera positioning, tessellation, and texture mipmaps. The JOGL version of GLUT (OpenGL Utility Toolkit) doesn't include its windowing functionality, which is handled by Java, but does offer geometric primitives (both in solid and wireframe mode). JOGL's utility classes include frame-based animation, texture loading, file IO, and screenshot capabilities.

JOGL has evolved into the reference implementation for the JSR-231 specification for binding OpenGL to Java (`http://jcp.org/en/jsr/detail?id=231`). JOGL 1.1.1 was superseded by JSR-231 in October 2005, and the current JSR-231 release candidate, 1.1.0-rc2, came out in January 2007. I'll be using that version in the following chapters, but will keep using the name JOGL.

To become JSR-231 compliant, many JOGL classes, methods, and packages have been modified, mostly in minor ways. This means that older examples need some tweaking to get them to compile and run. Details about the changes can be found in the JOGL forum thread `http://www.javagaming.org/forums/index.php?topic=11189.0`.

The new GLDrawable and GLContext classes are the most important for this chapter since they allow direct access to OpenGL's drawing surface and state information. These new classes support a new style of coding, called *active rendering*, which I use as the basis of the second programming framework.

The OpenGL API is accessed via Java Native Interface (JNI) calls, leading to a very direct mapping between the API's C functions and JOGL's Java methods. As a consequence, it's extremely easy to translate most OpenGL examples into JOGL. The drawback is that the OpenGL programming style is based around affecting a global graphics state, which makes it difficult to structure Java code into meaningful classes and objects. JOGL does provide class structuring for the OpenGL API, but the vast majority of its methods are in the very large GL and GLU classes.

OpenGL is a vast, complex, and powerful API, with entire books dedicated to its explanation. In the next three chapters, I'll only explain the OpenGL features I need for my examples. For an all-around knowledge, you'll need other sources, and I point you toward some at the end of this chapter.

Installing JOGL

JOGL will work with J2SE 1.4.2 or later; I used Java 1.6.0 for my tests and downloaded the JSR-231 1.1.0 release candidate 2 of JOGL from https://jogl.dev.java.net/. I chose the Windows build from January 23, 2007, jogl-1.1.0-rc2-windows-i586.zip, which contains a lib\ subdirectory holding two JAR files (jogl.jar and gluegen-rt.jar) and four DLLs (jogl.dll, gluegen-rt.dll, jogl_awt.dll, and jogl_cg.dll).

The JOGL user guide (which is part of the ZIP file) recommends that the JARs and DLLs should be installed in their own directory rather than inside the JRE directories. Consequently, I extracted the lib\ directory, renamed it to jogl\, and stored it on my test machine's d: drive (d:\jogl\).

The JARs and DLLs can be utilized at compile time and runtime by supplying suitable classpath and java.library.path parameters on the command line. For example, when I compile the JOGL demo PrintExt.java, I type the following:

```
javac -classpath "d:\jogl\jogl.jar;d:\jogl\gluegen-rt.jar;." PrintExt.java
```

Its execution requires the following:

```
java -cp "d:\jogl\jogl.jar;d:\jogl\gluegen-rt.jar;."
    -Djava.library.path="d:\jogl"
    -Dsun.java2d.noddraw=true  PrintExt
```

The java.exe command is a single line, which I've reformatted so it's easier to read.

The sun.java2d.noddraw property disables Java 2D's use of DirectDraw on Windows. This avoids any nasty interactions between DirectDraw and OpenGL, which can cause application crashes, poor performance, and flickering. The property is only needed if you're working on a Windows platform.

Another useful command-line option is -Dsun.java2d.opengl=true, which switches on the Java2D OpenGL pipeline. The pipeline provides hardware acceleration for many Java 2D rendering operations (e.g., text, images, lines, fills, complex transforms, composites, clips). It's essential when JOGL's GLJPanel class is employed as a drawing surface (as explained in the "Rotating a GLJPanel Cube with Callbacks" section). Unfortunately, -Dsun.java2d.opengl=true may cause crashes on older graphics hardware and drivers. If you don't like lengthy command-line arguments, another approach is to modify the CLASSPATH environment variable and PATH (Windows), LD_LIBRARY_PATH (Solaris and Linux), or DYLD_LIBRARY_PATH (Mac OS X). More details can be found in the JOGL user guide.

I packaged up the compilation command line in compileGL.bat:

```
@echo off
echo Compiling %1 with JOGL...
javac -classpath "d:\jogl\jogl.jar;d:\jogl\gluegen-rt.jar;." %1
```

```
echo Finished.
```

The call to java.exe is in runGL.bat:

```
@echo off
echo Executing %1 with JOGL...
java -cp "d:\jogl\jogl.jar;d:\jogl\gluegen-rt.jar;."
     -Djava.library.path="d:\jogl"
     -Dsun.java2d.noddraw=true %1 %2
echo Finished.
```

The batch variables (%1 and %2) allow up to two arguments to be passed to runGL.bat.

The Callback Framework

The two main JOGL GUI classes are GLCanvas and GLJPanel, which implement the GLAutoDrawable interface, allowing them to be utilized as *drawing surfaces* for OpenGL commands.

GLCanvas is employed in a similar way to AWT's Canvas class. It's a heavyweight component, so care must be taken when combining it with Swing. However, it executes OpenGL operations very quickly due to hardware acceleration.

GLJPanel is a lightweight widget that works seamlessly with Swing. In the past, it's gained a reputation for being slow since it copies the OpenGL frame buffer into a BufferedImage before displaying it. However, its speed has improved significantly in Java SE 6, as I show with some timing tests later in the "Timing the GLJPanel" section of this chapter.

A key advantage of GLJPanel over GLCanvas is that it allows 3D graphics (courtesy of OpenGL) and 2D elements in Swing to be combined in new, exciting ways.

Using GLCanvas

A GLCanvas object is paired with a GLEventListener listener, which responds to changes in the canvas and to drawing requests.

When the canvas is first created, GLEventListener's init() method is called; this method can be used to initialize the OpenGL state.

Whenever the canvas is resized, including when it's first drawn, GLEventListener's reshape() is executed. It can be overridden to initialize the OpenGL viewport and projection matrix (i.e., how the 3D scene is viewed). reshape() is also invoked if the canvas is moved relative to its parent component.

Whenever the canvas' display() method is called, the display() method in GLEventListener is executed. Code for rendering the 3D scene should be placed in that method.

Aside from the canvas and listener, most games will need a mechanism for triggering regular updates to the canvas. This functionality is available through JOGL's FPSAnimator utility class, which can schedule a call to the canvas' display() method with a frequency set by the user. All these elements are shown in Figure 15-1.

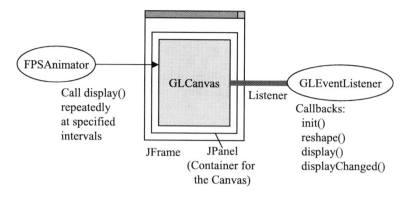

Figure 15-1. *A callback application with GLCanvas*

The GLCanvas can be placed directly inside the JFrame, but by wrapping it in a JPanel the JFrame can contain other (lightweight) GUI components as well.

The GLEventListener callbacks include displayChanged(), which should be called when the display mode or device has changed. This might occur when the monitor's display settings are changed or when the application is dragged to another monitor in a multidisplay configuration. displayChanged() is not currently implemented in JOGL.

Missing from Figure 15-1 is how user interactions, such as mouse and keyboard activity, affect the canvas. The basic technique is to set up mouse and keyboard listeners in the usual Java manner and have them change global variables in GLEventListener. When its display() method is called, it can check these globals to decide how to act. The next chapter has an extended example that employs this approach.

A common source of coding errors with JOGL is to have a mouse or keyboard listener call OpenGL functions directly, which usually results in the application crashing. The OpenGL state can only be safely manipulated via the GLAutoDrawable interface, which is exposed in GLEventListener's callback methods. Many vendors' OpenGL drivers aren't that reliable when faced with multithreading so should not be accessed from listener threads.

Using GLJPanel

Since the GLJPanel is a lightweight Swing component, it can be added directly to the enclosing JFrame, as shown in Figure 15-2.

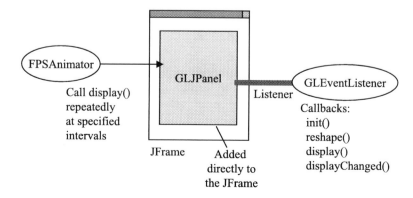

Figure 15-2. *A callback application with GLJPanel*

The rest of the callback framework is identical to Figure 15-1: FPSAnimator drives the anima-tion, and GLEventListener catches changes to the drawing area. This means that it's just a matter of changing a few lines of code to switch between GLCanvas and GLJPanel, as I show in the rotating cube example in the following sections.

A commonly used variant of Figure 15-2 is to place GLJPanel inside a JPanel, which renders a "background" image such as a gradient fill or picture. For the background to be visible, GLJPanel's own background must be made transparent. I'll explain how to do this for the rotating cube application.

Rotating a GLCanvas Cube with Callbacks

The GLCanvas and callback technique outlined in the last section is used in the CubeGL application to rotate a colored cube around the x-, y-, and z- axes. Figure 15-3 shows a screenshot of the cube in action.

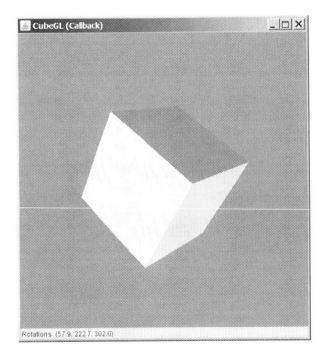

Figure 15-3. *CubeGL with GLCanvas and callbacks*

The window consists of a JPanel in the center holding the GLCanvas and a text field at the bottom that reports the current x-, y-, and z-axis rotations of the cube.

Class diagrams for the application are given in Figure 15-4, showing only public methods.

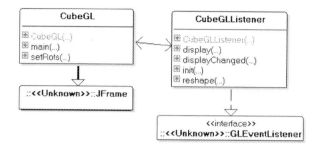

Figure 15-4. *Class diagrams for CubeGL with GLCanvas and callbacks*

CubeGL is the top-level JFrame that creates the GLCanvas and FPSAnimator objects. CubeGLListener is the canvas' listener, a subclass of GLEventListener that implements the callbacks init(), reshape(), and display(). (displayChanged() is empty since JOGL doesn't support it.)

CubeGL is an example of the GLCanvas callback coding style illustrated by Figure 15-1.

Building the Top-Level Window

CubeGL's constructor builds the GUI and sets up a window listener for responding to a window closing event:

```
// globals
private FPSAnimator animator;
private JTextField rotsTF;   // displays cube rotations


public CubeGL(int fps)
{
  super("CubeGL (Callback)");

  Container c = getContentPane();
  c.setLayout( new BorderLayout() );
  c.add( makeRenderPanel(fps), BorderLayout.CENTER);

  rotsTF = new JTextField("Rotations: ");
  rotsTF.setEditable(false);
  c.add(rotsTF, BorderLayout.SOUTH);

  addWindowListener( new WindowAdapter() {
    public void windowClosing(WindowEvent e)
    { new Thread( new Runnable() {
        public void run() {
          animator.stop();
          System.exit(0);
        }
      }).start();
    } // end of windowClosing()
  });

  pack();
  setVisible(true);
```

```
    animator.start();
} // end of CubeGL()
```

The frame/second (FPS) input argument comes from the command line, or a default value of 80 is used. The aim is to update the rotating cube at the specified rate.

The windowClosing() terminates the FPSAnimator object (*animator*) and makes the application exit. The code is carried out in its own thread instead of the one associated with the window listener to ensure that the animator stops before System.exit() is called.

Connecting the Canvas

The GLCanvas is embedded inside a JPanel by makeRenderPanel() and connected to its animator and listener:

```
// globals
private static final int PWIDTH = 512;    // initial size of panel
private static final int PHEIGHT = 512;

private CubeGLListener listener;


private JPanel makeRenderPanel(int fps)
{
  JPanel renderPane = new JPanel();
  renderPane.setLayout( new BorderLayout() );
  renderPane.setOpaque(false);
  renderPane.setPreferredSize( new Dimension(PWIDTH, PHEIGHT));

  GLCanvas canvas = new GLCanvas();              // the canvas
  listener = new CubeGLListener(this, fps);  // the listener
  canvas.addGLEventListener(listener);

  animator = new FPSAnimator(canvas, fps, true);
                 // the animator uses fixed rate scheduling

  renderPane.add(canvas, BorderLayout.CENTER);
  return renderPane;
}  // end of makeRenderPanel()
```

The canvas' enclosing JPanel is given an initial size (512 by 512 pixels), but the window can be resized later, affecting the canvas.

The FPSAnimator constructor takes a reference to the GLAutoDrawable instance (i.e., the *canvas*). Its display() method will be called with a frequency set by the fps argument. FPSAnimator's third argument (set to true) indicates that *fixed-rate scheduling* will be used. Each task is scheduled relative to the scheduled execution time of the initial task. If a task is delayed for any reason (such as garbage collection), two or more tasks will occur in rapid succession to catch up.

Building the Listener

The rotating colored cube is implemented with OpenGL function calls inside the GLEventListener callback methods init(), reshape(), and display().

The listener also includes statistics-gathering code to report how well the application meets the requested frame rate.

The CubeGLListener constructor creates various statistics data structures. It then waits for the canvas to be displayed, which triggers a call to init().

Initializing OpenGL

The OpenGL initialization code in init() typically includes the setup of the z- (depth) buffer, the creation of lights, texture loading, and display-list building. This example doesn't use lights or textures:

```
// globals
private static final float INCR_MAX = 10.0f;    // rotation increments

private GLU glu;

private int cubeDList;    // display list for displaying the cube

// rotation variables
private float rotX, rotY, rotZ;       // total rotations in x,y,z axes
private float incrX, incrY, incrZ;    // increments for x,y,z rotations


public void init(GLAutoDrawable drawable)
{
  GL gl = drawable.getGL();     // don't make this gl a global!
  glu = new GLU();              /* this is okay as a global, but
                                   only use it in callbacks */

  // gl.setSwapInterval(0);
  // switch off vertical synchronization, for extra speed (maybe)

  // initialize the rotation variables
  rotX = 0; rotY = 0; rotZ = 0;
  Random random = new Random();
  incrX = random.nextFloat()*INCR_MAX;    // 0 - INCR_MAX degrees
  incrY = random.nextFloat()*INCR_MAX;
  incrZ = random.nextFloat()*INCR_MAX;

  gl.glClearColor(0.17f, 0.65f, 0.92f, 0.0f); //sky color background

  // z- (depth) buffer initialization for hidden surface removal
  gl.glEnable(GL.GL_DEPTH_TEST);

  // create a display list for drawing the cube
  cubeDList = gl.glGenLists(1);
  gl.glNewList(cubeDList, GL.GL_COMPILE);
    drawColourCube(gl);
  gl.glEndList();
} // end of init()
```

init()'s GLAutoDrawable input argument is the programmer's entry point into OpenGL. The GLAutoDrawable.getGL() call returns a GL object that can be employed to call OpenGL routines.

The JOGL documentation advises against making the GL instance global, since it might tempt programmers into calling OpenGL functions from mouse and keyboard listeners or other threads. This would almost certainly cause the application to crash, since the OpenGL context (its internal state) is tied to the GLEventListener. However, it is OK to make the GLU instance a global, but it should only be utilized in the callback methods.

The GL.setSwapInterval() call switches off vertical synchronization, which may increase the frame rate, depending on the display card and its settings. It makes no discernable difference on my three test machines, so is commented out here.

The cube's current x-, y-, and z- rotations are stored in the globals rotX, rotY, and rotZ. The rotation increments are randomly generated but have values somewhere between 0 and 10 degrees.

An OpenGL display list acts as a storage space for OpenGL rendering and state commands. The commands are compiled into an optimized form, which allows them to be executed more quickly. The benefit of a display list is that it can be called multiple times without OpenGL having to recompile the commands, thereby saving processing time. The cubeDList display list created in init() groups the commands that draw the cube.

Drawing the Colored Cube

The colored cube is made from six differently colored squares—an unchanging rendering task that's a good choice for a display list.

Figure 15-5 shows the cube's vertices, which are positioned so the box is centered on the origin, and has sides of length 2. Each vertex is assigned a number, which is used in the code that follows.

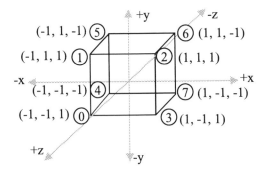

Figure 15-5. *The colored cube's numbered vertices*

The vertices are stored in a global array:

```
private float[][] verts = {
    {-1.0f,-1.0f, 1.0f},  // vertex 0
    {-1.0f, 1.0f, 1.0f},  // 1
    { 1.0f, 1.0f, 1.0f},  // 2
    { 1.0f,-1.0f, 1.0f},  // 3
    {-1.0f,-1.0f,-1.0f},  // 4
    {-1.0f, 1.0f,-1.0f},  // 5
    { 1.0f, 1.0f,-1.0f},  // 6
    { 1.0f,-1.0f,-1.0f},  // 7
};
```

The array positions of the vertices are used by drawPolygon() to draw a cube face. drawPolygon() is called six times from drawColourCube():

```
private void drawColourCube(GL gl)
// six-sided cube, with a different color on each face
{
    gl.glColor3f(1.0f, 0.0f, 0.0f);   // red
    drawPolygon(gl, 0, 3, 2, 1);      // front face

    gl.glColor3f(0.0f, 1.0f, 0.0f);   // green
    drawPolygon(gl, 2, 3, 7, 6);      // right
```

```
gl.glColor3f(0.0f, 0.0f, 1.0f);    // blue
drawPolygon(gl, 3, 0, 4, 7);       // bottom

gl.glColor3f(1.0f, 1.0f, 0.0f);    // yellow
drawPolygon(gl, 1, 2, 6, 5);       // top

gl.glColor3f(0.0f, 1.0f, 1.0f);    // light blue
drawPolygon(gl, 4, 5, 6, 7);       // back

gl.glColor3f(1.0f, 0.0f, 1.0f);    // purple
drawPolygon(gl, 5, 4, 0, 1);       // left
} // end of drawColourCube()


private void drawPolygon(GL gl, int vIdx0, int vIdx1,
                                int vIdx2, int vIdx3)
// the polygon vertices come from the verts[] array
{
  gl.glBegin(GL.GL_POLYGON);
    gl.glVertex3f(verts[vIdx0][0],verts[vIdx0][1], verts[vIdx0][2] );
    gl.glVertex3f(verts[vIdx1][0],verts[vIdx1][1], verts[vIdx1][2] );
    gl.glVertex3f(verts[vIdx2][0],verts[vIdx2][1], verts[vIdx2][2] );
    gl.glVertex3f(verts[vIdx3][0],verts[vIdx3][1], verts[vIdx3][2] );
  gl.glEnd();
}  // end of drawPolygon()
```

GL.glBegin() and GL.glEnd() bracket a sequence of vertex definitions, and glBegin()'s argument specifies the vertices' collective shape. Other modes include GL.GL_POINTS (a collection of points) and GL.GL_LINES (a set of lines).

Reshaping the Canvas

reshape() is called when the canvas is moved or resized, which includes when it's first drawn onscreen. That makes reshape() the natural place to hold OpenGL commands for setting the viewport and projection matrix:

```
public void reshape(GLAutoDrawable drawable, int x, int y,
                                    int width, int height)
{
  GL gl = drawable.getGL();

  if (height == 0)
    height = 1;     // to avoid division by 0 in aspect ratio below

  gl.glViewport(x, y, width, height);  // size of drawing area

  gl.glMatrixMode(GL.GL_PROJECTION);
  gl.glLoadIdentity();
  glu.gluPerspective(45.0, (float)width/(float)height, 1, 100);
          // FOV, aspect ratio, near & far clipping planes

  gl.glMatrixMode(GL.GL_MODELVIEW);
  gl.glLoadIdentity();
} // end of reshape()
```

reshape()'s (x, y) input arguments specify the canvas' position relative to its enclosing container. In this example, they're always (0, 0).

A GL object is freshly created from the GLAutoDrawable input argument.

The GL.glViewport() call defines the size of 3D drawing window (viewport) in terms of a lower-left corner (x, y), width, and height.

The matrix mode is switched to PROJECTION (OpenGL's projection matrix) so the mapping from the 3D scene to the 2D screen can be specified. GL.glLoadIdentity() resets the matrix, and GLU.gluPerspective() creates a mapping with perspective effects (which mirrors what happens in a real-world camera). FOV is the camera's angle of view.

The matrix mode is switched to MODELVIEW at the end of reshape() so OpenGL's model-view matrix can be utilized from then on. It defines the scene's coordinate system, used when positioning, or moving, 3D objects. It's set up at the end of reshape() since display(), which draws the scene, will be called next.

Scene Rendering

As FPSAnimator ticks, it calls display() in the canvas, triggering a call to display() in CubeGLListener. Its display() method holds code that updates and redraws the scene:

```
// global
private static final double Z_DIST = 7.0;    // for camera position


public void display(GLAutoDrawable drawable)
{
  // update the rotations
  rotX = (rotX + incrX) % 360.0f;
  rotY = (rotY + incrY) % 360.0f;
  rotZ = (rotZ + incrZ) % 360.0f;
  top.setRots(rotX, rotY, rotZ);  // report at top-level

  GL gl = drawable.getGL();

  // clear color and depth buffers
  gl.glClear(GL.GL_COLOR_BUFFER_BIT | GL.GL_DEPTH_BUFFER_BIT);
  gl.glLoadIdentity();

  glu.gluLookAt(0,0,Z_DIST, 0,0,0, 0,1,0);   // position camera

  // apply rotations to the x,y,z axes
  gl.glRotatef(rotX, 1.0f, 0.0f, 0.0f);
  gl.glRotatef(rotY, 0.0f, 1.0f, 0.0f);
  gl.glRotatef(rotZ, 0.0f, 0.0f, 1.0f);
  gl.glCallList(cubeDList);   //execute display list for drawing cube
  // drawColourCube(gl);

  reportStats();
} // end of display
```

The cube's x-, y-, and z- rotations in rotX, rotY, and rotZ are updated. The new values are reported onscreen by writing them to the text field in the top-level JFrame (see Figure 15-3).

After the new rotations have been applied to the world coordinates, the cube is drawn via its display list. Alternatively, display() could call drawColourCube() directly.

Measuring FPS Accuracy

reportStats() is called at the end of display(). It prints an average frame rate value roughly every second, as shown in the following CubeGL execution:

```
> runGL CubeGL
Executing CubeGL with JOGL...
fps: 80
period: 12 ms
54.4
64.18
68.42
70.93
72.63
73.84
74.78
75.53
76.13
Finished.
```

The average is calculated from the previous ten FPS values (or less, if ten numbers haven't been calculated yet). This weighted approach discounts earlier slow frame rate data.

In the previous example, CubeGL is started with a requested frame rate of 80, which is converted into a millisecond time period using integer division:

```
int period = (int) 1000.0/fps;    // in ms
```

This is later converted back to a frame rate of 1000/12, which is 83.333. This means an optimally running application should report an average frame rate of around 83 FPS. The example is slowly approaching that and reaches 83 after about 30 seconds.

The implementation of reportStats() doesn't have anything to do with JOGL or OpenGL, so I'll skip its explanation.

Table 15-1 shows the reported average FPS on different versions of Windows when the requested FPS are 20, 50, 80, and 100. Windows XP appears twice since I ran the tests on two different machines using XP.

Table 15-1. *Average FPS for GLCanvas CubeGL with FPSAnimator (Fixed Rate Scheduling)*

Requested FPS	20	50	80	100
Windows 2000	20	50	79	80
Windows XP (1)	20	50	83	100
Windows XP (2)	20	50	81	99

Each test was run three times on a lightly loaded machine running for a few minutes.

The average frame rates are excellent for 80 FPS, although the average hides the fact that it takes a minute or so for the frame rate to rise toward the average. Also, JVM garbage collection reduces the FPS for a few seconds every time it occurs.

The Windows 2000 machine is not capable of achieving 100 FPS, due to its slow hardware.

The FPSAnimator constructor can also be instructed to use a fixed *period* scheduler rather than fixed-rate scheduling. This only requires the change of the boolean argument in FPSAnimator's constructor in makeRenderPanel():

```
// makeRenderPanel() in CubeGL
animator = new FPSAnimator(canvas, fps, false);
                // the animator uses fixed period scheduling
```

The timing tests were run again on the same machines under the same load conditions. The results are shown in Table 15-2.

Table 15-2. *Average FPS for GLCanvas CubeGL and FPSAnimator (Fixed Period Scheduling)*

Requested FPS	20	50	80	100
Windows 2000	19	49	49	98
Windows XP (1)	16	32	63	62
Windows XP (2)	16	31	62	62

The results show a wide variation in FPS accuracy, but the results for the 80 FPS request (the refresh rate on my test machines) are quite poor.

The fixed period scheduler in FPSAnimator uses java.util.Timer.schedule() to repeatedly trigger actions. Unfortunately, the timer's frequency can drift because of extra delays introduced by the garbage collector or long-running game updates and rendering.

Best results are obtained by using FPSAnimator's fixed rate scheduler, as Table 15-1 shows.

Rotating a GLJPanel Cube with Callbacks

An alternative to GLCanvas is GLJPanel, a lightweight widget. Its interface is almost the same as GLCanvas, so the two components can be interchanged easily. This is illustrated by the callback frameworks for GLCanvas and GLJPanel in Figures 15-1 and 15-2.

GLJPanel has historically been much slower than GLCanvas, but its speed has significantly improved in J2SE 5 and Java SE 6. Its key advantage over GLCanvas is that it allows Java 2D and JOGL to be combined in new ways.

Figure 15-6 shows one such combination, a GLJPanel with a background supplied by an enclosing JPanel.

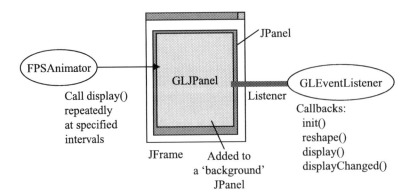

Figure 15-6. *A callback application with GLJPanel and JPanel background*

The callback framework is the same as in Figure 15-2; only the background JPanel is new.

Figure 15-7 shows the rotating cube example again, implemented using the Figure 15-6 approach. The 3D parts are rendered in a GLJPanel with a transparent background. The gradient fill and "Hello World" text are drawn by Java 2D in the JPanel enclosing the GLJPanel.

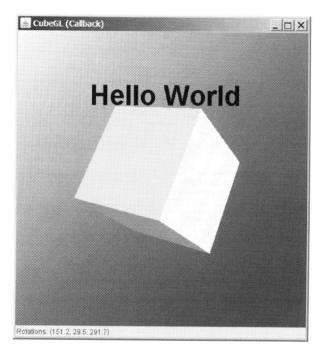

Figure 15-7. *Rotating cube inside a GLJPanel and JPanel background*

The required code changes to convert from a GLCanvas to the GLJPanel are quite small, as I outline in the next three subsections.

A very important command-line change is to include -Dsun.java2d.opengl=true to switch on the Java2D OpenGL pipeline and so increase Java 2D's rendering speed. The application will still run without -Dsun.java2d.opengl=true but much slower. My runGL.bat batch file becomes the following:

```
@echo off
echo Executing %1 with JOGL...
java -cp "d:\jogl\jogl.jar;d:\jogl\gluegen-rt.jar;."
    -Djava.library.path="d:\jogl"
    -Dsun.java2d.noddraw=true
    -Dsun.java2d.opengl=true %1 %2
echo Finished.
```

There have been reports of problems with -Dsun.java2d.opengl=true at the JOGL forum at javagaming.org. For example, it appears to affect rendering speeds when the window is maximized and sometimes crashes the application. On my oldest test machine, which uses a Radeon 9000 PRO AGP graphics chip, the -Dsun.java2d.opengl=true argument causes the gradient fill to disappear, and the application crashes when the window is closed.

The most common response from forum readers is to suggest that people update their graphics cards and drivers. This lack of backward-compatibility is an important concern when using GLJPanel in games aimed at older machines.

Building the Panels

makeRenderPanel() in CubeGL now creates a GLJPanel object rather than a GLCanvas instance and embeds it inside a background panel:

```
private JPanel makeRenderPanel(int fps)
{
  // JPanel renderPane = new JPanel();
  JPanel renderPane = createBackPanel();    // for the GLJPanel

  renderPane.setLayout( new BorderLayout() );
  renderPane.setOpaque(false);
  renderPane.setPreferredSize( new Dimension(PWIDTH, PHEIGHT));

  // GLCanvas canvas = new GLCanvas();
  // create the GLJPanel
  GLCapabilities caps = new GLCapabilities();
  caps.setAlphaBits(8);
  GLJPanel canvas = new GLJPanel(caps);
  canvas.setOpaque(false);

  listener = new CubeGLListener(this, fps);
  canvas.addGLEventListener(listener);

  animator = new FPSAnimator(canvas, fps, true);

  renderPane.add(canvas, BorderLayout.CENTER);
  return renderPane;
}   // end of makeRenderPanel()
```

The old code for creating the GLCanvas object and its JPanel have been commented out.

A transparent GLJPanel requires a nonzero alpha depth, set using a GLCapabilities object and a call to GLJPanel.setOpaque().

The Background Panel

The JPanel acting as the background draws a gradient fill and text:

```
// global
private Font font;

private JPanel createBackPanel()
{
  font = new Font("SansSerif", Font.BOLD, 48);

  JPanel p = new JPanel() {
    public void paintComponent(Graphics g)
    {
      Graphics2D g2d = (Graphics2D) g;
      int width = getWidth();
      int height = getHeight();
      g2d.setPaint( new GradientPaint(0, 0, Color.YELLOW,
                              width, height, Color.BLUE));
      g2d.fillRect(0, 0, width, height);

      g2d.setPaint(Color.BLACK);
      g2d.setFont(font);
      g2d.drawString("Hello World", width/4, height/4);
```

```
    } // end of paintComponent()
  };
  return p;
} // end of createBackPanel()
```

The gradient fill and text change position when the application is resized since they utilize the panel's current width and height values.

Making the 3D Background Transparent

The OpenGL background drawn into the GLJPanel must be transparent (or at least translucent) so the background JPanel's gradient fill and text will be visible.

The rotating cube's background (a light-blue color) is set up inside init() inside CubeGLListener. It is changed to be transparent (or translucent).

The effect shown in Figure 15-7 is achieved with the following:

```
gl.glClearColor(0.0f, 0.0f, 0.0f, 0.0f);    // no OpenGL background
```

The important argument is the fourth, which sets the alpha value for the RGB color preceding it. *0.0f* means fully transparent; *1.0f* is opaque. The 0.0f value in the example means that all the background color comes from the background panel.

A translucent effect (a mix of the background panel and OpenGL's background colors) is obtained with the following:

```
gl.glClearColor(0.17f, 0.65f, 0.92f, 0.3f);
                        // translucent OpenGL sky
```

The 0.3f alpha value makes the OpenGL sky translucent.

The result is shown in Figure 15-8.

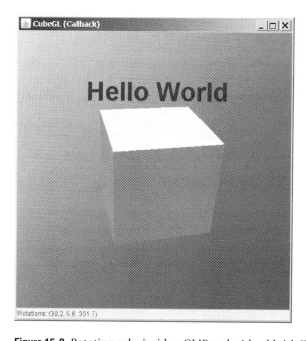

Figure 15-8. *Rotating cube inside a GLJPanel with a bluish JPanel background*

The effect is hard to see (especially when rendered in shades of gray), but the yellow parts of the JPanel's gradient fill have turned green due to the blue OpenGL background.

Timing the GLJPanel

Timing tests were run using the same Windows XP machines under the same load conditions as the GLCanvas callback code with fixed rate scheduling. The results are shown in Table 15-3.

Table 15-3. *Average FPS for GLJPanel CubeGL and FPSAnimator (Fixed Rate Scheduling)*

Requested FPS	20	50	80	100
Windows XP (1)	20	50	71	87
Windows XP (2)	20	50	75	90

The results are very good but slower at higher frame rates than the GLCanvas code.

The speeds are substantially less when the OpenGL pipeline is not enabled (i.e., when -Dsun.java2d.opengl=true isn't part of the command line). For instance, the application only manages about 25 FPS when 80 FPS are requested.

No results are shown for my antiquated Windows 2000 machine since the background rendering didn't work with its old ATI graphics card; the background was always drawn in black.

More Visual Effects with GLJPanel

Chris Campbell's blog entry, "Easy 2D/3D Mixing in Swing" (`http://weblogs.java.net/blog/campbell/archive/2006/10/easy_2d3d_mixin.html`), is a good starting point for more examples of how to integrate 2D and 3D effects in a GUI.

His PhotoCube application includes a CompositeGLJPanel class that offers methods for common types of 2D/3D mixing (e.g., render2DBackground(), render3DScene(), and render2DForeground()). There are also pointers to other articles and online code.

Callback Summary

The callback technique (for GLCanvas and GLJPanel) delivers great frame rates, as long as fixed rate scheduling is utilized and the hardware is fast enough. GLJPanel's successful operation is particularly sensitive to the underlying hardware and graphics driver.

An important advantage of the JOGL callback coding style is its similarity to the callback mechanism used in OpenGL's GLUT. This allows numerous OpenGL examples to be ported over to JOGL with minimal changes.

One drawback of the callback approach is the way that the application life cycle (initialization, resizing, frame-based animation, and termination) is divided across multiple disjoint methods. Also, the use of a timer (inside the animator class) makes it difficult to vary the application's timing behavior at runtime and to separate the frame rate (FPS) from the application's update rate (UPS). The active rendering framework described in the next section addresses these concerns.

The Active Rendering Framework

The active rendering framework utilizes the new features in JSR-231 for directly accessing the drawing surface and context (OpenGL's internal state). This means that there's no longer any need to utilize GUI components that implement the GLAutoDrawable interface, such as GLCanvas. An application can employ a subclass of AWT's Canvas, with its own rendering thread, as illustrated by Figure 15-9.

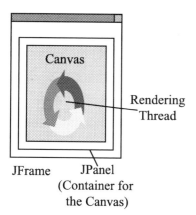

JFrame   JPanel
(Container for
the Canvas)

Figure 15-9. *An active rendering application*

The rendering thread can be summarized using the following pseudocode:

```
make the context current for this thread;
initialize rendering;
while game isRunning {
  update game state;
  render scene;
  put the scene onto the canvas;

  sleep a while;
  maybe do game updates without rendering them;
  gather statistics;
}
discard the rendering context;
print the statistics;
exit;
```

The tricky aspect of this code is remembering that OpenGL should be manipulated from the rendering thread only. Any mouse, key, or window events must be processed there, rather than in separate listeners.

The OpenGL callback code, located inside GLEventListener's init(), reshape(), and display() methods, can be moved without many changes into the active rendering thread. The init() code is carried out in the "initialize rendering" stage, while reshape() and display() are handled inside "render scene."

The principal advantage of the active rendering approach is that it allows the programmer to more directly control the application's execution. For example, it's straightforward to add code that suspends updates when the application is iconified or deactivated (i.e., when it's not the topmost window). Also, access to the timing code inside the animation loop permits a separation of frame rate processing from application updates. I'll illustrate these points by implementing the rotating cube application once again.

Rotating a Cube with Active Rendering

The active rendering CubeGL looks the same as the GLCanvas callback version, as shown in Figure 15-10.

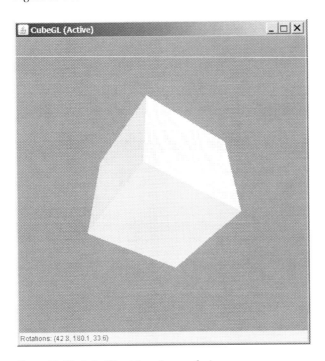

Figure 15-10. *CubeGL with active rendering*

The application has new functionality, courtesy of active rendering; when the window is iconified or deactivated, the cube stops rotating until the window is deiconified or activated again. The class diagrams for this version of CubeGL are given in Figure 15-11.

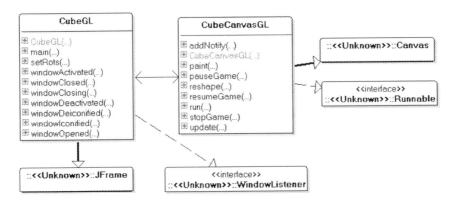

Figure 15-11. *Class diagrams for CubeGL with active rendering*

CubeGL creates the GUI, embedding the threaded canvas, CubeCanvasGL, inside a JPanel. It also captures window events and component resizes and calls methods in CubeCanvasGL to deal with them.

Building the Application

CubeGL creates the threaded canvas inside makeRenderPanel():

```
// globals
private static final int PWIDTH = 512;    // size of panel
private static final int PHEIGHT = 512;

private CubeCanvasGL canvas;


private JPanel makeRenderPanel(long period)
// construct the canvas inside a JPanel
{
  JPanel renderPane = new JPanel();
  renderPane.setLayout( new BorderLayout() );
  renderPane.setOpaque(false);
  renderPane.setPreferredSize( new Dimension(PWIDTH, PHEIGHT));

  canvas = makeCanvas(period);
  renderPane.add(canvas, BorderLayout.CENTER);

  canvas.setFocusable(true);
  canvas.requestFocus();    //canvas has focus, so receives key events

  // detect window resizes, and reshape the canvas accordingly
  renderPane.addComponentListener( new ComponentAdapter() {
    public void componentResized(ComponentEvent evt)
    { Dimension d = evt.getComponent().getSize();
      canvas.reshape(d.width, d.height);
    }
  });

  return renderPane;
}  // end of makeRenderPanel()
```

The panel has two roles: it surrounds the canvas, protecting lightweight GUI widgets from the heavyweight AWT Canvas and is a convenient place to connect a component listener to detect window resizes. A resize generates a call to CubeCanvasGL.reshape(), which triggers a recalculation of the OpenGL viewport and perspective.

The period input to makeRenderPanel() comes from the frame rate supplied on the command line. It's calculated as the following:

```
long period = (long) 1000.0/fps;
```

makeCanvas() obtains an optimal graphics configuration for the canvas. It passes this information to an instance of the threaded canvas, CubeCanvasGL:

```
private CubeCanvasGL makeCanvas(long period)
{
  // get a configuration suitable for an AWT Canvas
  GLCapabilities caps = new GLCapabilities();
```

```
AWTGraphicsDevice dev = new AWTGraphicsDevice(null);
AWTGraphicsConfiguration awtConfig =
   (AWTGraphicsConfiguration)GLDrawableFactory.getFactory().
              chooseGraphicsConfiguration(caps, null, dev);

GraphicsConfiguration config = null;
if (awtConfig != null)
   config = awtConfig.getGraphicsConfiguration();

return new CubeCanvasGL(this, period, PWIDTH, PHEIGHT,
                                          config, caps);
} // end of makeCanvas()
```

Dealing with Window Events

CubeGL is a window listener:

```
public void windowActivated(WindowEvent e)
{ canvas.resumeGame();  }

public void windowDeactivated(WindowEvent e)
{  canvas.pauseGame();  }

public void windowDeiconified(WindowEvent e)
{  canvas.resumeGame();  }

public void windowIconified(WindowEvent e)
{  canvas.pauseGame(); }

public void windowClosing(WindowEvent e)
{  canvas.stopGame();  }

public void windowClosed(WindowEvent e) {}
public void windowOpened(WindowEvent e) {}
```

pauseGame(), resumeGame(), and stopGame() trigger extra processing inside CubeCanvasGL's rendering loop to pause, resume, or terminate the application.

Preparing the Canvas

Before the rendering thread can start inside CubeCanvasGL, the rendering surface and context for the canvas need to be accessed. This is done in CubeCanvasGL's constructor:

```
// globals
private GLDrawable drawable;   // the rendering 'surface'
private GLContext context;
    // the rendering context (holds rendering state info)


// in the CubeCanvasGL constructor:
drawable =
  GLDrawableFactory.getFactory().getGLDrawable(this, caps, null);
context = drawable.createContext(null);
```

The GLCapabilities instance, caps, comes from CubeGL's makeCanvas(), which creates the canvas object.

Rendering should be delayed until the canvas is visible onscreen, which occurs once the canvas calls its addNotify() method. This behavior can be implemented by starting the thread from addNotify() in CubeCanvasGL:

```
// global
private Thread animator;     // thread that performs the animation


public void addNotify()
// wait for the canvas to be added to the JPanel before starting
{
  super.addNotify();           // make the component displayable
  drawable.setRealized(true); // canvas can now be used for rendering

  // initialize and start the animation thread
  if (animator == null || !isRunning) {
    animator = new Thread(this);
    animator.start();
  }
} // end of addNotify()
```

Thread Rendering

The run() method in CubeCanvasGL follows the pseudocode given earlier. This is the first version; I describe a slightly modified version later in this section:

```
public void run()
// initialize rendering and start frame generation; first version
{
  makeContentCurrent();

  initRender();
  renderLoop();

  // discard the rendering context and exit
  context.release();
  context.destroy();
  System.exit(0);
} // end of run()


private void makeContentCurrent()
// make the rendering context current for this thread
{
  try {
    while (context.makeCurrent() == GLContext.CONTEXT_NOT_CURRENT) {
      System.out.println("Context not yet current...");
      Thread.sleep(100);
    }
  }
  catch (InterruptedException e)
  { e.printStackTrace(); }
}  // end of makeContentCurrent()
```

makeCurrentContext() calls GLContext.makeCurrent(), which should immediately succeed since no other thread is using the context. The while-loop around the GLContext.makeCurrent() call is extra protection since the application will crash if OpenGL commands are called without the thread holding the current context.

When execution returns from the rendering loop inside renderLoop(), the context is released and destroyed and the application exits.

This coding approach means that the context is current for the entire duration of the thread's execution. This causes no problems on most platforms (e.g., it's fine on Windows), but unfortunately there's an issue when using X11. On X11 platforms, a AWT lock is created between the GLContext.makeCurrent() and GLContext.release() calls, stopping mouse and keyboard input from being processed.

The only solution is to periodically release the context, giving the JRE under X11 time to act on mouse and keyboard events.

This means that run() must have its calls to makeCurrentContext() and GLContext.release() commented out. This leads to a second version of the code:

```
public void run()
// initialize rendering and start frame generation; 2nd version
{
  // makeContentCurrent();   // commented out due to X11

  initRender();
  renderLoop();

  // discard the rendering context and exit
  // context.release();      // commented out due to X11
  context.destroy();
  System.exit(0);
} // end of run()
```

Instead, the context will be made current and released inside initRender() and renderLoop().

Rendering Initialization

The initRender() method in CubeCanvasGL corresponds to the init() callback in GLEventListener with one important OpenGL-related change:

```
// globals
private GL gl;
private GLU glu;


private void initRender()
{
  makeContentCurrent();

  gl = context.getGL();  // gl is now global
  glu = new GLU();

  resizeView();

  gl.glClearColor(0.17f, 0.65f, 0.92f, 0.0f); // sky color backgrnd

  // z- (depth) buffer initialization for hidden surface removal
  gl.glEnable(GL.GL_DEPTH_TEST);

  // create a display list for drawing the cube
  cubeDList = gl.glGenLists(1);
```

```
gl.glNewList(cubeDList, GL.GL_COMPILE);
  drawColourCube(gl);
gl.glEndList();

/* release the context, otherwise the AWT lock in X11
   will not be released */
context.release();
} // end of initRender()
```

The recommended coding style in GLEventListener callbacks, such as init(), is to obtain a fresh GL reference inside each method via the GLAutoDrawable input argument. This is unnecessary in the active rendering approach since there's only a single thread executing inside the canvas. Therefore, the GL instance is made global and initialized once at the start of initRender().

The initialization of the rotation variables has been moved to CubeCanvasGL's constructor so only OpenGL code is left in initRender().

The color cube drawing code in drawColourCube() (and its helper method drawPolygon()) are unchanged from the callback version of CubeGL, so I'll skip them here.

resizeView() sets the viewpoint and perspective and corresponds to the initial call to the reshape() callback in GLEventListener:

```
// globals
private int panelWidth, panelHeight;


private void resizeView()
{
  gl.glViewport(0, 0, panelWidth, panelHeight); // drawing area

  gl.glMatrixMode(GL.GL_PROJECTION);
  gl.glLoadIdentity();
  glu.gluPerspective(45.0, (float)panelWidth/(float)panelHeight, 1, 100);
      // fov, aspect ratio, near & far clipping planes
} // end of resizeView()
```

panelWidth and panelHeight are assigned their initial values in CubeCanvasGL's constructor.

I explain how resizeView() is called in the "Rendering the Scene" section when I describe how the application's window is resized.

The Rendering Loop

renderLoop() implements the while-loop in the active rendering pseudocode:

```
while game isRunning {
  update game state;
  render scene;
  put the scene onto the canvas;

  sleep a while;
  maybe do game updates without rendering them;

  gather statistics;
}
```

The loop is complicated by having to calculate the amount of time it takes to do the update-render pair. The sleep time that follows must be adjusted so the time to complete the iteration is as close to the desired frame rate as possible.

If an update-render takes too long, it may be necessary to carry out some game updates without rendering their changes. The result is a game that runs close to the requested frame rate by skipping the time-consuming rendering of the updates.

The timing code distinguishes between two rates: the actual frame rate that measures the number of renders/second (FPS), and the update rate that measures the number of updates/second (UPS).

FPS and UPS aren't the same. It's quite possible for a slow platform to limit the FPS value, but the program performs additional updates (without rendering) so that its UPS number is close to the requested frame rate.

This separation of FPS and UPS makes the animation loop more complicated, but it's one of the standard ways to create reliable animations. It's especially good for games where the hardware is unable to render at the requested frame rate.

The following is the code for renderLoop():

```
// constants
private static final int NO_DELAYS_PER_YIELD = 16;
  /* Number of iterations with a sleep delay of 0 ms before the
     animation thread yields to other running threads. */

private static int MAX_RENDER_SKIPS = 5;
  /* no. of renders that can be skipped in any one animation loop;
     i.e. the games state is updated but not rendered. */

// globals
private long prevStatsTime;
private long gameStartTime;
private long rendersSkipped = 0L;

private long period;       // period between drawing in nanosecs
private volatile boolean isRunning = false;
                          // used to stop the animation thread


private void renderLoop()
{
  // timing-related variables
  long beforeTime, afterTime, timeDiff, sleepTime;
  long overSleepTime = 0L;
  int noDelays = 0;
  long excess = 0L;

  gameStartTime = System.nanoTime();
  prevStatsTime = gameStartTime;
  beforeTime = gameStartTime;

  isRunning = true;

  while(isRunning) {
    makeContentCurrent();

    gameUpdate();
    renderScene();    // rendering
    drawable.swapBuffers();  // put the scene onto the canvas
      // swap front and back buffers, making the rendering visible

    afterTime = System.nanoTime();
```

```
    timeDiff = afterTime - beforeTime;
    sleepTime = (period - timeDiff) - overSleepTime;

    if (sleepTime > 0) {    // some time left in this cycle
      try {
        Thread.sleep(sleepTime/1000000L);  // nano -> ms
      }
      catch(InterruptedException ex){}
      overSleepTime = (System.nanoTime() - afterTime) - sleepTime;
    }
    else {  // sleepTime <= 0; this cycle took longer than the period
      excess -= sleepTime;  // store excess time value
      overSleepTime = 0L;

      if (++noDelays >= NO_DELAYS_PER_YIELD) {
        Thread.yield();    // give another thread a chance to run
        noDelays = 0;
      }
    }

    beforeTime = System.nanoTime();

    /* If the rendering is taking too long,
       then update the game state without rendering it, to
       get the UPS nearer to the required frame rate. */
    int skips = 0;
    while((excess > period) && (skips < MAX_RENDER_SKIPS)) {
      excess -= period;
      gameUpdate();     // update state but don't render
      skips++;
    }
    rendersSkipped += skips;

    /* release the context, otherwise the AWT lock in X11
       will not be released */
    context.release();

    storeStats();
  }

  printStats();
} // end of renderLoop()
```

The "sleep a while" code in the loop is complicated by dealing with inaccuracies in Thread.sleep(). sleep()'s execution time is measured and the error (stored in overSleepTime) adjusts the sleeping period in the next iteration.

The if-test involves Thread.yield():

```
if (++noDelays >= NO_DELAYS_PER_YIELD) {
  Thread.yield();
  noDelays = 0;
}
```

It ensures that other threads get a chance to execute if the animation loop hasn't slept for a while.

renderLoop calls makeContentCurrent() and GLContext.release() at the start and end of each rendering iteration. This allows the JRE under X11 some time to process AWT events.

Updating the Game

gameUpdate() should contain any calculations that affect gameplay, which for CubeGL are only the x-, y-, and z- rotations used by the cube:

```
// globals
private volatile boolean gameOver = false;
private volatile boolean isPaused = false;

private CubeGL top;    // reference back to the top-level JFrame

// rotation variables
private float rotX, rotY, rotZ;      // total rotations in x,y,z axes
private float incrX, incrY, incrZ;   // increments for x,y,z rotations


private void gameUpdate()
{ if (!isPaused && !gameOver) {
    // update the rotations
    rotX = (rotX + incrX) % 360.0f;
    rotY = (rotY + incrY) % 360.0f;
    rotZ = (rotZ + incrZ) % 360.0f;
    top.setRots(rotX, rotY, rotZ);
  }
}  // end of gameUpdate()
```

The isPaused and gameOver booleans allow the updates to be skipped when the game is paused or has finished.

Rendering the Scene

The scene generation carried out by renderScene() is similar to what display() does in the callback version of CubeGL:

```
// global
private boolean isResized = false;    // for window resizing


private void renderScene()
{
  if (context.getCurrent() == null) {
    System.out.println("Current context is null");
    System.exit(0);
  }

  if (isResized) {    // resize the drawable if necessary
    resizeView();
    isResized = false;
  }

  // clear color and depth buffers
  gl.glClear(GL.GL_COLOR_BUFFER_BIT | GL.GL_DEPTH_BUFFER_BIT);

  gl.glMatrixMode(GL.GL_MODELVIEW);
  gl.glLoadIdentity();

  glu.gluLookAt(0,0,Z_DIST, 0,0,0, 0,1,0);    // position camera
```

```
// apply rotations to the x,y,z axes
gl.glRotatef(rotX, 1.0f, 0.0f, 0.0f);
gl.glRotatef(rotY, 0.0f, 1.0f, 0.0f);
gl.glRotatef(rotZ, 0.0f, 0.0f, 1.0f);
gl.glCallList(cubeDList);  // execute display list for drawing cube
// drawColourCube(gl);

  if (gameOver)
    System.out.println("Game Over");    //report that the game is over
} // end of renderScene()
```

One of the new things that renderScene() does is to check that the thread still has the current context; if it doesn't, the application exits. A more robust response would be to try to regain the context by calling GLContext.makeCurrent() again, reinitializing the scene, and restarting the animation loop.

renderScene() calls resizeView() to update the OpenGL view if isResized is true. The boolean is set to true by CubeGL calling reshape() in CubeCanvasGL when the window is resized:

```
public void reshape(int w, int h)
/* Called by the JFrame's ComponentListener when the window
   is resized. */
{
  isResized = true;
  if (h == 0)
    h = 1;   // to avoid div by 0 in aspect ratio in resizeView()
  panelWidth = w; panelHeight = h;
}  // end of reshape()
```

This illustrates the single-threaded coding style needed for OpenGL. reshape() does *not* call OpenGL routines itself since it's being executed by a component listener in CubeGL. Instead, it sets isResized and lets the rendering thread handle the resizing.

renderScene() finishes by checking the gameOver boolean and printing a simple message. In a real game, the output would be more complicated.

The Game Life Cycle Methods

Window events detected in CubeGL are processed by calling CubeCanvasGL methods:

```
public void resumeGame()
// called when the JFrame is activated / deiconified
{ isPaused = false;  }

public void pauseGame()
// called when the JFrame is deactivated / iconified
{ isPaused = true;    }

public void stopGame()
// called when the JFrame is closing
{ isRunning = false;    }
```

In the same way as reshape(), these methods do not call OpenGL functions since they're being executed by the window listener in CubeGL. Instead, they set global booleans checked by the rendering thread.

Statistics Reporting

CubeCanvasGL utilizes two statistics methods: storeStats() and printStats(). storeStats() collects a range of data, and printStats() prints a summary just before the application exits. Neither method utilizes JOGL features, so I won't explain their implementation here. Typical output from printStats() is shown here:

```
> runGL CubeGL
Executing CubeGL with JOGL...
fps: 80; period: 12 ms
Average FPS: 82.47
Average UPS: 83.28
Time Spent: 33 secs
Finished.
```

The averages are calculated from the last ten recorded FPS and UPS values. If the FPS and UPS numbers are the same, the game was able to match the requested frame rate without skipping the rendering of any updates.

Table 15-4 shows the average FPS and UPS figures for different requested FPS on different versions of Windows.

Table 15-4. *Average FPS/UPS for CubeGL with Active Rendering*

Requested FPS	20	50	80	100
Windows 2000	20/20	43/50	73/83	79/100
Windows XP (1)	20/20	50/50	80/83	95/100
Windows XP (2)	20/20	50/50	81/83	97/100

Each test was run three times on a lightly loaded machine, executing for a few minutes.

The numbers are very good for the machines hosting Windows XP, but the frame rates on the Windows 2000 machine plateau at about 80. This behavior is due to the age of the machine.

The Windows 2000 figures show that active rendering can deal with slow hardware. The processing power of the machine isn't able to deliver the requested frame rate, but the application doesn't seem slow since the UPS stays near to the request FPS. When 80 FPS are requested, about 12% of the updates aren't rendered ($(83-73)/83$). This isn't apparent when the cube is rotating, which shows the benefit of decoupling updates from rendering.

Java 3D and JOGL

Most of the examples in this book utilize Java 3D, so it's natural to wonder whether Java 3D and JOGL can be used together. The news as of March 2007 was disappointing, but matters may improve in the future.

A posting to the Java Desktop 3D forum in 2004 (http://forums.java.net/jive/thread.jspa?threadID=5465) describes the use of JOGL's GLCanvas to create a HUD (heads-up display) within a Java 3D application. The canvas was manipulated in the pre- and postrendering phases of Java 3D's immediate mode (or *mixed mode*) to allow JOGL-generated objects to appear in the background and foreground of the scene.

When I tried to duplicate this approach, the objects had a tendency to disappear when the camera position was moved, and sometimes the Java 3D parts of the scene didn't appear.

(For readers unfamiliar with Java 3D's immediate and mixed modes, Chapter 8 explains how to use mixed mode to draw purely Java 3D backgrounds and overlays.)

On a brighter note, Java 3D 1.6 is scheduled for release early in 2008. One of its stated aims is to allow Java 3D and JOGL code to be utilized together. The first steps have already been taken in version 1.5, which offers three versions of Java 3D implemented on top of OpenGL, DirectX, *and* JOGL.

One of the reasons for using JOGL is its access to shading languages for special effects such as fish eyes, shadow textures, and spherization. However, both GLSL and Cg are already supported in Java 3D.

A user who needs scene graph functionality and OpenGL functions today may want to look at Xith3D (`http://xith.org/`).

More Information on JOGL and OpenGL

The JOGL web site (`https://jogl.dev.java.net/`) hosts the latest software releases together with demos, presentation slides, and a user guide.

The principal source for JOGL help is its forum site at `http://www.javagaming.org/forums/index.php?board=25.0`. A good (but old) JOGL introduction by Gregory Pierce is at `http://www.javagaming.org/forums/index.php?topic=1474.0`. Another introductory article, "Jumping into JOGL" by Chris Adamson in 2003, is at `http://today.java.net/pub/a/today/2003/09/11/jogl2d.html`.

A minor drawback of the forum is that search results will include informationfor the out-of-date JOGL 1.1. However, it's possible to date-limit the searches to exclude older threads. JSR-231 implementations started appearing in October 2005.

The first stop for information on OpenGL is `http://www.opengl.org/`, which offers a lot of documentation, coding resources, and links to applications, games, and code samples.

The NeHe site (`http://nehe.gamedev.net/`) is an excellent place to start learning OpenGL. It contains an extensive collection of tutorials, articles, examples, and other programming materials. The tutorial, starting from first principles, consists of 48 lessons and has been ported to a variety of languages, including JOGL/JSR-231. The tutorial examples were ported to JOGL by Kevin Duling, Pepijn Van Eeckhoudt, Abdul Bezrati, and Nicholas Cambel. Van Eeckhoudt placed them in a common framework and ported them to JSR-231. The examples are available at `http://pepijn.fab4.be/?page_id=34`.

There are a growing number of textbooks on OpenGL (e.g., see `http://www.opengl.org/documentation/books/`). For a quick overview that covers the basics without a great deal of computer graphics theory you could try *OpenGL: A Primer* (Second Edition) by Edward Angel (Pearson, 2005). The book's code is available at `http://www.cs.unm.edu/~angel/BOOK/PRIMER/SECOND_EDITION/PROGRAMS/`.

If you don't have a background in computer graphics you should probably switch to Angel's more technical book, *Interactive Computer Graphics: A Top-Down Approach Using OpenGL* (Fourth Edition) (Addison Wesley, 2005).

A good OpenGL text with a gaming slant is *OpenGL Game Programming* by Kevin Hawkins and David Astle (Premier Press, 2001). The examples use the complex Microsoft windowing library, wgl, but they're still fun and informative. The online support page is `http://glbook.gamedev.net/oglgp.asp`.

Astle and Hawkins have released two more recent books: *Beginning OpenGL Game Programming* (Course Technology, 2004) and *More OpenGL Game Programming* (Course Technology, 2005), which cover similar ground and more advanced topics, such as programmable shaders. Details are available at `http://glbook.gamedev.net/`.

The ultimate OpenGL programming text, *OpenGL Programming Guide: The Official Guide to Learning OpenGL Version 2* (Fifth Edition) by the OpenGL Architecture Review Board (Addison-Wesley, 2005), is known as the "red book" in OpenGL circles. An early version, for OpenGL 1.0, is online at `http://www.opengl.org/documentation/red_book/` in PDF and HTML formats and at `http://www.gamedev.net/download/redbook.pdf`.

Summary

I introduced JOGL in this chapter by coding a simple rotating multicolored cube using several approaches.

The *callback framework* utilizes an animator, an event listener, and a drawing surface. I coded two variants of it—one with the fast GLCanvas class, the other using GLJPanel. Their speeds were roughly equivalent, but GLJPanel's performance depends on the suitability of the hardware, graphics driver, and Java version. Its main advantage is its ability to closely integrate with other Swing components to create novel, fun 2D/3D GUIs. An important issue is that the -Dsun.java2d.opengl=true argument needed for GLJPanel's speed may cause crashes on older graphics hardware and drivers.

The cube application was also implemented using *active rendering*, a technique only made possible with the recent extensions to JOGL to make it JSR-231 compliant. Active rendering is as fast as the callback approach and allows finer control over the application's timing behavior. For example, a poor frame rate on a slow machine can be compensated for by performing updates without the slow rendering. The downside is the increased complexity of the rendering loop and the fact that most JOGL/OpenGL examples use the callback approach, offering more help to novice programmers.

CHAPTER 16

∎∎∎

Touring the World

The previous chapter was about two programming frameworks for JOGL (callbacks and active rendering), with a simple rotating cube as the example. This chapter utilizes the active rendering framework to build a more substantial application: a small 3D world containing a checkerboard floor, a skybox, lighting, a rotating sphere, and billboards. The user moves around the scene using keyboard controls with the aim of finding shapes lying on the ground. The game begins with a start screen and finishes with a "Game Over" message.

The application illustrates a number of useful techniques, including texturing images with transparent parts, using 2D overlays, and writing text with bitmaps and Java 2D fonts.

Application Details

This chapter focuses on a single example, the TourGL application, which is shown in Figure 16-1.

Figure 16-1. *The TourGL application*

The following are the visual elements of the application:

- A green and blue checkerboard floor with a red square at its center and numbers along its x- and z- axes.
- A skybox of stars.
- An orbiting "earth" (a textured sphere).
- A billboard showing a tree, which rotates around its y-axis to always face the camera.
- Several shapes randomly placed flat on the ground. The shape image is a red *R* but it can be easily changed.

The user can move around the world using the arrow keys to go forward and backward, to translate left, right, up, and down, and to turn left and right, but the player can't travel off the checkerboard or beyond the borders of the skybox. The game is terminated by pressing ESC, q, END, or Ctrl-c, or by clicking the close box.

TourGL is a very basic game: the user must navigate over the shapes lying on the ground to make them disappear. The game ends when all the shapes are deleted, and a score is calculated based on how long it takes to delete them.

Since TourGL utilizes the active rendering framework, the game automatically suspends when the window is iconified or deactivated and can be resized. TourGL also offers two extensions to the framework:

- A message is displayed in the canvas while the world is being initialized (see Figure 16-2).
- A "Game Over" 2D image with text is displayed when all the ground shapes have disappeared (see Figure 16-3). This stays onscreen until the application is terminated.

Figure 16-2. *The loading message*

Figure 16-3. *The "Game Over" message*

Various OpenGL (JOGL) techniques are illustrated in this example, including transparent images as textures, 2D overlays, and bitmap and Java 2D fonts.

The class diagrams for TourGL in Figure 16-4 highlight its use of active rendering.

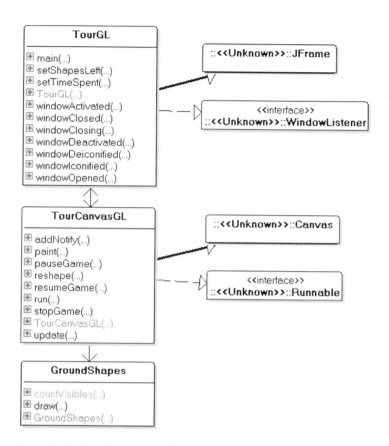

Figure 16-4. *Class diagrams for TourGL*

The TourGL class creates the GUI, which consists of the threaded canvas, TourCanvasGL, and two text fields at the bottom of the window.

TourGL captures window and component resizing events and calls methods in TourCanvasGL to pause, resume, stop, and resize the 3D scene. It also has two set methods for its text fields: setShapesLeft() and setTimeSpent(). They're called by TourCanvasGL to report the number of remaining shapes and the game's running time.

GroundShapes positions the shapes on the floor and manages their drawing at runtime.

Constructing the Canvas

The TourCanvasGL constructor obtains the OpenGL drawing surface and context, standard tasks for active rendering applications:

```
// globals
private TourGL tourTop;        // reference back to top-level JFrame
private long period;           // period between drawing in nanosecs

private int panelWidth, panelHeight;

private GLDrawable drawable;   // the rendering 'surface'
private GLContext context;     // rendering state info
```

```
// used by the 'loading' message
private Font font;
private FontMetrics metrics;
private BufferedImage waitIm;


public TourCanvasGL(TourGL top, long period, int width, int height,
                    GraphicsConfiguration config, GLCapabilities caps)
{
  super(config);

  tourTop = top;
  this.period = period;
  panelWidth = width;
  panelHeight = height;

  setBackground(Color.white);

  // get a rendering surface and a context for this canvas
  drawable = GLDrawableFactory.getFactory().getGLDrawable(this, caps, null);
  context = drawable.createContext(null);

  initViewerPosn();

  addKeyListener( new KeyAdapter() {
    public void keyPressed(KeyEvent e)
    { processKey(e);  }
  });

  // 'loading' message font and image
  font = new Font("SansSerif", Font.BOLD, 24);
  metrics = this.getFontMetrics(font);
  waitIm = loadImage("hourglass.jpg");

  // axes labels renderer
  axisLabelRenderer = new TextRenderer(font);

  // statistics initialization
     // not shown here...
} // end of TourCanvasGL()
```

TourCanvasGL performs four application-specific jobs: it initializes the camera coordinates (in initViewerPosn()), sets up a key listener (processKey()), prepares the font and image used in the loading message, and creates a TextRenderer object for drawing the floor axes. TextRenderer is a JOGL utility class for employing Java 2D fonts.

The Camera Position

initViewerPosn() stores the camera position in xCamPos, yCamPos, and zCamPos, and the point being looked at in xLookAt, yLookAt, and zLookAt.

The camera's orientation is recorded in viewAngle and is used to calculate the x- and z-axis "step," which moves the camera forward:

```
// camera related constants
private final static double LOOK_AT_DIST = 100.0;
private final static double Z_POS = 9.0;

// camera movement
private double xCamPos, yCamPos, zCamPos;
private double xLookAt, yLookAt, zLookAt;
private double xStep, zStep;
private double viewAngle;


private void initViewerPosn()
{
  xCamPos = 0; yCamPos = 1; zCamPos =  Z_POS;   // camera position

  viewAngle = -90.0;    // along negative z-axis
  xStep = Math.cos( Math.toRadians(viewAngle));   // step distances
  zStep = Math.sin( Math.toRadians(viewAngle));

  xLookAt = xCamPos + (LOOK_AT_DIST * xStep);   // look-at posn
  yLookAt = 0;
  zLookAt = zCamPos + (LOOK_AT_DIST * zStep);
} // end of initViewerPosn()
```

By setting the viewAngle to -90, the initial xStep and zStep values become (0, -1), which is a step "forward" into the scene along the negative z-axis.

The camera looks forward into the distance, represented by the coordinate (LOOK_AT_DIST*xStep, 0, LOOK_AT_DIST*zStep), which is (0, 0, -100) initially.

These variables are used to adjust the camera in renderScene() (explained in the "Rendering the Scene" section), which calls GLU.gluLookAt():

```
glu.gluLookAt(xCamPos, yCamPos, zCamPos,
                       xLookAt, yLookAt, zLookAt, 0,1,0);
```

The camera and lookAt coordinates are changed whenever the user presses an arrow key to move the camera. Key processing is handled by processKey(), described next.

Responding to Key Presses

TourGL assigns focus to the canvas when it's created:

```
canvas.setFocusable(true);
canvas.requestFocus();
```

This means that key events will be passed to TourCanvasGL, where they're dealt with by processKey().

Two groups of keys are handled: those triggering the application's termination (ESC, q, END, Ctrl-c) and those for moving the camera (the arrow keys, possibly combined with the Ctrl key, and page-up and page-down).

The arrow keys cause the camera to move forward and backward and rotate left and right. When the left or right arrow keys are pressed with the Ctrl key, the camera translates left or right. The page-up and page-down keys send the camera up and down.

The user can travel around the scene freely but isn't allowed to go beyond the confines of the floor, which lie between -FLOOR_LEN/2 and FLOOR_LEN/2 in the x- and z- directions. Vertical movement is limited to be between 0 and FLOOR_LEN/2 (the height of the skybox).

The camera is moved by adding the xStep and zStep values to the camera's (x, z) position. xStep and zStep are calculated using Math.cos() and Math.sin() applied to the camera's current viewAngle, as illustrated by the forward vector in Figure 16-5.

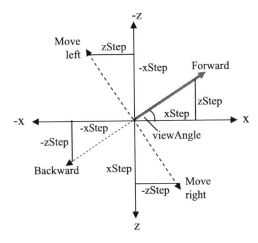

Figure 16-5. *Camera movements*

Figure 16-5 also shows how xStep and zStep can be employed to make left, right, and backward vectors. One tricky aspect is that the zStep value for the forward vector is negative (since it represents a step along the negative z-axis), so its sign must be changed if a positive number is required (i.e., for translating right and backward).

The following is the processKey() method:

```
// camera related constants
private final static double SPEED = 0.4;    // for camera movement
private final static double LOOK_AT_DIST = 100.0;
private final static double ANGLE_INCR = 5.0;    // degrees
private final static double HEIGHT_STEP = 1.0;


private void processKey(KeyEvent e)
// handles termination, and the game-play keys
{
  int keyCode = e.getKeyCode();

  // termination keys
  // listen for esc, q, end, Ctrl-c on the canvas
  if ((keyCode == KeyEvent.VK_ESCAPE) ||
      (keyCode == KeyEvent.VK_Q) ||
      (keyCode == KeyEvent.VK_END) ||
      ((keyCode == KeyEvent.VK_C) && e.isControlDown()) )
    isRunning = false;

  // game-play keys
  if (isRunning) {
    // move based on the arrow key pressed
```

```
  if (keyCode == KeyEvent.VK_LEFT) {    // left
    if (e.isControlDown()) {    // translate left
      xCamPos += zStep * SPEED;
      zCamPos -= xStep * SPEED;
    }
    else {  // turn left
      viewAngle -= ANGLE_INCR;
      xStep = Math.cos( Math.toRadians(viewAngle));
      zStep = Math.sin( Math.toRadians(viewAngle));
    }
  }
  else if (keyCode == KeyEvent.VK_RIGHT) {  // right
    if (e.isControlDown()) {    // translate right
      xCamPos -= zStep * SPEED;
      zCamPos += xStep * SPEED;
    }
    else {  // turn right
      viewAngle += ANGLE_INCR;
      xStep = Math.cos( Math.toRadians(viewAngle));
      zStep = Math.sin( Math.toRadians(viewAngle));
    }
  }
  else if (keyCode == KeyEvent.VK_UP) {   // move forward
    xCamPos += xStep * SPEED;
    zCamPos += zStep * SPEED;
  }
  else if (keyCode == KeyEvent.VK_DOWN) {  // move backward
    xCamPos -= xStep * SPEED;
    zCamPos -= zStep * SPEED;
  }
  else if (keyCode == KeyEvent.VK_PAGE_UP) {  // move up
    if ((yCamPos + HEIGHT_STEP) < FLOOR_LEN/2) {
      // stay below stars ceiling
      yCamPos += HEIGHT_STEP;
      yLookAt += HEIGHT_STEP;
    }
  }
  else if (keyCode == KeyEvent.VK_PAGE_DOWN) {  // move down
    if ((yCamPos - HEIGHT_STEP) > 0) {    // stay above floor
      yCamPos -= HEIGHT_STEP;
      yLookAt -= HEIGHT_STEP;
    }
  }

  // don't allow player to walk off the edge of the world
  if (xCamPos < -FLOOR_LEN/2)
    xCamPos = -FLOOR_LEN/2;
  else if (xCamPos > FLOOR_LEN/2)
    xCamPos = FLOOR_LEN/2;

  if (zCamPos < -FLOOR_LEN/2)
    zCamPos = -FLOOR_LEN/2;
  else if (zCamPos > FLOOR_LEN/2)
    zCamPos = FLOOR_LEN/2;

  // new look-at point
  xLookAt = xCamPos + (xStep * LOOK_AT_DIST);
```

```
    zLookAt = zCamPos + (zStep * LOOK_AT_DIST);
  }
}  // end of processKey()
```

The termination keys don't directly cause the application to exit; instead they set the isRunning boolean to false, which stops the game but keeps the application running. This permits a program to do other things after the end of the game.

The xStep and zStep values are added to the camera's current position with an additional SPEED multiple, as shown in the following code fragment:

```
xCamPos += xStep * SPEED;
zCamPos += zStep * SPEED;
```

This allows the distance moved to be changed by adjusting the SPEED constant.

Rotation is handled by altering viewAngle. When viewAngle is decremented the camera rotates to the left; an increment causes a right rotation.

Aside from calculating a new camera location, it's also necessary to update the *look-at* location, which is in front of the camera, off into the distance. It's obtained by multiplying the xStep and zStep values by a suitably large constant and adding them to the camera position:

```
xLookAt = xCamPos + (xStep * LOOK_AT_DIST);
zLookAt = zCamPos + (zStep * LOOK_AT_DIST);
```

The y- components of the camera and the look-at location are usually 0 since the camera moves along the ground. However, the yCamPos and yLookAt values are affected by the page-up and page-down keys, which move the camera up and down.

Let the Rendering Commence

The top-level parts of TourCanvasGL's active rendering thread are the same as in the rotating cube example in the previous chapter:

```
public void run()
// initialize rendering and start frame generation
{
  initRender();
  renderLoop();

  // discard the rendering context and exit
  context.destroy();
  System.exit(0);
} // end of run()
```

The initialization phase in initRender() may take a few seconds, especially if many large textures are being loaded. During this time the canvas will remain blank, which may worry users. A simple alternative, employed in TourCanvasGL, is to draw something on to the canvas by overriding its paint() method:

```
// globals
private volatile boolean isRunning = false;
private volatile boolean gameOver = false;


public void paint(Graphics g)
// display a loading message while the canvas is being initialized
{
  if (!isRunning && !gameOver) {
```

```
        String msg = "Loading. Please wait...";
        int x = (panelWidth - metrics.stringWidth(msg))/2;
        int y = (panelHeight - metrics.getHeight())/3;
        g.setColor(Color.blue);
        g.setFont(font);
        g.drawString(msg, x, y);

        // draw image underneath text
        int xIm = (panelWidth - waitIm.getWidth())/2;
        int yIm = y + 20;
        g.drawImage(waitIm, xIm, yIm, this);
    }
} // end of paint()
```

paint() is called automatically when the canvas first becomes visible onscreen; its output is shown in Figure 16-2.

The if-test in paint() ensures that the text and image will only be drawn before the game starts being rendered.

Rendering Initialization

initRender() in TourCanvasGL is an extended version of initRender() in CubeCanvasGL from the previous chapter:

```
// OpenGL globals
private GL gl;
private GLU glu;
private GLUT glut;

private int starsDList;        // display lists for stars
private GLUquadric quadric;    // for the sphere

private void initRender()
{
    makeContentCurrent();

    gl = context.getGL();
    glu = new GLU();
    glut = new GLUT();

    resizeView();

    gl.glClearColor(0.0f, 0.0f, 0.0f, 0.5f);        // black background

    // z- (depth) buffer initialization for hidden surface removal
    gl.glEnable(GL.GL_DEPTH_TEST);

    gl.glShadeModel(GL.GL_SMOOTH);      // use smooth shading

    // create a textured quadric
    quadric = glu.gluNewQuadric();
    glu.gluQuadricTexture(quadric, true);    // creates texture coords

    loadTextures();
    addLight();
    groundShapes = new GroundShapes(FLOOR_LEN);
```

```
// create a display list for drawing the stars
starsDList = gl.glGenLists(1);
gl.glNewList(starsDList, GL.GL_COMPILE);
    drawStars();
gl.glEndList();

/* release the context, otherwise the AWT lock on X11
   will not be released */
context.release();
} // end of initRender()
```

References to the GL, GLU, *and* GLUT classes are obtained during the initialization stage. A GLUT instance is needed in order to utilize bitmap fonts.

Smooth shading is switched on to improve the appearance of the sphere when it's drawn later.

The sphere is created with the help of a textured quadric, a GLU feature that also supports cylinders and disks. Incidentally, GLUT also offers complex shapes, including the sphere, cone, torus, several regular polyhedra (e.g., the dodecahedron), and the Utah teapot.

Loading Textures

The JOGL reference implementation for JSR-231 has several utility classes for texture manipulation.

loadTextures() calls loadTexture() to load each of the texture graphics, and that method utilizes JOGL's TextureIO utility class:

```
// globals
private Texture earthTex, starsTex, treeTex, robotTex;


private void loadTextures()
{
  earthTex = loadTexture("earth.jpg");  // for the sphere
  starsTex = loadTexture("stars.jpg");  // for the skybox
  treeTex = loadTexture("tree.gif");    // for the billboard
  robotTex = loadTexture("robot.gif");  // the game-over image

  // repeat the skybox texture in every direction
  starsTex.setTexParameteri(GL.GL_TEXTURE_WRAP_S, GL.GL_REPEAT);
  starsTex.setTexParameteri(GL.GL_TEXTURE_WRAP_T, GL.GL_REPEAT);
}  // end of loadTextures()


private Texture loadTexture(String fnm)
{
  String fileName = "images/" + fnm;
  Texture tex = null;
  try {
    tex = TextureIO.newTexture( new File(fileName), false);
    tex.setTexParameteri(GL.GL_TEXTURE_MAG_FILTER, GL.GL_NEAREST);
    tex.setTexParameteri(GL.GL_TEXTURE_MIN_FILTER, GL.GL_NEAREST);
  }
  catch(Exception e)
  { System.out.println("Error loading texture " + fileName);  }
```

```
    return tex;
}  // end of loadTexture()
```

TextureIO supports a wide variety of image types, including GIF, JPEG, and PNG.

TextureIO.newTexture() returns a Texture object, an instance of another JOGL utility class. Texture offers a convenient way of setting/getting texture parameters, binding the texture, and computing texture coordinates.

All the textures use the fast resizing option, GL.GL_NEAREST, when they're magnified or minified. In addition, the stars texture used in the skybox is set to repeat when pasted onto a large surface.

Several of the images have transparent backgrounds, but no special settings are needed to load them.

Texture mapping isn't switched on in these methods; instead it's enabled as needed inside the methods for rendering the skybox, billboard, sphere, the ground shapes, and "Game Over" message.

Lighting the Scene

OpenGL's lighting model supports multiple light sources, which may have ambient, diffuse, specular, or emissive components, in much the same way as Java 3D.

Lighting interacts with the material settings for objects, which specify the color reflected when the object is exposed to ambient, diffuse, or specular light. Materials can also emit light, and have a shininess value.

addLight() only deals with light properties; material properties are set when an object is being rendered:

```
private void addLight()
{
  // enable a single light source
  gl.glEnable(GL.GL_LIGHTING);
  gl.glEnable(GL.GL_LIGHT0);

  float[] grayLight = {0.1f, 0.1f, 0.1f, 1.0f};  // weak gray ambient
  gl.glLightfv(GL.GL_LIGHT0, GL.GL_AMBIENT, grayLight, 0);

  float[] whiteLight = {1.0f, 1.0f, 1.0f, 1.0f};
                     // bright white diffuse & specular
  gl.glLightfv(GL.GL_LIGHT0, GL.GL_DIFFUSE, whiteLight, 0);
  gl.glLightfv(GL.GL_LIGHT0, GL.GL_SPECULAR, whiteLight, 0);

  float lightPos[] = {1.0f, 1.0f, 1.0f, 0.0f};
                     // top right front direction
  gl.glLightfv(GL.GL_LIGHT0, GL.GL_POSITION, lightPos, 0);
}  // end of addLight()
```

The scene uses a single source, GL.GL_LIGHT0, producing a grayish ambient light, with white diffuse and specular components. White is the default color for LIGHT0's diffuse and specular elements, so the second and third GL.glLightfv() calls aren't necessary, but I've left them in as examples.

The final GL.glLightfv() call sets the light's position; the 0 argument specifies that lightPos defines a *vector* passing through the origin. The light becomes *directional*, corresponding to rays hitting all parts of the scene with the same vector (e.g., somewhat like sun rays hitting the earth). The (1, 1, 1) vector creates parallel light coming from the front top-right of the scene.

If the final argument of GL.glLightfv() was a 1, the light would become *positional*, more like a lightbulb, emitting light in all directions from the (1, 1, 1) coordinate.

OpenGL supports up to eight light sources, called LIGHT0 to LIGHT7, and aside from the features in addLight() offers spotlights and various forms of attenuation (decreasing light intensity based on the distance from the source).

Creating the Ground Shapes

The constructor of the GroundShape class generates the coordinates for its ground shapes and loads the image that will be used for rendering the shapes:

```
// globals
private final static String TEX_FNM = "r.gif";  // the shape image file
private Texture shapeTex;

public GroundShapes(int floorLen)
{
  generatePosns(floorLen);
  shapeTex = loadTexture(TEX_FNM);
} // end of GroundShapes()
```

The loadTexture() method is the same as the one in TourCanvasGL, already described in the "Loading Textures" section.

The shapes' positions are calculated by generatePosns():

```
// globals
private final static int FLOOR_LEN = 20;  // should be even
private final static int NUM_SHAPES = 5;

private float[] xCoords, zCoords;   // placement of shapes
private boolean[] visibles;         // if the shapes are visible
private int numVisShapes;


private void generatePosns(int floorLen)
{
  Random rand = new Random();
  xCoords = new float[NUM_SHAPES];
  zCoords = new float[NUM_SHAPES];
  visibles = new boolean[NUM_SHAPES];
  numVisShapes = NUM_SHAPES;

  for (int i=0; i < NUM_SHAPES; i++) {
    xCoords[i] = (rand.nextFloat()*(floorLen-1)) - floorLen/2;
    zCoords[i] = (rand.nextFloat()*(floorLen-1)) - floorLen/2;
    visibles[i] = true;
  }
}  // end of generatePosns()
```

The x- and z-axis coordinates are stored in two arrays, xCoords[] and zCoords[], which are used later to specify the center of each shape image. The values are randomly generated but lie on the floor. (The *floor* is a square of sides floorLen centered on (0, 0)).

The rendering of the shapes is controlled by the boolean array visibles[]. When a shape is "run over" by the camera it becomes "invisible," and will no longer be drawn.

The Rendering Loop

TourCanvasGL's rendering cycle in renderLoop() is almost unchanged from the one explained in the previous chapter. It can be summarized using a mix of code and pseudocode:

```
isRunning = true;
while (isRunning) {
  makeContentCurrent();
  gameUpdate();
  renderScene();
  drawable.swapBuffers();

  // sleep a while;
  // maybe do extra game updates;
  // gather statistics;
}
// print statistics;
glu.gluDeleteQuadric(quadric);
```

The new element is the call to GLU.gluDeleteQuadric(), which deletes the textured sphere quadric at the end of rendering.

Updating the Game

The changing parts of the scene are the rotating sphere and which shapes are visible on the floor:

```
// globals
private volatile boolean isRunning = false;
private volatile boolean isPaused = false;

// sphere movement
private float orbitAngle = 0.0f;
private float spinAngle = 0.0f;


private void gameUpdate()
{
  if (!isPaused && !gameOver) {
    // update the earth's orbit and the R's
    orbitAngle = (orbitAngle + 2.0f) % 360.0f;
    spinAngle = (spinAngle + 1.0f) % 360.0f;
    checkShapes();
  }
}
```

The if-test in gameUpdate() stops the game updating if it's been paused (i.e., minimized or deactivated) or if the game is over (i.e., all the ground shapes are invisible).

The sphere's position is dictated by two rotation variables: orbitAngle is the sphere's current angle around a central point (similar to the way the earth orbits the sun), and spinAngle is the sphere's rotation around its own y-axis.

checkShapes() gets the number of visible ground shapes, and if it's dropped to 0, the game is over. The number of shapes is also written to a text field in the top-level TourGL JFrame:

```
// globals
private TourGL tourTop;      // reference back to top-level JFrame
private volatile boolean gameOver = false;
private int score = 0;
```

```
private void checkShapes()
{
  int numVis = groundShapes.countVisibles(xCamPos, zCamPos);
  tourTop.setShapesLeft(numVis);

  // when all the shapes are gone, the game is over
  if (numVis == 0) {
    gameOver = true;
    score =  25 - timeSpentInGame;    // hack together a score
  }
}  // end of checkShapes()
```

The counting of the shapes is carried out by GroundShapes.countVisibles(). It also uses the current camera position to make a nearby shape invisible:

```
// the GroundShapes class
// globals
private final static int NUM_SHAPES = 5;
private final static double CLOSE_DIST = 1.0;
            // how near the camera must get to 'touch' a shape

private float[] xCoords, zCoords;    // (x, z) placement of shapes
private boolean[] visibles;          // if the shapes are visible
private int numVisShapes;


public int countVisibles(double xCamPos, double zCamPos)
{
  if (numVisShapes == 0)     // no shapes left
    return 0;

  int nearIdx = isOverShape(xCamPos, zCamPos);    // is the camera near a shape?
  if (nearIdx != -1) {
    visibles[nearIdx] = false;    // make that shape invisible
    numVisShapes--;
  }
  return numVisShapes;
}  // end of countVisibles()


private int isOverShape(double xCamPos, double zCamPos)
// returns index of shape that the camera is 'near', or -1
{
  for(int i=0; i < NUM_SHAPES; i++) {
    if (visibles[i]) {
      double xDiff = xCamPos - (double) xCoords[i];
      double zDiff = zCamPos - (double) zCoords[i];
      if (((xDiff*xDiff) + (zDiff*zDiff)) < CLOSE_DIST)
        return i;
    }
  }
  return -1;
}  // end of isOverShape()
```

isOverShape() checks the camera position against all the visible shapes, with nearness based on the squared distance between each shape and the camera. Only the x- and z-axis values are considered, so it doesn't matter how high the camera is in the air.

Rendering the Scene

TourCanvasGL.renderScene() draws the scene and also checks that the context is current, resizes the OpenGL viewport if necessary, and responds to the gameOver boolean being true:

```
private void renderScene()
{
  if (context.getCurrent() == null) {
    System.out.println("Current context is null");
    System.exit(0);
  }

  if (isResized) {
    resizeView();
    isResized = false;
  }

  // clear color and depth buffers
  gl.glClear(GL.GL_COLOR_BUFFER_BIT | GL.GL_DEPTH_BUFFER_BIT);

  gl.glMatrixMode(GL.GL_MODELVIEW);
  gl.glLoadIdentity();

  glu.gluLookAt(xCamPos, yCamPos, zCamPos,
          xLookAt, yLookAt, zLookAt, 0,1,0); // position camera

  drawTree();
  groundShapes.draw(gl);
  drawSphere();
  drawFloor();

  // execute display list for drawing the stars
  gl.glCallList(starsDList);  // it calls drawStars();

  if (gameOver)
    gameOverMessage();
} // end of renderScene()
```

The game-specific parts of renderScene() are drawing the tree billboard, the ground shapes, the sphere, the floor, and the skybox, which are carried out by the highlighted draw methods and the display list.

Drawing the Tree Billboard

drawTree() wraps a tree image over a quadrilateral (*quad*), without drawing its transparent background. It also rotates the quad to face the current camera position. The tree billboard is shown in Figure 16-6.

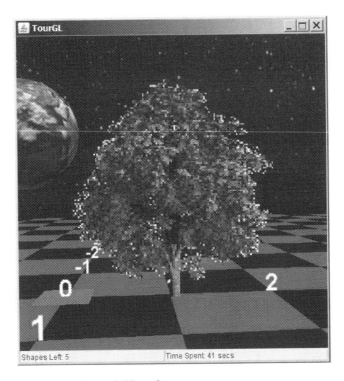

Figure 16-6. *The tree billboard*

drawTree() specifies the quad's coordinates so it rests on the XZ plane, initially facing along the positive z-axis, with its base centered at (1, 0, 0). Figure 16-7 shows the billboard's coordinates.

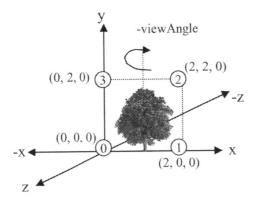

Figure 16-7. *The tree billboard's coordinates*

The numbered circles in Figure 16-7 indicate the order that the vertices are specified in the quad, starting with the lower left and progressing counterclockwise. The order is used when mapping the texture onto the quad's surface.

drawTree() lets drawScreen() do most of the work of creating the quad:

```
private void drawTree()
{
  float[] verts = {0,0,0, 2,0,0, 2,2,0, 0,2,0};  // posn of tree
  gl.glPushMatrix();
  gl.glRotatef(-1*((float)viewAngle+90.0f), 0, 1, 0);
      // rotate in the opposite direction to the camera
  drawScreen(verts, treeTex);
  gl.glPopMatrix();
}  // end of drawTree()
```

The billboard's rotation is derived from the camera's rotation stored in viewAngle. viewAngle has an initial value of -90, which needs to be subtracted away. Also, the billboard must rotate in the opposite direction from the camera to keep facing it, so viewAngle is multiplied by -1.

drawScreen() is used in several places in the code to render the billboard, the ground shapes, and the "Game Over" image. It's supplied with four vertices (in an array) that it uses to draw a quad wrapped with the supplied texture. Transparent parts of the texture aren't rendered:

```
private void drawScreen(float[] verts, Texture tex)
{
  boolean enableLightsAtEnd = false;
  if (gl.glIsEnabled(GL.GL_LIGHTING)) {
              // switch lights off if currently on
    gl.glDisable(GL.GL_LIGHTING);
    enableLightsAtEnd = true;
  }

  // do not draw the transparent parts of the texture
  gl.glEnable(GL.GL_BLEND);
  gl.glBlendFunc(GL.GL_SRC_ALPHA, GL.GL_ONE_MINUS_SRC_ALPHA);
          // don't show source alpha parts in the destination

  // determine which areas of the polygon are to be rendered
  gl.glEnable(GL.GL_ALPHA_TEST);
  gl.glAlphaFunc(GL.GL_GREATER, 0);  // only render if alpha > 0

  // enable texturing
  gl.glEnable(GL.GL_TEXTURE_2D);
  tex.bind();

  // replace the quad colors with the texture
  gl.glTexEnvi(GL.GL_TEXTURE_ENV, GL.GL_TEXTURE_ENV_MODE, GL.GL_REPLACE);

  TextureCoords tc = tex.getImageTexCoords();

  gl.glBegin(GL.GL_QUADS);
  gl.glTexCoord2f(tc.left(), tc.bottom());
  gl.glVertex3f(verts[0], verts[1], verts[2]);

  gl.glTexCoord2f(tc.right(), tc.bottom());
  gl.glVertex3f(verts[3], verts[4], verts[5]);

  gl.glTexCoord2f(tc.right(), tc.top());
  gl.glVertex3f(verts[6], verts[7], verts[8]);

  gl.glTexCoord2f(tc.left(), tc.top());
```

```
gl.glVertex3f(verts[9], verts[10], verts[11]);
gl.glEnd();

gl.glDisable(GL.GL_TEXTURE_2D);

// switch back to modulation of quad colors and texture
gl.glTexEnvi(GL.GL_TEXTURE_ENV, GL.GL_TEXTURE_ENV_MODE, GL.GL_MODULATE);
gl.glDisable(GL.GL_ALPHA);  // switch off transparency
gl.glDisable(GL.GL_BLEND);

if (enableLightsAtEnd)
  gl.glEnable(GL.GL_LIGHTING);
}  // end of drawScreen()
```

Lighting is disabled since it affects the texture rendering.

The nondrawing of the transparent parts of the image involve the use of blending, alpha testing, and the replacement of the quad's colors. Blending and alpha testing are switched off at the end of the method, and quad color replacement is switched back to modulation (the default behavior).

The texture coordinates for the entire image are obtained using Texture.getImageCoords(). The s- and t- coordinates stored in the TextureCoords object are accessed with the left(), right(), bottom(), and top() methods.

The texture coordinates are mapped to the quad coordinates by assuming the vertices are stored in counterclockwise order, with the first vertex at the bottom-left of the quad. This ordering is represented in Figure 16-7 by the numbered circles at the four corners of the tree quad.

Drawing the Ground Shapes

Figure 16-8 shows several ground shapes (red *R*s) lying on the ground.

Figure 16-8. *Ground shapes*

The coordinates for a shape are derived from the (x, z) value produced by GroundShapes.generatePosns(). The (x, z) becomes a shape's center point on the ground, with the quad orientated so its base is farther down the positive z-axis than its top; the idea is illustrated by Figure 16-9.

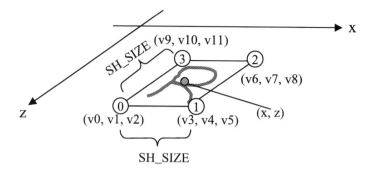

Figure 16-9. *The coordinates for a ground shape*

GroundShapes.draw() generates four vertices for each shape quad and renders them by calling a slightly modified version of drawScreen():

```
// in the GroundShapes class
// global
private final static float SH_SIZE = 0.5f;    // size of shape quad


public void draw(GL gl)
{
  if (numVisShapes == 0)     // nothing to draw
    return;

  float[] verts = new float[12];    // to hold 4 (x, y, z) vertices
  float xc, zc;
  for (int i=0; i < NUM_SHAPES; i++) {
    if (visibles[i]) {
      xc = xCoords[i];
      zc = zCoords[i];
      /* make a quad with center (xc, zc) with sides SH_SIZE,
         lying just above the floor */
      verts[0] = xc-SH_SIZE/2; verts[1] = 0.1f; verts[2] = zc+SH_SIZE/2;
      verts[3] = xc+SH_SIZE/2; verts[4] = 0.1f; verts[5] = zc+SH_SIZE/2;
      verts[6] = xc+SH_SIZE/2; verts[7] = 0.1f; verts[8] = zc-SH_SIZE/2;
      verts[9] = xc-SH_SIZE/2; verts[10] = 0.1f; verts[11] = zc-SH_SIZE/2;
      drawScreen(gl, verts, rTex);
    }
  }
} // end of draw()
```

The (x, z) point in Figure 16-9 is represented in draw() by (xc, zc), and the diagram's vertices, v0, v1, v2, and so on, correspond to the cells of the verts[] array.

Each shape image is lifted a little bit off the floor by having its vertices utilize a y-axis value of 0.1.

The Planet Earth

The rotating and spinning earth is shown in Figure 16-10.

Figure 16-10. *The earth.*

The sphere is built with the textured quadric created in initRender():

```
quadric = glu.gluNewQuadric();
glu.gluQuadricTexture(quadric, true);
```

It's necessary to define material properties for the sphere's surface to specify how light is reflected. Also, since the sphere is orbiting a point and spinning around its y-axis, the sphere will need to be translated and rotated.

The following is the code for drawSphere():

```
private void drawSphere()
{
  // enable texturing and choose the 'earth' texture
  gl.glEnable(GL.GL_TEXTURE_2D);
  earthTex.bind();

  // set how the sphere's surface responds to the light
  gl.glPushMatrix();
  float[] grayCol = {0.8f, 0.8f, 0.8f, 1.0f};
  gl.glMaterialfv(GL.GL_FRONT, GL.GL_AMBIENT_AND_DIFFUSE,grayCol,0);
```

```
float[] whiteCol = {1.0f, 1.0f, 1.0f, 1.0f};
gl.glMaterialfv(GL.GL_FRONT, GL.GL_SPECULAR, whiteCol, 0);
gl.glMateriali(GL.GL_FRONT, GL.GL_SHININESS, 100);

gl.glTranslatef(0.0f, 2.0f, -5.0f);  // position the sphere (1)
gl.glRotatef(orbitAngle, 0.0f, 1.0f, 0.0f);
                                // orbit around the point (2)
gl.glTranslatef(2.0f, 0.0f, 0.0f);   // the orbit's radius (3)

gl.glRotatef(90.0f, 1.0f, 0.0f, 0.0f);
                /* rotate sphere upward around the x-axis so
                   the texture is correctly orientated (4) */
gl.glRotatef(spinAngle, 0.0f, 0.0f, 1.0f);
        // spin around the z-axis (which looks like the y-axis) (5)

glu.gluSphere(quadric, 1.0f, 32, 32);  // generate textured sphere
                    // radius, slices, stacks
gl.glPopMatrix();

gl.glDisable(GL.GL_TEXTURE_2D);
} // end of drawSphere()
```

The sphere reflects gray for ambient and diffuse light, and white for specular light, with a large shininess value that makes the specular region bigger.

The sphere's translations and rotations are illustrated in Figure 16-11.

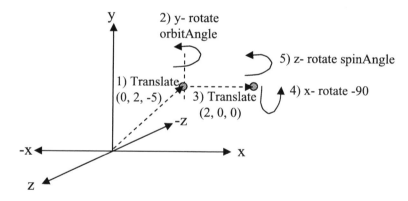

Figure 16-11. *Translating and rotating the earth*

The five transformations are numbered in the figure and in the code.

The earth orbits around (0, 2, -5), with a y-axis rotation using orbitAngle, at a distance of 2 units.

Unfortunately, the automatic texturing for a quadric sphere wraps the texture around the z-axis so the bottom of the texture (the Antarctic region) is facing out of the scene along the positive z-axis. This orientation is shown in Figure 16-12, which employs a version of drawSphere() without the x-axis rotation labeled as operation 4 in Figure 16-11.

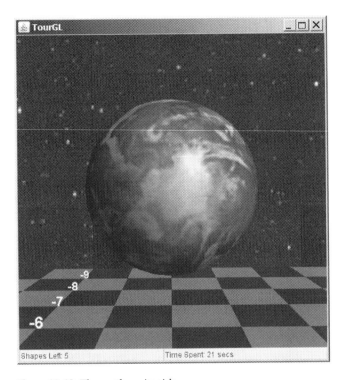

Figure 16-12. *The earth on its side*

The simplest solution is to rotate the sphere 90 degrees clockwise around its x-axis so the texture is facing upward. This also means that what appears to be the earth's y-axis (straight up) is really the z-axis. Consequently, the earth's y-axis spin must be coded as a spin around its z-axis, with the rotation amount supplied by spinAngle.

The Skybox

The skybox is a series of quads acting as four walls and a ceiling. Each wall is covered with two copies of a stars texture, and the ceiling with four copies. The walls and ceiling, with texture divisions, are shown in Figure 16-13.

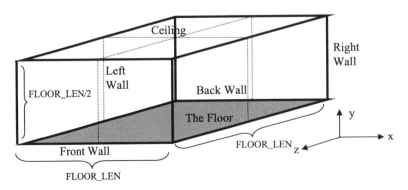

Figure 16-13. *The skybox with texture divisions*

The walls and ceiling are edged in thick lines in Figure 16-13, while the texture divisions are dotted lines. The walls and ceiling are divided so that each texture will occupy a square of sides FLOOR_LEN/2.

This type of skybox encloses the entire scene and is stationary. Another approach is to move the skybox so it follows the camera. This allows the skybox to stay a constant distance from the camera, so the player never reaches its walls or ceiling.

The texture divisions in Figure 16-13 are hard to see in the application, due to the use of stars as the texture. So that texture has been replace by an *R* image in Figure 16-14. I've also disabled the constraints on camera movement so the camera can be moved off the floor to get an overview of the entire scene.

Figure 16-14. *A skybox of red Rs*

A skybox of transparent *R* images may seem a bit strange. The *R* was chosen because of its lack of symmetry—it looks quite different if it's rotated or reflected. This makes it a good choice when the orientation of a texture needs to be checked. The transparent parts of the *R* also have a purpose: they allow you to see what's behind the texture, a useful debugging feature for a skybox.

To further aid the visual checking of the texture orientation and placement, the scene's background color is altered from its default pitch-black to blue using GL.glClearColor() in initRender():

```
gl.glClearColor(0.17f, 0.65f, 0.92f, 0.0f);
```

Figure 16-14 clearly shows that the wall textures are orientated so they face inward, since the user will be looking at them from inside the scene. This means that the texture coordinates must be supplied in a clockwise order. Figure 16-15 shows the ordering of the coordinates for the front face of the skybox.

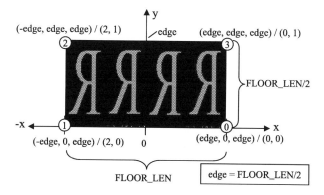

Figure 16-15. *Coordinates for the front face of the skybox*

Multiple copies of the texture are drawn by mapping the physical coordinates to texture coordinates larger than 1 in the s- and/or t- directions. The (s, t) texture coordinates for the front wall are shown after the slash marks(/) in Figure 16-15.

It's also necessary to switch on texture repetition in loadTextures():

```
starsTex.setTexParameteri(GL.GL_TEXTURE_WRAP_S, GL.GL_REPEAT);
starsTex.setTexParameteri(GL.GL_TEXTURE_WRAP_T, GL.GL_REPEAT);
```

drawStars() creates the skybox:

```
private void drawStars()
{
  gl.glDisable(GL.GL_LIGHTING);

  // enable texturing and choose the 'stars' texture
  gl.glEnable(GL.GL_TEXTURE_2D);
  starsTex.bind();

  TextureCoords tc = starsTex.getImageTexCoords();
  float lf = tc.left();
  float r = tc.right();
  float b = tc.bottom();
  float t = tc.top();

  // replace the quad colors with the texture
  gl.glTexEnvf(GL.GL_TEXTURE_2D, GL.GL_TEXTURE_ENV_MODE,
                                      GL.GL_REPLACE);

  gl.glBegin(GL.GL_QUADS);
    // back wall
    int edge = FLOOR_LEN/2;
    gl.glTexCoord2f(lf, b); gl.glVertex3i(-edge, 0, -edge);
    gl.glTexCoord2f(2*r, b); gl.glVertex3i(edge, 0, -edge);
    gl.glTexCoord2f(2*r, t); gl.glVertex3i(edge, edge, -edge);
    gl.glTexCoord2f(lf, t); gl.glVertex3i(-edge, edge, -edge);

    // right wall
    gl.glTexCoord2f(lf, b); gl.glVertex3i(edge, 0, -edge);
    gl.glTexCoord2f(2*r, b); gl.glVertex3i(edge, 0, edge);
    gl.glTexCoord2f(2*r, t); gl.glVertex3i(edge, edge, edge);
    gl.glTexCoord2f(lf, t); gl.glVertex3i(edge, edge, -edge);

    // front wall
    gl.glTexCoord2f(lf, b); gl.glVertex3i(edge, 0, edge);
    gl.glTexCoord2f(2*r, b); gl.glVertex3i(-edge, 0, edge);
    gl.glTexCoord2f(2*r, t); gl.glVertex3i(-edge, edge, edge);
    gl.glTexCoord2f(lf, t); gl.glVertex3i(edge, edge, edge);

    // left wall
    gl.glTexCoord2f(lf, b); gl.glVertex3i(-edge, 0, edge);
    gl.glTexCoord2f(2*r, b); gl.glVertex3i(-edge, 0, -edge);
    gl.glTexCoord2f(2*r, t); gl.glVertex3i(-edge, edge, -edge);
    gl.glTexCoord2f(lf, t); gl.glVertex3i(-edge, edge, edge);

    // ceiling
    gl.glTexCoord2f(lf, b); gl.glVertex3i(edge, edge, edge);
    gl.glTexCoord2f(2*r, b); gl.glVertex3i(-edge, edge, edge);
    gl.glTexCoord2f(2*r, 2*t); gl.glVertex3i(-edge, edge, -edge);
```

```
      gl.glTexCoord2f(1f, 2*t); gl.glVertex3i(edge, edge, -edge);
  gl.glEnd();

  // switch back to modulation of quad colors and texture
  gl.glTexEnvi(GL.GL_TEXTURE_ENV, GL.GL_TEXTURE_ENV_MODE,
                                    GL.GL_MODULATE);

  gl.glDisable(GL.GL_TEXTURE_2D);
  gl.glEnable(GL.GL_LIGHTING);
} // end of drawStars()
```

Adding a 2D Overlay

A 2D overlay is a way of drawing a 2D image in front of the 3D scene so it always stays at the front, even as the camera moves around the scene. The most common example is a HUD displaying player information during the course of a game.

In TourGL, the 2D overlay technique is used to show a "Game Over" message consisting of a robot image with a transparent background and the player's score inside a red rectangle (see Figure 16-3).

The gameOver boolean is checked at the end of renderScene():

```
if (gameOver)
  gameOverMessage();
```

gameOverMessage() draws the robot image, the rectangle, and the text:

```
private void gameOverMessage()
{
  gl.glDisable(GL.GL_LIGHTING);

  String msg = "Game Over. Your Score: " + score;
  int msgWidth =
        glut.glutBitmapLength(GLUT.BITMAP_TIMES_ROMAN_24, msg);
        // use a bitmap font (since no scaling required)

  // get (x,y) for centering the text on screen
  int x = (panelWidth - msgWidth)/2;
  int y = panelHeight/2;

  begin2D();  // switch to 2D viewing

  drawRobotImage(x+msgWidth/2, y-12, msgWidth*1.5f);

  // draw a medium red rectangle, centered on the screen
  gl.glColor3f(0.8f, 0.4f, 0.3f);    // medium red
  gl.glBegin(GL.GL_QUADS);
    gl.glVertex3i(x-10, y+10, 0);
    gl.glVertex3i(x+msgWidth+10, y+10, 0);
    gl.glVertex3i(x+msgWidth+10, y-24, 0);
    gl.glVertex3i(x-10, y-24, 0);
  gl.glEnd();

  // write the message in the center of the screen
  gl.glColor3f(1.0f, 1.0f, 1.0f);    // white text
  gl.glRasterPos2i(x, y);
  glut.glutBitmapString(GLUT.BITMAP_TIMES_ROMAN_24, msg);
```

```
  end2D();   // switch back to 3D viewing

  gl.glEnable(GL.GL_LIGHTING);
} // end of gameOverMessage()
```

The text message employs GLUT library methods for bitmap strings. Bitmap fonts can be rendered quickly but don't have 3D depth and can't be transformed (e.g., rotated and scaled). These drawbacks don't matter when the text is being used as part of a 2D overlay, as in this section.

2D viewing is turned on while the overlay is being drawn, then switched back to 3D afterward, a technique I've borrowed from an example posted by ozak at http://www.javagaming.org/forums/index.php?topic=8110.0.

The begin2D() method switches the view to use an orthographic projection, which is suitable for 2D-style rendering. Orthographic projection doesn't perform perspective correction, so objects close or far from the camera appear the same size. This is useful for 2D or isometric gaming:

```
private void begin2D()
{
  gl.glMatrixMode(GL.GL_PROJECTION);
  gl.glPushMatrix();     // save projection settings
  gl.glLoadIdentity();
  gl.glOrtho(0.0f, panelWidth, panelHeight, 0.0f, -1.0f, 1.0f);
          // left, right, bottom, top, near, far
  /* In an orthographic projection, the y-axis runs from
     the bottom-left upward. This is reversed to the
     more familiar top-left downward by switching
     the top and bottom values in glOrtho().
  */

  gl.glMatrixMode(GL.GL_MODELVIEW);
  gl.glPushMatrix();    // save model view settings
  gl.glLoadIdentity();
  gl.glDisable(GL.GL_DEPTH_TEST);
} // end of begin2D()
```

One concern is to save the 3D projection and model view settings so they can be restored at the end of gameOverMessage(). They're pushed onto their respective matrix stacks with GL.glPushMatrix() calls and retrieved with GL.glPopMatrix() in end2D().

The orthographic projection can be thought of as a 2D drawing surface with its y-axis starting at the *bottom* of the screen and increasing upward. This is the opposite of the y-axis used by Java when doing 2D painting into a JPanel or Canvas.

The orthographic y-axis can be reversed with GL.glOrtho(). The following is the call in begin2D():

```
gl.glOrtho(0.0f, panelWidth, panelHeight, 0.0f, -1.0f, 1.0f);
```

GL.glOrtho() defines a *viewing volume* for the projection: a rectangular box within which things are drawn. The x-axis of the volume is defined by the first two arguments (its left and right edges), the y-axis by the third and fourth arguments (bottom and top), and the z-axis by the last two arguments (front and back of the box).

The GL.glOrtho() call specifies that the y-axis "bottom" is panelHeight, and its "top" is 0. This means that the bottom is actually the top of the orthographic volume and extends downward to y == 0 (the "top"). This reverses the y-axis in the projection, making it correspond to the one used by Java components.

Subsequent (x, y) calculations for positioning the image, rectangle, and text can now use the familiar Java 2D view of things: the x-axis runs left to right and the y-axis runs top to bottom.

The drawing of the robot image utilizes drawScreen() again, so the robot's transparent background won't be rendered:

```
private void drawRobotImage(float xc, float yc, float size)
/* The screen is centered on (xc, yc), with sides of length size,
   and standing upright. */
{
  float[] verts = { xc-size/2, yc+size/2, 0,
                    xc+size/2, yc+size/2, 0,
                    xc+size/2, yc-size/2, 0,
                    xc-size/2, yc-size/2, 0};
  drawScreen(verts, robotTex);
}
```

end2D() pops the stored projection and model view matrices from their stacks and restores them:

```
private void end2D()
// switch back to 3D viewing
{
  gl.glEnable(GL.GL_DEPTH_TEST);
  gl.glMatrixMode(GL.GL_PROJECTION);
  gl.glPopMatrix();    // restore previous projection settings
  gl.glMatrixMode(GL.GL_MODELVIEW);
  gl.glPopMatrix();    // restore previous model view settings
} // end of end2D()
```

Drawing the Floor

The floor consists of a series of green and blue tiles in a checkerboard pattern, a single red square over the origin, and x- and z- axes labels:

```
// globals
private final static int BLUE_TILE = 0;    // floor tile color types
private final static int GREEN_TILE = 1;

private void drawFloor()
{
  gl.glDisable(GL.GL_LIGHTING);

  drawTiles(BLUE_TILE);
  drawTiles(GREEN_TILE);
  addOriginMarker();
  labelAxes();

  gl.glEnable(GL.GL_LIGHTING);
}  // end of CheckerFloor()
```

Drawing the Tiles

The trick to tiles creation is the calculation of their coordinates. Figure 16-16 shows a simplified view of the floor from above (*B* is for blue tile, *G* for green).

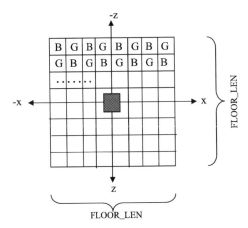

Figure 16-16. *The floor from above*

drawTiles() calculates the top-left (x, z) coordinate for all the tiles of the given color type. Each coordinate is passed to drawTile() to generate the other three coordinates for a tile:

```
private void drawTiles(int drawType)
{
  if (drawType == BLUE_TILE)
    gl.glColor3f(0.0f, 0.1f, 0.4f);
  else  // green
    gl.glColor3f(0.0f, 0.5f, 0.1f);

  gl.glBegin(GL.GL_QUADS);
  boolean aBlueTile;
  for(int z=-FLOOR_LEN/2; z <= (FLOOR_LEN/2)-1; z++) {
    aBlueTile = (z%2 == 0)? true : false;   // set color for new row
    for(int x=-FLOOR_LEN/2; x <= (FLOOR_LEN/2)-1; x++) {
      if (aBlueTile && (drawType == BLUE_TILE))
        drawTile(x, z);                      // blue tile and drawing blue
      else if (!aBlueTile && (drawType == GREEN_TILE))   // green
        drawTile(x, z);
      aBlueTile = !aBlueTile;
    }
  }
  gl.glEnd();
} // end of drawTiles()
```

The (x, z) coordinate passed to drawTile() is the top-left corner of the desired quad, and the sides of the quad will be unit length. drawTile() creates a quad with the coordinates shown in Figure 16-17.

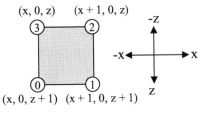

Figure 16-17. *Coordinates for a single tile*

The numbered circles in Figure 16-17 indicate the order the vertices are passed to OpenGL. They're supplied in counterclockwise order so the resulting quad faces upward.

The following is the drawTile() code:

```
private void drawTile(int x, int z)
{
  // points created in counterclockwise order
  gl.glVertex3f(x, 0.0f, z+1.0f);    // bottom left point
  gl.glVertex3f(x+1.0f, 0.0f, z+1.0f);
  gl.glVertex3f(x+1.0f, 0.0f, z);
  gl.glVertex3f(x, 0.0f, z);
}  // end of drawTile()
```

The red origin square, centered at (0, 0.01, 0) with sides 0.5, is created with code very similar to drawTile():

```
private void addOriginMarker()
{
  gl.glColor3f(0.8f, 0.4f, 0.3f);    // medium red
  gl.glBegin(GL.GL_QUADS);

  // points created counterclockwise, a bit above the floor
  gl.glVertex3f(-0.25f, 0.01f, 0.25f);  // bottom left point
  gl.glVertex3f(0.25f, 0.01f, 0.25f);
  gl.glVertex3f(0.25f, 0.01f, -0.25f);
  gl.glVertex3f(-0.25f, 0.01f, -0.25f);

  gl.glEnd();
} // end of addOriginMarker();
```

The red square is raised slightly above the XZ plane (0.01 up the y-axis) so it's visible above the tiles.

Drawing the Axes

labelAxes() places numbers along the x- and z-axes at the integer positions. The axes labels are drawn using a scaled Java 2D font. Figure 16-18 shows some of the numbers.

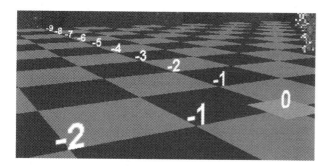

Figure 16-18. *Some of the axes labels*

```
private void labelAxes()
{
  for (int i=-FLOOR_LEN/2; i <= FLOOR_LEN/2; i++)
    drawAxisText(""+i, (float)i, 0.0f, 0.0f);  // along x-axis
```

```
  for (int i=-FLOOR_LEN/2; i <= FLOOR_LEN/2; i++)
    drawAxisText(""+i, 0.0f, 0.0f, (float)i);  // along z-axis
}
```

drawAxisText() draws the specified text string at a given coordinate, with the text centered in the x- direction and facing along the z-axis. It utilizes the JOGL TextRenderer utility class for drawing with Java 2D fonts:

```
// global
private TextRenderer axisLabelRenderer;

// in the TourCanvasGL constructor...
font = new Font("SansSerif", Font.BOLD, 24);
axisLabelRenderer = new TextRenderer(font);
```

The drawAxisText() method uses the axisLabelRenderer object:

```
// global
private final static float SCALE_FACTOR = 0.01f;


private void drawAxisText(String txt, float x, float y, float z)
{
  Rectangle2D dim = axisLabelRenderer.getBounds(txt);
  float width = (float)dim.getWidth() * SCALE_FACTOR;

  axisLabelRenderer.begin3DRendering();
  axisLabelRenderer.draw3D(txt, x-width/2, y, z, SCALE_FACTOR);
  axisLabelRenderer.end3DRendering();
} // end of drawAxisText()
```

The scaling factor (0.01) was arrived at by experimentation. A full-size character is almost too big to be seen.

Summary

This chapter employed the active rendering framework from Chapter 15 to build a simple 3D world containing a checkerboard floor, a skybox, lighting, and a mix of objects including a rotating sphere and billboards. Keyboard controls allow the user to navigate around the world (in search of ground shapes), and the game is rounded out with a start screen and a "Game Over" message. These features use a wide variety of techniques that are useful across different applications, including texture images with transparent backgrounds, 2D overlays, and bitmap and Java 2D fonts.

CHAPTER 17

Loading Models

This chapter continues using the 3D world of Chapter 16, but as a setting to demonstrate four new coding techniques:

* The *loading and positioning* of 3D models created using the Wavefront OBJ file format.

• The selection (*picking*) of objects in the scene by clicking them with the mouse. OpenGL's selection mode is utilized to implement this feature.

• 3D *sound*, in this case the chirping of a penguin, which varies as the user moves around the scene (nearer and farther from a penguin model). It's implemented using JOAL and the JOALSoundMan class introduced in Chapters 13.

• *Fog* shrouding the scene, making it harder to find the models.

The vast majority of this chapter (nearly two-thirds of it) is concerned with the first technique, leading to the development of an OBJ model loader package called OBJLoader and an application called ModelLoaderGL that uses the loader. The loader *and* the other three topics (picking, sound, and fog) are required by the chapter's other example, TourModelsGL.

ModelLoaderGL and TourModelsGL are briefly explained in the next section.

Overviews of the Examples

ModelLoaderGL is a simple model viewer, shown in Figure 17-1, displaying a penguin.

Figure 17-1. *Displaying a penguin*

The model's name is specified on the command line, along with the display size and whether the model should rotate. The model is loaded and positioned using the OBJLoader package developed in this chapter. ModelLoaderGL can be employed to check what an object looks like before it's loaded into a more complex application.

TourModelsGL is a simple game based around trying to find a penguin and a couch hidden in the fog. The search is made a bit harder by including other models in the scene, but the player is given some aural help because the penguin is constantly chirping. When the user clicks the mouse on the penguin or the couch, a message is printed to standard output. Needless to say, a lot could be done to make this a more exciting gaming experience. Figures 17-2 and 17-3 show TourModelsGL without the fog and with it. The four OBJ models are a penguin wrapped in a single texture, a red couch, a red rose in a blue vase, and a racing car decorated with several colors and textures.

Figure 17-2. *TourModelsGL with a clear blue sky*

Figure 17-3. *TourModelsGL after the fog has descended*

TourModelsGL reuses the checkerboard floor from the previous chapter, but I've removed the skybox, the billboard trees, the rotating sphere, the splash screen, and the "Game Over" message in order to simplify the code.

The OBJ File Format

The complete Wavefront OBJ file format offers many advanced elements, such as free-form curves and surfaces, rendering interpolation, and shadowing. However, most OBJ exporters and loaders (including the Java 3D loader from Chapter 7) only support polygonal shapes. A polygon's face is defined using vertices, with the optional inclusion of normals and texture coordinates. Faces can be grouped together, and different groups can be assigned materials made from ambient, diffuse, and specular colors and textures. The material information is stored in a separate MTL text file.

A list of OBJ features can be found at http://www.csit.fsu.edu/~burkardt/data/obj/obj.html, and examples of MTL are at http://www.csit.fsu.edu/~burkardt/data/mtl/mtl.html. The description in this chapter will focus on the core elements found in the Java 3D loader (accessed via the ObjectFile class). Some unnecessary details will be left out, but they can be found in the ObjectFile class documentation.

An OBJ file is a text file consisting of lines of statements, comments, and blank lines. Comments start with # and are ignored. Each statement begins with an operator name indicating how to process the data that follows it on the line. There are three types of basic OBJ statements: those that are shape-related, those for grouping, and those for materials. I'll briefly explain the format of each.

Shape Statements

The three floats in a v statement specify a vertex's position:

```
v float float float
```

The first vertex listed in an OBJ file (i.e., the first v statement) is assigned an index value of 1, and subsequent vertices are numbered sequentially.

The floats in a vn statement specify a normal:

```
vn float float float
```

The first normal in the file (i.e., the first vn statement) is assigned index 1, and subsequent normals are numbered sequentially.

A vt statement is used to define a 2D or 3D texture coordinate:

```
vt float float [float]
```

The square brackets mean that the third float argument is optional.

The first texture coordinate in a file (i.e., the first vt statement) is index 1, and subsequent textures are numbered sequentially.

A polygonal face is specified using an f statement, which can employ three different formats:

```
f int int int ...
```

or

```
f int/int int/int int/int ...
```

or

```
f int/int/int int/int/int int/int/int ...
```

A face can be defined as a sequence of vertex indices (the first format), or vertices and textures indicies (the second format), or vertices, textures, and normal indices (the last format). I'll call each collection of indices (e.g., int/int/int) a *term*.

When a term has three elements, it's possible for the texture indices to be left out if they haven't been defined for the model, resulting in the f statement:

```
f int//int  int//int  int//int ...
```

The number of terms making up a face depends on its shape; often it's a triangle (which needs three terms to define it) or a quadrilateral (four terms).

The first face in the file (i.e., the first f statement) is assigned index 1, and subsequent faces are numbered sequentially.

Grouping Statements

A g statement specifies a group name:

```
g name
```

Faces defined after a g statement will be added to the named group. Named groups are a useful way of referring to a collection of faces; for example, Java 3D maps each named group to a Shape3D object at load time. This makes it easier to apply transformations or appearance changes to sub-components of the model:

The s statement defines a "smoothing" group:

```
s int
```

Subsequent face definitions will be members of the numbered group and have their normals calculated as if they form part of the same surface.

Material Use Statements

The MTL file named in the mltlib statement contains material definitions that can be used in the rest of the OBJ file:

```
mltlib filename
```

When a usemtl statement is encountered in the OBJ file, all subsequent faces will be rendered with the named material obtained from the MTL file:

```
usemtl name
```

The MTL File Format

An MTL file consists of a series of material definitions made up of statements, comments, and blank lines. Comments start with # and are ignored.

Each new material definition begins with a newmtl statement that specifies a material's name:

```
newmtl name
```

The name is used by the usemtl statement in an OBJ file to refer to the material.

A material's properties (e.g., its color, transparency, texture) are defined using material statements (e.g., Ka, Kd) given on the lines after the newmtl statement, as in this example:

```
newmtl penguinMat
# material properties for the penguin model
```

```
Ka 0.01 0.75 0.75
Kd 0.90 0.69 0.90
Ks 0.93 0.93 0.93
Ns 445
illum 2
map_Kd penguin.gif
```

The following are the basic material statements:

```
Ka r g b
```

The three floats (r, g, and b) define the ambient RGB color of the material.

```
Kd r g b
```

The three floats specify the diffuse RGB color of the material.

```
Ks r g b
```

The r, g, and b floats represent the specular color of the material.

```
d alpha
```

or

```
Tr alpha
```

The alpha value specifies the transparency of the material. Java 3D doesn't support either the d or Tr statement.

```
Ns s
```

The shininess of the material is set with the s float value. If no Ns statement is supplied for a material, the material's default shininess will be 0.0f (i.e., it will not be shiny).

```
illum n
```

The illum statement sets the illumination mode for a material. If n is 1, the material has no specular highlights and the Ks values are ignored. If n is 2, specular highlights are present and will utilize the Ks value. When n is 0, lighting is disabled.

```
map_Ka filename
```

The named file contains a texture for the material. The MTL specification states that this should be an ASCII dump of RGB values, but most tools (including the Java 3D loader) also support standard image files (GIF, JPG, PNG). The image must have a size that is a power of 2 (e.g., 64 by 64, 128 by 128).

The OBJ File Loader

My OBJLoader package can load models and materials from simple OBJ and MTL files. The shape statements (v, vt, vn, f) and material statements (mtllib and usemtl) are understood, but grouping operations are ignored (g and s). MTL statements are processed, except for transparency (d, Tr) and illumination (illum). Textures and colors can't be blended together; the presence of a texture for a material (map_Ka) disables any color settings (e.g., Ka, Kd, Ks).

Class diagrams for the OBJLoader package are shown in Figure 17-4.

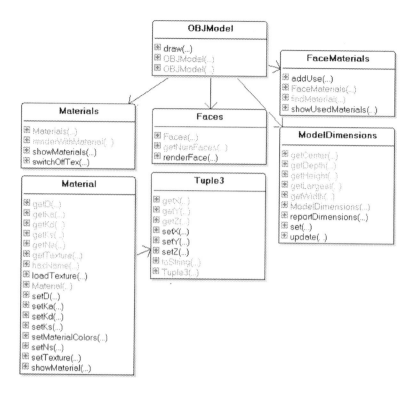

Figure 17-4. *The class diagrams for the OBJLoader package*

The OBJModel class loads the OBJ model, centers it at the origin and scales it to a size supplied in its constructor. The OpenGL commands for rendering the model are stored in a display list and are executed by calling OBJModel.draw().

The Faces class stores information about each face of the model. When OBJModel is constructing the display list, it calls Faces.renderFace() to render a face in terms of the loaded model's vertices, texture coordinates, and normals.

The Materials class loads material details from the MTL file, storing them as Material objects in an ArrayList.

FaceMaterials stores the face indices where materials are first used. This information is used to load the right material when a given face needs to be drawn.

ModelDimensions holds the smallest and largest coordinates for the model along its three dimensions. These are utilized to calculate the model's width, height, depth, its largest dimension, and its center point. ModelDimensions is employed by OBJModel to resize and center the loaded model.

Tuple3 is a general-purpose class for storing a three-element tuple. It's used in several places in the package to store vertices, normals, and texture coordinates as Tuple3 objects.

While writing the OBJLoader package, I got a lot of help and inspiration from examining the loaders written by Evangelos Pournaras in his *JautOGL* game (http://today.java.net/pub/a/today/2006/10/10/development-of-3d-multiplayer-racing-game.html and https://jautogl.dev.java.net/) and Kevin Glass's *Asteroids* tutorial (http://www.cokeandcode.com/asteroidstutorial/).

Reading in the OBJ File

OBJModel is responsible for reading in the OBJ file, line by line, and processing the statements it finds. The shape data (vertices, texture coordinates, and normals) is stored in ArrayLists of Tuple3 objects:

```
private ArrayList<Tuple3> verts;
private ArrayList<Tuple3> normals;
private ArrayList<Tuple3> texCoords;
```

OBJModel also initializes the other package objects:

```
private Faces faces;              // holds model faces
private FaceMaterials faceMats;   // materials used by the faces
private Materials materials;      // materials defined in MTL file
private ModelDimensions modelDims;  // model dimensions
```

The parsing of the OBJ file is carried out in readModel():

```
private void readModel(BufferedReader br)
{
  boolean isLoaded = true;    // hope things will go okay

  int lineNum = 0;
  String line;
  boolean isFirstCoord = true;
  boolean isFirstTC = true;
  int numFaces = 0;

  try {
    while (((line = br.readLine()) != null) && isLoaded) {
      lineNum++;
      if (line.length() > 0) {
        line = line.trim();

        if (line.startsWith("v ")) {   // vertex
          isLoaded = addVert(line, isFirstCoord);
          if (isFirstCoord)
            isFirstCoord = false;
        }
        else if (line.startsWith("vt")) {   // tex coord
          isLoaded = addTexCoord(line, isFirstTC);
          if (isFirstTC)
            isFirstTC = false;
        }
        else if (line.startsWith("vn"))     // normal
          isLoaded = addNormal(line);
        else if (line.startsWith("f ")) {  // face
          isLoaded = faces.addFace(line);
          numFaces++;
        }
        else if (line.startsWith("mtllib "))   // load material
          materials = new Materials( line.substring(7) );
        else if (line.startsWith("usemtl "))    // use material
          faceMats.addUse( numFaces, line.substring(7));
        else if (line.charAt(0) == 'g') {  // group name
          // not implemented
        }
```

```
      else if (line.charAt(0) == 's') {  // smoothing group
        // not implemented
      }
      else if (line.charAt(0) == '#')   // comment line
        continue;
      else
        System.out.println("Ignoring line " + lineNum +
                                    " : " + line);
    }
  }
}
catch (IOException e) {
  System.out.println( e.getMessage() );
  System.exit(1);
}

if (!isLoaded) {
  System.out.println("Error loading model");
  System.exit(1);
}
} // end of readModel()
```

The v, vt, and vn statements trigger code that adds a vertex, a texture coordinate, and a normal Tuple3 object to the verts, texCoords, and normals ArrayLists. For example, addVert() adds a tuple to verts and updates the model dimension's information:

```
private boolean addVert(String line, boolean isFirstCoord)
{
  Tuple3 vert = readTuple3(line);
                    // store (x,y,z) from "v x y z" in a tuple
  if (vert != null) {
    verts.add(vert);
    if (isFirstCoord)
      modelDims.set(vert);      // add first coordinate
    else
      modelDims.update(vert);   // add a later coordinate
    return true;
  }
  return false;
} // end of addVert()
```

In readModel(), an f statement is handled by addFace() in the Faces class, and mtllib triggers the creation of a Materials object that reads in the named MTL file. A usemtl statement causes the FaceMaterials object to record the current face index and the named material. The material will be utilized when that face and subsequent ones need to be rendered.

Reading a Face

The Faces object stores information about all the face statements in the OBJ file.

The data for a single face is stored in three arrays of vertex indices, texture coordinate indices, and normal indices; the indices come from the face's f statement.

For example, if the statement is

```
f 10/12/287 9/14/287 8/16/287
```

the vertex indices array will hold {10, 9, 8}; the texture coordinate indices array will contain {12, 14, 16}; and the normal indices array is {287, 287, 287}.

All the faces data is held in three ArrayLists called facesVertIdxs, facesTexIdxs, and facesNormIdxs. facesVertIdxs stores all the vertex indices arrays, facesTexIdxs all the texture coordinate indices arrays, and facesNormIdxs the normal indices arrays:

```
private ArrayList<int[]> facesVertIdxs;  // for the vertices indices
private ArrayList<int[]> facesTexIdxs;   // texture coords indices
private ArrayList<int[]> facesNormIdxs;  // normal indices
```

The Faces.addFace() method (called from OBJModel.readModel()) pulls the terms out of an f line, builds arrays for the vertices, texture coordinates, and normals indices, and adds those arrays to the ArrayLists.

Things are complicated by the fact that terms may be missing texture and normal information:

```
public boolean addFace(String line)
{
  try {
    line = line.substring(2);   // skip the "f "
    StringTokenizer st = new StringTokenizer(line, " ");
    int numTokens = st.countTokens();   // number of v/vt/vn tokens
    // create arrays to hold the v, vt, vn indices
    int v[]  = new int[numTokens];
    int vt[] = new int[numTokens];
    int vn[] = new int[numTokens];

    for (int i = 0; i < numTokens; i++) {
      String faceToken = addFaceVals(st.nextToken());
                            // get a v/vt/vn token

      StringTokenizer st2 = new StringTokenizer(faceToken, "/");
      int numSeps = st2.countTokens();
                            // how many '/'s are there in the token

      v[i]  = Integer.parseInt(st2.nextToken());
      vt[i] = (numSeps > 1) ? Integer.parseInt(st2.nextToken()) : 0;
      vn[i] = (numSeps > 2) ? Integer.parseInt(st2.nextToken()) : 0;
          // add 0s if the vt or vn index values are missing;
          // 0 is a good choice since real indices start at 1
    }
    // store the indices for this face
    facesVertIdxs.add(v);
    facesTexIdxs.add(vt);
    facesNormIdxs.add(vn);
  }
  catch (NumberFormatException e) {
    System.out.println("Incorrect face index");
    System.out.println(e.getMessage());
    return false;
  }
  return true;
}  // end of addFace()
```

Reading in an MTL File

The processing of an MTL file is handled by a Materials object. readMaterials() parses the MTL file line by line, adding Material objects to a materials ArrayList:

```
// global
public ArrayList<Material> materials;
    // stores the Material objects built from the MTL file data


private void readMaterials(BufferedReader br)
{
  try {
    String line;
    Material currMaterial = null;  // current material

    while (((line = br.readLine()) != null)) {
      line = line.trim();
      if (line.length() == 0)
        continue;

      if (line.startsWith("newmtl ")) {  // new material
        if (currMaterial != null)   // save previous material
          materials.add(currMaterial);

        // start collecting info for new material
        currMaterial = new Material(line.substring(7));
      }
      else if (line.startsWith("map_Kd ")) {  // texture filename
        String fileName = MODEL_DIR + line.substring(7);
        currMaterial.loadTexture( fileName );
      }
      else if (line.startsWith("Ka "))    // ambient color
        currMaterial.setKa( readTuple3(line) );
      else if (line.startsWith("Kd "))    // diffuse color
        currMaterial.setKd( readTuple3(line) );
      else if (line.startsWith("Ks "))    // specular color
        currMaterial.setKs( readTuple3(line) );
      else if (line.startsWith("Ns ")) {  // shininess
        float val = Float.valueOf(line.substring(3)).floatValue();
        currMaterial.setNs( val );
      }
      else if (line.charAt(0) == 'd') {    // alpha
        float val = Float.valueOf(line.substring(2)).floatValue();
        currMaterial.setD( val );
      }
      else if (line.startsWith("illum ")) { // illumination model
        // not implemented
      }
      else if (line.charAt(0) == '#')    // comment line
        continue;
      else
        System.out.println("Ignoring MTL line: " + line);

    }
    materials.add(currMaterial);
  }
```

```
  catch (IOException e)
  { System.out.println(e.getMessage());  }
} // end of readMaterials()
```

When a newmtl statement is encountered, the current Material object is added to the materials ArrayList, and a new object is created, ready to be filled with color and texture information read from subsequent statements.

The Ka, Kd, Ks, Ns, and d values are passed to the Material object via set methods. When readMaterials() sees a map_Kd statement, it calls loadTexture() in the current Material object:

```
// in the Material class
// global  texture info
private String texFnm;
private Texture texture;

public void loadTexture(String fnm)
{
  try {
    texFnm = fnm;
    texture = TextureIO.newTexture( new File(texFnm), false);
    texture.setTexParameteri(GL.GL_TEXTURE_MAG_FILTER, GL.GL_NEAREST);
    texture.setTexParameteri(GL.GL_TEXTURE_MIN_FILTER, GL.GL_NEAREST);
  }
  catch(Exception e)
  { System.out.println("Error loading texture " + texFnm);  }
}  // end of loadTexture()
```

Recording Material Use

A subtle aspect of the OBJ format is how materials are linked to faces. After a material is named in a usemtl statement, all subsequent faces will use it for rendering until another usemtl line is encountered, as in the following example:

```
usemtl couch
f 10/10/287 9/9/287 8/8/287
f 10/10/287 8/8/287 7/7/287
f 10/10/287 7/7/287 6/6/287
f 10/10/287 6/6/287 5/5/287
   // many more faces ...
```

All the faces defined after the usemtl line will use the couch material at render time.

When OBJModel.readModel() encounters a usemtl statement, it stores the information by passing the current face index and material name to a FaceMaterials object:

```
else if (line.startsWith("usemtl "))   // use materials
  faceMats.addUse( numFaces, line.substring(7));
```

numFaces contains the current index, and the substring is the material name.

A HashMap in the FaceMaterials object is employed to connect face indices to material names:

```
private HashMap<Integer, String>faceMats;
```

FaceMaterials.addUse() adds a new face index and material name to faceMats:

```
public void addUse(int faceIdx, String matName)
{
  // store the face index and the material it uses
  if (faceMats.containsKey(faceIdx))  // face index already present
    System.out.println("Face index " + faceIdx +
                    " changed to use material " + matName);

  faceMats.put(faceIdx, matName);

  // other non-relevant code...
} // end of addUse()
```

Centering and Resizing a Model

After the OBJ and MTL files have been read in, OBJModel calls centerScale() to center the model at the origin and resize it. The size is either specified in OBJModel's constructor or defaults to 1 unit.

centerScale() relies on the ModelDimensions object, which stores the minimum and maximum coordinates for the model and includes methods for calculating the model's largest dimension and center point:

```
// global
private float maxSize;      // for scaling the model

private void centerScale()
{
  // get the model's center point
  Tuple3 center = modelDims.getCenter();

  // calculate a scale factor
  float scaleFactor = 1.0f;
  float largest = modelDims.getLargest();
  if (largest != 0.0f)
    scaleFactor = (maxSize / largest);
  System.out.println("Scale factor: " + scaleFactor);

  // modify the model's vertices
  Tuple3 vert;
  float x, y, z;
  for (int i = 0; i < verts.size(); i++) {
    vert = (Tuple3) verts.get(i);
    x = (vert.getX() - center.getX()) * scaleFactor;
    vert.setX(x);
    y = (vert.getY() - center.getY()) * scaleFactor;
    vert.setY(y);
    z = (vert.getZ() - center.getZ()) * scaleFactor;
    vert.setZ(z);
  }
} // end of centerScale()
```

centerScale() directly modifies the model's vertices to modify its scale. An alternative approach, which may seem more efficient, is to apply translation and scaling transformations to the geometry. Unfortunately, a scaling transformation also affects the model's normals, so they're no longer guaranteed to be of unit length. This will cause the model's color to change at render time and textures to be positioned incorrectly.

Creating a Display List for the Model

Once OBJModel has centered and scaled the model, it can render it to a display list. Subsequent calls to OBJModel.draw() will execute the list, greatly improving the drawing speed.

OBJModel.drawToList() creates the display list:

```
// globals
private int modelDispList;  // the model's display list
private boolean flipTexCoords = false;
    // whether the texture coords should be vertically flipped


private void drawToList(GL gl)
{
  modelDispList = gl.glGenLists(1);
  gl.glNewList(modelDispList, GL.GL_COMPILE);

  gl.glPushMatrix();
  // render the model face-by-face
  String faceMat;
  for (int i = 0; i < faces.getNumFaces(); i++) {
    faceMat = faceMats.findMaterial(i);
                        // get material used by face i
    if (faceMat != null)
      flipTexCoords = materials.renderWithMaterial(faceMat, gl);
                        // render using that material
    faces.renderFace(i, flipTexCoords, gl);       // draw face i
  }
  materials.switchOffTex(gl);
  gl.glPopMatrix();

  gl.glEndList();
} // end of drawToList()
```

drawToList() draws each face by calling Faces.renderFace() in a loop. Before rendering a face, it checks whether the face's index is associated with a material (with FaceMaterials.findMaterial()). If a material change is required, it is loaded into OpenGL by Materials.renderWithMaterial().

Materials.renderWithMaterial() assigns a value to the flipTexCoords boolean, which is passed to FaceMaterials.findMaterial(). The boolean indicates whether the texture's coordinates need to be vertically flipped when they're mapped to the shape's coordinates at render time.

Texturing may still be enabled at the end of the loop, so a call to Materials.switchOffTex() makes sure that it's switched off and that the lights are reenabled.

Finding a Material

The FaceMaterial instance, faceMats, stores a HashMap of face indices mapped to material names. When FaceMaterial.findMaterial() is called with a face index, the retrieval of the associated material name is a fast lookup:

```
// in the FaceMaterial class
private HashMap<Integer, String>faceMats;
    // the face index (integer) where a material is first used

public String findMaterial(int faceIdx)
{ return (String) faceMats.get(faceIdx); }
```

If the index isn't in the HashMap, the method returns null, which is tested for back in OBJ-Model.drawToList().

Rendering with a Material

If the face that's about to be rendered has an associated material, it needs to be loaded first.

Materials.renderWithMaterial() has two types of material to deal with colors and textures. Also, before a new material can be loaded, any existing texturing must be disabled:

```
// in the Materials class
// globals
private String renderMatName = null;
  // stores the material currently being used for rendering
private boolean flipTexCoords = false;
  // whether the model's texture coords should be vertically flipped


public boolean renderWithMaterial(String faceMat, GL gl)
{
  if (!faceMat.equals(renderMatName)) { // is faceMat new?
    renderMatName = faceMat;
    switchOffTex(gl);   // switch off any previous texturing

    // set up new rendering material
    Texture tex = getTexture(renderMatName);
    if (tex != null) {   // use the material's texture
      switchOnTex(tex, gl);
      flipTexCoords = tex.getMustFlipVertically();
    }
    else  // use the material's colors
      setMaterialColors(renderMatName, gl);
  }
  return flipTexCoords;
}  // end of renderWithMaterial()
```

renderWithMaterial() checks the new material name (stored in faceMat) with the name of the currently loaded material (in renderMatName) and makes no changes if the names are the same.

The method returns a boolean indicating whether the texture's coordinates need to be vertically flipped when they're mapped to the shape's coordinates. The current value is stored in a global so it can be returned by future calls to renderWithMaterial() when the material name hasn't changed.

The method doesn't allow color and texturing to be mixed (i.e., blended). Any face color is ignored when a texture is applied.

switchOffTex() switches off 2D texturing (and enables lighting lighting). switchOnTex() turns texturing on (and disables lighting):

```
// global
private boolean usingTexture = false;


public void switchOffTex(GL gl)
{
  if (usingTexture) {
    gl.glDisable(GL.GL_TEXTURE_2D);
    usingTexture = false;
    gl.glEnable(GL.GL_LIGHTING);
```

```
  }
} // end of switchOffTex()


private void switchOnTex(Texture tex, GL gl)
{
  gl.glDisable(GL.GL_LIGHTING);
  gl.glEnable(GL.GL_TEXTURE_2D);
  usingTexture = true;
  tex.bind();
}  // end of switchOnTex()
```

getTexture() iterates through the materials ArrayList until it finds the named material and retrieves its texture:

```
// global
private ArrayList<Material> materials;
  // stores the Material objects built from the MTL file data


private Texture getTexture(String matName)
{
  Material m;
  for (int i = 0; i < materials.size(); i++) {
    m = (Material) materials.get(i);
    if (m.hasName(matName))
      return m.getTexture();
  }
  return null;
} // end of getTexture()
```

setMaterialColors() performs a similar iteration through materials, but gets the Material object to turn on its own colors:

```
private void setMaterialColors(String matName, GL gl)
{
  Material m;
  for (int i = 0; i < materials.size(); i++) {
    m = (Material) materials.get(i);
    if (m.hasName(matName))
      m.setMaterialColors(gl);
  }
}  // end of setMaterialColors()
```

Material.setMaterialColors() consists of several calls to GL.glMaterialfv() to switch on the ambient, diffuse, and specular colors for the material and its shininess:

```
// in the Material class
// global color info
private Tuple3 ka, kd, ks;  // ambient, diffuse, specular colors
private float ns, d;        // shininess and alpha

public void setMaterialColors(GL gl)
{
  if (ka != null) {   // ambient color
    float[] colorKa = { ka.getX(), ka.getY(), ka.getZ(), 1.0f };
    gl.glMaterialfv(GL.GL_FRONT_AND_BACK, GL.GL_AMBIENT, colorKa,0);
  }
  if (kd != null) {  // diffuse color
```

```
      float[] colorKd = { kd.getX(), kd.getY(), kd.getZ(), 1.0f };
      gl.glMaterialfv(GL.GL_FRONT_AND_BACK, GL.GL_DIFFUSE, colorKd,0);
    }
    if (ks != null) {    // specular color
      float[] colorKs = { ks.getX(), ks.getY(), ks.getZ(), 1.0f };
      gl.glMaterialfv(GL.GL_FRONT_AND_BACK, GL.GL_SPECULAR,colorKs,0);
    }

    if (ns != 0.0f)    // shininess
      gl.glMaterialf(GL.GL_FRONT_AND_BACK, GL.GL_SHININESS, ns);

    if (d != 1.0f) {    // alpha
      // not implemented
    }
  } // end of setMaterialColors()
```

I haven't implemented transparency, although the Material object stores an alpha value (in the d variable). It would require the use of blending and depth testing and the inclusion of the d value in the three calls to GL.glMaterialfv().

Rendering a Face

The code for rendering a face is complicated by the use of indices in the OBJ data. Each face is defined by a sequence of terms, with each term consisting of *indices* pointing to the actual vertex, texture coordinate, and normal data, as shown in the following example:

```
f 104/22/188 114/45/198 78/78/138
f 81/56/144 104/87/188 78/21/138
  :
```

The numbers are indices for the vertices, texture coordinates, and normals data.

Faces.renderFace()'s task is to draw the *i*th face of the model. The i value is used to access the *i*th arrays in facesVertIdxs, facesTexIdxs, and facesNormIdxs:

```
private ArrayList<int[]> facesVertIdxs;
private ArrayList<int[]> facesTexIdxs;
private ArrayList<int[]> facesNormIdxs;
```

The array retrieved from facesVertIdxs contains vertex *indices* for the *i*th face. The array extracted from facesTexIdxs holds texture coordinate *indices*, and the array from facesNormIdxs has normal *indices*.

The actual data is stored in the verts, normals, or texCoords ArrayLists:

```
private ArrayList<Tuple3> verts;
private ArrayList<Tuple3> normals;
private ArrayList<Tuple3> texCoords;
```

When an index (e.g., index value j) is read from one of the indices arrays, such as facesVertIdxs, renderFace() uses it to access the j-1th tuple in verts. This tuple contains the model's vertex for index j.

I use j-1 since the OBJ format starts its indices at 1, while the tuples in the verts, normals, and texCoords ArrayLists start at position 0.

The following is Faces.renderFace():

```
// global
private static final float DUMMY_Z_TC = -5.0f;

public void renderFace(int i, boolean flipTexCoords, GL gl)
```

```
{
  if (i >= facesVertIdxs.size())    // i out of bounds?
    return;

  int[] vertIdxs = (int[]) (facesVertIdxs.get(i));
        // get the vertex indices for face i

  int polytype;  // the shape of the faces
  if (vertIdxs.length == 3)
    polytype = gl.GL_TRIANGLES;
  else if (vertIdxs.length == 4)
    polytype = gl.GL_QUADS;
  else
    polytype = gl.GL_POLYGON;


  gl.glBegin(polytype);

  // get the normal and tex coords indices for face i
  int[] normIdxs = (int[]) (facesNormIdxs.get(i));
  int[] texIdxs = (int[]) (facesTexIdxs.get(i));

  /* render the normals, tex coords, and vertices for face i
     by accessing them using their indices */
  Tuple3 vert, norm, texCoord;
  float yTC;
  for (int f = 0; f < vertIdxs.length; f++) {
    if (normIdxs[f] != 0) {  // if there are normals, render them
      norm = (Tuple3) normals.get(normIdxs[f] - 1);
      gl.glNormal3f(norm.getX(), norm.getY(), norm.getZ());
    }

    if (texIdxs[f] != 0) {    // if there are tex coords, render them
      texCoord = (Tuple3) texCoords.get(texIdxs[f] - 1);
      yTC = texCoord.getY();
      if (flipTexCoords)     // flip tuple's y-value (the texture's t-value)
        yTC = 1.0f - yTC;

      if (texCoord.getZ() == DUMMY_Z_TC)  // using 2D tex coords
        gl.glTexCoord2f(texCoord.getX(), yTC);
      else // 3D tex coords
        gl.glTexCoord3f(texCoord.getX(), yTC, texCoord.getZ());
    }

    vert = (Tuple3) verts.get(vertIdxs[f] - 1);
                              // render the vertices
    gl.glVertex3f(vert.getX(), vert.getY(), vert.getZ());
  }

  gl.glEnd();
} // end of renderFace()
```

The vertex, texture coordinates, and normals data is rendered using the GL methods: glVertex3f(), glTexCoord2f(), and glNormal3f().

If 3D texture coordinates are detected, glTexCoord3f() is called, but only the 2D part will be drawn due to the use of 2D texture rendering in switchOnTex().

renderFace() is passed a boolean called flipTexCoords that indicates whether the texture's coordinates need to be vertically flipped when they're mapped to the shape's coordinates. This is done by subtracting the texture's t-value from 1.0.

OBJ face data may leave out texture coordinate and normal indices. For example, a face without texture coordinates will have the following form:

```
f 104//188 114//198 78//138
f 81//144 104//188 78//138
   :
```

If faces don't use normals or texture coordinates, the indices arrays will contain 0s. This is tested for in renderFace(), and the calls to glTexCoord2f() and glNormal3f() are skipped.

Drawing a Model

The lengthy code needed to create a display list has its payoff in the brevity and speed of the drawing operation, OBJModel.draw():

```
// in the OBJModel class
private int modelDispList;  // the model's display list

public void draw(GL gl)
{ gl.glCallList(modelDispList);  }
```

draw() is the only public method in OBJModel, aside from its constructors.

When to Create the Display List

The display list technique employed in draw() has a drawback: the display list (in modelDispList) must already exist. The list is created in drawToList() (described previously in the "Creating a Display List for the Model" section), which is called at the end of the loading phase.

This approach can be criticized since display list creation is arguably not part of loading. In practical terms, it means that the loader can only start once it has a valid reference to the OpenGL state. This makes it impossible for the loader to be used for offline batch processing tasks where there is no rendering phase and no OpenGL state.

OBJLoader could be rewritten to not finish its loading phase with a call to drawToList(). The call could be moved to the start of draw() instead, with the addition of testing code so that drawToList() was only called once, when draw() was executed for the first time. This would free the loading phase from its dependency on the OpenGL state, but with the small penalty of having draw() take a little longer to render the model initially.

Viewing a Model

Before moving on to TourModelGL, I'll demonstrate the OBJLoader package by using it inside a simple model display application, ModelLoaderGL (shown in action in Figure 17-1).

ModelLoaderGL utilizes the callback coding approach, described in Chapter 15 and illustrated by Figure 17-5.

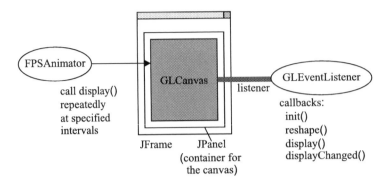

Figure 17-5. *The callback coding framework*

The ModelLoaderGL JFrame contains a JPanel that holds a GLCanvas. The GLCanvas displays the OBJ model, which may be rotating. The model is scaled and centered at the origin.

The canvas's listener is ModelLoaderGLListener (a subclass of GLEventListener), and the canvas's display is updated by an FPSAnimator instance using fixed-rate scheduling.

The simplicity of the application is reflected in the class diagrams for ModelLoaderGL in Figure 17-6 (only the public methods are listed).

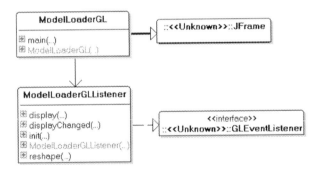

Figure 17-6. *Class diagrams for ModelLoaderGL*

Loading the Model

The name of the model is supplied on the command line and passed to the ModelLoaderGLListener constructor where it's stored in the global string modelName.

When init() is called, the model is loaded using its name:

```
// in the ModelLoaderGLListener class
// globals
private String modelName;
private OBJModel model;


public void init(GLAutoDrawable drawable)
{
  GL gl = drawable.getGL();
    // other non-relevant lines...
```

```
   model = new OBJModel(modelName, maxSize, gl, true);
} // end of init()
```

The maxSize value in the OBJModel constructor specifies the maximum size of the model's largest dimension. The true argument switches on verbose reporting of the model's details, which includes the number of vertices, normals, and texture coordinates found and its dimensions and colors used. They're printed to standard output.

Drawing the Model

OBJModel.draw() is called in the display() callback method:

```
public void display(GLAutoDrawable drawable)
{
  GL gl = drawable.getGL();
  // other nonrelevant lines...

  model.draw(gl);
  gl.glFlush();
} // end of display()
```

Other JOGL Model Loaders

Pournaras's *JautOGL* is a 3D multiplayer racing game with many interesting features, such as use of the full-screen exclusive mode (FSEM), 3D sound through JOAL, multiple camera views, and a UDP client-server model employing nonblocking sockets (http://today.java.net/pub/a/today/2006/10/10/development-of-3d-multiplayer-racing-game.html and https://jautogl.dev.java.net/).

The loader part of the game consists of two classes, GLModel and MtlLoader. The former is responsible for parsing and displaying the OBJ file, the latter for loading the MTL file. Texturing isn't supported, and coloring is implemented using GL.GL_COLOR_MATERIAL and calls to GL.glColor4f().

Glass's loader is part of his 3D asteroid game tutorial (http://www.cokeandcode.com/asteroid-stutorial/) built using LWJGL (which is quite similar to JOGL). He also develops a game framework, utilities for drawing the GUI (e.g., menus), a texture loader, classes for 3D sprites, a particle system, and sound based around LWJGL's binding of OpenAL and JOrbis for decoding OGG files.

His loader handles v, vt, vn, and f OBJ statements, but there's no MTL capability. Instead, a texture is loaded separately and wrapped around the entire model.

An OBJ loader is under development by Chris Brown at https://jglmark.dev.java.net/. As of March 2007, it didn't handle materials or textures.

A 3DS loader can be found at http://joglutils.dev.java.net/. The ThreeDS package by Greg Rodgers supports colors and textures, but 3DS features such as keyframe animation aren't in place yet. It is part of the full joglutils JAR, which is downloadable from the Documents & Files folder at the web site.

The NeHe site (http://nehe.gamedev.net/) is an excellent resource for OpenGL tutorials. Lesson 31 by Brett Porter explains how to build a MilkShape3D model loader. Color and texturing is available but not animation. The JOGL port by Nikolaj Ougaard can be found at http://pepijn.fab4.be/?page_id=34. Interestingly, it includes code for keyframe positioning of joints, but it was incomplete as of March 2007.

The need for model loaders in JOGL will undoubtedly drive development forward at a rapid pace, so it's a good idea to regularly search the JOGL forum at http://www.javagaming.org/forums/index.php?board=25.0 for announcements about new and improved packages.

The TourModelsGL Application

Having developed the OBJLoader package and tested it with ModelLoaderGL, it's time to consider TourModelsGL. It reuses a lot of code from the TourGL example in Chapter 16. It implements the active rendering framework, and the 3D scene reuses TourGL's green and blue checkerboard floor with numbers along its x- and z- axes.

The class diagrams for TourModelsGL are shown in Figure 17-7; only public methods are shown.

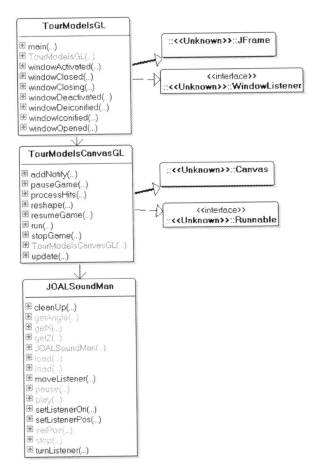

Figure 17-7. *Class diagrams for TourModelsGL*

TourModelsGL creates the JFrame and JPanel around the heavy-weight TourModelsCanvasGL canvas and handles window events such as resizing and iconification.

TourModelsCanvasGL spawns a single thread that initializes rendering, then loops, carrying out an update/render/sleep cycle with a fixed period.

Aside from the checkerboard, TourModelsCanvasGL makes use of TourCanvasGL's user navigation code, which converts key presses into camera movement forward, backward, left, and right. One change is that the user can't move vertically. This simplifies the 3D audio requirements for the game and lets me reuse JOALSoundMan from Chapter 13 (it assumes that a listener stays on the XZ plane).

TourModelsCanvasGL doesn't display a skybox, billboard trees, a rotating sphere, or the splash screen and "Game Over" message. Instead, the scene contains four OBJ models, shown in Figure 17-8 (and also in Figure 17-2).

Figure 17-8. *The models in TourModelsGL*

The other new elements in TourModelsCanvasGL are the following:

- The ability to select (pick) the penguin or couch with the mouse. OpenGL's selection mode is utilized to implement this feature.

- The penguin singing with the help of JOALSoundMan.

- The spooky fog (which is switched off in Figures 17-2 and 17-8 but can be seen in Figure 17-3).

Each of these is explained in detail in the rest of this chapter.

Adding Models

The four models (penguin, rose and vase, racing car, and couch) were chosen to illustrate the features (and limitations) of the OBJLoader package.

The penguin is a mesh wrapped with a single texture. The use of texturing means that the color lighting values defined in the penguin's MTL file are ignored.

The couch employs a single diffuse color, but the model's normals allow it to be affected by the scene's light source.

The rose and vase model has several colors using various ambient, diffuse, and specular settings.

I borrowed the racing car model from Pournaras's *JautOGL* game and modified its MTL file so the car uses different colors and textures on different faces.

Loading the Models

The models are loaded during the initialization phase in TourModelsCanvasGL.initRender():

```
// globals for the four OBJ models
private OBJModel couchModel, carModel, penguinModel, roseVaseModel;

// loading done in initRender()
couchModel = new OBJModel("couch", 2.0f, gl, false);
carModel = new OBJModel("formula", 4.0f, gl, false);
penguinModel = new OBJModel("penguin", gl);
roseVaseModel = new OBJModel("rose+vase", 3.2f, gl, false);
```

OBJModel attempts to load an OBJ file with the specified name. The four-argument version of the constructor includes a maximum size, a reference to the GL state, and a boolean that determines whether verbose model details are printed to standard output.

It's important to set the model's size using a constructor argument rather than a later call to GL.glScalef(), since a scaling transformation will affect the model's normals and so will modify the model's coloring and/or texturing.

The two-argument version of the OBJModel constructor assumes that the maximum size of the model will be 1.0f and that its details shouldn't be output.

The previous code fragments show a potential drawback of this loader: the need for a reference to the OpenGL state (the gl argument) in the call to the OBJModel constructor. As explained previously in the "When to Create the Display List" section, the reference is required so a display list can be created for the model at the end of the loading phase.

Drawing the Models

renderScene() calls drawModels() to render the models. Each model is drawn after being translated and rotated:

```
private void drawModels()
{
  drawCouch();

  // the racing car
  gl.glPushMatrix();
    gl.glTranslatef(-3.0f, 0.5f, -3.0f);   // move left, up, back
    carModel.draw(gl);
  gl.glPopMatrix();

  drawPenguin();

  // the rose vase
  gl.glPushMatrix();
    gl.glTranslatef(0f, 1.6f, 0f);   // move up
    roseVaseModel.draw(gl);
```

```
  gl.glPopMatrix();
}  // end of drawModels()


private void drawCouch()
{
  gl.glPushMatrix();
    gl.glTranslatef(4.0f, 0.5f, -4.0f);   // move right, up, back
    gl.glRotatef(-90.0f, 1.0f, 0.0f, 0.0f);
                           // rotate clockwise around x-axis
    couchModel.draw(gl);
  gl.glPopMatrix();
}  // end of drawCouch()


private void drawPenguin()
{
  gl.glPushMatrix();
    gl.glTranslatef(2.0f, 0.5f, 0f);   // move right, up
    gl.glRotatef(-90.0f, 0.0f, 1.0f, 0.0f);  // rotate clockwise
    penguinModel.draw(gl);
  gl.glPopMatrix();
}  // end of drawPenguin()
```

The couch and penguin are drawn by separate methods so these functions can be reused by the picking code described in the next section.

The calls to GL.glPushMatrix() and GL.glPopMatrix() stop the translation and rotation operations from affecting other elements in the scene. If a model isn't moved from its default position at the origin, stack pushing and popping isn't needed.

The rotation of a model around the x-axis (e.g., for the couch) is a fairly common requirement since many drawing packages use the XY plane as a "floor" rather than XZ.

Let's Be Picky

OpenGL supports a selection (or *picking*) mode that makes it fairly straightforward to click an object inside a scene with the mouse and retrieve details about it, such as its ID and distance from the camera.

Picking is enabled for the penguin and the couch in TourModelsCanvasGL. For example, I can click the penguin's eye when the camera is orientated as in Figure 17-9.

Figure 17-9. *The penguin in front of the couch*

The application then prints the following:

```
No. of hits: 2
Hit: 1
 minZ: 0.7478; maxZ: 0.769
 Name(s): couch
Hit: 2
 minZ: 0.3818; maxZ: 0.4625
 Name(s): penguin
Picked the penguin
```

The positioning of the penguin in front of the couch means that both models are selected when the user clicks the penguin's eye. Their depth information (stored in minZ and maxZ) allows the application to determine that the penguin is nearest to the camera, so it is chosen from the two possibilities.

If the camera is moved so the models don't overlap, picking will only return details for the one clicked upon.

The picking code has four main stages:

1. The cursor coordinates of a mouse press are recorded.

2. *Selection mode* is entered when it's time to render the scene, and the viewing volume is reduced to a small area around the cursor location.

3. The scene is *rendered*, which means that details about named objects inside the viewing volume are stored in *hit records* in a *selection buffer*. *Rendering* is a misleading word since nothing is drawn to the frame buffer.

4. Once the selection mode has been exited, name and depth information can be extracted from the hit records.

An object is named with an integer (not a string), which is pushed onto the *name stack* prior to the object's "rendering" in selection mode, and popped afterward. The names stored in the hit records are copied from the name stack when the viewing volume is examined in stage 3.

Capturing Mouse Presses

A mouse listener is set up in TourModelsCanvasGL's constructor:

```
// in TourModelsCanvasGL()
addMouseListener( new MouseAdapter() {    // used for picking
  public void mousePressed(MouseEvent e)
   { mousePress(e); }
});
```

mousePress() stores the cursor coordinates and switches on the inSelectionMode boolean:

```
// globals for picking
private boolean inSelectionMode = false;
private int xCursor, yCursor;

private void mousePress(MouseEvent e)
{
  xCursor = e.getX();
  yCursor = e.getY();
  inSelectionMode = true;
}
```

Switching to Selection Mode

In renderScene(), the inSelectionMode boolean is used to distinguish between normal rendering and selection mode:

```
// global
private GLDrawable drawable;  // the rendering 'surface'


// in renderScene()
if (inSelectionMode)
  pickModels();
else {   // normal rendering
  drawFloor();
  drawModels();
  drawable.swapBuffers(); // put the scene onto the canvas
  // swap front and back buffers, making the new rendering visible
}
```

All the normal scene rendering (e.g., of the floor and models) should be moved to the else part of the if-test since there's no point drawing objects unrelated to picking when selection mode is enabled.

In previous active rendering examples (e.g., TourCanvasGL in the previous chapter), the call to GLDrawable.swapBuffer() occurs after renderScene() has returned, back in renderLoop(). The call has been moved so it only occurs after the scene has really been rendered. Selection mode rendering only affects the selection buffer, so there's no need to swap the front and back buffers.

If the swapBuffers() call is left in renderLoop() in TourModelsCanvasGL, it triggers a nasty flicker since the back buffer is empty after picking but filled after normal rendering. This means the user will see a white screen for a moment after each selection.

Model Picking

pickModels() illustrates the picking code stages:

```
// global names (IDs) for pickable models
private static final int COUCH_ID = 1;
private static final int PENGUIN_ID = 2;


private void pickModels()
// draw the couch and penguin models in selection mode
{
  startPicking();

  gl.glPushName(COUCH_ID);
  drawCouch();
  gl.glPopName();

  gl.glPushName(PENGUIN_ID);
  drawPenguin();
  gl.glPopName();

  endPicking();
}  // end of pickModels()
```

Picking initialization (stage 2) is carried out in startPicking(), then the objects are rendered (stage 3) and picking is terminated by endPicking() (stage 4), which also processes the hit records in the selection buffer.

The drawCouch() and drawPenguin() methods are reused without change, but their calls are bracketed by the pushing and popping of their names onto OpenGL's name stack.

A common mistake is to forget to pop a name after its object has been rendered. Also, GL.glPushName() and GL.glPopName() only work after the selection mode has been enabled (which is done in startPicking()).

The Start of Picking

startPicking() switches to the selection mode, initializes the selection buffer and name stack, and creates a reduced-size viewing volume around the cursor:

```
// globals
private static final int BUFSIZE = 512;    // size of buffer
private IntBuffer selectBuffer;


private void startPicking()
{
  // initialize the selection buffer
  int selectBuf[] = new int[BUFSIZE];
  selectBuffer = BufferUtil.newIntBuffer(BUFSIZE);
  gl.glSelectBuffer(BUFSIZE, selectBuffer);

  gl.glRenderMode(GL.GL_SELECT);  // switch to selection mode

  gl.glInitNames();    // make an empty name stack

  // save the original projection matrix
  gl.glMatrixMode(GL.GL_PROJECTION);
  gl.glPushMatrix();
  gl.glLoadIdentity();

  // get the current viewport
  int viewport[] = new int[4];
  gl.glGetIntegerv(GL.GL_VIEWPORT, viewport, 0);

  // create a 5x5 pixel picking volume near the cursor location
  glu.gluPickMatrix((double) xCursor,
                    (double) (viewport[3] - yCursor),
                    5.0, 5.0, viewport, 0);

  /* set projection (perspective or orthogonal) exactly as it is in
     normal rendering (i.e. duplicate the gluPerspective() call
     in resizeView()) */
  glu.gluPerspective(45.0,
        (float)panelWidth/(float)panelHeight, 1, 100);

  gl.glMatrixMode(GL.GL_MODELVIEW);   // restore model view
} // end of startPicking()
```

JOGL's BufferUtil utility class was utilized to create an integer buffer (BufferUtil.newIntBuffer()). The selection buffer in OpenGL is an array of *unsigned* integers, a slightly different thing, which impacts how depth values are extracted later.

The first two arguments of GLU.gluPickMatrix() are the cursor's (x, y) location, but it needs to be converted from Java coordinate's scheme (x and y starting at the top left) to OpenGL's scheme (x and y starting at the bottom left). This is done by subtracting the cursor's y-value from the viewport's height: (viewport[3] - yCursor).

A common problem is forgetting to set the selection mode's projection (perspective or orthogonal) to be the same as in normal rendering. In the active rendering framework, this is done with a call to GLU.gluPerspective() in resizeView(), which is duplicated in startPicking().

The End of Picking

endPicking() switches rendering back to normal, which has the side-effect of making the selection buffer available:

```
private void endPicking()
{
  // restore original projection matrix
  gl.glMatrixMode(GL.GL_PROJECTION);
  gl.glPopMatrix();
  gl.glMatrixMode(GL.GL_MODELVIEW);
  gl.glFlush();

  // return to normal rendering mode, and process hits
  int numHits = gl.glRenderMode(GL.GL_RENDER);
  processHits(numHits);

  inSelectionMode = false;
}  // end of endPicking()
```

The buffer is examined in processHits().

Processing the Hit Records

processHits() simply lists all the hit records in the selection buffer and reports the name of the object that was picked closest to the viewport.

Each hit record contains the following:

- The number of names assigned to the hit object (usually there's only one, but it's possible to assign more)

- The minimum and maximum depths of the hit

- The names assigned to the hit object (which come from the name stack)

One source of confusion is that the depth values are for the part of an object that intersects with the viewing volume; they do not correspond to the object's z-axis dimensions.

Also, although the OpenGL specification talks about names on the name stack and in the hit records, it's more accurate to think of them as integer name IDs:

```
public void processHits(int numHits)
{
  if (numHits == 0)
    return;    // no hits to process

  System.out.println("No. of hits: " + numHits);

  // storage for the name ID closest to the viewport
  int selectedNameID = -1;    // dummy initial values
  float smallestZ = -1.0f;
```

```
boolean isFirstLoop = true;
int offset = 0;

/* iterate through the hit records, saving the smallest z value
   and the name ID associated with it */
for (int i=0; i < numHits; i++) {
  System.out.println("Hit: " + (i + 1));

  int numNames = selectBuffer.get(offset);
  offset++;

  // minZ and maxZ are taken from the Z buffer
  float minZ = getDepth(offset);
  offset++;

  // store the smallest z value
  if (isFirstLoop) {
    smallestZ = minZ;
    isFirstLoop = false;
  }
  else {
    if (minZ < smallestZ)
      smallestZ = minZ;
  }

  float maxZ = getDepth(offset);
  offset++;

  System.out.println(" minZ: " + df4.format(minZ) +
                     "; maxZ: " + df4.format(maxZ));

  // print name IDs stored on the name stack
  System.out.print(" Name(s): ");
  int nameID;
  for (int j=0; j < numNames; j++){
    nameID = selectBuffer.get(offset);
    System.out.print( idToString(nameID) );
    if (j == (numNames-1)) {
      // if the last one (the top element on the stack)
      if (smallestZ == minZ)     // is this the smallest min z?
        selectedNameID = nameID;  // then store it's name ID
    }
    System.out.print(" ");
    offset++;
  }
  System.out.println();
}

System.out.println("Picked the " + idToString(selectedNameID));
System.out.println("-------------");
} // end of processHits()
```

Typical output from processHits() was shown earlier. Here's another example, when only the couch is picked:

```
No. of hits: 1
Hit: 1
 minZ: 0.6352; maxZ: 0.6669
 Name(s): couch
Picked the couch
```

A depth is in the range 0 to 1 but is stored after being multiplied by 2^32 -1 and rounded to the nearest unsigned integer. The number will be negative due to the multiplication and being cast to a signed integer in the buffer.

The conversion of the integer back to a float is done by getDepth():

```
private float getDepth(int offset)
{
  long depth = (long) selectBuffer.get(offset);  // large -ve number
  return  (1.0f + ((float) depth / 0x7fffffff));
                            // return as a float between 0 and 1
}  // end of getDepth()
```

The depths aren't linearly proportional to the distance to the viewpoint due to the nonlinear nature of the Z buffer, but different depths can be compared to find the one closest to the camera.

The mapping from a name ID to a string is carried out by idToString():

```
private String idToString(int nameID)
{
  if (nameID == COUCH_ID)
    return "couch";
  else if (nameID == PENGUIN_ID)
    return "penguin";

  // we should not reach this point
  return "nameID " + nameID;
}  // end of idToString()
```

Gleem: A Different Way of Picking

The picking described in this chapter relies on OpenGL's selection mode, which is simple to use but has a reputation for being slow. A more advanced solution is to utilize ray-to-triangle intersection tests, as found in gleem (OpenGL Extremely Easy-to-Use Manipulators), a library used in many of the JOGL demos (http://jogl-demos.dev.java.net/).

Gleem supports several forms of object selection and dragging based on the manipulators idea first introduced in Silicon Graphics's Open Inventor 3D graphics API (http://oss.sgi.com/projects/inventor/). Gleem includes manipulators for translating a selected object along a line and across a plane and for rotating it about various axes and for scaling.

The manipulator functionality employs ray casting to find intersections with the triangles in the scene's objects. A *ray* is the path followed by a light beam from the camera to the object.

Gleem includes useful camera navigation controls in its ExaminerViewer class, such as trackball-style rotation, translation, and zooming.

Gleem was developed by Ken Russell, who is also one of the main developers of JOGL. The source is included with the JOGL demos source code, downloadable from http://jogl-demos.dev.java.net. Some older background information can be found at http://www.media.mit.edu/~kbrussel/gleem/.

A Singing Penguin

JOALSoundMan (developed in Chapter 13) is employed to set up a 3D sound for the penguin model and to attach an audio listener to the camera.

A JOALSoundMan instance is created in TourModelsCanvasGL's constructor:

```
// global
private JOALSoundMan soundMan;

// in TourModelsCanvasGL()
soundMan = new JOALSoundMan();
```

Locating the Penguin Sound

The penguin sound is positioned at (2, 0, 0) in initRender(), and set to play repeatedly:

```
// in initRender()
if (!soundMan.load("penguin", 2, 0, 0, true))
  System.out.println("Penguin sound not found");
else
  soundMan.play("penguin");
```

Although the penguin model is also loaded in initRender(), it isn't positioned until drawPenguin() is called at rendering time:

```
private void drawPenguin()
{
  gl.glPushMatrix();
    gl.glTranslatef(2.0f, 0.5f, 0f);  // move up, right, to (2,0.5,0)
    gl.glRotatef(-90.0f, 0.0f, 1.0f, 0.0f);
                  // rotate the model to face left
    penguinModel.draw(gl);
  gl.glPopMatrix();
}  // end of drawPenguin()
```

There's no direct link between the audio source and the penguin model, so it's up to the programmer to ensure they stay colocated. That's easy here since the penguin doesn't move.

Connecting the Camera and the Listener

As the camera moves and rotates about the scene, so should the listener. The connection is made by updating the listener's position and y-axis orientation to match those of the camera.

Obtaining the positional data is straightforward since the camera details are stored in three globals, xPlayer, yPlayer, and zPlayer, updated by processKey(). The listener moves by using xPlayer and zPlayer (yPlayer isn't utilized since JOALSoundMan assumes the listener always stays on the floor).

Linking the rotation of the camera to the listener is a bit trickier. The camera's rotation angle is stored in the viewAngle global, which initially has the value -90 degrees to point it along the negative z-axis. When the camera rotates clockwise around the y-axis, a positive amount is added to viewAngle (see Figure 17-10). However, JOAL initializes its listener to point down the negative z-axis, so it starts at 0 degrees. Also, a clockwise rotation reduces the angle rather than increases it (as shown in Figure 17-10).

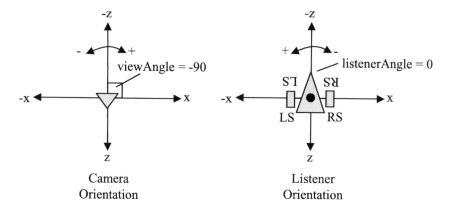

Figure 17-10. *Rotating the camera and listener*

TourModelsCanvasGL includes a new global, listenerAngle, which stores the current rotation angle of the listener around the y-axis. It starts with the value 0, which corresponds to it pointing down the negative z-axis. Both viewAngle and listenerAngle are initialized in initViewerPosn():

```
// globals
private double viewAngle, listenerAngle;

// in initViewerPosn()
viewAngle = -90.0;   // along negative z-axis
listenerAngle = 0;
```

When processKey() adjusts the camera's rotation value (in viewAngle) it also changes the listener's rotation (in listenerAngle) but with the opposite operation (e.g., addition instead of subtraction). For instance, the following code fragment deals with the camera turning left:

```
// globals
private final static double ANGLE_INCR = 5.0;    // degrees

// turning left in processKey()
viewAngle -= ANGLE_INCR;      // subtract
listenerAngle += ANGLE_INCR;  // add
```

The positional and rotational data are employed in renderScene() to move the listener:

```
// in renderScene()
soundMan.setListenerPos( (float)xPlayer, (float)zPlayer );
soundMan.setListenerOri( (int) listenerAngle );
```

The casting of listenerAngle to an integer is a requirement of the JOALSoundMan.setListenerOri() method, and perhaps the code should be rewritten to accept doubles (or floats).

The Fog Descends

The fog shown in Figure 17-3 makes it much harder to find the models, which could be used as the basis of a time-constrained search game. Also, the fog reduces the amount of geometry that needs to be rendered, thereby improving the application's speed.

Almost all the fog-related code is in one method, addFog(), which is called from initRender():

```
private void addFog()
{
  gl.glEnable(GL.GL_FOG);

  gl.glFogi(GL.GL_FOG_MODE, GL.GL_EXP2);
    // possible modes are: GL.GL_LINEAR, GL.GL_EXP, GL.GL_EXP2

  float[] fogColor = {0.7f, 0.6f, 0.6f, 1.0f};
                            // same color as background
  gl.glFogfv(GL.GL_FOG_COLOR, fogColor, 0);

  gl.glFogf(GL.GL_FOG_DENSITY, 0.35f);

  gl.glFogf(GL.GL_FOG_START, 1.0f);  // start depth
  gl.glFogf(GL.GL_FOG_END, 5.0f);  // end depth

  gl.glHint(GL.GL_FOG_HINT, GL.GL_DONT_CARE);
    /* possible hints are: GL.GL_DONT_CARE, GL.GL_NICEST,
       GL.GL_FASTEST */
}  // end of addFog()
```

The fog is enabled and its various characteristics are set. OpenGL implements fog by blending each pixel with the fog's color, depending on the distance from the camera, the fog density, and the fog mode.

Possible fog modes are GL.GL_LINEAR, GL.GL_EXP, and GL.GL_EXP2, with GL.GL_EXP2 looking the most realistic but also being the most computationally expensive. If the linear blend is chosen, start and end depths for the fog must be defined using the GL_FOG_START and GL.GL_FOG_END attributes. If GL.GL_EXP or GL.GL_EXP2 is employed, the GL_FOG_DENSITY attribute needs to be set.

I've used the GL.GL_EXP2 mode in addFog(), so the GL_FOG_START and GL.GL_FOG_END values aren't really needed; I've included them to show how they're used.

The fog color is set with the GL.GL_FOG_COLOR argument, and the scene generally looks better if its background is the same color as well. In initRender(), I set the background to be the following:

```
gl.glClearColor(0.7f, 0.6f, 0.6f, 1.0f);   // same color as the fog
```

In the clear sky screenshots (Figures 17-2, 17-8, and 17-9), the blue background was generated with the following:

```
gl.glClearColor(0.17f, 0.65f, 0.92f, 1.0f);  // sky blue
```

The GL.GL_FOG_HINT argument *may* be utilized by OpenGL to switch to faster or higher-quality blending; its default value is GL.GL_DONT_CARE.

Fog can be switched off with GL.glDisable(), so it's possible to have the fog only selectively affect objects in the scene.

Summary

This chapter was primarily about the development of a loader for Wavefront OBJ models, resulting in the OBJLoader package that can load polygonal shapes utilizing multiple colors and textures defined using the Wavefront MTL format.

The main example, TourModelsGL, is the beginning of a search-type game, which utilizes OBJLoader to load and position models. The needs of the application also led to the discussion of three other programming techniques: picking with OpenGL's selection mode, 3D sound, and fog.

The 3D sound (a chirping penguin) employs JOAL via the JOALSoundMan class introduced in Chapter 13.

Index